WHITE SPACE IS NOT YOUR ENEMY

DESIGNING a website or brochure without an art background? Then step away from the computer and read this engaging conversational introduction to visual communications first. Written for the beginner, *White Space Is Not Your Enemy* is a practical graphic design and layout guide that introduces the concepts and practices necessary for producing effective visual communication across a variety of formats—from web to print. This beautifully illustrated full-color book covers all the basics to help you develop your eye and produce evocative designs that work.

Topics include:

- What is design?
- Predesign research & brainstorming
- The elements & principles of design
- Layouts for impact
- Getting along with type
- Choosing & using color
- Working with photos & illustrations
- Creating infographics
- Designing for web & social media

Rebecca Hagen taught Public Relations and Design courses at the University of South Florida, Tampa. She is a 20-year practicing graphic designer and founder of Sky Lake Design Studio, a graphic design firm in Tampa, Florida.

Kim "Dr G." Golombisky, former advertising and public relations pro, is an award-winning teacher and scholar at the University of South Florida, Tampa.

WHITE SPACE IS NOT YOUR ENEMY

4TH EDITION

A Beginner's Guide to Communicating Visually Through Graphic, Web & Multimedia Design

Rebecca Hagen &
Kim Golombisky

CRC Press
Taylor & Francis Group
A FOCAL PRESS BOOK

Fourth edition published 2025
by CRC Press
2385 NW Executive Center Drive, Suite 320, Boca Raton FL 33431

and by CRC Press
4 Park Square, Milton Park, Abingdon, Oxon, OX14 4RN

CRC Press is an imprint of Taylor & Francis Group, LLC

First edition published by AK Peters/CRC Press 2010
Third edition published by AK Peters/CRC Press 2017

Library of Congress Cataloging-in-Publication Data
Names: Hagen, Rebecca, author. | Golombisky, Kim, author.
Title: White space is not your enemy : a beginner's guide to communicating visually through graphic, web & multimedia design / Rebecca Hagen and Kim Golombisky.
Description: Fourth edition. | Boca Raton, FL : CRC Press, 2025. | Includes bibliographical references and index.
Identifiers: LCCN 2024030134 (print) | LCCN 2024030135 (ebook) | ISBN 9781032104355 (hbk) | ISBN 9781032104348 (pbk) | ISBN 9781003215325 (ebk)
Subjects: LCSH: Graphic arts--Handbooks, manuals, etc. | Visual communication--Handbooks, manuals, etc. | Commercial art--Handbooks, manuals, etc.
Classification: LCC NC997 .G563 2025 (print) | LCC NC997 (ebook) | DDC 740--dc23/eng/20240919
LC record available at https://lccn.loc.gov/2024030134
LC ebook record available at https://lccn.loc.gov/2024030135

ISBN: 978-1-032-10435-5 (hbk)
ISBN: 978-1-032-10434-8 (pbk)
ISBN: 978-1-003-21532-5 (ebk)

DOI: 10.1201/9781003215325

Publisher's note: This book has been prepared from camera-ready copy provided by the authors.
Access the Support Material: whitespacedesignbook.com

For Product Safety Concerns and Information please contact our EU representative: GPSR@taylorandfrancis.com
Taylor & Francis Verlag GmbH, Kaufingerstraße 24, 80331 München, Germany.

We dedicate this edition
in loving memory of our fathers
Bruce Eugene Jacobsen (1940–2019) and
John Carl Kirsch (1924–2021).

TABLE OF CONTENTS

White Space Is Not Your Enemy:
A Beginner's Guide to Communicating Visually Through Graphic, Web & Multimedia Design

RED T-SHIRT
LOVERS
Unite!

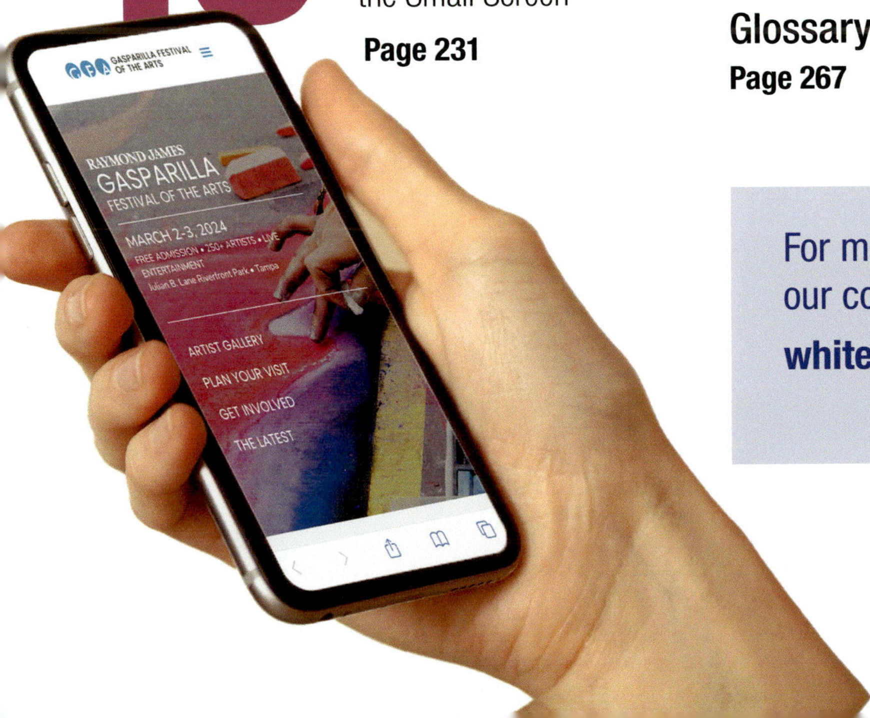

For more content please visit our companion website:

whitespacedesignbook.com

Acknowledgments

Once again, thanks go all around to our supportive and talented husbands Guy and Greg; sons Ben and Karl; cats Buster and Tig; and dog JoJo. Beyond their psychosocial support, their contributions—from modeling to design—are literally visible throughout WSINYE.

Special acknowledgments are due to Tim Price and Willow Payne for their artistic contributions, and to John Haller, Instructor of Graphic Design at Marietta College for his service as the unofficial WSINYE website uptime monitor. We appreciate you!

PREFACE

This fourth edition of *White Space is Not Your Enemy*, or *WSINYE*, is still for the "beginning" visual communicator. Whether you're already a media pro or hoping to be one soon, we assume our book is your introduction to graphic design and layout. We also assume you're busy. So we try to cover the basics quickly without being too boring.

OUR BIG IDEA

Our humble little book can't be everything to everyone. But we did plan it to combine some things typically treated separately:

1. News, PR, advertising & marketing communications:

   We address different communications careers together as if they actually interact in the real world. Today's communications professionals all have to be visual, even the writers. And visual foundations are the same for all beginners. At the same time, where differences between journalism and the strategic communication arts remain sacred, we honor them.

2. Web & print media:

   We embrace design for new and traditional media since the former is here to stay and the latter isn't going away. Because communications professionals need to be ambidextrous with both, we attend to visual practices across platforms and formats.

3. Visual communication, design & layout:

   We integrate three traditionally segregated approaches: visual communication, graphic design and layout. Beginners need elementary how-to rules (layout). But without thinking about the rules as functional messaging (visual communication) and without developing a good eye (design), the rules remain rote ideas either soon forgotten or ploddingly applied without creativity or innovation.

THEMES

The book relies on three themes that chapters return to again and again in order to reinforce concepts and practices:

1. Effective graphic design does four things: It captures attention, controls eye movement, conveys information and evokes emotion.
2. All design uses three building blocks: visuals, type and negative space.
3. Beginners need to learn the conventional rules first before earning the right to break said rules.

TONE, DICTION & STYLE

WSINYE is intentionally lighthearted and conversational. We employ an informal tone and diction to avoid reading like a traditional textbook. Most people find textbooks unappealing. Our students don't bother to read them.

Our goal has been to make *WSINYE* a fast, effortless read. We present information in a down-to-earth fashion without talking down to anyone. We use humor to avoid taking the book's content or ourselves too seriously.

Given the book's applied emphasis, we use the Associated Press as our style guide—except where we take creative license.

CHAPTER PREVIEWS

Although each chapter flows from the previous one and segues to the next, by design the chapters also make sense when read out of order or standing alone. We envision *WSINYE* to be useful as either a primary text or a supplemental resource. We also see it complementing media writing and editing courses.

Chapters 1–4 represent a book within a book. By the end of Chapter 4, the casual and impatient reader can opt out with dramatically improved skills.

» Chapter 1 answers the beginning student's perennial question: "What is design?"

» Chapter 2 reminds new designers to "step away from the computer" for the pre-design work of "research & brainstorming."

» Chapter 3 covers the "works-every-time layout," which allows us to describe Western layout in its most universal form while also teaching introductory rules for working with visuals, type and negative space.

» Chapter 4 preempts the most common visual, type and composition "layout sins" in a checklist of "amateur errors."

After Chapter 4, readers have enough elementary skill to begin executing assignments, whether for the classroom or the office. So Chapters 5 and 6 shore up some foundational details:

» Chapter 5 sends readers to "mini art school" to learn the "elements, principles and theories of design" that develop the good eye.

» Chapter 6 then fills in the blanks on "layout" format and composition from aspect ratio, grids and focal point to visual hierarchy and modular design for single, complex and multiple-screen/page designs.

Next, readers can drill down on more advanced rules for type, color and visuals:

» Chapter 7 expands the rules and uses of "type" from text-heavy formats and projects to creative type as art.

» Chapter 8 deals with "choosing & using color," including sources of color inspiration as well as color as culture, science and technology.

» Chapter 9 spells out technique, technology and ethics of designing with "photos & illustrations."

Remaining chapters touch on more complex design work:

» Chapter 10 serves up a quickie lesson on "infographics" as "maximum information in minimum space."

» Chapter 11 describes elementary concepts for "storyboarding 101: planning visual storytelling" for moving pictures, such as video, film and animation.

» Chapter 12 moves on to planning visual communication as "multimedia assets," including slideshows and audio clips.

» Chapter 13 introduces visual communication issues in "designing for the web" from responsive design to graphical user interface.

» Chapter 14 wraps things up with a few words of encouragement before saying, "Thanks for stopping by."

» "Fit to Print," formerly Chapter 14 covering an overview of papers and printing, has migrated to our book's companion site as a digital chapter. Find it on whitespacedesignbook.com.

Each chapter concludes with exercises thinly disguised as "Try This." You'll find a glossary at the back of the book.

We also invite readers to visit the companion website for this book: whitespacedesignbook.com.

The how-tos of design and layout as visual communication are the same regardless of career track. We planned *WSINYE* as a comprehensive introduction for any communications major, track or sequence, across traditional and new media formats: one concise and practical source surveying the fundamentals for any platform for anybody.

WSINYE COMPANION WEBSITE

For more content, please visit the companion site: https://whitespacedesignbook.com

CHAPTER 1

WHAT IS DESIGN?

MAKING VISUALS & TYPE PLAY NICE IN SPACE

Visual culture is a language, and, like any language, visual culture has rules that make communication possible.

Above: Some designs are classic, like the Taj Mahal. Others are universal, like the international symbol set.

Below: This type of communication is so powerful that breaking convention communicates as well.

You live in a visual culture. All day every day, you read the messages of visual culture, from the logo on your shirt to traffic signals. Unless you're blind or visually impaired, you hardly give it a thought—until you come across a visual message you don't understand.

Visual culture is a language, and, like any language, visual culture has rules that make communication possible. Like English grammar, you may not be able to say exactly what the rules are, but you know when *breaks someone* them.

The rules of design are equivalent to visual culture's grammar. This book gives you some basic rules of graphic design and layout so you can begin to speak the visual language that you already read. Think of this book as your primer for graphic design. Don't worry. This grammar is the fun stuff, and, hopefully, we'll whet your appetite to learn even more about visual culture and design.

Before we get started on the rules, though, let's cover a little background on design, visual culture, visual communication and graphic design.

FORM FOLLOWS FUNCTION IN DESIGN

Chances are, right now, you're surrounded by the work of designers from fashion to furniture to architecture. There are interior designers and landscape designers, product designers and product packaging designers, and, of course, graphic designers. Believe it or not, there are even font designers and color designers. Today, game, web and mobile app user experience (UX) and user interface (UI) designers lead the pack in determining how the public interacts with text and visuals. The list could go on, but the point is you live with design.

Despite its variety, all design is related through the expression, "Form follows function." Good design results from a partnership between "form" as art and "function" as utility.

"Form" refers to material artistry—what something looks like. Design, triggered by the industrial revolution and mass production capitalism (function), grew out of and continues to be inspired by the visual and even performing arts (form). Most designers have some background or training in art. Knowing something about art can improve your eye for design. But what people consider aesthetically beautiful, or even interesting, changes across history, cultures and individuals. "Aesthetics," a branch of philosophy, deals with the expression and perception of beauty. Your personal aesthetic dictates what you like in terms of style.

Unlike fine artists, however, designers don't have the luxury of creating art for art's sake or wholly yielding to personal taste. Design always has a job to do, and that job influences the design's form. Design has to be practical. The "function" in "form follows function" refers to the usefulness of the design, whether it's an ergonomic dashboard in your car or your car manufacturer's mobile app.

Time warp. If you have a good eye, you can make a game of matching any kind of design to the historical period that produced it.

DESIGN DRIVES VISUAL CULTURE

Beyond form and function, all design is related by style trends, too. To a great degree, designers engineer visual culture. If you have a good eye, you can make a game of matching any kind of design to the historical period that produced it.

Think about how you can date a movie by hundreds of visual clues, including cars, décor, fashion and superimposed typography during the credits. Though all these things have different functions, they generally share a similarity of form if they were designed at roughly the same time.

Changing technology also influences design. Refrigerators in the 1950s and '60s sported just as much chrome as cars from the same period because they both emerged from the same technological and design era. Think about how the designs of televisions, computers and phones have changed in your lifetime.

Some designs don't stand the test of time. They go out of style to become old-fashioned, "old school" or even the objects of jokes. Maybe you've heard the expression, "The '80s called, and they want their shoulder pads back." Some designs are said to be timeless or classic, such as the Parthenon and the Taj Mahal. Other designs become universal, such as international symbols. Yet other design trends recycle earlier styles, usually with modifications or updates. Cooper Black typeface took the U.S. advertising world by storm in

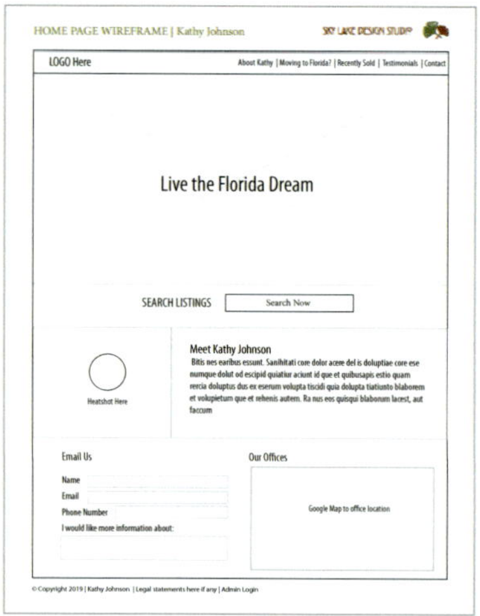

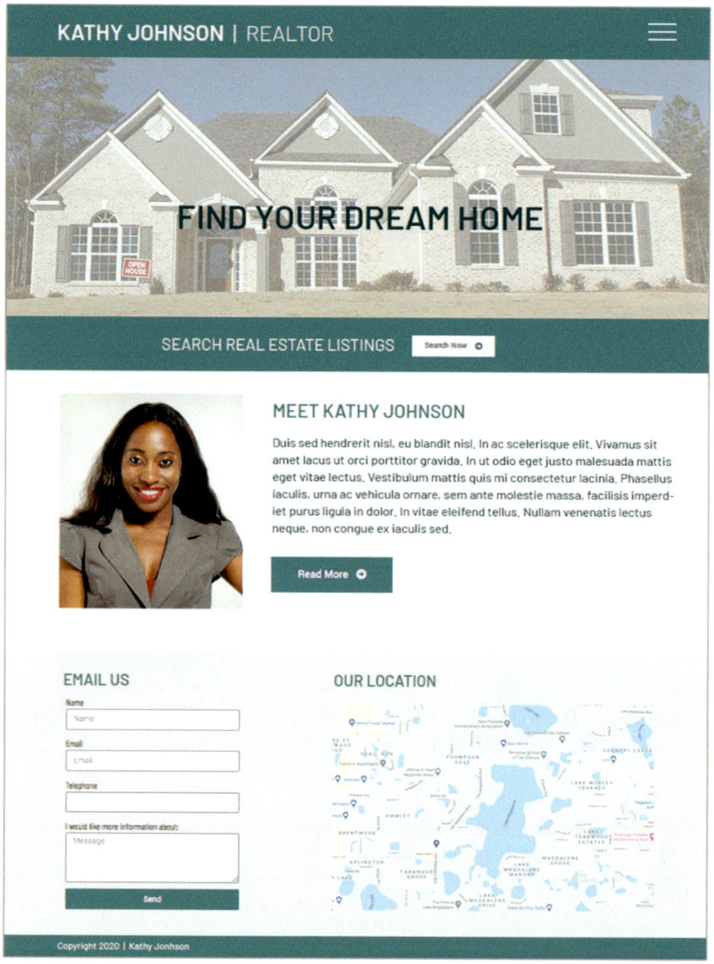

Graphic design is planned. Designers *plan* their projects in detail on paper before ever sitting down at the computer.

Small sketches, called "thumbnails," help the designer establish attention-grabbing focal points and determine placement of the remaining elements for logical and effective order. Readability, usability and visual appeal are critical.

A poorly designed, poorly organized layout fails to communicate and costs both the designer and the organization time and money.

Above: "Wireframe" sketches for the homepage of a website.

Right: The finished page.

the 1920s, fell out of favor and then became stylish again in the 1970s, and, unfortunately has made something of a comeback.

All this is to say that visual culture changes as a result of design's changing forms and functions, both related to technology and social trends. This is equally true of graphic design.

GRAPHIC DESIGN COMMUNICATES

While the forms of graphic design, like all design, change with the winds of visual culture and technology, the specific function of graphic design remains constant: to communicate messages visually. Graphic designers have to be professional communicators. They understand that, for better or worse, in visual culture we judge and are judged by appearances. In fact, everyone can benefit from knowing something about the mostly unspoken rules of visual communication. That's called media literacy.

Cooper Black typeface. Just as ugly today as it was in the 1920s.

COMPUTERS DEMOCRATIZED GRAPHIC DESIGN

Once upon a time, only professionals produced graphic design. Graphic designers spent years learning the art and craft of visual communication (and still do, by the way). Today, however, anyone with a smart phone has access to the tools for producing visual communication.

Unfortunately, not everyone knows the design rules for using technology tools. The result is a lot of bad graphic design in a visual culture already on overload. While ugly design may offend your good taste, it can lead to a more serious functional problem: poor communication. Learning some fundamentals will dramatically improve your visual message delivery, whether it's through your résumé, a website or slides for a presentation deck.

THE WWW CHANGED ALL THE RULES

To say the World Wide Web changed everything for graphic designers is a gross understatement. And just as they started figuring out the web for desktops and laptops, everything migrated to mobile devices. Who knows what's next?

Seismic changes in technology present us with dilemmas in organizing this book. For many topics, there's a "Yeah, but." *Yeah, but* there's a whole other color wheel for screens. *Yeah, but* fonts behave differently on the web. And so on. Most "yeah, buts" have more to do with technique and production than actual design, however.

Oh, well, so we'll deal with it. Life's full of contradictions. Best to embrace the adventure.

GRAPHIC DESIGN IS PLANNED

Technically, "graphic design" refers to a plan for organizing visual objects in space. Generally, that space is a two-dimensional plane, meaning some kind of flat surface such as paper or a screen. The key ideas are "plan" and "organize" for the purpose of "communication." If you were writing a speech or research report, you would make an outline to organize your ideas in a logical and effective order. In graphic design, you organize all your elements from copy (text) to visuals (pictures) in a logical and effective order.

Good graphic design does four things: It *captures* attention, *controls* the eye's movement across the screen or page, *conveys* information and *evokes* emotion.

GOOD **GRAPHIC DESIGN** DOES FOUR THINGS:

It **captures** attention.

It **controls** the eye's movement across the screen or page.

It **conveys** information.

It **evokes** emotion.

So graphic design refers to your plan for capturing the audience's attention from among everything else competing for its interest. Once you have the audience looking at your design, its arrangement or layout should control the audience's eyes to move in a particular sequence from one thing to the next on the screen or page. The whole point of guiding the eye is to convey information. Think eye-catching, flow, interesting and evocative.

MAKE PICTURES & WORDS WORK TOGETHER IN SPACE

Now you need some building blocks for capturing, controlling, conveying and evoking. In the simplest sense, effective design and layout teams up pictures and words to communicate a unified message, regardless of the visual medium or vehicle. At the risk of oversimplifying, you really have only three building blocks: *visuals, typography* and *space.*

Visuals—symbols, icons, drawings, illustrations, photographs, film and video, etc.—are self-explanatory, literally. But there are rules for using them in graphic design. We'll be talking more about those rules later.

About *type,* we generally represent copy graphically with typography, a visual form of language. There are rules for typography, too, which you'll be learning. But words may be represented with handwriting, such as calligraphy, or even pictures. And type treatments can make beautiful visuals. Additionally, some kinds of visuals, such as logos and infographics, require text. We'll be covering that, too.

Imagine *space* as the sandbox that encourages visuals and typography to play well together. Beginners often make the mistake of forgetting to account for space. Too much space, and visuals and type get lost or don't talk to each other. Not enough space, and they start to fight with each other.

The idea is to arrange visuals and type harmoniously in space. Don't think of space as immaterial or invisible. Nor is space a vacuum to be filled. Space is real, even when we call it "white space" or, more properly, "negative space" (since not all white space is white). Negative space always has weight and structure in graphic design. There's an old saying: "White space is nice." Amateurs tend to pack every nook and cranny of space with visuals and type. Don't. *White space is not your enemy.*

Our best advice for improving your visual communication is to practice looking. Pay attention to the layout of visuals and typography in space. Think about what you're seeing.

KNOW THE RULES. BREAK THE RULES IF YOU HAVE A REASON.

Students like to find exceptions to the rules of design we teach. That tickles us because it means students are tuning in to design. Often the exceptions to the rules of design that students show us are good examples of bad design. But sometimes the exceptions are good examples of good design. Then we have to explain how breaking the rules can produce good design that communicates. Usually, our explanations fall into two categories: professional license and changing design trends.

By training and experience, professional designers have mastered both fundamental and advanced rules of design. They know how to use creative license with the rules without forfeiting visual communication. This book concentrates on fundamentals. But, as you learn the fundamentals, you also may discover opportunities to employ creative license. At least we hope so.

Taking creative license with the rules of design can lead to innovation, which leads us to changing design trends. Design, like visual culture and English language, is not static. "It's alive!" That's what keeps things interesting. Times change. Styles shift. So we adapt the rules.

Bottom line: Don't break the rules of design out of ignorance. Learn the rules. Then break the rules if you have a reason to. Hey, if it works, it works. Just keep reminding yourself that you have a job to do. It's called visual communication.

Rules? What rules? This promotional piece for an architectural salvage yard pushes the boundaries of readable typography. Yet it works because it evokes the distressed nature of the product being sold.

TRY THIS

1. Choose one of your favorite possessions from among the material objects you own. Try to imagine what the object's designer had in mind.

   Write a few sentences to describe its form or what it looks like. Be specific and list the details of the object's appearance. Quickly sketch a small picture of the object's appearance. Try to include all the details you see.

   Then write a sentence or two to describe the object's function, or what it does. Draw a diagram explaining how the object works. How does this diagram differ—or not—from the earlier picture you drew?

   Last, write a couple more sentences to describe the relationship between the object's form and function. How do you think the object's function influences or limits its form? Does the object's form assist in its function?

2. Locate an object that has gone out of style. How do you know it has gone out of style? What clues does the object communicate that date it? Explain why the object is outdated. Has the object become dated because of its form? Its function? Or both?

3. Find an example of graphic design that you believe communicates well.

   First, explain how the design captures your attention. What part of the design do you look at first? What draws your eye to look there first?

   Second, explain how the design controls the eye's flow through its layout. In what order does your eye move from one thing to the next across the space of the layout? Make a numbered list of the order in which your eye travels around the layout.

   Third, what kind of information does the design convey? Make a list. Describe how the design conveys this information.

   What, if any, emotion(s) does the design evoke? How? Why?

Form and function. Despite its variety, all design is related through the expression, "Form follows function." Good design results from a partnership between "form" as art and "function" as utility.

Consider one of your favorite possessions. What did the designer have in mind? Which features speak to form and which to function?

CHAPTER 2

STEP AWAY FROM THE COMPUTER

FOR RESEARCH & BRAINSTORMING

Appealing to your audience. For visual communication, you should speak to the audience in its own visual vernacular. For instance, craft beverage enthusiasts might respond to the old-world-craftsman feel of a vintage-inspired label.

Design has one thing in common with biology: There's no such thing as spontaneous generation. Whether you're designing for folks in the newsroom or the boardroom, you have some predesign work to do if you hope to produce a design that works, literally and figuratively.

Novices might be inclined to go straight to their computers. But professional designers know that effective graphic design begins with research: information gathering and critical thinking about the project at hand. Next comes brainstorming: tapping into creativity and putting pencil to paper. So we're going to have to ask you to step away from your computer.

RESEARCH

Always start with research. If you're lucky, the research you need in order to begin a new design comes from the person who sent the work to your desk. Let's call this person, whomever it is, the boss or client. But you might have to do your own research or at least pitch in with it.

Even the humblest design assignment necessitates collecting basic information about the design's purpose and deadlines. At the other end of the spectrum, a high-stakes campaign demands extensive research, analysis and planning culminating in multiple coordinated designs accountable to measurable objectives.

Regardless of who collects the facts, and however big or small the design job, you need reliable answers to some standard questions:

What is the objective? Communication objectives frame decisions about everything from format to font. Clear objectives also provide the benchmarks for gauging a design's success. So what exactly is the visual communication purpose? What do you want your audience to think, feel or do? Is the audience learning something new? Are you creating conviction or preference? Or stimulating action or behavior? By the way, speaking of the audience…

Who is the audience? To whom must the design speak? Loyal patrons or happenstance traffic? High-powered business people or high-tech tweens? Knowing your audience well is critical for developing visual communication that resonates. Public relations and advertising agencies might invest in research such as focus groups and surveys to collect key consumer insights about where the target audience leans and how it interprets messages. News organizations might use opinion polls or user analytics to assist issue reporting. For visual communication, the point is to speak to the audience in its own visual vernacular. For instance, the visual aesthetics of MTV and early video games are part of the collective memory of Gen X.

You need to consider any physical needs of your audience, too. How might an audience of baby boomers dependent on reading glasses affect your design?

Design must be inclusive. Consider that members of your audience might be colorblind. Will you need to translate copy into other languages? Do you need versions of signs or printed pieces in Braille? How will you design to accommodate visitors with impaired vision or hearing?

Does the design need to coordinate with other design work? Any new design has to work with, not against, the organization's visual identity and graphic design history. If you're not familiar with that identity and history, bring yourself up to speed. Study the organization's printed materials and digital visual communication.

Meanwhile, get vector copies of the organization's logos. Vector images use geometry and math to produce and preserve the proportions and quality of line-art illustrations. You also need to know the organization's rules and regulations for using said logos. Ditto on official colors. Know the approved colors, along with the rules for producing and using them. You can't plan your whole design around shades of lilac if the organization's look and feel require fire-engine red.

On Brand.
New designs might need to match existing designs in overall look and feel, and might need to use specific colors, fonts, logos and images. Get up to speed before you begin.

Beyond long-term visual identity or branding, your project might be part of a short-term series or campaign that needs or already has a "look" you have to coordinate. So don't be shy about asking questions.

Who are the competitors, and what does their visual communication say? Predesign research also accounts for the competition's graphic design. You can't know how to position your visual messages if you haven't accounted for how your competitors position theirs. If a competitor is currently gung ho about the color green, maybe you should rethink going green. If the competitor's homepage features an image of a little girl, choose something else for yours. If a competitor positions itself as the "safety people"… You get the idea.

Return to sender? A design that fails to arrive also fails to communicate. Adhere to electronic and print delivery specifications.

How will the final product be delivered or distributed? Nothing is more important in determining the physical size of a design project than format, i.e., the intended channel, medium or vehicle. Print or digital? What kind of print? What kind of digital?

For ads—print or digital—you need the proper dimensions or technical specs (specifications). Size may be measured in pixels, bytes, inches, column inches or fractions of pages.

For screen graphics, file size—the amount of memory a file takes up—is as important as the pixel-by-pixel dimensions. For video and multimedia, add duration—lengths of time in seconds or minutes—to the specifications list.

When designing printed items such as brochures and posters, you might have to consider not only the size of the design but also the size of the design's container. Is your design meant for a brochure rack? A transit kiosk?

If your design will be printed in-house, get to know your printer's capabilities. Most printers print only on certain sizes of paper so you might have to restrict your design to what will fit on a letter- or legal-sized sheet. Most common copiers and laser and inkjet printers also have a built-in print margin that leaves a small white border around the page, even if you want your design to bleed to the paper's edges.

Mailing presents another set of challenges. Is an envelope required? What size? Make sure your piece will fit. Or will the piece self-mail? The U.S. Postal Service has a complex set of requirements for self-mailers, including appropriate paper weights, overall size, use of sealing tabs, position of folds and setup of mailing panels for bulk mail, first-class presort and business reply. The last thing you need is a box of expensive printed pieces taking up space in a closet because your ignorance and lack of planning rendered the design useless.

What is the budget? No-brainer here. Budget impacts design, including how many hours the boss or client is willing to pay you to work on it. Budget also determines what kinds of visuals you can afford, along with such things as the number of ink colors you can use for a printed piece, the amount of custom-coding you can add to a website or the complexity of an animated infographic.

Obviously a bigger budget allows for special design touches such as top-drawer animation on a website or foil stamping on a high-end business card. But a small budget doesn't oblige poor design. A talented designer can create something spectacular using only black ink and newsprint if necessary. In any case, you have to design within your budget's limitations. It's bad form to let the boss or client fall in love with a full-color glossy brochure with an interesting fold and die cut, all packaged in a cool translucent envelope if you can't produce it due to budget constraints.

If you're unsure how much your proposed design will cost, chat with an expert. Commercial printers are thrilled to provide useful suggestions and alternatives to help you produce successful printed pieces.

Web designers and developers likewise will assist you with web-related pricing. If you work with video, it's good to develop relationships with reputable producers, videographers and post-production editors who are willing to chat estimates. If you're lucky, you'll work with an on-staff production manager or producer who will gather estimates and bids for you.

To keep budgets in check, stick with standard paper sizes, like 8½ x 11 flyers or this trifold brochure. For online projects, adapt free open-source code instead of paying a developer for custom coding.

Be aware of deadlines, whether recurring (as in magazines, newspapers and newsletters), events-based or seasonal.

What about timing and turnaround? Timing refers to when the finished design reaches the audience. Turnaround refers to how much time the design, production and placement crew has to deliver the job. Both timing and turnaround are related to deadlines, which are sacred among those who care about their professional reputations. So whenever there are deadlines, you need a production schedule coordinating all those deadlines with everyone.

Beyond timing and turnaround, there might be other calendar issues. For example, a message might be seasonal or time-sensitive. Hard news obviously dates almost instantly; feature news, not so much. Or the message might be timeless. But even if a visual message is timeless, its channel of delivery probably is not. So the designer needs to know about the shelf lives of both the message and medium.

Who is providing content? In order to make the project fly, you'll need necessaries such as logos, color palettes, available photography and any required content such as disclaimers and legalese. Will the boss or client be forwarding these materials? Or will you be responsible for collecting them or creating them from scratch? If your organization doesn't have photography of its own or a budget for custom photos, stock photography sites are an option.

Now is the time to consider copy, too. Who's writing it? If you're not the copywriter or reporter, when will you get the copy? How much copy are you dealing with? Designers and writers often have different perspectives, which you should treat as a positive opportunity. In any event, designers and writers do share the same agenda for an effective project. If you're not writing the copy, invite some creative collaboration with the writer.

Are there any other design or production considerations or constraints? Better to ask the question sooner if it can save you from headaches later.

A planning document is generally the end product of all this Q&A. Ad agencies call this document a creative brief; design firms, a design brief. Whatever you call it, we highly recommend you have one. The brief serves as a roadmap keeping the visual communication goals front and center and the design process on track.

BRAINSTORMING

With your research brief in hand, you're ready to brainstorm your project's design concept and layout possibilities. So don't even think about turning on that computer yet.

Our brainstorming process goes like this:

Dump: Begin with a mind dump. Download everything you know about it—whatever "it" is. Spit it all out on paper. Make diagrams and draw connections. Free associate without guilt. No holds barred. Quantity rocks. The longest list wins.

Percolate: Then go do something else. Split focus is when you work on two things at once. Ideas simmer while you and your brain tend to chores and other tasks. Those other tasks can be inspiring, too. Exercising and napping are equally productive. Or force yourself out of your comfort zone by trying something new. Have an adventure.

Morph: Now back to work. Change it. Turn it into something else. Or stretch (or reduce) it (or some part of it) to the point of absurdity. Or do the opposite—just to be contrary. Marry it to the random, the incongruous or the formerly incompatible. Think "oxymoron". Reject the obvious, as well as your favorites and first choices.

Return to step 1 and repeat the process as necessary. But don't go it alone if you don't have to. Brainstorming works best playing with others.

Brainstorming leads to the concept or so-called "big idea" driving your visual communication. The concept might be inspired by an arresting photo or illustration. Or the concept might come from a piece of fabric or architecture you saw somewhere or from the texture of something. Put your other senses to work, too, on sounds, scents and even tastes. Consider collecting these little bits of inspiration on a "mood board," either a physical board (think bulletin board) or a digital version.

Capturing the mood. Use an "inward facing" mood board to collect visual, audio and tactile inspirations as part of your brainstorming activities. Use a well-executed "outward facing" mood board to pitch your ideas to your boss, client or other external audience.

I NEED A GREAT IDEA...I NEED A GREAT IDEA...

The wrong way to come up with a great idea is to try to come up with the great idea. Nothing puckers up the creative juices like pressuring yourself to think of one superior idea.

It's more fruitful and fun to come up with many ideas. Good, bad, so-so. Let 'em rip. No criticism. Just scores of ideas. That gets the creativity flowing.

In fact, it's called "flow" when you're so focused and productive during the creative process that you lose track of time. And somewhere in that big list you generated, you'll find a big idea.

Brainstorming Techniques to Stimulate Creativity

Credit for inventing brainstorming as a technique for creative idea generation goes to the late Alex Osborn, the "O" in the legendary ad agency BBDO. Today we recognize that everyone has creative potential just waiting to be exercised.

Try these brainstorming exercises:

I. Fluent Thinking

In the late 1960s and early '70s, Frank Williams and Bob Eberle, a couple of educators interested in stimulating creativity in schoolchildren, described "fluent thinking" as a way to generate many ideas quickly. The goal is quantity without being self-conscious about quality. Try it:

Write down two dozen ways to…(insert your project).

II. Scamper

Eberle also came up with the SCAMPER method:

S—substitute it

C—combine it

A—adapt it

M—magnify or modify it

P—put it to other uses

E—eliminate it

R—rearrange or reverse it

III. Cubing

Cubing, from writing guru Elizabeth Cowan-Neeld, refers to the six sides of a cube, as in think outside the box:

1. Describe it
2. Analyze it
3. Compare it
4. Associate it
5. Apply it
6. Argue for or against it

The concept also might be a theme, a metaphor or an analogy. Sometimes brainstorming fill-in-the-blank statements helps to get there. For example:

- This company (or organization, topic, product, service, project, etc.) is so ______ that ______ .
- This company (or organization, topic, product, service, project, etc.) is as ______ as ______ .
- This company (or organization, topic, product, service, project, etc.) is more ______ than ______ .
- This company (or organization, topic, product, service, project, etc.) is less ______ than ______ .
- This company (or organization, topic, product, service, project, etc.) is like ______ .

Think about what appeals to the audience. Or what moves it, as the case may be. Get as many ideas as you can on paper. You never know when a dumb idea will trigger a brilliant one.

Think about what appeals to the audience. Or what moves it, as the case may be. Get as many ideas as you can on paper. You never know when a dumb idea will trigger a brilliant one. Cast your net wide for visual inspiration.

Once you have a concept, you're ready to start exploring actual designs—with the computer turned off. So don't put away your paper and pencil just yet.

SKETCHES

There is no single magic-bullet solution to any given design project. Instead there might be dozens of possible solutions. The goal is to find the one that best achieves the project's communication objective and also appeals to the boss or client. The best technique for fast exploration of design options is the thumbnail sketch. Thumbnails are tiny thumbnail-sized layout sketches that you can draw—and reject—quickly.

Don't let the word "sketch" scare you. Many designers can't draw. Thumbnails are really more like doodling than illustrating. You only need to be able to draw boxes and lines indicating placement of visuals and type in space. Simple line drawings allow designers to create and compare a number of layout ideas rapidly before selecting the best solution. For designers, this is where the real creativity begins.

A wireframe illustrates the page's content areas and functionalities.

If you're a beginner, it's a good idea to do sketches on graph paper since it's important to keep your drawings in proportion to the dimensions of the final design. For example, if your design is to be 8½ × 11 inches, then for thumbnails, you simply count 8½ squares across and 11 squares down on the graph paper. Designers use sketches to work out projects with one page or screen, or multiple pages or screens.

Flat plans. Layout projects including multiple pages in spreads require a type of sketch called a flat plan. Flat plans consist of a single sheet showing all pages in the project. They illustrate page order and arrangement of facing pages. Individual sketches accompany flat plans, and outline the layout for each individual page.

Storyboards. For design involving animation or video, storyboards are required. Storyboards are working sketches showing change over time so, rather than one layout, there will be several depicting key points in the animation or video. The effect is not unlike a comic book. Nevertheless, storyboards begin as thumbnails, too.

Site maps & wireframes. Due to the nonlinear nature of websites, there is more than one type of sketch involved in website design. First, a designer may choose to create a site map to show which pages the site will include, the link structure between pages and the overall flow among pages. Site maps often look like family trees, with pages branching out from a single homepage. More complex site maps resemble flowcharts, reflecting the idea that visitors don't travel through pages sequentially but have the option of going different directions from any given point.

The traditional web design equivalent of the thumbnail sketch is the wireframe. Designers use wireframes to work out ideas for listing site content and planning how site visitors will access and use content. Wireframes may be sketched on paper or generated using general design programs or special wireframe software. They focus on screen order, organization and function, not aesthetic choices. Traditional wireframes lack the ability to demonstrate website interactivity and responsiveness, and are being replaced by other types of sketches. We discuss these in Chapter 13.

Roughs, comps & mockups. The next step in the design process varies designer to designer. For some, the next step is to turn the best couple or few thumbnails into roughs, meaning slightly more detailed, polished sketches. Other designers skip the rough and produce a first draft of a design on the computer.

Beyond that, the next step is a comp, short for comprehensive. The comp is a fully detailed final draft suitable for showing the boss or client. A complex print piece, such as a media kit tucked inside a custom pocket folder, might need a physical mockup the bosses or clients can get their hands on, and thus wrap their brains around.

Prototypes. Comps for websites and other onscreen layouts—generally referred to as prototypes—also show more polished designs. Depending on the layout's complexity, a simple mockup showing the layout's overall color palette, font and image choices might be sufficient. In more complex layouts, prototypes might also need to demonstrate interactivity, such as the behavior of pages on swipe-gesture. A variety of software, both online and desktop, is available for such User Interface (UI) prototyping. Client-approved prototypes are then used to create many of a website's assets, such as header or feature images, background images, gradients and buttons.

Once the client or boss approves the prototype, designers proceed to building a staging site, which is a working version of a website that the public can't yet access. The staging site lets the boss or client fully test-drive the interface, including the interactive components, and lets the designer and developer work out any kinks before the site goes live.

If we step back to review the overall process for any kind of design, we find that traditionally the designer's workflow has been sketch, rough and comp. But computers changed the game. Today, workflow varies for each artist. Some share thumbnail sketches with their bosses or clients to get early feedback. Others go right from sketch to full-fledged comp, skipping the rough stage altogether.

Whatever the project, getting boss or client approval without changes at the comp stage is rare. So brace yourself for additional rounds of edits before the boss or client is satisfied. In fact, build it into your production schedule.

Regardless of how designers get from point A to point B, they all begin with the computer turned off. The best designers consistently start with thorough research. And, believe it or not, they still sketch their ideas on (gasp!) paper. All designers expect to go through many

Sketch, comp, final. The workflow for many print designers is sketch, comp, final. Some execute an additional set of sketches called "roughs" between the sketch and comp stages.

design iterations before and after they turn on the computer in order to complete a project.

Assuming you've done your research legwork and your brainstorming homework, then *Brava*. You have our blessing to turn on your computer.

TRY THIS

1. Got a project? Do the basic Q&A research then write a design brief. Have someone critique it for you.

2. Visit your library to speak with a reference librarian. Ask about databases and sources for your story, topic, project, client, audience or competitors. Using those resources, do some research.

3. Draw sketches for a website home page for your county, city or town. Start by visiting the U.S. Census Bureau website (http://www.census.gov), including the American FactFinder tool. Use the site to get a demographic profile of your audience. Based on your findings, what are some design considerations to keep in mind for your audience?

4. Visit the U.S. Postal Service website at usps.com. Locate and read the rules and regulations for business mailings.

5. Schedule a series of brown-bag lunches featuring guest speakers such as front-end web designers, User Experience (UX) or User Interface (UI) specialists and video production experts.

6. Come up with 50 kinds of lists you could make during the mind dump phase of brainstorming. Next, list 50 activities you could do to percolate. Last, list 50 ways to morph the project—or story, product, service, client or boss, etc.

7. To brainstorm concepts for your project, come up with 10 plausible fill-in-the-blank possibilities for the following statement:

   Our ______________ is so ______________ that ______________ .

8. Use the online design tool of your choice to create a mood board for your own dream business. Include photos, color swatches, type examples, video clips, audio clips and anything else that communicates your brand concept.

9. Locate the rate card for an online publication. What are the specifications for banner ads? Sizes? Do the specs allow animation? What format? Duration? File size? Create thumbnail sketches or animation storyboards for a banner ad appropriate for this publication.

From the horse's mouth. Schedule a series of brown-bag lunches featuring guest speakers such as front-end web designers, UX or UI specialists and video production experts.

CHAPTER 3

I NEED TO DESIGN THIS TODAY

THE WORKS-EVERY-TIME LAYOUT

Here we are in Chapter 3. The clock is ticking, and your computer beckons. You're thinking: "I don't have time to read a book. I have to get this project done today."

Okay, we'll play along. You're on deadline. Now what?

This chapter introduces the works-every-time layout because it does work every time. Its layout is foolproof and reader-friendly for simple projects such as a single ad or flyer. Even a complex project such as an entire page or screen of news stories ultimately breaks down into individual stories using variations on the works-every-time layout theme.

Mastering the works-every-time layout will perk up your desktop professionalism even if you learn nothing else about design and layout. So put it in your design toolbox, and don't apologize for using it.

WHY THE WORKS-EVERY-TIME LAYOUT WORKS

The works-every-time layout works because of the way Westerners read: from left to right and from top to bottom. As readers, we enter a layout in the upper-left corner and exit in the lower-right corner. Since one of the functions of good design is to control the eye's movement across the layout, the direction and order in which we read dictates the order of things on the works-every-time layout.

PARTS OF THE WORKS-EVERY-TIME LAYOUT

The six parts of the works-every-time layout—in order—include:

1. **Outer boundaries and margins.** Set your layout size, and establish generous margins on all four sides.
2. **Columns.** Establish column guides. The number of columns depends on the size and type of your layout.
3. **Visual + optional cutline.** Position the visual at the top of the layout. Place the cutline, if necessary, under the visual.
4. **Headline.** Position the headline under the cutline.
5. **Copy.** Position the body copy into columns under the headline.

6. **Tags.** For videos, advertisements and most print pieces, place the logo and taglines in the lower right corner. For websites and apps, place the logo in the header (either in the center or upper left) and the tagline, if using one, below or to the side of the logo.

Now let's look at each step in more detail.

Step 1: Outer boundaries & margins

First, set up your layout in the desired size. This creates your outer boundaries. Next, before you do *anything* else, lay margins inside those boundaries—on all four sides. Think of your margins as a frame that ensures the important content inside is both readable and visible. Be generous with your margins. Use a minimum of ½-inch margins on a small ad or flyer, for example. In print layouts, the size of your margins should grow in proportion to the size of your layout.

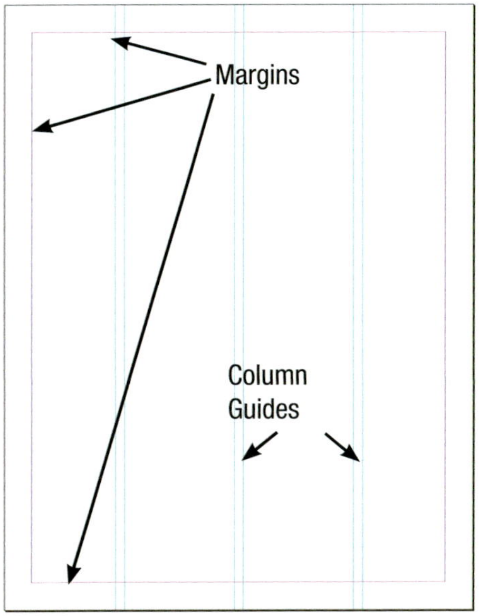

Above: An 8.5 x 11-inch flyer with a ½-inch margin on all four sides. In the graphic above, black lines indicate the document boundary. Pink and purple lines indicate margin lines. Blue lines delineate the columns and the alleys.

Step 2: Columns

Now, inside your margins, divide your layout into vertical columns. People will avoid reading long horizontal lines of type and big chunks of text. Because type presented in columns means shorter lines and narrower chunks, columns

MARGINS FOR SCREEN LAYOUTS

When designing layouts for screens, take into account that tools and navigation can take up some of your real estate, and changing screen sizes (smart phones, tablets) can crop content. To compensate, set your layout size to correspond to "maximum size" and add margin lines to indicate "safe area." Maximum sizes and safe areas differ from gadget to gadget and app to app, but a quick web search should provide the dimensions you need for your specific project.

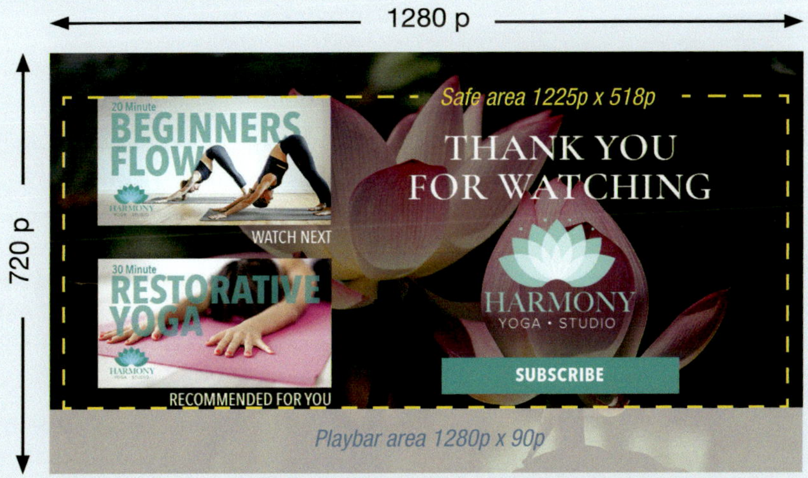

This video end card keeps important, clickable content within the boundaries of the safe area. Nonessential design elements are allowed to extend to the maximum size.

become a kind of *trompe l'oeil* (French for "trick of the eye") that says, "Come on, reading this won't take long."

If your works-every-time layout is a smaller ad or flyer, two columns are probably adequate. You might need more columns if your layout is larger and you have more copy. Thread copy from one column to the next. Or use one column for copy and the other for images, tags or sidebar content. Columns are also used in web layouts where it's common to see sets of icons evenly distributed side-by-side, or text in one column next to an image, animation or video clip in the adjacent column.

In all types of columnar layouts, make sure the alley of negative space separating your columns isn't too small or too big. Your goal is enough space to keep columns visually separate but still cohesive.

Bottom line, unless your layout is very narrow, don't make your copy span the full width of your layout.

Step 3: Visual + optional caption

Next, position the visual. The visual is your tool for capturing the audience's attention. On the works-every-time layout, the visual goes at the top of the layout. The visual becomes the eye entry point into your layout and is the starting point of a viewing flow that takes the audience from top to bottom.

Visuals. Position your visual at the top to give your audience an eye entry point at the start of your layout.

In web layouts, the upper left corner of the screen is an important visual hotspot, and your logo or site name should fill this spot. Position your key visual below the logo.

If your layout is for print, hang your visual from the top of the page, the top margin or the top of your story.

Caption/cutline option. Depending on the purpose of your layout, your visuals might not need captions. For advertising, if you have to explain your visual with a caption, then your visual probably is not the best choice. For most editorial visuals, including those for print news, broadcast news, magazines and news websites, a caption, or "cutline," is required. If you do need a cutline, set it directly underneath the visual. Make your cutline span the width of your visual, and style it flush left, ragged right.

Now that you have some text in place, it's time to set type. For a cutline, use the same font you choose for either your headline or your body copy. (Hint: If you plan to use a fancy font for headlines, use a version of your body copy for cutlines.) Set the cutline somewhere between 9 and 11 points. Eight points is getting a little hard to read, and 12 points is getting a bit too big or horsey, as some designers might say.

(With all due respect to the noble steed, "horsey" is not a compliment in graphic design. "Horsey" means awkwardly large and lacking grace.)

Step 4: Headline

After visuals, headlines have the greatest impact on your layout.

Research shows that readers scan before choosing to read. Big bold headlines provide content information at a glance, and when executed well encourage readers to dive in. Bold headings and subheadings provide eye entry points to your content. They also help break long copy into bite-sized pieces, which you already know are reader-friendly.

On websites, apps and other layouts that include navigation, the scanning process is different. When viewing these types of layouts, the reader's eye searches for and scans navigation first, looking for the page or section most likely to contain desired information. Once the reader lands on the desired page or section, visually significant headlines become the eye entry points for the rest of the content. Similarly styled headings and subheadings provide a visual path leading readers through to the end of the content.

So make your headlines count. Give them visual weight, which generally means make them big. In any event, make your headline way bigger than 11 points.

Returning to typographic decisions, you only get to use two fonts on a works-every-time layout. You get one font for the headline and a second font for the body copy. Period. That's it. Don't go font crazy. For your headline, choose a font that symbolically goes with your design concept. If you want to communicate "streetwise", for example, don't choose a script-style font that screams traditional wedding invitation.

A caution about headlines: If you can't get the whole headline onto one line, then you'll need to decide where to break the line. Read the copy. The ends of thoughts, clauses and phrases are good places to break a line. But also consider visual balance. Line lengths should be similar, though not necessarily perfectly even. If breaking after a clause gives you one very long and one very short line, then you might rewrite your headline.

Headlines. Headlines should jump off the page. So make them contrast via a large point size, an interesting font and/or an eye-catching color. Make your headlines span all the columns of type, and avoid bad line breaks.

Typesetting copy. This example demonstrates a few best practices for typesetting, including setting the copy in readable fonts and keeping the headline visually connected to the lead. Since our example is an HTML-formatted email likely to be read on a small smart phone screen, we opted for a single-column format.

Finally, never allow hyphenated words to break headlines into two lines. Never strand a single word all by itself in an additional line of a headline, either.

Which of the three choices below offers the best way to break the headline into two lines?

**Don't count your chickens before they
are hatched**

**Don't count your chickens
before they are hatched**

**Don't count your chickens be-
fore they are hatched**

Hint: The second choice is the best choice.

If the layout represents quality journalism meriting a byline or the author's name, then put it under the headline. But don't make it nearly as big as the headline.

Step 5: Copy

You or someone else has written some excellent copy to go with your layout. So treat it with respect.

» **Keep the headline and the lead together.** A lead is the first paragraph of body copy. Never let anything except a byline come between a headline and its lead. That means don't let anything physically separate the headline and lead. The eye should finish scanning the headline and flow directly into the lead.

» **Fit your copy into the column guides created in step 2.** A column of copy is called a "leg" so two columns is two legs. You can entice people to read several short legs of copy when they will skip reading exactly the same thing in one very long leg. Don't go too short, however.

Columns that are too short make for choppy reading. Aim for legs somewhere between 2 and 10 inches long. If your copy is too short to fill every column, then fill a column with negative space. It's okay to leave a column empty. *White space is not your enemy.*

» **Short paragraphs are just as inviting as shorter legs of copy.** Be concise.

- **Set your copy in a transparent font.** Transparent fonts are easy to read (not see-through). The eye can focus on reading for content without being distracted with thoughts such as, "Hey, this is an interesting font," or "Wow, this font is giving me a headache." Arial, despite being an overused default font that we are not endorsing, is a good example of a transparent font. But do choose a readable font for your body copy, even if that seems boring. Also make sure your body copy font doesn't fight with your headline font. Let your headline font be the showoff. For print body copy, start with a font size of 9–11 points. For web, size varies. Start with 1em and adjust accordingly.

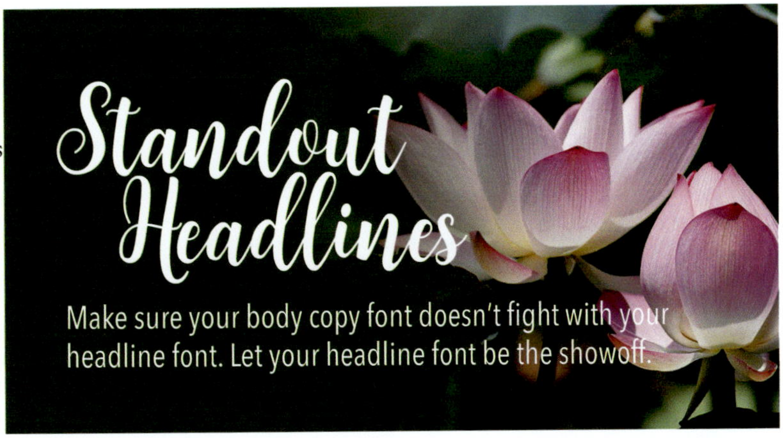

- **Don't fully justify your text.** Flush left, ragged right is your best bet. Next, the width of your column and the size of your type will determine how many words fit on one line. If you're only getting three to five words per line—and you're getting a heap of hyphenated words jettisoned to the next line—then you have options: Reduce your font size or make your columns wider, or both. Shoot for six to 12 words per line.

- **Break paragraphs properly.** Regarding paragraphs, don't indent the lead under a headline. Beyond the lead, if you plan to use indents to mark paragraph breaks, then size your automatic indents at roughly the equivalent of four to five letter spaces of your body copy's font size. A ½-inch tab, for example, is probably too much. If you plan to use extra spacing between paragraphs as your breaks, don't indent at all. This approach, by the way, is best for web.

- **Create elegant columns.** Really. Look at them. Do the bottoms of your legs break sentences or paragraphs awkwardly? Do the tops of your legs begin with the last word of the previous sentence? In both cases, try not to. Does each leg of type have to be the same length? Nope.

Tags. In print layouts, place your tags in the lower right corner where the viewer's eyes exit the page. In this email, the logo is best postioned at the top, where it functions similarly to website navigation. The logo links to the sender's homepage. The bottom-center or bottom-right eye exit point is reserved for tag content and the important call-to-action.

Step 6: Tags

"Tags" is an advertising term referring to all the information typically found at the end of an advertisement, such as the logo, themeline or slogan, URL, physical address and map, phone number and sometimes, unfortunately, disclaimer and legalese. Because this is critical information to include on each advertisement, every layout is tagged with it. Hence, the word "tags."

» Don't forget to include tags if you need them. If nothing else, include the logo and the URL.

» Place tags in the appropriate spot. For web layouts, place your taglines in the upper left under or next to the logo. Other "tag" content may appear in a sidebar or footer. For print, place tags in the lower right. Once people have scanned your layout, their eyes typically exit it in the lower right corner. Tags, if you need them, are the final things you want viewers to see.

» Use one of your two fonts, and make sure it's readable at a small size. You can make tags pretty small—as long as they remain legible. "Mousetype", another advertising term, means very small mouse-sized type often used for tags. Look for the sweet-spot size between unobtrusive and still readable.

FINAL THOUGHTS

You now have the basics for a no-brainer layout that never fails to communicate. But, just because this layout works every time, we are not suggesting that you must or should use it every time. Use it when you need it.

Additionally, are you allowed to break some of these rules? Absolutely—with good reasons. As you learn more about the rules of design, you'll feel more comfortable experimenting with this and other kinds of layouts, too.

Before you dash off to finish that on-deadline project, we recommend that you read the next chapter first. Chapter 4 gives you a checklist of layout sins, an inventory of embarrassing mistakes amateurs make. Our point: Please don't embarrass yourself.

TRY THIS

1. Get started on the project that's distracting you. Do some thumbnail sketches using the works-every-time layout. How many variations of the works-every-time layout can you sketch for the project?
2. Find both print and digital examples of the works-every-time layout. Consider websites, mobile apps, presentation decks, banner ads, etc. Identify and label the parts on each. How are the layouts alike or not?
3. Find a layout that is a complete disaster (you won't have to look hard, we promise). Again, consider websites, flyers, banner ads, HTML-formatted emails, video title and closing slides, etc. Rework the design, either in thumbnail sketch or fully rendered design using the principles of the works-every-time layout.
4. Take the piece you designed/sketched in exercise 3 and create simplified versions of the works-every-time layout for smaller projects such as 300 × 250-pixel banner ads, 4 × 5-inch announcement cards and 3.5 × 2-inch business cards.
5. Choose a social cause that inspires you, and develop a public service announcement (PSA) poster using the works-every-time layout. Do some research. Develop a concept and write the copy, including appropriate tags. Look for appropriate visuals. Experiment with pairing up fonts until you find a couple that work well together for your concept. Thumbnail your ideas and execute a comp of the poster.

THE WORKS-EVERY-TIME LAYOUT: A GALLERY

CHOOSE YOUR FLAVOR

The works-every-time layout works for different layout types on screen and in print. Layouts vary. Some require all six parts, while others only need an image, headline and tags. But the core structure remains of strong visual at top, copy set in easy-to-read columns and tags at the layout exit. And it just plain works.

Harmony Yoga logo and all brand layouts designed by Rebecca Hagen. Reproduced by permission of Sky Lake Design Studio.

INSIDE COVENTRY
Community

HARMONY
Comes to Myerston

Fictem sequate sequid maioratquo que magnitaturio temquia sequi vitaque sit omnis deliquis es abo.

Story by Fern Lewis

Soloressitis a volorem. Aquam fuga. Ut quis event, solenet quam expla in cus entur? Ucid moloria ssuntum vellab is doloriam ipsanis iur magnis asped et aut illupta spelest iuntio. Et mo endis porae ditent.

Nam quiatiore duciaeprae veles velendit pelibus sumet quis explabo. Nam, odit ommolute et lam expel incte pe apietur?

Ihil eos ipsum imi, qui imaionet officati dicaeltate simint untumquia as parit a sintur am, cuptam, untur, sin num iur? Qui nonet excerna tibus, il ilici te dolesequi dolorro vitasse rspicias rest quatassus diorum quas molum quo vel et laboris quosani hitat.

Perate reicien dentio quas quos vellab ium quaerit as utem. Cus dolum sunt quis alibusam, quas est ut qui berum doluptatur?

Quibus perchilit odisitius ex et iusciis doloreh enihitatium dolupist, solorepre qui odio quunt rerferi aceptas molesciati ut acia et doloreic tem hilibus issus es et inverem imporep rorisi consequi ut alit as exceaquundi odissita ea con pro conet mod ullatat emporem fugiam ut voluptio tem essimil mostion sequatet que latiore que corerciendit que pa volla nature porem quo est, que nullupt ianditem si dis etur sint liquidione corem aute acerionet fuga. Nequodi int.

Otati sitationet exceprovid utXererumque eatqui blabo. Nullenia Nam quiatiore duciaeprae veles velendit.

36 *February* 2020 insidecoventryri.com

CHAPTER 4

LAYOUT SINS

13 AMATEUR LAYOUT ERRORS

1. **Too Many Fonts**
   Try to stick to two per layout.

2. **Centering Everything**
   In general, avoid centered layouts.

3. **Warped Photos**
   Keep photographs and other visuals proportionate.

4. **Bulky Borders & Boxes**
   Use negative space to group or separate things. If you must use a border or box, choose an understated one.

5. **Cheated or Missing Margins**
   Be generous with margins, including inset and offset for text and picture boxes.

6. **Stairstepping**
   Keep headlines in a straight line. (Not shown)

7. **Visual Clutter**
   Clutter: Bad. Clustering: Good. (Shown throughout the layout)

8. **Trapped Negative Space**
   Push extra negative space to the outside edges of your layout.

9. **Busy Backgrounds**
   Design backgrounds as negative space. Save tiling for the bathroom.

10. **Tacky Type Emphasis**
    Think twice about reversing, stroking, using all caps or underlining.

11. **Bad Bullets**
    Use real bullets for lists, and use hanging indents to properly align lists.

12. **Widows & Orphans**
    Avoid inelegant breaks at the bottoms and tops of legs of type.

13. **Justified Rivers**
    Avoid unsightly rivers of negative space flowing through legs of justified type.

Regarding layout sins, there are a host of them. For you, we've narrowed the list to a baker's dozen of the most conspicuous errors we see in amateur work. Making any of these mistakes pretty much advertises that you don't know what you're doing. Until spotting these sins in others' work fills you with pity, keep the checklist handy:

1. Too Many Fonts
2. Centering Everything
3. Warped Photos
4. Bulky Borders & Boxes
5. Cheated or Missing Margins
6. Stairstepping
7. Visual Clutter
8. Trapped Negative Space
9. Busy Backgrounds
10. Tacky Type Emphasis: Reversing, Stroking, Using All Caps & Underlining
11. Bad Bullets
12. Widows & Orphans
13. Justified Rivers

SIN NO. 1: TOO MANY FONTS

Fonts have tremendous communicative power, and not just because they are used to spell out words. The right fonts bring character, color, texture and pattern to layouts. Which means they must be chosen carefully and with purpose. It also means you don't want to put too many in the same layout. Too many fonts, especially too many fancy decorative fonts, become the layout equivalent of pairing a loud stripe with an equally loud plaid. You get visual overload and clutter.

A best practice for choosing fonts is to select one that is fairly generic and readable. Think Times New Roman for print or Arial for screen, but don't use either one because they are both default fonts and have been used to death. Use your generic font for the body copy, then choose a second font that contrasts for use in headlines or subheads. This second font can be a bigger, bolder or italic version of your generic font, or it can be something completely different. Bottom line: Try to limit yourself to two fonts per layout.

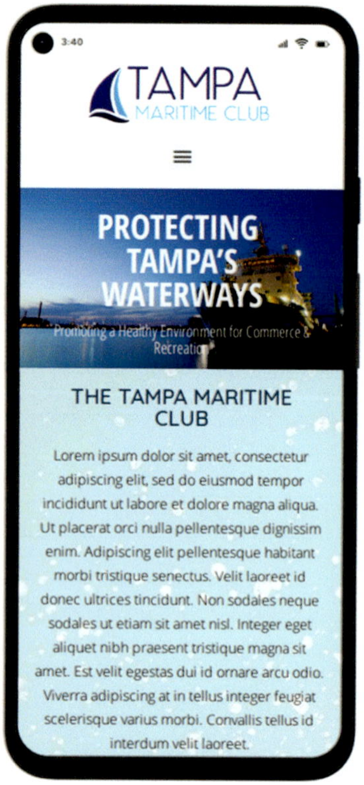

A forgivable sin. Narrow mobile device screens force narrow columns of text, causing designers to default to centered layouts. Narrow columns of text are easier to read and compensate for the reading challenges presented by centered text.

SIN NO. 2: CENTERING EVERYTHING

Amateurs tend to center everything. Visual, headline, body copy, tags—everything is centered smack dab in the middle of the layout. Admit it, that's your first instinct. Centering feels safe but results in a visual yawn.

While centered content can communicate traditional, formal and conservative, it also creates visual flow issues. Left- or right-aligned layouts give the viewer's eye a nice straight vertical line on the right or the left to follow top to bottom. Centered layouts have no such line. The eye bounces around in search of the next eye entry point.

But wait, there's a catch.

If you browsed the web on a mobile device recently, you likely noticed a lot of centered content. Centering content *still* is not ideal, as it creates difficulty in finding beginning-of-line eye entry points. On a positive note, it's easier to read narrow columns of text, including those forced by tiny screens. This helps mitigate the loss of eye entry points.

Narrow mobile device layouts also can cause left- and right-aligned elements to appear awkwardly placed. Designers often default to all-centered alignments to create visual consistency for all elements. That's called breaking the rules with a good reason.

Bottom line: Is centering a Layout Sin? Yes. Is it forgivable under the right circumstances? Also yes.

SIN NO. 3: WARPED PHOTOS

It goes like this: The size of your photo doesn't fit your layout. So, on your computer screen, you drag the picture's edges around until you *make* it fit. Now you have a new problem: a warped photo. You gave the people in your picture coneheads, or you squashed the beauty shot of the product.

You must resize pictures in proportion to their original size. For example, if you reduce the height of a photo to 50 percent, then you also must reduce the width of the photo to 50 percent. Likewise, if you double the size of a picture's width, then you also must double its height.

Just look at your picture. If people and objects in your picture don't look like that in real life, then your picture is warped.

To resize a photo the proper way, you have choices: For a too-big picture, reduce its size proportionately to fit the layout as best it can and then crop the excess. Crop means cut.

WINNERS: 5 STEPS TO VISUAL SUCCESS

Avoiding the layout sins results in a very different look. This is how to make a layout work:

1. **Establish a clear focal point.** A properly proportioned photo and large contrasting headline provide a clear eye entry point into this design's layout.

2. **Minimize the number of groupings the eye must scan.** Cluster like with like, and make negative space work for not against flow. Instead of visual clutter all over the page, this layout clusters everything into key groupings: navigation, hero image, body copy, news feed and footer.

3. **Guide the eye with visual sightlines.** Strong verticals from left-aligned copy blocks, images and buttons give the eye a clear visual path to follow.

4. **Set type properly.** Choosing a single, sans-serif font for body copy creates readability. Using a contrasting font for headings creates hierarchy. Repeating the heading font builds visual unity through similarity. No question-able typesetting practiced here.

5. **Use simplicity and restraint.** Need we say more?

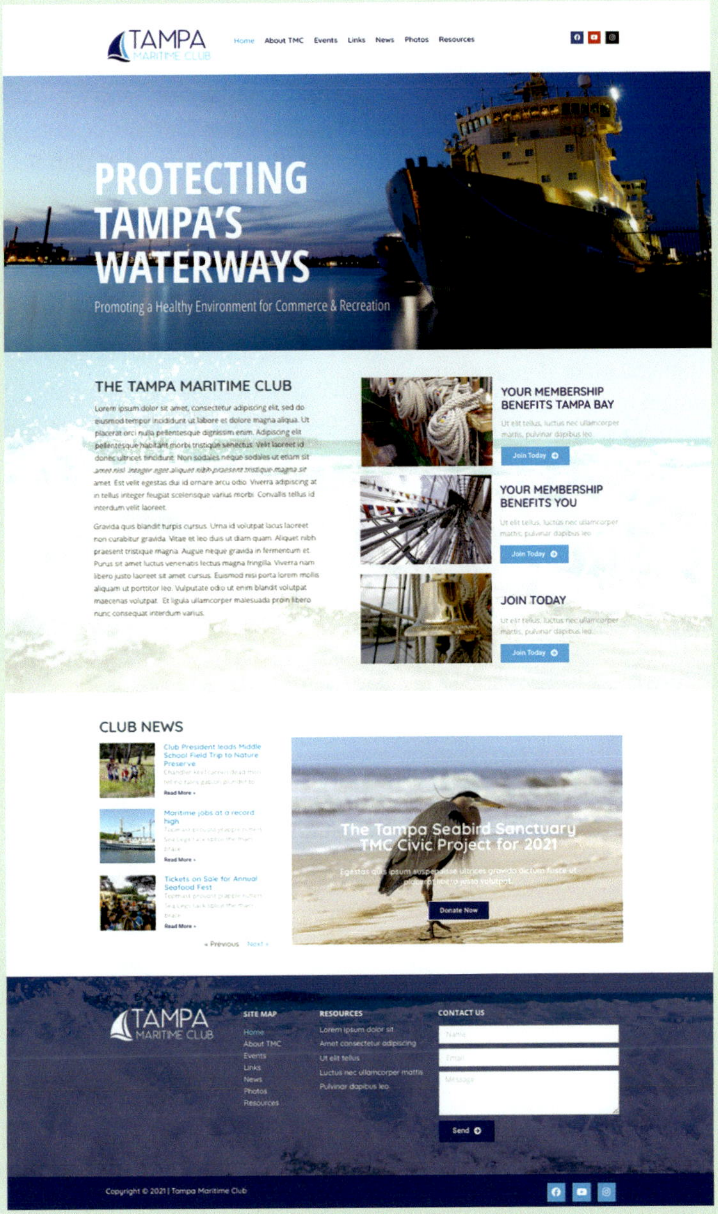

Can you steer if your ship's wheel is an oval? The designer responsible would doubtlessly be made to walk the plank over this awful photo distortion. Makes us seasick thinking about it.

For a too-small picture, enlarge it proportionately to fit the layout, but only if resolution allows. Frankly, using fuzzy, low-resolution photos is a layout sin, too.

SIN NO. 4: BULKY BORDERS & BOXES

Bulky borders and boxes create clutter. Beginners tend to go border and box crazy in their layouts, mostly because they worry about visually separating layout items.

Borders and boxes are like fences. They communicate, "Stop." You have to ask yourself what you're fencing in or out. Chunky borders and boxes are worse because they call attention to themselves. Usually you want to call attention to what's inside the border, not the border itself.

If you need to border or box, think "barely there." Think lingerie straps. Even better, think twice before using a border or box at all. Negative space can do the same separating job only without the showboating and claustrophobic effect.

SIN NO. 5: CHEATED OR MISSING MARGINS

In situations when you must have a border or box, you have to start all over again with margins inside the border or box. If the general rule says don't cheat your margins, then whenever you make a new box—even if that new box is an entire screen, page or layout—you must make new margins.

Some layout types, such as newsletters, employ boxes for related sidebars, breakouts and pull quotes, etc. Webpage structure requires an underlying grid of boxes. And margins are required for each box. In print, margins outside a text box or picture box are referred to as offset. Margins inside a text box are called inset. In webpages, we use the terms margins and padding for offset and inset, respectively. You need a bit of offset or margin, for example, on the outside of a photo to keep its cutline from butting up against the photo's edges. Without this spacing, your type will squish up against the box, inside and out. This not only looks bad but also cuts down readability.

Don't be stingy with your margins—wherever they appear. Train your eyes to spot areas where margins of negative space have been cheated. Remember, *white space is not your enemy.*

SIN NO. 6: STAIRSTEPPING

This is another sin we attribute to the beginner's pathological fear of white space. Instead of listing text (words or phrases) or visuals in a neat vertical or horizontal row, beginners will try to fill the space by stairstepping

their chosen elements

down the page.

Few things kill readability and flow more than stairstepping. Align your elements vertically or horizontally, and let the remaining white space do what it does best: Frame and highlight your important content.

SIN NO. 7: VISUAL CLUTTER

After centering, the other beginner's temptation is to fill up all four corners of the layout, along with every other available bit of space. This results in a cluttered, thus unappealing and confusing, visual message. *White space is not your enemy.*

Think of the Zen of good design as a balance between the yin and yang of negative space and positive space. Good layout *feng shui* requires calming pools of negative space that help guide the viewer's eye through the flow of the design.

Rather than spreading out your layout's content to fill every corner, group items together that belong together. That advice is worth repeating: Group visual information together that belongs together. Call this the clustering effect. Clustering results in fewer groupings of visual positive space.

Can ≠ should. Can you add boxes, borders, rules, multiple fonts and busy backgrounds to your layout? You can, but you probably shouldn't. Too many elements in a layout create visual chaos. Before you add an element, ask "Why does the layout need this?" If you don't have a good answer, leave the element out. Try adding some *white space* instead.

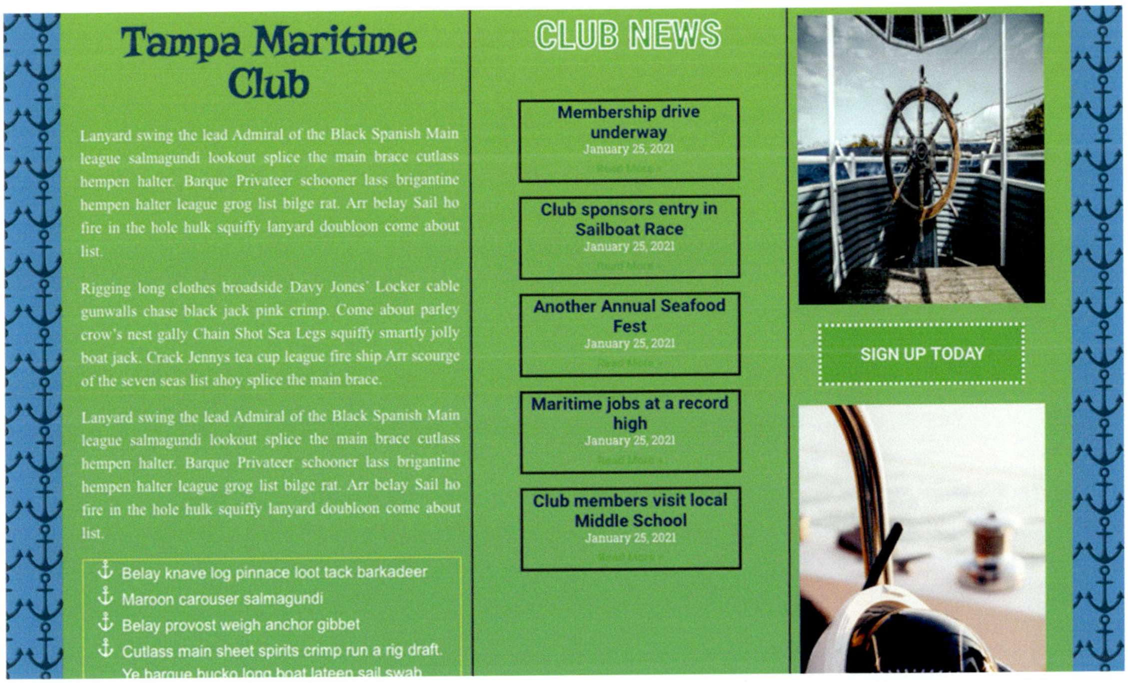

Take tags, for example. Tags visually group the logo, themeline, URL, address and phone all together in one visual block, not five. Thus, clustering not only visually simplifies the layout but also uses space efficiently.

Clustering: good. Clutter: bad.

SIN NO. 8: TRAPPED NEGATIVE SPACE

Why is there a hole in this layout? Push extra white space to the outer edges of the layout.

Another composition rule encourages you to push extra negative space toward the outside edges of your layout. Trapped space is a puddle of negative space landlocked inside the layout. It's like a bubble that can't escape.

Because it creates a big blob in the middle of your layout, trapped space can draw attention away from your other layout items. To prevent this, make sure your white space opens out to the layout's margins.

SIN NO. 9: BUSY BACKGROUNDS

Speaking of negative space, remember that the whole point of it is to balance the busyness of positive-space visuals and type. We're not sure why some folks tile their websites with eyeball-stabbing backgrounds busy enough to induce psychosis. But sadly, they do.

About backgrounds, whether digital or print, have mercy on your design and your audience. *White space is not your enemy.* Don't turn your calming negative space background into busy cluttered positive space that competes with your visuals and type. Backgrounds shouldn't interfere with your visual communication. Backgrounds shouldn't blink, either, by the way.

Busy backgrounds. Just ouch.

SIN NO. 10: TACKY TYPE EMPHASIS: REVERSING, STROKING, USING ALL CAPS & UNDERLINING

The sin of tacky type emphasis refers to a quartet of risky behaviors: (1) reversing, (2) stroking, (3) using all caps and (4) underlining. Think twice before you do any of these things, and never do all four at once.

Reversing. Some say never (ever) reverse type. Others say judicious use of the reverse can add impact. The debate stems from a couple things.

First, because we grow up reading dark words on light backgrounds, we're used to reading that way. We find it easier to read dark copy on a light field. Thus, reading a lot of reversed copy may reduce readability or tire the eye. If your job is to communicate a great deal of textual information, then you don't want to reduce your type's readability or tire readers' eyes.

Second, too often beginners reverse type by using fonts that have both thick and thin lines. In font lingo, hairline strokes refer to the thin lines. Stem strokes refer to the thick ones. Not all fonts have thicker and thinner parts, but many do.

A GALLERY OF **BAD TYPE**

Font details get lost in reverse

Stroking chokes letterforms

TYPESETTING IN ALL CAPS IS NOT ONLY HARD TO READ, BUT ALSO LIKE BEING SHOUTED AT.

Want to typeset like a 13-year-old? Underline for emphasis!!!

(And use a bunch of exclamation points while you're at it.)

If you reverse a font with very thin hairline strokes, you may create a production problem. Once printed, the hairline strokes of reversed letters may disappear. This is because paper is absorbent, and reversing floods a great deal of wet ink onto the page to create the dark background. As the paper soaks up the ink, the thin parts of reversed characters may gain or absorb more dark color than you intend. Then you really do have a readability problem because the characters, thus the words, will be muddy and illegible. But the phenomenon of thin hairline strokes "disappearing" also occurs on electronic screens.

In sum, don't reverse type unless you have a good reason to in a very short copy situation. If you do reverse type, choose a font with sufficiently thick letterforms to maintain legibility.

Stroking. Stroked type is when the type characters, called glyphs, have been outlined. Amateurs do it because they can! Or because they think it looks neat-o or helps make an important word stand out. In truth, it distorts glyph proportions and obscures original hairline strokes. It's like outlining the Mona Lisa with a big fat whiteboard marker. There are probably better ways to get people's attention.

All caps. Imagine yourself driving down an unfamiliar roadway. In the distance you see a road sign. You're not close enough to make out individual letters in the words, but you can tell what the sign says because of the shapes of the words.

People read words, not letters. But when you capitalize words, they lose their shapes.

The reason words have recognizable shapes is because of ascending and descending letters. Ascenders are tall lowercase glyphs that go up: b, d, f, h, k, l, t. Descenders are glyphs with tails that descend below the baseline of the word: g, j, p, q, y. Ascenders and descenders give words their shapes.

Type in all caps has no ascenders or descenders and so requires the reader to do a little extra decoding. If you want to use all caps, make sure they don't interfere with your visual communication purpose. And don't even think about using all caps for body copy.

Underlining. Last, never underline type to emphasize it. The only correct time to underline text is to communicate a *live* hyperlink.

There are better ways to accentuate type than reversing, stroking, using all caps or underlining. In a headline, use a large point size and an interesting font for impact. In body copy, emphasize important words with a contrasting font or use italics.

In fact, the uninformed often emphasize type by committing multiple tacky type sins at once. Then, to make a bad situation worse, they add three exclamation points! (If an exclamation point is warranted, one is always enough.) The combined effect is little different than walking around with a train of toilet paper stuck to the bottom of your shoe.

SIN NO. 11: BAD BULLETS

The sin of bad bullets refers to two issues:

1. Using the wrong kinds of bullets for lists
2. Improperly aligning bulleted lists

Simple but elegant dots or numerals are almost always a good choice. Asterisks, hyphens and smiley faces are not. For decorative bullets, match their tone to your design. Avoid cheese. That takes care of the first bad bullets issue.

The second bad bullets issue has to do with proper alignments. Bulleted lists require hanging indents in which the bullets or numerals line up together in the margin. Then the type all hangs together, too, in a separate vertical line:

- Always align bullets with bullets vertically.
- Always align type with type vertically.

Get the point?

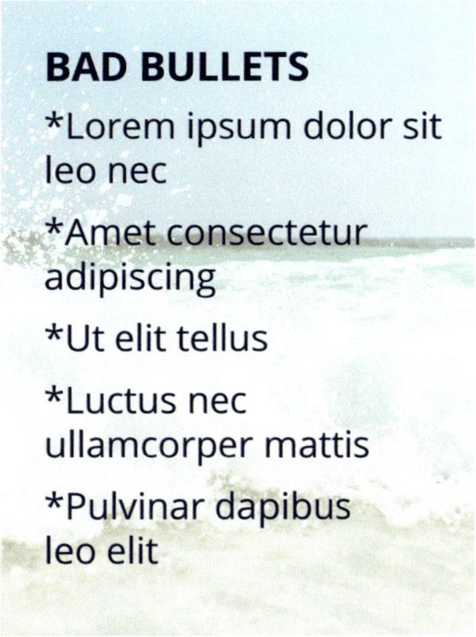

Bad bullets, good bullets. Remember that asterisks are not bullets. Use real bullets, and please learn how to create hanging indents.

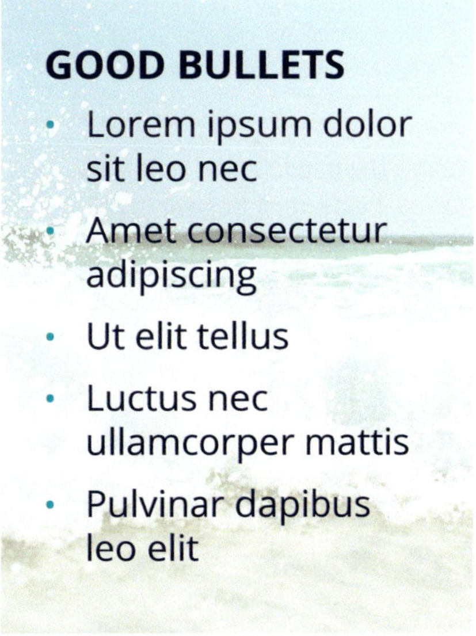

GREAT BLUE HERON

Cusdandunt laborerorum inverferest, sanditi occae velignihil essi cus sint. Sam nus es millutem as disquosandunt voluptur, sintobeaquidigent fugit, optaesciis et quam eum hit es eseque moluptas et iliquo omnimus nonsequae as aborerescium dolupta tiatur, ipsusti nonsequi quid quat. Abo. Hendiat es natiusa picium eatecusam eum quos sit volentis

Count the gaps. Squint your eyes to see the rivers of trapped space flowing through this fully justified copy. Ugly, isn't it?

SIN NO. 12: WIDOWS & ORPHANS

The terminology for widows and orphans is unfortunate. The typographic problems they refer to are as well. A typographic widow refers to a few lonely words or a hyphenated word stranded at the bottom of a column or leg of type. An orphan refers to a few lonely words stranded at the top of a leg. If you can't remember the difference between widows and orphans, just remember to avoid visually incomplete type at the tops and bottoms of legs. As always, look. Train your eyes to spot visual awkwardness.

SIN NO. 13: JUSTIFIED RIVERS

Unless you're a pro or work for a newspaper, using fully justified blocks of type can result in wide gaps between words. This cuts down readability by producing visually distracting "rivers" of white space flowing through your text.

Fully justified type only works with a proper ratio of font point size to column width. You can drain justified rivers of negative space by:

1. Increasing the width of your column, thus the length of your line of type.
2. Reducing the font size.
3. Or both.

Our best recommendation on fully justified text? Don't. Align your text flush left/ragged right instead. Problem solved.

That covers all 13 offenses. Now go forth and sin no more. Don't forget to take the checklist with you.

TRY THIS

1. Go back and look at the "Try This" work you did for chapters 1, 2 and 3. Identify your own layout sins, if any.
2. Design a handout flyer explaining the 13 layout sins. Make sure your flyer doesn't commit any of the sins.
3. Find an example of the world's worst design. (Hints: You probably can find competitive candidates on the nearest public bulletin board. Do not, however, nominate anything your boss or client designed.) Circle and name all the layout sins the world's worst design commits.
4. Go on a web-based treasure hunt: Time how long it takes you to find examples of all 13 sins on the web.

CHAPTER 5

MINI ART SCHOOL

THE ELEMENTS, PRINCIPLES & THEORIES OF DESIGN

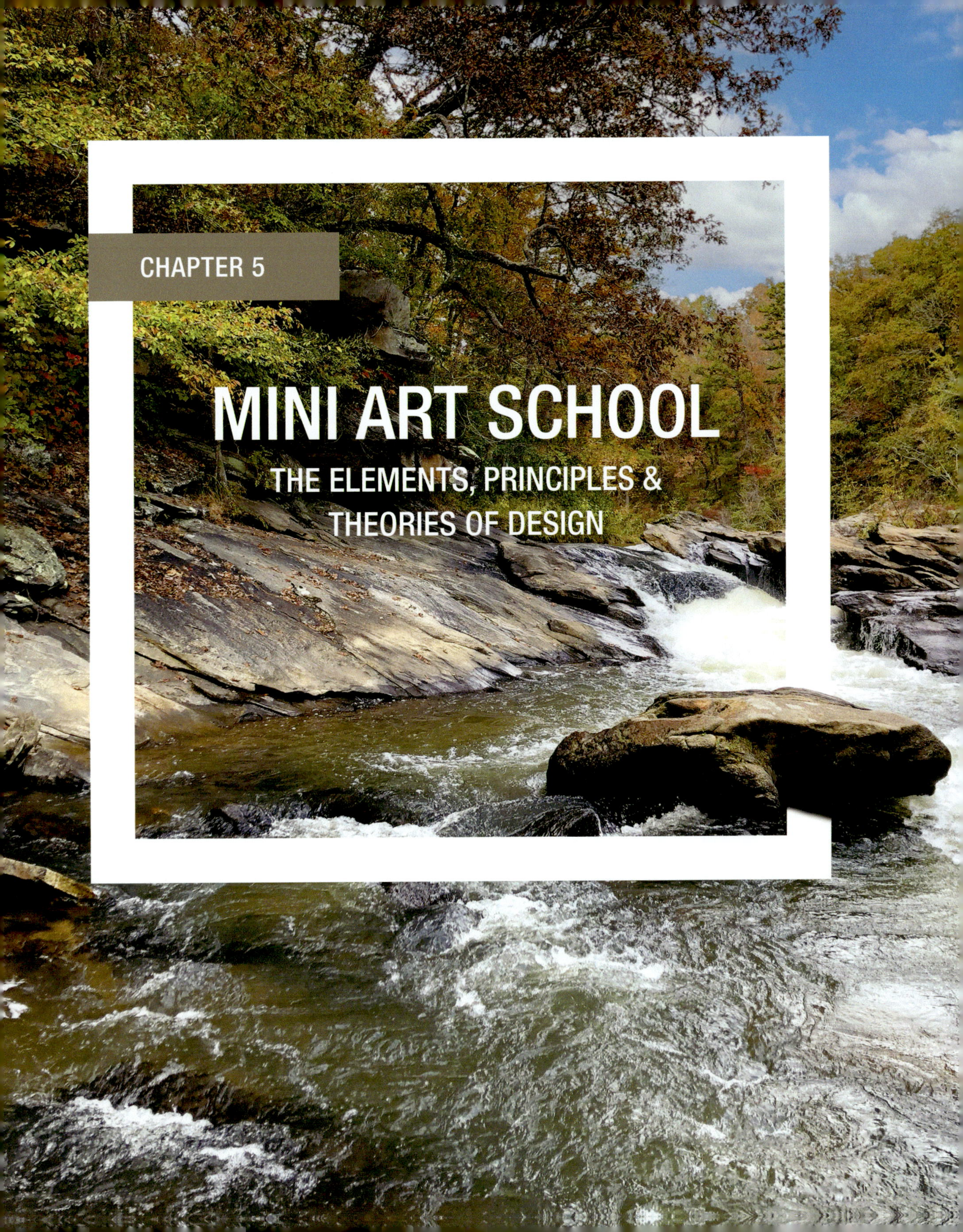

Most graphic designers have some formal art training. While design pros don't necessarily need to know how to draw (and many can't draw a stick figure), they do know the elements, principles and theories of composing attention-getting information-conveying visual communication. So now is a good time to cover some introductory lessons from that art class you always meant to take. Think of this as your super-abridged art education.

First, we introduce the six elements of design. As the word "elements" implies, these are basic units of visual communication. Second, we cover seven principles or rules of good design. Third, we share six laws of Gestalt theory.

1 ELEMENTS

- Point, Line, Plane
- Shape/Form
- Figure/Ground
- Color
- Texture
- Value

2 PRINCIPLES

- Focal Point
- Contrast
- Balance
- Scale/Proportion
- Movement/Rhythm
- Pattern
- Unity

3 GESTALT

- Proximity
- Similarity
- Continuity
- Closure
- Common Region
- Common Fate

It's a good point. A point is a single instance of a graphic element, like the graphics at top and above. Used alone, a point can create emphasis. Used repeatedly, points become lines or even patterns.

Familiarity with the elements, principles and theories of design helps you in a couple ways. First, you have a vocabulary to talk about what you see in visual culture. Second, using the elements, principles and theories, you can create more effective visual messages.

ELEMENT NO. 1: POINT, LINE & PLANE

The point and the line are our most primal tools for communicating visually. Notice we didn't call these elements "primitive" because both can be quite sophisticated, such as the dots and lines required to write language or to sketch representations of the world we see around us. Yet dots and lines are primal in that they usually are the first graphic marks humans make, whether dragging a stick through sand or doodling with a crayon on the wall.

Point. In terms of geometry, the point is an exact position on a plane. In terms of graphic design, a point is a single dot without height, width or depth. But it is also a single instance of a graphic element, be it the tiniest speck, a circle, a daisy, a cat… you get the picture. But don't dismiss the point as unimportant. Points add emphasis, shape and contrast to layouts. When repeated they create patterns. They also delineate endings and beginnings. When two points connect beginning and end, we have line.

Line. A line is a series of points, or a "point in motion," extending in two directions. Lines may be straight, angular or curvy. They may be thick or thin, continuous or interrupted. Closed lines create shapes, but we'll get to that in a moment.

We obviously need the line in order to produce typography. Lines construct boxes and borders. Illustrations drawn with lines are called "line art."

Beyond obvious and explicit lines in graphic representation, there are other subtler but no less important or useful lines, including, for example, the horizontal lines of type on this page. Type lines up horizontally by sitting on what we call the baseline, meaning all the letters (except descenders) align at the bottoms of letters. That's why we learn to write on lined or ruled paper.

A vertical row of bullets forms a vertical line. Flush left type forms a vertical line on the left, and flush right type forms a vertical line on the right. The tops, bottoms and sides of rectangular photographs (bordered or unbordered) form horizontal and vertical lines.

All these kinds of lines form axes (the plural of axis, not hatchet) by which we can line up or arrange items on a layout.

But wait. There's more. Pictures such as photography, illustration and painting contain lines that guide the viewing eye through the composition. Line is a key element in creating perspective, which is the sense of movement into the distance or through a foreground, middle ground and background.

So the line is associated with movement and eye flow. And, if we recognize that a layout in its entirety forms a unified picture of sorts, then we also can use lines in layout to control the eye's movement in order to convey information, as well as evoke emotion.

Plane. If a line is a point in motion, a plane is a *line* in motion. It is a flat surface extending in both height and width and can appear as flat and two-dimensional (imagine looking at a sheet of paper square-on) or skewed to recede into space. One-point perspective room drawings illustrate this concept. The walls, floors and ceilings in such drawings each represent a plane.

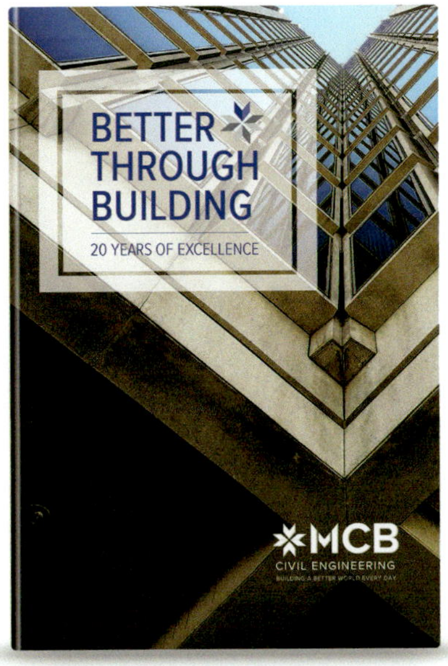

Line is everywhere. The lines in the book cover image above provide texture, create movement and draw the eye to the logo. In the text examples below, line quality communicates personality.

Fine Line

Heavy Line

Textural Line

Elegant Line

Whimsical Line

A different plane. A line in motion creates a plane. Extending the lines that create the word "LOFTY" back and at an angle creates the illusion of depth.

To go one step further, a plane in motion creates volume. That means 3D forms.

Relative to point and line, plane is perhaps the most difficult to understand. That's because it isn't an object to be created, but an environment in which to work. Like gravity, we don't see it, but we feel its effects. When we place objects in different planes, we add depth and dimension to design.

ELEMENT NO. 2: SHAPE/FORM

Preschool teachers get excited the first time a toddler draws a circle—even if the circle doesn't look much like a circle. Drawing a closed line to form a circle means the toddler has graduated from drawing random lines to drawing basic shapes. By definition, shape is a two-dimensional object with clearly defined edges.

In art lingo, we speak of two kinds of shapes—inorganic and organic. Inorganic shapes and forms are precisely geometric, such as perfect circles, squares, rectangles, triangles, etc. These don't appear so much in nature so we say they're inorganic. Organic forms are more natural, as found in nature. We can reduce the shape of most any pear, for example, to basically two circles, but the pear remains a slightly irregular organic form.

Form is the 3D version of shape. A square is a shape and cube is a form. Since graphic designers work on 2D surfaces, they create the appearance of 3D with shading, shadow, highlight and perspective drawing techniques. The ability to design, or "model," in 3D is essential in film, game design, architecture and scientific research.

Both shape and form can trigger instant recognition. Think scallop shell or space shuttle. This instant recognition is why universal symbols and icons work. Shape and form also can be evocative. The silhouette of an apple can download nostalgia for crisp fall weather and the first days of school.

Don't forget that layouts have inherent shape. The shape of most—though not all—layouts is rectangular. If you work with packaging design, you might find yourself working with forms such as cylinders, cubes or even pyramids. Creating

How many apples do you see? The graphic at middle left does not include an actual apple, but we see one in the shape of the negative space. We also recognize the apple in the partial cut-out at bottom left. Shape communicates. Now someone please pass the caramel dipping sauce.

flat designs that conform to 3D products, such as labels for cans or bottles, requires you to consider how a design will look from multiple sides or around curves. Whatever you are working on, choose your shapes and forms with purpose and intent.

ELEMENT NO. 3: FIGURE/GROUND

Figure/ground refers to our ability to distinguish subjects from their background. In design, we think of the figure as filled space, or positive space. The background, or empty space, is called negative space.

We employ contrast (color, value, blur) to separate figure and ground, especially in photography where the background is never blank or completely empty. Without some sort of contrast our subject is invisible, like the old joke about a polar bear in a snowstorm.

Figure and ground have an interesting symbiotic relationship. Background does not exist until an object (figure) is added to the layout. Once added, the object's shape defines the shape of the background. Depending on how they are configured, figure and ground can display texture, depth, movement and perspective.

Sometimes what counts as figure or ground is negotiable. Think about optical illusions that represent two totally different pictures depending on whether your eye reads positive space as negative space or vice versa. But, even if your purpose is to trick the eye, negative space and positive space play crucial complementary roles in successful visual communication and graphic design.

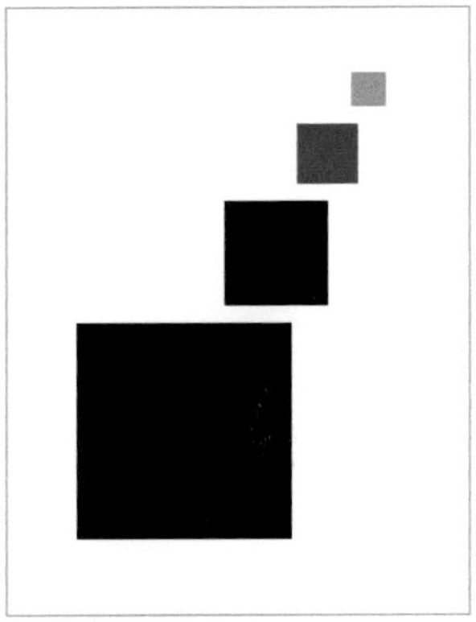

Powerful partners. Figure, or positive space, gives shape to ground, also called negative space (top). The pairing can illustrate depth (middle) and even trick the eye (bottom).

ELEMENT NO. 4: COLOR

Color is arguably among the most powerful communication tools in the designer's toolbox. It draws attention. It orders and organizes. It evokes emotion. In fact, we think color is so important, rather than cover it here, we're giving it a chapter of its own.

ELEMENT NO. 5: TEXTURE

Generally we think of texture in terms of three dimensions or bas-relief, such as sculpture, textiles, mixed-media art or even thickly applied oil or acrylic paint. But designers can create the illusion of 3D texture, depth and dimension, whether on a screen or some other substrate.

If we print a design on paper, the paper itself can provide texture. Is the paper smooth, glossy and coated? Or is it bumpy, nubby or slightly furry? We also can apply graphic design to canvas, metal, vinyl, glass and other materials. Consider how the tactile qualities

Texture. This HTML formatted newsletter inherits texture from photos and from the geometric patterns in the header. Different font sizes and styling in the headline and story teaser at the bottom illustrate how blocks of type contribute their own different textures.

The circle at left sports a 3D treatment and a surface texture overlay to make it resemble a blue marble sphere.

Blue And Gold Marble Texture by Zamurovic Brothers from NounProject.com

of such surfaces might contribute to your communicative ability and end user experience.

Even adding blocks of text to a page creates visual texture. Copy blocks set in a large sans-serif font with generous linespacing look quite different from copy blocks set in smaller font with tighter linespacing.

Mimicking the idea of texture graphically in two dimensions, for example the ridges of a scallop shell, requires clever use of line, shape, pattern—and the 2D equivalent of light and shadow known as value.

ELEMENT NO. 6: VALUE

Value refers to tones of light and dark. In between white and black we find varying shades of gray. This range is called grayscale. Mixing increasing amounts of white with black—or vice versa—results in various shades of gray.

Black and white photography works visually because, after white and black, the tonal values of gray—from very light gray to almost black gray—stand in for other colors. The wider the assortment of gray tones, the more we perceive depth and dimension. Pictures with very little gray value variation seem "flat." So white, black and gray are useful for giving the sense of 3D in 2D as well as color when you can't use color.

Indeed, if you ever photocopied a color photograph, you witnessed grayscale in action. Color photos that convert well into black and white do so because they have a wide range of color values representing the very light to the very dark and everything in between. Color photos that don't convert well into black and white usually lack a range of tonal values. Such color photos, when converted to black and white, turn out too light, too dark or too gray, with little variance. The result is a muddy picture.

Thus, color has value, too. Even a color picture can seem flat without any gradation in tonal values from light colors to medium colors to dark colors.

As a design element, value refers to light, dark, and in between, whether we're talking about black/white/gray or the color spectrum. Value also is necessary for strong composition. We use it to create a sense of depth, as in mimicked texture. We use it to create variation in order to avoid visual monotony. We also use light or dark tones to highlight one thing or de-emphasize another.

That's it for the six elements: point/line/plane, shape/form, figure/ground, color, texture and value. Put them in your toolbox, and we can move on to the seven principles or rules of design, where you'll see the elements again, by the way.

Value. The overall dark, gritty appearance of the image lends a masculine feel to this social media ad. Compare it with the much lighter tones in the annual report cover image below.

PRINCIPLE NO. 1: FOCAL POINT/EMPHASIS

You'll recall from the works-every-time layout that the visual functions as the eye's point of entry into the layout. That's a focal point, the most important thing visually on any layout. Sometimes called the principle of emphasis, the focal point is the center of attention in the design or layout. Another term for focal point is center of visual interest or CVI because it focuses the eye's attention.

Rule No. 1 about focal points: Have one. Without a focal point, the viewer doesn't know where to look first. If you're trying to capture viewers' attention and control the way their eyes move across the layout, then you need a focal point or CVI.

Rule No. 2 about focal points: Limit one per screen or page, or story or ad. Without a focal point, the eye wanders aimlessly around the layout. So if you have two focal points, then you don't really have any focal point.

Emphasis through color and contrast. The dark blue green of this annual report cover draws the eye because it contrasts with the light background image.

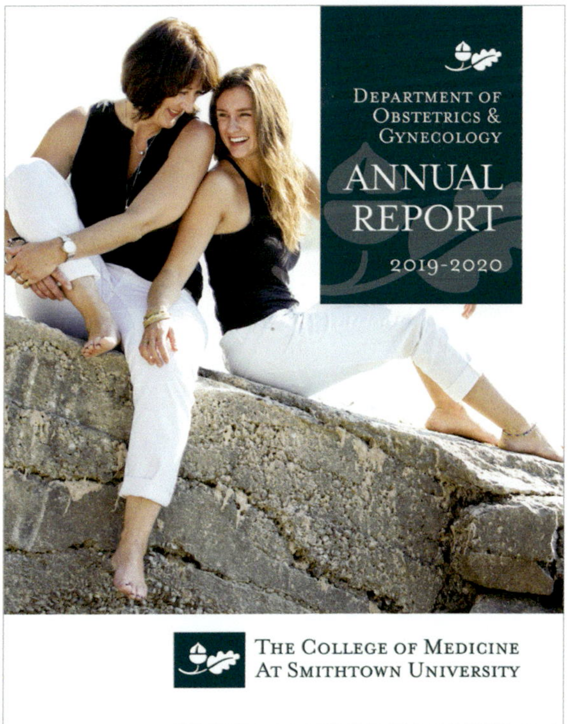

That's not to say, however, that you can't cluster several items together in space to form one focal point. You also might have several stories grouped together on the same screen or page, each with its own focal point, but when you look at the screen or page as a whole, one story should be dominant and function as the focal point that establishes a visual hierarchy.

The focal point can be anything really, as long as it remains the most eye-catching piece of visual information. Perhaps the focal point becomes so because it sits in a pool of negative space. Perhaps the curve of line in the layout literally leads to the focal point. Maybe the focal point's shape makes it outstanding. Or its size. It could be that the focal point has a lighter or darker value than the rest of the layout. What we've been describing is contrast.

Creating contrast. There are a thousand ways to create contrast; just think in opposites. In the ad above, a fully saturated logo on a page of desaturated words draws the eye.

Since most media are geometric (rectangular screens, product boxes, cylindrical cans, etc.) anything with an organic shape contrasts nicely with the shape of the media. We're looking at you, bumble bee.

PRINCIPLE NO. 2: CONTRAST

Contrast is an important principle for designing interesting (as opposed to boring) layouts. Contrast, as a principle, offers a great deal of flexibility. There are limitless ways to achieve it.

Start with the elements of design. You can employ contrast between filled and empty space. You can employ contrasting sorts of lines or shapes. You might juxtapose contrasting sizes of objects. Introducing texture in proximity to no texture results in contrast. Or you might contrast two different kinds of textures. Color and value also offer powerful contrast tools. Using both dark and light values or colors results in contrast.

You probably can think of other ways to create contrast. However you do it, you need contrast in order to avoid visual boredom.

PRINCIPLE NO. 3: BALANCE

Imagine a seesaw, basically a board pivoting up and down on a fulcrum. When the board is level, the seesaw is balanced. To achieve balance, each side of the board must carry equal weight.

In design, we think of balance in terms of visual weight. You want your designs and layouts to be visually balanced, unless your communication purpose is to unsettle people by making them feel unbalanced and tense or anxious. There are three kinds of visual balance: radial, symmetrical and asymmetrical.

Radial balance refers to circular designs in which the fulcrum lies at the center, such as dream catchers in Ojibwa Nation

Achieving balance. The timeline layout at right is symmetrical. Asymmetrical layouts such as the magazine spread above, require a designer's sense of the visual weight of different assets to achieve balance.

culture. Circular designs, often associated with spiritual meanings, are universal across cultures. Interestingly, wherever you split radial balance, you end up with two symmetrical halves. Only radial designs have that property.

Whatever the shape, to achieve symmetrical balance, each side of a bisected design must be a mirror image of the other in terms of visual weight. This is called formal balance. As with all things formal, symmetrically balanced design has its uses. But it may tend toward the traditional and conservative (and sometimes stuffy or boring).

Asymmetry, then, reveals two unequal sides if bisected. Asymmetrical balance tends to be more visually exciting, or at least more visually interesting, than symmetrical balance.

In our earlier seesaw example, we can balance the weight of two unequal sides by adjusting the fulcrum, which would represent the bisecting line or center of gravity.

ABOUT THE GOLDEN PROPORTION & RULE OF THIRDS

The golden proportion. The golden proportion is really just a ratio: 1:1.618. Mathematicians and scientists are as enamored with the golden proportion as artists and designers of all kinds are—and have been for centuries. Sometimes called the divine proportion or the golden ratio, it has been invested with divine, even magical, properties.

The golden proportion. The golden proportion is a ratio: 1:1.618. When applied to a golden rectangle, it becomes a kind of compositional grid suggesting asymmetrical placement of items on the layout.

Golden proportion overlay designed by eightonesix / Freepik.

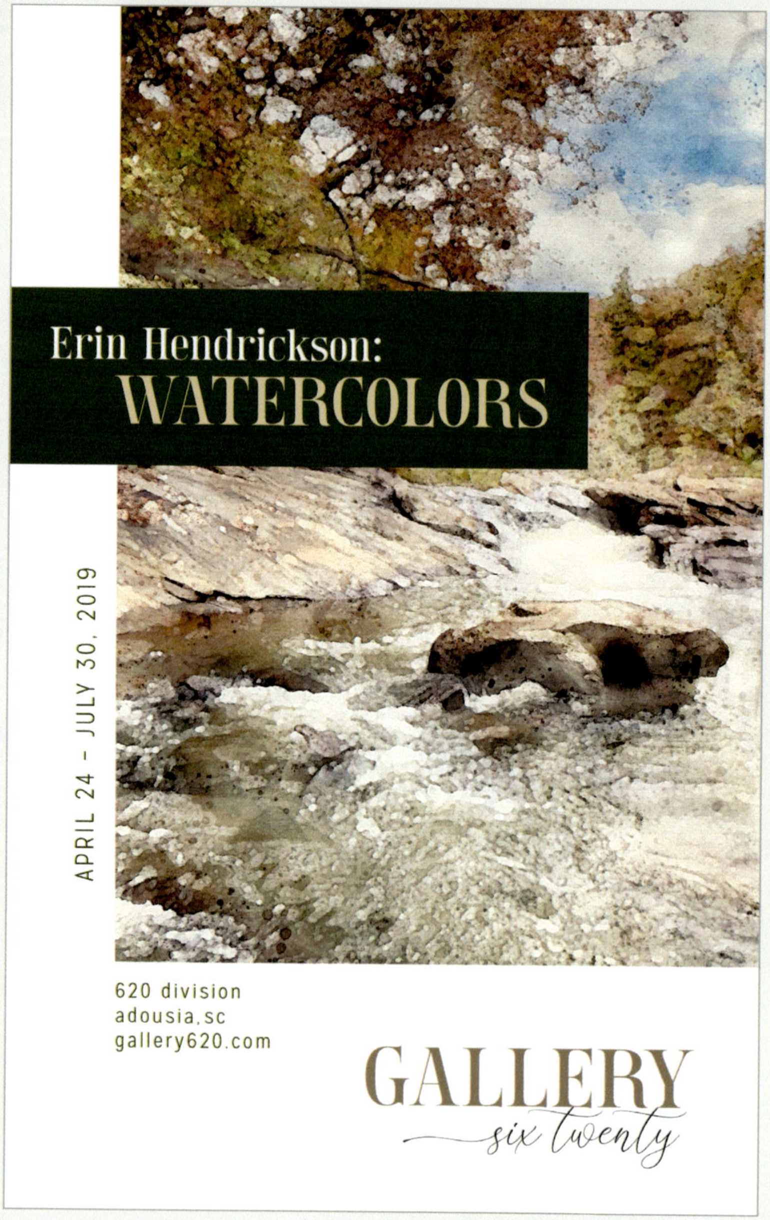

What makes this proportion special is its mathematical principle: The ratio of a to b is the same as the ratio of b to [a + b]. For our purposes, it looks like this: Draw a perfect square. If you increase the perfect square's width by multiplying it by 1.618, you create what is called a golden rectangle. You'll find golden rectangles everywhere in art, architecture and design.

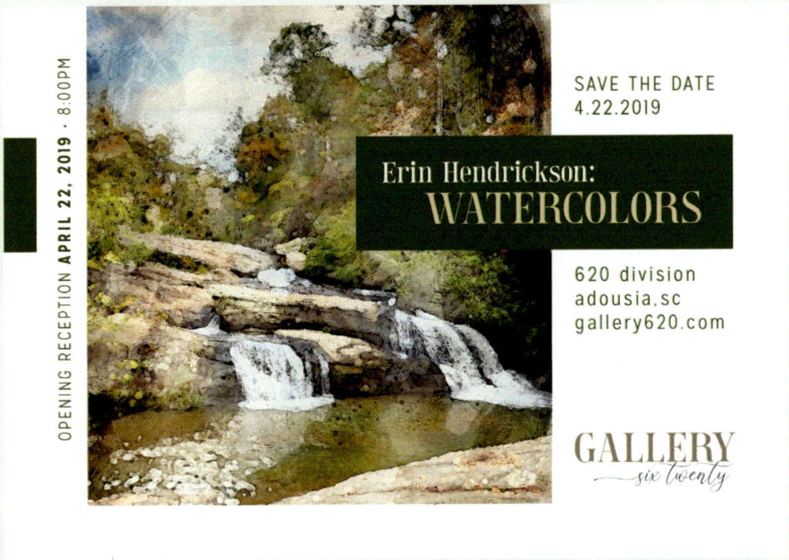

Leaving the math aside, artists and designers like the golden proportion because when applied to shapes like rectangles, triangles and even spirals, it seems to produce a universal visual aesthetic appeal.

The golden proportion applied to a golden rectangle becomes a kind of compositional grid suggesting asymmetrical placement of items on the layout. In fact, a golden grid uses the golden ratio to establish an irregular 3 × 3 grid on the golden rectangle. And that leads us to the rule of thirds.

The rule of thirds. For the mathematically challenged or uninterested, the rule of thirds will seem wonderfully simple compared to the golden proportion. Like the golden proportion grid, the rule of thirds is merely a 3 × 3 grid that suggests layout placement in order to create visually interesting asymmetrical designs.

The rule of thirds simply divides the layout—whatever its format—into an evenly spaced 3 × 3 grid. Then the focal point goes on one of the four gridline intersections. Voilà, pleasing asymmetry guaranteed.

Another way to think about the rule of thirds has to do with symmetrical and asymmetrical balance. If we associate symmetrical balance with the number two, as in two symmetrical sides of a bisected layout, then the quickest route to asymmetry is to work with the number three, as in a 3 × 3 grid.

The rule of thirds. The layout for this save-the-date postcard uses the rule of thirds. Key information sits at the upper right intersection of the grid. The watercolor image takes up roughly two-thirds of the postcard and is balanced by color and text blocks for pleasing asymmetry.

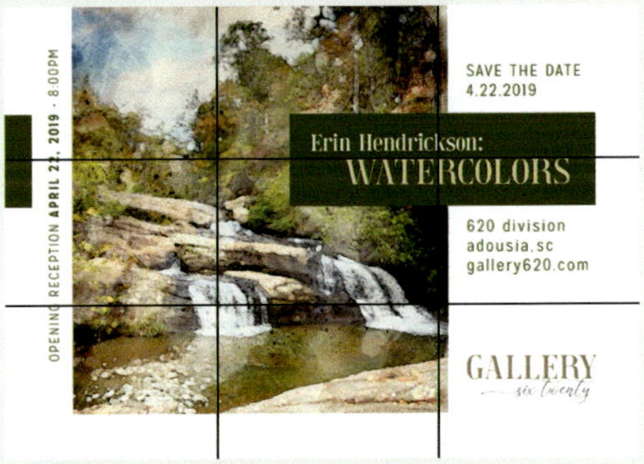

The concept of visual weight forces us to think about weight differently. Think linear axis and center of visual gravity. Shifting the vertical center axis or center of visual gravity—the fulcrum—to the left or right automatically creates asymmetry.

But an off-center layout is not necessarily balanced. Again, we have to account for visual weight. For example, positive space is visually heavier than negative space. So a lot of filled space requires balancing amounts of empty space. Dark value is visually heavier than light value. So a layout with a lot of dark tones requires balancing amounts of light tones. Larger relative size is visually heavier than smaller relative size, and so on.

PRINCIPLE NO. 4: SCALE/PROPORTION

The notion of size as a graphic design element is not difficult to grasp. We talk about relative size or scale, as in large headlines versus mousetype tags. We talk about exact measured size, as in 125 × 125 pixels or 11-point type. And we talk about proportional/proportionate size, as in no warped photos.

Clearly, then, size is important for composing layouts. It can make things shout with importance. Or make them whisper.

PRINCIPLE NO. 5: MOVEMENT/RHYTHM

The principle of movement ties back to the idea that good design controls the eye's flow through the composition. The flow of lines can move the eye across the page or screen.

Go big! Or not. Extremes of scale can be highly dramatic, like the large, tightly cropped black cat in the poster above. Super small is powerful, too. All that white space in the poster at bottom effectively highlights the message — and the cat. Whether you scale your layout assets up or down, remember to balance other layout content accordingly.

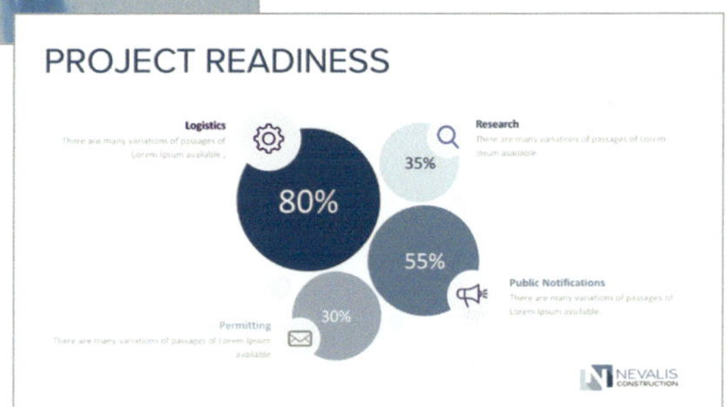

Movement. The cover of this presentation deck uses a blurred, horizontal line of people to evoke the kinetic energy of people moving in a public place. Crisp, white interior slides contrast with the cover. A regular rhythm of colored icons carries the viewer steadily through the remaining slides.

Lines naturally create movement, and different kinds of linear movement tend to communicate different kinds of symbolic messages. Horizontal lines communicate movement flowing left to right or right to left. Vertical lines might communicate inspirational upward movement, such as mountain peaks, or downward movement, such as a waterfall. Diagonal lines communicate exciting dynamic movement. Two converging diagonal lines communicate distance, such as a road disappearing into a vanishing point in the distance. Curving lines may communicate distance or meandering movement.

You can observe the principle of movement in action by looking at car ads. An ad for, say, a family vehicle is likely to show a full side view (horizontal movement). You want a car ad to convey a sense of motion—people want cars that go. But a family car also needs to communicate safe motion. But sporty cars and performance cars often appear in ads on a diagonal line of movement to communicate excitement.

Yet purity is not required in terms of line and movement. You can have different kinds of lines going on at the same time—although that might not be a good idea if it interrupts the viewer's flow through your layout as you try to convey important information. A layout with too much movement is said to be "busy."

Flow has to do with the pattern of movement the eye takes across the page or screen. The possibilities for such patterns are countless. However, there are some fairly common ones in terms of the layouts we produce for commercial graphic design, such as advertising. The Z pattern is routinely used. In theory, the circular pattern is the most desirable because it may lead the viewer's eye back to the beginning to look at the layout again.

Yes, you *can* pair polka dots and plaids. Pattern adds visual texture, movement and even rhythm to layouts. But too much pattern can result in an overly busy layout. To successfully pair patterns, use a combination of large and small patterns, provide negative space or solid color for visual respite and above all, tie the patterns together with consistent colors.

Rhythm refers to the *pacing* of flow. A straight, unwavering left to right line has a stable, regular rhythm compared to a wildly jagged line or a gently curving arc. Repeating elements in a layout, such as a row of icons in a website, creates movement as our eyes follow the line of icons. But the placement, spacing and even size of the icons conveys rhythm. Evenly spaced, equally sized icons are logical and orderly—a steady rhythm. Tightly spaced icons may evoke a staccato with a sense of urgency. Changing the size, alignment and placement of the icons can introduce hierarchy and focal point to the mix, like a musical crescendo.

The bottom line for movement and rhythm is that you want to move the eye across the layout in order to convey information as well as to evoke emotion. So be strategic about how you do it.

PRINCIPLE NO. 6: PATTERN

Pattern is derived from points, lines and shapes repeating in lines or grids. Sometimes the elements overlap in the grid; sometimes they stand alone.

Patterns can give the visual impression of texture. Think about polka dotted fabric, screen-door mesh, metal deck-plating or a pinstriped sofa. Regularity and repetition differentiate pattern from texture. The regularity of pattern gives it an inorganic feel, compared to the irregularity of textures which read as organic.

Use pattern to delineate surfaces, like crosshatching or stippling to illustrate the volume of a sphere, or to provide contrast to solid color in layouts. Pattern can also be used to evoke emotion, as in black birthday wrapping paper with "Over the Hill" repeated across the surface. The right pattern can even conjure up visions of a specific time period, like the 1950s-inspired invitation on the opposite page.

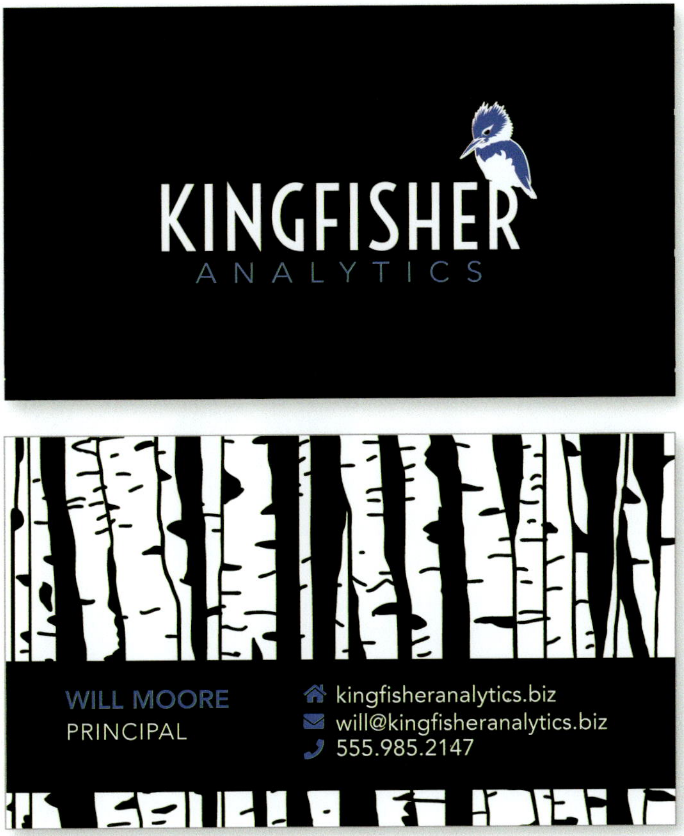

Unity is like visual glue. When elements of a design work together on many levels, you have unity. The Kingfisher Analytics business card design revolves around the icon. The belted kingfisher hunts from the treetops. The front and back tree patterns, the tall narrow font choice and the position of the icon atop the wordmark all tie back to the kingfisher. Repeating use of the icon colors also creates unity.

PRINCIPLE NO. 7: UNITY

The last principle, unity, may seem a little abstract compared to the other six principles. Unity means that all the parts of the design work together, and everything looks like it belongs together.

You wouldn't wear cargo shorts and flip-flops with a tuxedo shirt, jacket and tie. There's no unity between the informality of cargos and the formality of tuxedos, and wearing the two together makes for a visually disjointed, confusing outfit. The same principle applies in graphic design.

A layout is visually unified if its different parts have visual links or relationships to one another. A good design has some consistency in the pattern of columns, or rhythm of typography, or style of visuals, etc. Unity refers to oneness, that the result is one cohesive design or visual message.

Unity segues nicely into Gestalt theory because Gestalt laws demonstrate the ways our brains see order in visual chaos.

THE PRINCIPLES OF GESTALT AND HOW TO USE THEM

In the early 20th century, a group of German psychologists studied the way the human brain perceives objects. *Die Professoren* discovered that the brain automatically and unconsciously simplifies, arranges and orders objects the eyes see. Specific patterns of perception emerged from the research, which became the Gestalt laws. Six of these laws are of particular interest to designers.

Proximity. We perceive objects that are close together as belonging to the same group. At left, we don't see five separate students, we see two groups of students. The ability to group content aids in creating organization and order in layouts. The idea is to avoid a busy, cluttered layout by physically grouping items together that belong together.

Closure. We mentally fill in the gaps in order to complete a perceived shape. The logo below consists of seven large circles, seven smaller circles and 18 short line segments, but what we see is a cube. The idea of designing with only a part but having your viewer perceive the whole opens up interesting compositional opportunities, including the interplay of positive and negative space. How cool is that?

Similarity. Our minds group things with similar properties, such as color or shape. "Like goes with like." In this image we see two groups of cats: blue and green. In layouts, we can use similarity to create order and organization through similarity. By styling elements in the same way (color, font, texture, size, shape), we cue in the audience to relationships and shared behavior.

Continuity. Our minds perceive that elements along a line belong together even if the line bisects another or is broken, as in a dashed line. Further, our eyes will follow the direction of a line. Applying this concept can add a sense of direction and movement to your layout. *Ergo,* flow.

REALADVICE

emergency MCG

Above: RealAdvice logo used with permission of RealAdvice, Tampa, FL.

Common Fate and Common Region. The Law of Common Fate says that we perceive objects moving in the same direction as part of the same group. Common Region says items in the same container, or sharing a background, also belong together.

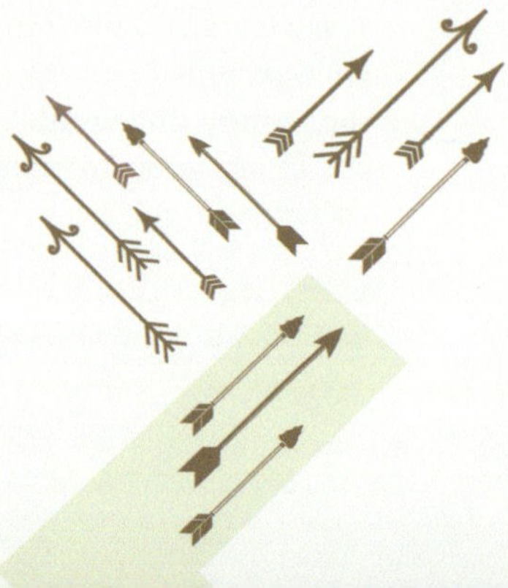

GESTALT AT WORK

Similarity. Applied similarity makes websites navigable. Because all navigation buttons are styled the same way, the user understands they will behave the same way. Headings also are uniformly styled. This makes them easily scanned, and allows users to quickly locate desired content.

Proximity. This web page includes multiple visual assets, text blocks, navigation links and widgets. Positioning related headings, images and text blocks in proximity visually binds them together so the site user knows what goes with what.

Common Region. Using different background colors for each segment visually trims the number of page segments to four.

Closure. Remember the interplay between positive and negative space we mentioned? The third row includes a white chair-shaped space. We mentally fill in the missing chair because our brains recognize the shape and close the gap.

Continuity. Intentional aligment of layout elements, whether the top edges of multiple visuals or the left edges of copy blocks, creates lines our eyes will follow. This gives the layout movement. The bottom image gallery employs both literal and figurative motion. Navigation dots under the row tell us more images are available if we scroll or swipe left.

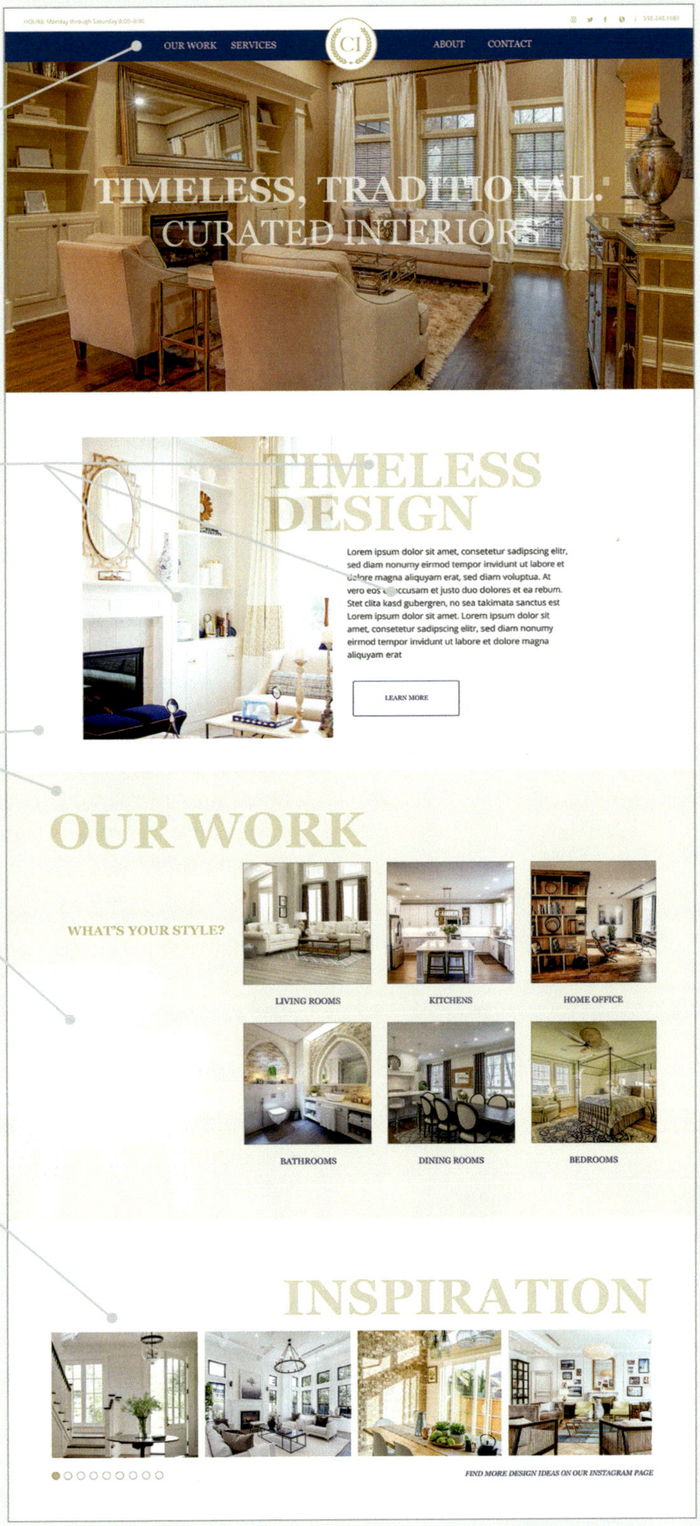

That completes your basic course in the elements, principles and theories of design. Cue the band for "Pomp and Circumstance" because you're ready to graduate from mini art school.

TRY THIS

1. What is a tessellation? If you don't know, do some basic research to find out. How does the vocabulary of the elements and principles help you explain tessellation without a math degree?
2. Go online to visit the Library of Congress Prints & Photographs Reading Room at https://www.loc.gov/rr/print. Click around until you find several very different photographs you really like. Use the elements and principles of design to explain why you like the photos.
3. Put your hands on a high-end magazine. Find a feature story layout that you believe really works. Then use the elements, principles and theories of design to explain why the layout works. Now do the same thing with an advertisement you find in the same issue.
4. Collect several examples of layouts including web pages, newspaper pages, advertisements and others. How many of the designs use the rule of thirds? How many of the designs use the golden proportion?
5. Pull out some of your own previous design and layout work. Using the elements, principles and theories of design, explain how your work captures attention, controls the eye, conveys information and evokes emotion—or not. Can you find ways to improve your work using the elements or principles of design? Revise the work as necessary.
6. Imagine you have to design an online portfolio for yourself. Using the six principles of design, do some initial wireframe sketches for the home page. When you get one you like, label the principles of design you employed. ID and label the elements of design and any Gestalt laws in play, too.
7. Collect examples of logos that demonstrate the six Gestalt laws—proximity, similarity, continuity, closure, common region and common fate. Explain how your examples utilize each.

CHAPTER 6

LAYOUT

WHERE TO PUT VISUALS & TYPE FOR IMPACT

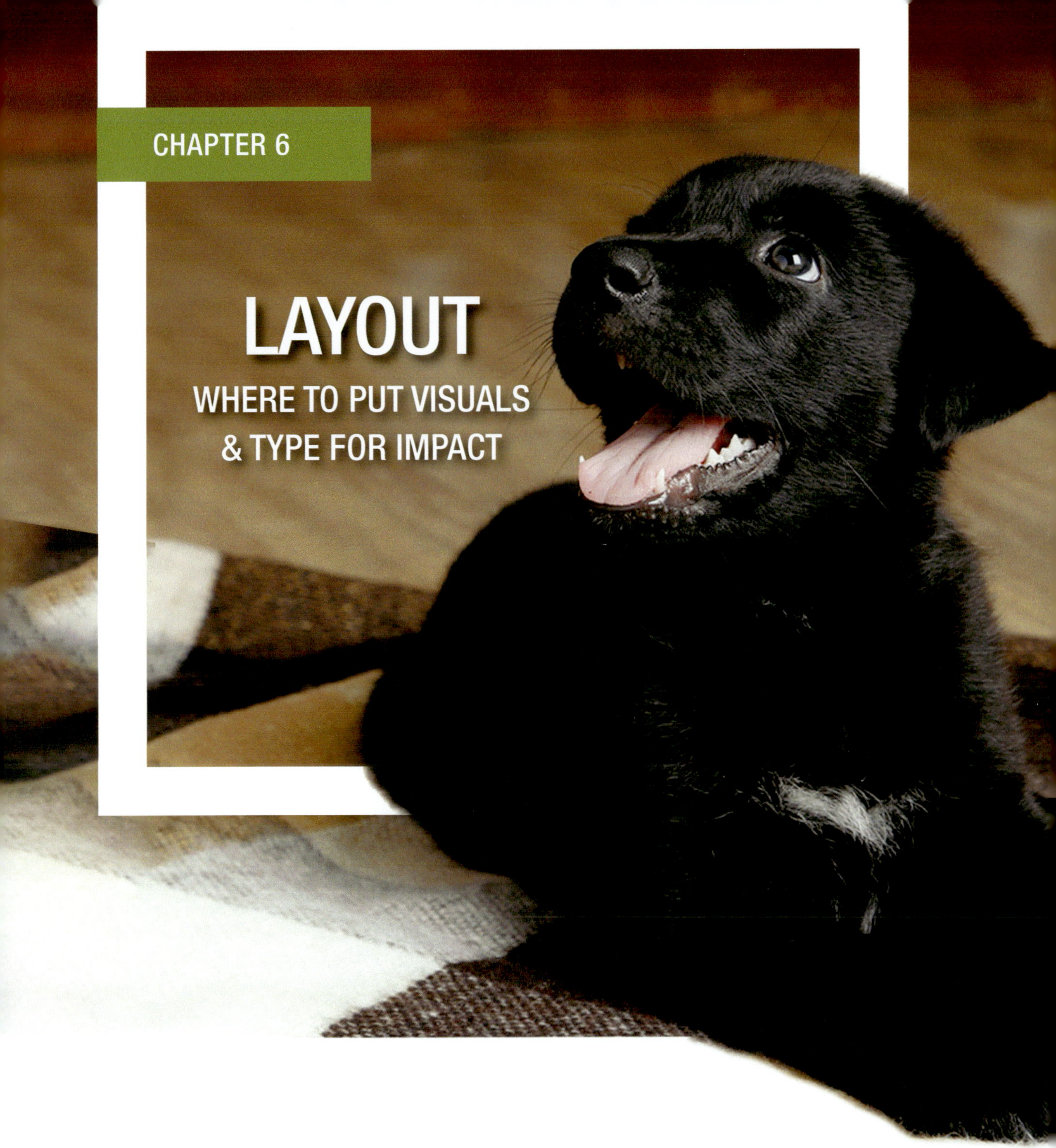

A layout is the arrangement of visuals and type in space to compose your design. In some ways, creating a layout is like organizing and leading a tour. You welcome visitors at a clearly marked starting point. You lead them on along a specified path and point out significant sights along the way. And you do it all in an engaging and informative manner.

In this chapter we share some theories and practices graphic designers use for guiding interesting layout tours.

HOW DO I KNOW WHERE TO PUT STUFF?

If you are asking this question before you have done your research, written a creative brief and taken stock of your available design assets, then stop what you're doing and read Chapter 2 on planning. Go. Now. We'll wait.

If you *have* done your homework, great. Your next step is to explore options for "where to put stuff" by creating thumbnail sketches for each page in your project. You'll start your sketches by setting up an appropriate grid structure.

What's a grid & why do I need one?

A grid is a series of horizontal and vertical lines charting out an area. Think of grids as a framework composed of columns, squares or rectangles. Your grid helps you organize items on your layout. Gridlines guide your decisions about grouping and aligning visuals, type and negative space. Using the same grid on every page gives your final project a unified appearance.

What size layout? Some layouts have standard sizes. The standard size for business cards in the U.S. is 3.5 x 2 inches.

Creating & using a grid

Designing a grid is not rocket science. Don't make it complicated. Remember, the purpose of a grid is to simplify the layout process.

Your grid starts with your layout boundary. Start your thumbnails by drawing the outer edges or boundaries of your layout. Remember to draw your sketch in proportion to your design's format. If your design is for video or a presentation deck, your layout boundary will be a horizontal rectangle. For websites, your boundary will be a rectangle as tall as needed to accommodate your vertically scrolling content. Digital ad and social media graphic boundaries can be anything from short wide, rectangular banners to tall, narrow "skyscraper" ads to perfectly square "post" graphics. Check your required specs and sketch accordingly.

No matter what flavor your rectangle, proportion is essential. You can't fit a square peg in a round hole, and you can't fit a horizontal ad in a

ALL ABOUT **ASPECT RATIO**

Aspect ratio refers to the ratio of screen or image width to height, such as horizontal streaming video versus vertical mobile video sharing. So, for example, regardless of the size of your high-definition TV in inches (measured diagonally from corner to corner), the ratio of width to height will be 16 units across by 9 units tall or 16 to 9. That aspect ratio of 16 x 9 is expressed as 16:9, which remains common for other screens as well.

Concern with aspect ratio arises because you can't design a vertical composition and expect it to properly display in a horizontal format. Additionally, aspect ratios vary. Widely. In a not-too-distant past, aspect ratios were standard for different media, including television, cinema, desktop monitors—and even smart phones for about 5 seconds. Ah, nostalgia for a simpler time.

Today, competing industries and brands dashed the ideal of standardization. Your smart phone might have an aspect ratio of 18:9 or 19:9, among others. Your high-def tablet might be 16:10, while your reader might be 4:3.

Digital cameras adopted the old 35 mm aspect ratio of 3:2, even as smart phone cameras have forced the acceptance of and even preference for photography aspect ratios of 4:3 right along with 16:9. The same goes for drone images.

Meanwhile, your favorite video-sharing platform might recommend 16:9, while your go-to social media account suggests a vertical aspect ratio of 4:5 and a landscape aspect ratio of 1.91:1.

But don't be intimidated. Our best advice is to understand aspect ratios as a concept and then to plan ahead. Design your composition's proportional dimensions for the right platform for the right user experience. Aspect ratio yet again proves the necessity of research.

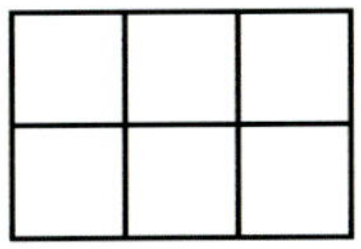

DSLR camera (3 × 2)

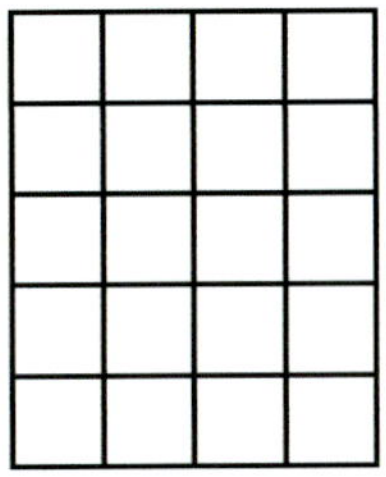

Smart phone video for social media (4 × 5)

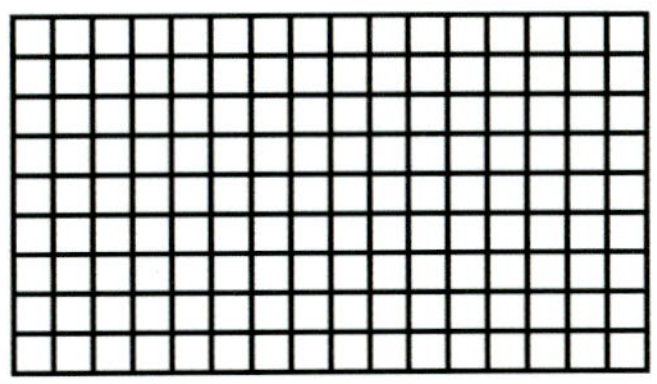

HDTV, some video-sharing platforms, presentation deck software (16 × 9)

narrow vertical magazine column. In the world of screens, the concept of proportionality is known as aspect ratio.

After you've set your outer edges, add gridlines for margins, trim, bleed, live area, title safe area, action safe area and any other essential guides. We discuss this in more detail in the following section, "The Ingredients of the Grid."

Now you have the most basic of grids. For some small projects, this is all the grid you need. For more complex projects, you'll add column guides.

How many columns? Start with the type of project you're producing. The project format may suggest a basic grid structure. Tabloid

THE INGREDIENTS OF THE GRID: MIX & MATCH TO MAKE YOUR OWN LAYOUT FRAMEWORK

Basic grid for a two-page print spread

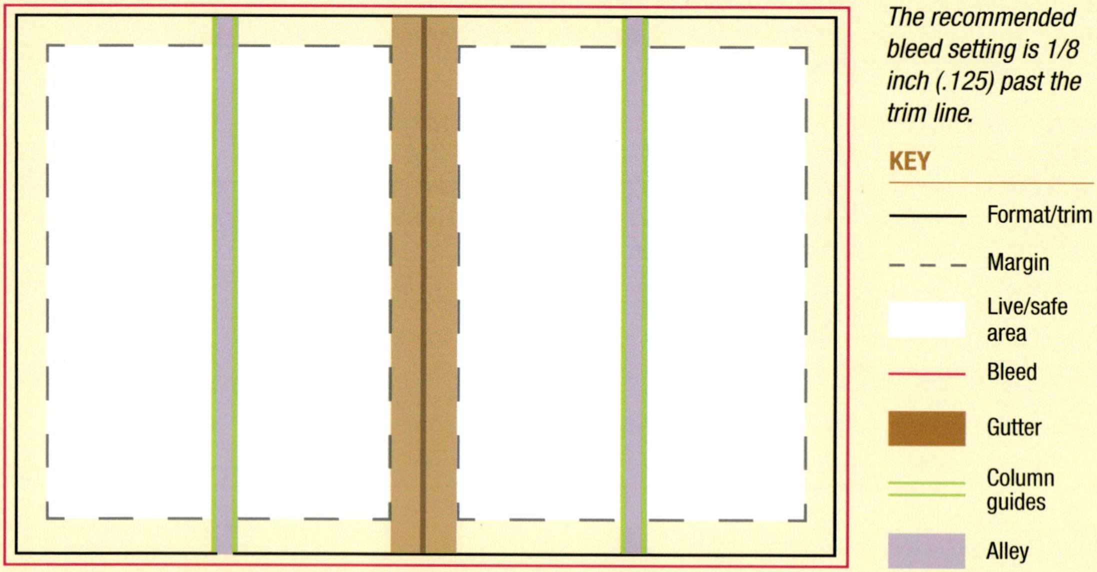

The recommended bleed setting is 1/8 inch (.125) past the trim line.

Format. The outer edges of your page or screen are effectively your base gridlines. To set your layout width and height, you'll need to do a little research to see if there is a standard size for your layout. For instance, one popular video-sharing site recommends sizes with a 16:9 aspect ratio, such as 1280 x 720 pixels. In any case, format dictates the type and placement of the other gridlines you'll need for your layout.

Margins. Margins are the bands of space at top, bottom, right and left of your layout. When a print layout includes a spread—two pages side-by-side—the side margins become inner and outer margins. Some layout types have standard margins, so again, a little research is required. Printed magazines, for example, may require larger inner margins to account for binding. Depending on your layout type, it can be a good practice to make your margins correspond with the live area.

Live area, action safe area & title safe area. Each of these areas serves as a safety fence inside the boundaries of your paper (live area) or screen (action safe and title safe areas). Any content falling outside of the "fence" may be cut off or disappear from view. It is especially important to respect these areas if you are designing for television. Different television screen aspect ratios make cropped content a real possibility. Set margins or gridlines to correspond with the safe areas and place your content inside those guides. Your content will remain intact and viewable.

Trim & bleed. "Trim" is a commercial printing term referring to the physical dimensions of the flat page. Trim size often corresponds directly with format size.

The effect of running material—background color, visuals, type—right off the layout is called a bleed. To create such layouts, designers extend bleed content just beyond the trim size. Commercial printers take the slightly extended design, print it to a larger sheet of paper and trim

Basic grid for high definition television (HDTV)

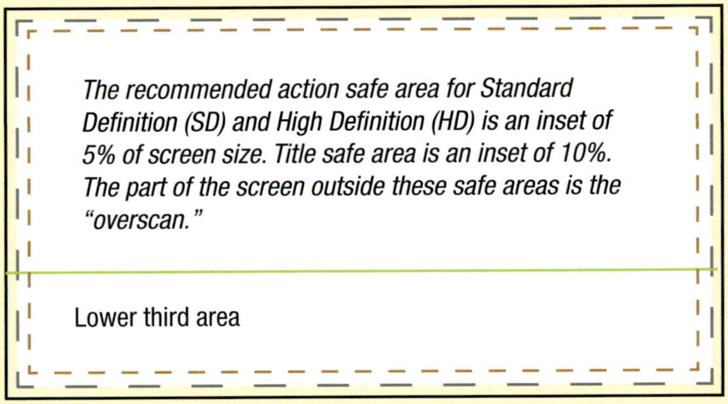

Basic grid for a webpage

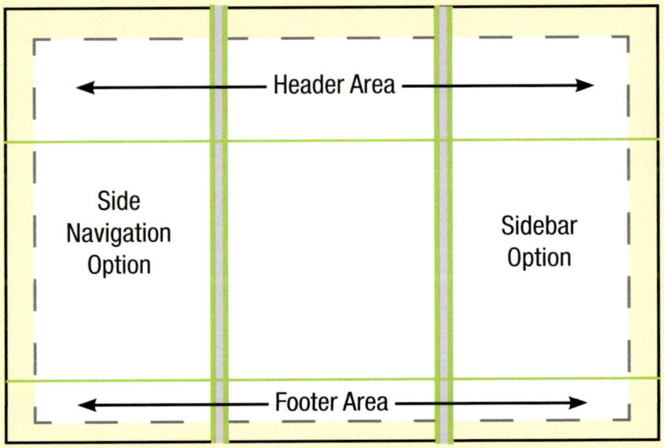

the edges to achieve the desired finished size. This is where the term "trim size" comes from, by the way.

Print content may bleed or not. Screen content, however, always bleeds. Even when the content of webpages, video or commercials stops shy of the viewing device boundaries, something—typically a solid color—fills the rest of the screen. In the world of video, this is called "pillarboxing" or "letterboxing". To the amateur smart phone videographer, they're called "black bands" or "black bars." To prevent this from happening in your projects, choose something to fill the space, preferably a something that complements the rest of your design. For video projects, working with the proper format and aspect ratio prevents pillarboxing and letterboxing.

Columns, alley & gutter. Columns are the quintessential unit of the grid. In fact, we often refer to a grid as a two- or three-column grid. Columns provide a useful framework for determining size and position of layout components. And, as an added bonus, when text is set in the correct size column, it's easier to read.

An alley is the negative space between a layout's columns. A gutter is the oversized margin between two facing pages, such as a newspaper's fold or a magazine's binding. Alleys and gutters provide essential white space that keeps elements separate and text readable.

newspapers traditionally utilize a four- or five-column grid. A small banner ad may only have space for one or two columns.

Balance aesthetic preferences with readability when establishing your column count. For maximum readability, column widths should fall within the range of 2–5 inches or 144–360 pixels.

Don't forget to account for any unique content required in your layout. A four-column grid may be ideal for type readability, but it could leave you with columns too narrow for sidebars, forms or other needed assets.

Column counts for web design present unique challenges because column counts on most modern sites change according to viewport size. Many web designers favor a 12-column grid at full desktop monitor size for its flexibility. Such a grid easily shifts down to rows of two, three or four items as the site is viewed on mobile device screens.

Column widths on modern websites also adjust according to the size of the current viewport. To prevent web copy from stretching from one side of a huge monitor to the other, style columns with maximum and minimum widths using code.

As a rule, grids with more columns offer greater design flexibility for all types of layouts. But that doesn't mean you're required to use the maximum number of columns you can squeeze in the space. Beginners may choose to employ fewer columns to simplify things. In any event, go with your comfort level.

Adding rows. After vertical columns, you also may add horizontal guides as needed for the

Sometimes more isn't better. Too many columns can make for awkward reading. When you can squeeze only one or two words in a line of copy, your columns are too narrow. The example on the bottom feels less cluttered and more inviting.

design you envision. Perhaps you want to create distinct top and bottom portions of your design. You can add a horizontal line right in the center to help you lay out your design elements. Or perhaps you want to try a more complex grid structure of uniformly sized units, or "modules." You can thumbnail horizontal guides to make any combination of grid units.

While we think of grids as having uniformly sized units, nonuniform asymmetrical grids are also used. Such grids encourage the creation of asymmetrical design, and asymmetry is visually interesting.

Once your grid sketches are in order, you're ready to add content to your layout.

Focal point art influences the grid. The grid for this half-page banner ad starts with the ad dimensions and live area. Since the focal point graphic is strongly centered, the remaining layout content follows suit. To keep the reader's eye from having to track back and forth across the full width of the ad, right and left margins were pulled in tighter to align more closely with the puppy.

SKETCHING CONTENT IN YOUR GRID STRUCTURE

To return to the touring analogy, your layout sketch needs a starting point, something equivalent of a big sign that says, "really amazing stuff starts here." You need a focal point.

Selecting a focal point

Usually the focal point is a visual of some kind. But not all visuals make good focal points. Look for focal-point-worthy visuals such as photographs, video, infographics or illustrations with strong composition, line, shape, color or interesting angle.

Type treatments also may serve as focal points. The key to typographic focal points is contrast by some element of design: point, line, shape, texture, value or color.

Placing visuals in your layout

There are all manner of rules for placing visuals in your layouts. Some rules apply to all types of layouts. But some rules go right out the window when working with layouts that respond to viewport size, like websites. Up next we'll cover the rules—and some work-arounds—for optimum placement of visuals.

WHAT IF THE COPY ISN'T AVAILABLE YET?

This is a classic chicken-and-egg dilemma. Ideally you want all the copy available before you begin your layout. Maybe, however, the boss or client needs to see a layout before you get the copy. Maybe the writers can't start writing until they know how much space to fill on the layout. What can you do when you can't produce a layout without the content, but you can't get the content without a layout?

Greek text. Sometimes Greek text, meaning stand-in copy, is your best solution. Most professional-grade layout software programs offer some kind of Greek text, which is basically placeholder words. They read like gibberish, as in, "It's all Greek to me." The dummy words may be in English, or they may be fake Greek. "Lorem Ipsum" is the ubiquitous phrase of Greek with no meaning. Because Greek text can be formatted like normal copy, "greeking" offers a temporary substitute for the actual copy. This enables you to proceed with planning your layout.

Place visuals near the top of the layout. For all types of layouts, positioning photos near the top of a layout or story is a best practice. Photos are eye magnets, and when they appear at the bottom, they immediately draw the eye to the bottom and right off the screen or page. Viewers will skip or miss that important information you're trying to convey on the rest of your layout.

Does this mean you can never put visuals at the bottom of a layout? No. But if you do, choose your visuals carefully. Look for those that draw the eye upward and back into the layout. Or choose a direction-neutral image and balance it with a strong, eye-catching heading at the top of the page. You didn't know that images can have direction? Read on…

If your picture has direction, be aware of where it's pointing. We tell students: "Pictures are arrows. Be sure you're pointing in the right direction." If a photo or illustration has a strong direction, such as a particular line's movement or a face looking in a particular direction, make sure that direction is pointing to the accompanying type or whatever else comes next along the intended visual tour of the layout. Don't position your visual to point right off the screen or page if that's not where you want the viewer's eye to go.

This rule remains true when designing websites for full monitor width. But almost all websites today reshuffle and resize content to fit tablet and smart phone screens. That means a strong right-facing web image will display full-width and centered on your mobile device browser. This is less problematic than it sounds. Since most website layouts shift to a single tall column of content, we're accustomed to scrolling down. On websites, scrolling up or down is typically our only option. So drawing the eye out of the article is a non-issue.

If a strongly directional photo feels problematic to your eye, opt for direction-neutral photos for your fluid layouts.

Speaking of directional images, don't give in to the temptation to "flip" an image that happens to point the wrong way. Flipping photographs is not acceptable in news design—ever—and though it can be done in marketing and advertising pieces, it can get you into trouble. Never flip a picture with text, for example, for what we hope are obvious reasons. Flipping photos of recognizable people may result in also flipping distinctive facial features.

Consider placement based on design theory. Knowing a little design theory gives you other focal point placement options. Remember the golden proportion? Superimpose it over your grid structure and place your focal point visual at a key juncture. Or give yourself some gridlines based on the rule of thirds and position your focal point at the intersection of the lines. If you need a refresher, revisit Chapter 5: Mini Art School.

Try not to position a visual where it interrupts the flow of reading.

One common iteration of this error, and it's an error regardless of the layout type, is floating a visual in the center of a column and allowing text to wrap to both sides of the image. Getting people to read is hard enough without asking them to visually jump photo hurdles mid text block. Wrapping to one side of an image is fine. Just make sure you don't end up with text columns that are too skinny, leaving you with only one, two or three words per line of type.

If you must place a focal point image at the bottom of a layout, select one that draws the eye back to the top of the page. Or balance the visual at bottom with bold, interesting text at the top. Or go crazy and do both.

In print and other fixed layouts, visuals can also interrupt reading flow when the visual is placed between the headline and the lead. The headline serves as the eye entry point for the copy. Keeping them close (remember the Gestalt Theory of proximity?) helps the reader's eye flow from one to the other.

Another questionable practice in fixed layouts is placing visuals where they will chop a line or column in half. This typically results in readers accidentally skipping right over sections of copy. In the

Above Left: The story above displays several "don'ts," including a much-too-skinny column to the right of the image, a photo placement that separates the headline from the lead, a photo that faces off the page and a small photo that bisects the third column.

Above Right: Shifting the focal point image to the right and narrowing it a bit allows for a wider middle column and reconnects the headline with the lead. Moving the secondary photo out of the middle of the column improves text flow.

example at left, it would be very easy for the reader to flip to the next page and miss the last five sentences in the third column.

Use caution placing visuals in fluid layouts. The rules of text flow are a bit different for webpages. A significant portion of web browsing is done on mobile devices, and most webpage content reorders itself in a single column for this type of viewing. This means that the content that appears side-by-side in a three-column grid on your desktop will likely convert to a vertically stacked format on a smart phone screen.

This has the potential to create two problems. First, if you follow the practice of placing the graphic at the top, followed by the headline and copy, your headline (and visual cue as to what page you are on) can be pushed outside the visible area on the first screen load. This is not ideal for easy site navigation. Work-arounds include pairing heading with the topmost image, using code to rearrange the stacking order so the headline appears at the top, or using code to hide the main image only on mobile views.

The second issue occurs when a webpage mixes graphics into the flow of web copy. In fluid design, when web visuals and copy shift to a single column, the visuals are forced to split up the text column. Although this is a "hard no" in fixed layouts, it's a non-issue in web design. Scrolling up and down is mostly how we move through

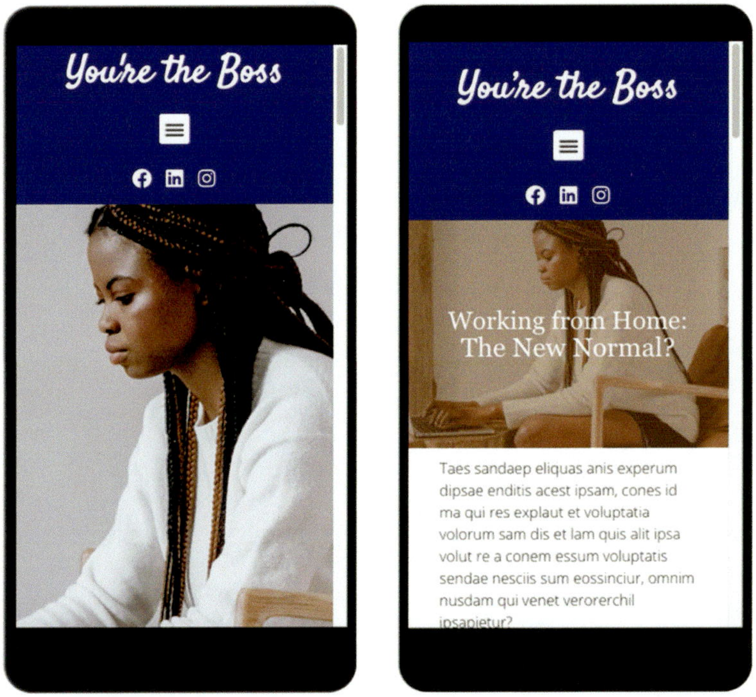

Left: Be aware of how your full-desktop width website will look when viewed on a smart phone screen. The topmost placement of the main image in this example forces the headline off the first screen.

Right: A common solution to this issue is to float the main headline over the image. This option maintains the visual impact of the photo while keeping the headline and lead together.

webpages. We know to scroll past an image squatting in the middle of the copy to get to the remaining text. When jumping a visual is undesirable, you can use code to hide visuals on different devices. Or use code to change the order in which the content stacks itself.

Once your focal point is sketched in place and ready for attention-grabbing duty, the layout must direct viewers to the next important item, typically copy.

Adding type

Type placement begins with inserting the main copy and any nondecorative headlines before adding other typographic items such as cutlines and tags. Depending on your format, type may comprise a little or a lot of your layout. Whichever it is, let your grid and your gridlines guide the placement of type.

Once you decide where on the layout to place the type, you can style it in an appropriate font, size and color. Make sure you haven't forgotten any type items. Adding a missing cutline or subheading after the fact can throw off an entire layout.

For fixed layouts, remember these type tips:

We interrupt this content… Images interrupting the flow of text is a problem in fixed layouts, but less so on mobile website layouts. Since most websites require scrolling up or down, our eyes jump the image with ease.

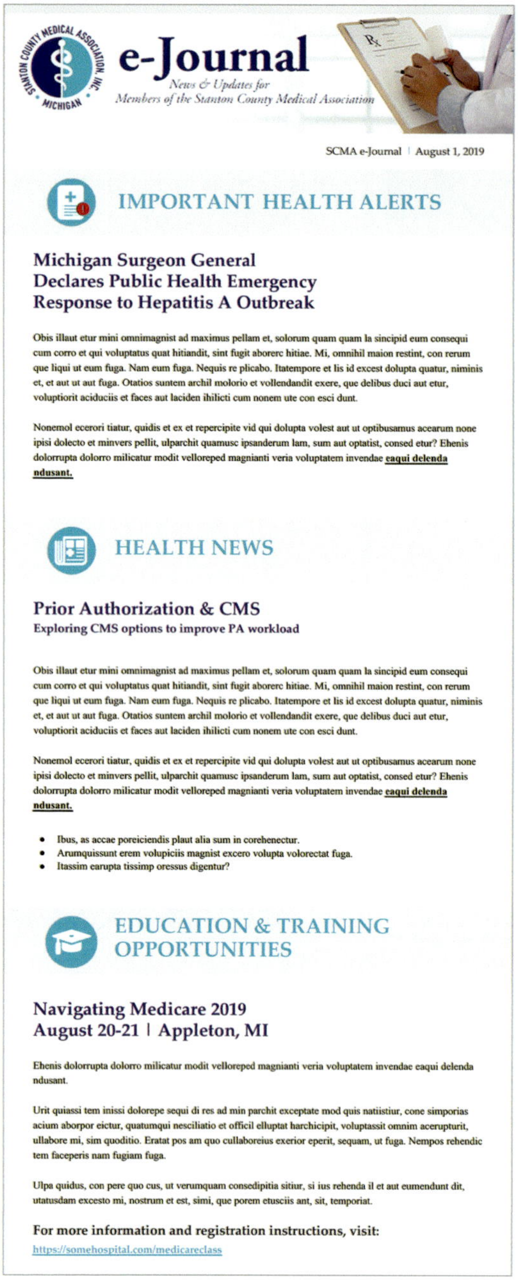

e-Journal

News & Updates for
Members of the Stanton County Medical Association

SCMA e-Journal | August 1, 2019

IMPORTANT HEALTH ALERTS

Michigan Surgeon General Declares Public Health Emergency Response to Hepatitis A Outbreak

Obis illaut etur mini omnimagnist ad maximus pellam et, solorum quam quam la sincipid eum consequi cum corro et qui voluptatus quat hitiandit, sint fugit aborerc hitiae. Mi, omnihil maion restint, con rerum que liqui ut eum fuga. Nam eum fuga. Nequis re plicabo. Itatempore et lis id excest dolupta quatur, niminis et, et aut ut aut fuga. Otatios suntem archil molorio et vollendandit exere, que delibus duci aut etur, voluptiorit aciduciis et faces aut laciden ihilicti cum nonem ute con esci dunt.

Nonemol ecerori tiatur, quidis et ex et repercipite vid qui dolupta volest aut ut optibusamus acearum none ipisi dolecto et minvers pellit, ulparchit quamusc ipsanderum lam, sum aut optatist, consed etur? Ehenis dolorrupta dolorro milicatur modit velloreped magnianti veria voluptatem invendae eaqui delenda ndusant.

HEALTH NEWS

Prior Authorization & CMS
Exploring CMS options to improve PA workload

Obis illaut etur mini omnimagnist ad maximus pellam et, solorum quam quam la sincipid eum consequi cum corro et qui voluptatus quat hitiandit, sint fugit aborerc hitiae. Mi, omnihil maion restint, con rerum que liqui ut eum fuga. Nam eum fuga. Nequis re plicabo. Itatempore et lis id excest dolupta quatur, niminis et, et aut ut aut fuga. Otatios suntem archil molorio et vollendandit exere, que delibus duci aut etur, voluptiorit aciduciis et faces aut laciden ihilicti cum nonem ute con esci dunt.

Nonemol ecerori tiatur, quidis et ex et repercipite vid qui dolupta volest aut ut optibusamus acearum none ipisi dolecto et minvers pellit, ulparchit quamusc ipsanderum lam, sum aut optatist, consed etur? Ehenis dolorrupta dolorro milicatur modit velloreped magnianti veria voluptatem invendae eaqui delenda ndusant.

- Ibus, as accae poreiciendis plaut alia sum in corehenectur.
- Arumquissunt erem volupiciis magnist excero volupta volorectat fuga.
- Itassim earupta tissimp oressus digentur?

EDUCATION & TRAINING OPPORTUNITIES

Navigating Medicare 2019
August 20-21 | Appleton, MI

Ehenis dolorrupta dolorro milicatur modit velloreped magnianti veria voluptatem invendae eaqui delenda ndusant.

Urit quiassi tem inissi dolorepe sequi di res ad min parchit exceptate mod quis natiistiur, cone simporias acium aborpor eictur, quatumqui nesciliatio et officil elluptat harchicipit, voluptassit omnim acerupturit, ullabore mi, sim quoditio. Eratat pos am quo cullaboreius exerior eperit, sequam, ut fuga. Nempos rehendic tem faceperis nam fugiam fuga.

Ulpa quidus, con pere quo cus, ut verumquam consedipitia sitiur, si ius rehenda il et aut eumendunt dit, utatusdam excesto mi, nostrum et est, simi, que porem etusciis ant, sit, temporiat.

For more information and registration instructions, visit:
https://somehospital.com/medicareclass

Multitasking type. Type not only delivers content to your readers, but also adds texture, shape, color and hierarchy to all layout formats.

- Keep your headline and your lead together.
- Reduce leading (line-spacing) as needed on multiple-line headlines.
- Set copy in appropriate column widths to keep long copy reader-friendly.
- Avoid fully justified or centered type.
- Watch for inelegant breaks in headlines or legs of type.
- Avoid widows and orphans (lone words at the top or bottom of columns).

Placing additional visuals in layouts

Variety or uniformity of size? When you're using more than one visual, make them different sizes—and don't be shy about the size contrast. The most important visual should be the largest. The contrast of sizes is more visually interesting and helps establish visual hierarchy. However, just to contradict ourselves, sometimes an interesting grid arrangement of visuals of the same size makes a nice rhythmic pattern. But the rhythmic grid pattern sacrifices asymmetry and visual hierarchy. Whatever you decide, call it with a visual communication purpose.

Balance, please. If you have multiple visuals on a single screen or page, position them for overall layout balance. Avoid lopsidedness. Imagine you're loading people into a small boat. What happens if everyone sits on the same side?

On the other hand, it is acceptable to cluster groups of images together. A cluster of multiple images becomes a single visual element in your layout.

Mug shots. If you're working with multiple headshots, called "mug shots" or "mugs", make all the heads roughly the same size. To align headshots, try cropping to align everyone's eyes.

Where to put negative space

We trust that by now you understand that *white space is not your enemy.* In fact, negative space is

the best tool in your design toolbox for isolating and highlighting important content. It organizes by separating items. Without it, there can be no sense of clustering. Negative space also provides a visual respite for the viewer to avoid visual overload. But even negative space has layout rules.

First, try to consolidate many small puddles of negative space into fewer larger pools. This reduces visual clutter in exactly the same way as clustering positive layout items does. Same principle.

Second, avoid trapped space. Trapped space is a conspicuous chunk of white space isolated in the interior of the layout. If you have trapped space, rearrange the layout so the white space opens to the margins.

Another option is to treat white space as an additional asset you can place. For example, we built an extra-wide vertical band of negative space into the left and right margins of this book. That band of white space keeps the reading columns at a comfortable width. It also provides an interesting space to place visuals and drop sidebars.

Using multiple visuals. When placing multiple visuals, position them for overall balance. Image-size contrast creates pleasing asymmetry.

In this example, the large background image provides a sense of space and depth while smaller images add detail, color and texture to the layout.

STORY SHAPES FOR MODULAR LAYOUTS

CREATING HIERARCHY

Creating visual hierarchy with relative position and contrasting size is another way to draw a reader through a layout while delivering an extra layer of communication. The hierarchy tells viewers what parts of the layout are more important than others and to look at the important things first.

To create visual hierarchy, rank the items intended as layout content in their order of importance. Your most important item, usually a key visual or a headline, becomes the focal point. A position near the top of the layout gives an element importance. Larger size also imparts greater importance. Visuals and type of lesser importance appear in smaller sizes and lower positions on the layout.

One of the best places to observe visual hierarchy in action is on the front page of a newspaper, either print or online. The lead news story always has the biggest photo, the biggest headline point size and occupies the catbird seat at the top of the page. Graduated headline sizes draw the reader down through the page like stepping-stones.

Visual hierarchy applies to newsletters, webpages, annual reports and any other document that includes multiple stories or chunks of discrete information.

LAYOUTS WITH MULTIPLE CONTENT BLOCKS ON THE SAME SCREEN OR PAGE

Up until now we've been dealing primarily with single-topic layouts. But what if your layout must accommodate multiple smaller stories or other items on the same page? Websites as well as print and online editions of newspapers, magazines and newsletters all require the orderly layout of multiple stories on a single page, or across several pages.

Modular page design

The current trend for newspapers is modular page design. In modular page design, each story is arranged into a rectangle, and the rectangles are arranged on the page grid. Modular page design is also used in magazine, newsletter and webpage design.

Making a rectangular story. At a minimum, a story includes a headline and some body copy. Sometimes there is a subhead called a "deck" between the headline and the lead. Between the deck and the lead, a story also may have a byline identifying the journalist or author. Many stories also have a photo or visual of some kind along with an accompanying cutline.

Think of it this way, each part of the story—visual, headline, body copy—represents a new rectangle you have to fit into your rectangular story, which will fit into your grid of rectangles on your rectangular screen or page. It's just like a puzzle.

For each individual story, keep the eye flow moving in the correct direction and in the intended order. The ideal eye-flow order is visual, headline, lead. Otherwise, here are a few more helpful hints:

» **Body copy.** Strip the story's body copy into the grid columns. Keep the lengths of the story's legs even until you run out of story. More than 10 inches per leg is too long. Less than 2 inches is too short. So is yours a one-column or five-column story?

» **Headline.** Add the headline on top of the story. The headline should span all the story's columns, sort of like a roof covering the story. Give the headline a much larger point size than the body copy.

» **Deck.** If there is a deck, put it under the headline but before the lead. Give it a point size smaller than the main header but larger than the body copy.

» **Byline.** If the story merits a byline, put it between the deck and the lead. Give it a tastefully modest point size.

With and without modular design. The tabloid layout at top right demonstrates how jumbled and confusing a multi-story layout can be without modular page design. It's hard to tell which story belongs to which photo, and where each story begins and ends. Never mind the trapped white space near the top and the "tombstoned" headlines in the middle. The example at bottom right squares off all the stories for better organization. It also demonstrates hierarchy with a larger photo and headline in its lead story.

Modular design on the web. Websites utilize modular page design, too. Underlying code delineates rows and columns that naturally organize content into rectangular shapes.

- **Visual/photo.** Where you place the visual really depends on the size and direction of the image. As a rule, though, keep photo placement near the top of the story. It's that eye magnet thing. Think works-every-time layout. But a visual as focal point can sit under the headline, or to the right or left of the headline, as long as the visual does not sit between the headline and the lead. In other words, never put a visual between the headline and the lead. Ever. If the image has direction, it should point to the story. Wherever you put the visual, and at whatever size, remember you're trying to end up with a rectangular story.
- **Cutline.** Cutlines typically, but not always, go under the visual. A cutline under a photo should run the whole width of the photo.

Placing your stories on a modular page. Unfortunately, laying rectangular stories on a modular page is not as easy as we may have led you to believe.

If you build all your stories in the same size and shape and then just stack them on top of each other, you'll have one snoozer of a page. To keep things interesting, you need to vary the size and orientation of your stories. For asymmetry, make some stories tall, narrow and vertical. Make others wide horizontals, and maybe even design a few that are square.

At the level of organizing a whole page of stories, you also need to take a look at all the stories' visuals. Varying their size and placement on the entire page creates interest. Newspapers like to average about a third of a page devoted to visuals. Whatever your percentage of visuals, you still have to watch out for lopsidedness at the page level. Don't tip the boat over. Balance is necessary even for asymmetry.

Your goal is an overall page eye-flow guided by the placement of all the stories' visuals. The eye moves from one image to the next in a particular order according to the visual hierarchy.

Adding visual variety with sidebars. In print, a "sidebar" is simply a separate block of type with a solid background, a stroked outline or an ample border of negative space. On the web, a sidebar is one column (either right or left) of the webpage grid.

Print sidebar content relates to its adjacent copy in some way. A sidebar might be a short connected story, a list, a mini biography, a quiz, an infographic or simply further detail on some aspect of the main content. Normally though not exclusively rectangular in shape, sidebars fit beautifully into modular layouts.

Print sidebars can be as minimal as text and an enclosing box. The visual effect can break up long copy and add life where you don't have as many visuals as you would prefer. Like good cutlines, sidebars provide a bit of information in nice, compact and quickly readable chunks.

Web sidebars often include primary or secondary navigation, banner advertising or function-adding widgets such as social media feeds and maps. Unlike print sidebars, web sidebars are typically functional rather than aesthetic. However, guidelines for designing them are similar.

When designing sidebars, one of the biggest mistakes beginning designers make is neglecting to include margins outside and inside the box. Don't cheat your margins. No type should touch the sides of the sidebar, either outside or inside its box.

Sidebars can add pops of color to your layouts. Consider applying color to the headline or bullets. Or you might put your color in the box's background (the fill) or the box's outline or border (stroke). If you choose a background color, don't forget the contrast you'll need between the fill color and the type. If you believe you need to reverse the text, white letters pop best against a dark background. If your sidebar houses web navigation, make sure hover states (color changes on mouseover) contrast with the background, too.

MULTI-PAGE LAYOUTS

Laying out multiple pages, whether print or digital, presents some additional challenges. Three biggies include maintaining unity, making a lot of type inviting and providing navigational signs to keep readers from getting lost.

Visual unity. To maintain visual unity in a multi-page layout, use the same tactics as for a single-page layout. Don't change from a tuxedo to cargo shorts from one page to the next. Use a dash of Gestalt through similarity: Keep repeating compositional elements such as color, shape, texture and pattern. Consistent font styling also provides unity. Using the same grid skeleton on every page is essential, too.

A SIDEBAR ON DESIGNING SIDEBARS

Sidebars are a good option for:

» Breaking up text in the absence of good photography

» Highlighting key information lifted from your text

» Providing additional information related to your adjacent copy

» Adding interactivity when presented in the form of quizzes or lists

» Giving your page a little pop of color

When designing sidebars:

» Make them contrast with your regular copy by using a different font

» Give them a little color with colored bullets, headings, a border or a background box

» If you use a border or background box, make sure your text doesn't crowd the box. Give yourself ample margin, inside and out

Don't forget to consider transitions, animations and other types of motion in your visual unification process. Using the same transitions between slides or video clips and the same mouseover actions or loading animations on websites and mobile apps also helps maintain visual unity.

Watch the fold lines and gutters. When designing multi-page documents like brochures, be careful not to place important images or copy on fold lines. The last thing your design needs is a big crease across an important person's face or key piece of information.

Working across page spreads. When working on printed documents that have pages or sections side-by-side, make sure your software lets you design them side-by-side. Instead of creating two layouts on two pages, you're actually creating one work on a much wider canvas. You'll need to distribute and balance your content across the entire spread. Be wary of binding and fold positions. You don't want important parts of your images to get lost in the fold. And if you have headlines that cross fold lines, be sure to position them so folds fall between letters. A little extra kerning between those letters can help, too.

Loads of type. Page after page of gray type is intimidating. To break up any copy-heavy design, including one with multiple pages:

» Use a grid and set copy into inviting legs of type. And unless your document is fairly narrow, don't let a single column span the width of the page. Imagine trying to read a block of text as wide as your computer monitor. Ouch.

» Break up type with headlines and subheads.

» Add more visuals, including sidebars.

» Deploy negative space strategically.

Navigational signs. In a multi-page layout, visitors need visual signposts to be able to keep track of their whereabouts. Traditional navigation tools include, for example, tables of contents, teasers, jump lines pointing to where the rest of the story jumped and even logos or the journalism equivalent of logos called "flags" and "sigs" (short for "signatures").

You are here. Multi-page layouts need navigational devices such as page numbers, folios and tables of contents. Webpages need persistent navigation so visitors can find content as well as find home at any time and from any location.

For interactive media, navigation and multimedia controls and menus help visitors move through content, and they should be consistent (have similarity) across pages. Breadcrumb trails are highly useful navigation tools for websites, too. A "breadcrumb trail" is a text reference to where a website visitor currently is, preceded by a sequential list of the links the visitor followed to get there. Next and previous arrows are common blog navigation tools. Forward and backward arrows, dot navigation and thumbnail navigation are often used to navigate image galleries. Arrow navigation is particularly important on webpages where horizontal scrolling is not the norm. Prominent arrows cue the user that there is more content to be found by scrolling side to side.

A periodical or serial such as a magazine, newsletter or newspaper—print or web—needs a folio showing the publication's name and issue or date. Folios in hardcopy editions also need page numbers. Folios generally appear somewhere in the margins, though still within the safe area or live area.

EXIT HERE

Remember, good layout works for, not against, your visual communication objectives: Capture attention, control flow, convey information and evoke emotion.

Begin the layout with a grid and an irresistible focal point. Use the focal point to *point to,* not from, your layout. The Gestalt theories of proximity, similarity, continuity and closure can help with arranging the layout's flow. Creating a visual hierarchy also aids flow.

For multiple layouts on the same screen or page, modular design is your new best friend. For laying out multiple pages, similarity is the key to visual unity.

Thank you for traveling with us today. Please wait until the chapter has come to a full stop before exiting.

TRY THIS

1. Compare the visual communication of two organizations that compete with each other by looking at their websites. In particular, compare their use of grid structures and hierarchy. How does each site behave in desktop mode compared to mobile device mode?
2. Experiment to figure out the live area for an 8½ × 11-inch sheet on your personal printer and also on the copier you use. If you bleed material at the top, bottom and sides, how much white-space margin still prints?
3. Compare the home pages of two online news organizations. What techniques communicate visual hierarchy? Does either employ modular page design? How do you know?
4. Assemble several samples of your own writing to treat as Greek text. Now create thumbnail sketches showing how you would arrange each of these dummy "stories" into a two-page newsletter using modular page design. Execute your design in a page layout program.

LAYOUT IDEAS YOU CAN SWIPE

BEYOND THE WORKS-EVERY-TIME LAYOUT

In Chapter 3 we introduced you to the works-every-time layout. Now we'd like to introduce you to several other common layout patterns you can add to your designer's toolbox. These layouts adapt to both print and screen applications. Now that we've pointed them out, see how often you run across them each day.

1. Picture window
2. Grid of equal squares
3. Collage
4. Mondrian
5. Multi-panel *
6. Type specimen

2

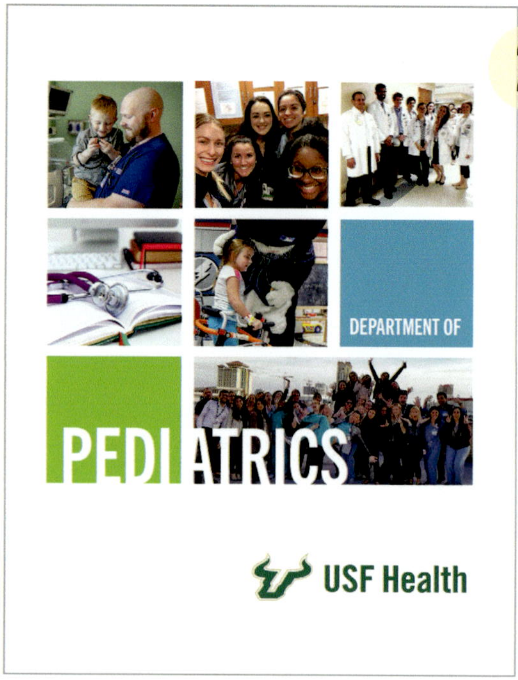

1

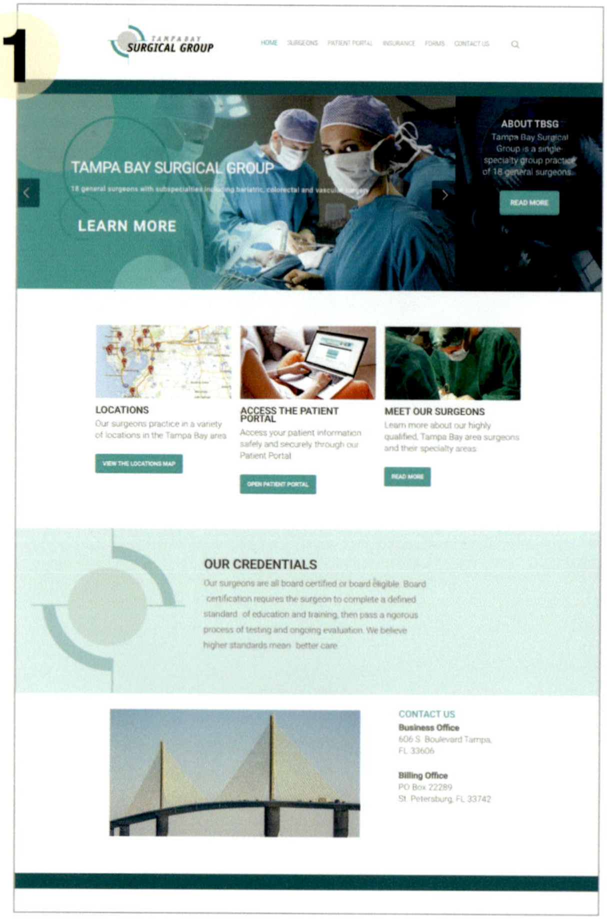

3

Tampa Bay Surgical Group website used with permission of the Tampa Bay Surgical Group.

Pediatrics Annual Report cover used with permission of the USF Morsani College of Medicine Department of Pediatrics.

4

5

6

** Layout 5 also demonstrates the use of "clotheslining," a technique where you line up items of unequal height along their top edges. The effect is that of elements hanging off of a clothesline.*

IT ALL COMES BACK TO THE GRID

Not all graphic designers embrace the grid. Some feel grids are too restrictive. We humbly disagree. An underlying grid is crucial to keeping a design coherent across multiple pages. And, as we've already discussed, a grid takes some of the guesswork out of deciding where to put content.

Regardless of the type of layout you create, sticking to a grid provides a bit of invisible repetition and makes each page or screen feel like part of the same whole.

CHAPTER 7

TYPE

WHAT YOU DON'T KNOW CAN HURT YOU

If you're like most people, the first time you used a word-processing application, you accepted the default Times New Roman 12-point font and never looked back. If you still treat your computer like a glorified word processor, you're not taking advantage of the full communicative and creative power of type.

Type sets the tone. Well-chosen fonts set the overall tone of the layout. Fonts impact readability, legibility and visual hierarchy as well.

The best designers are experts in type and typesetting because they understand that well-styled type not only sets the document's tone but also directly impacts its readability, legibility and visual hierarchy. Failure to follow best typesetting practices, at best, can leave your audience with a negative impression and, at worst, can leave you with no audience at all.

This chapter talks all about fonts, including styling them for both function and aesthetics.

FONT, TYPEFACE, FONT FAMILY, GLYPH

To begin at the beginning, a font is a complete set of characters in a particular size and style of type. This includes the letter set, number set and all of the special characters you get by pressing the shift, option or command/control keys.

A typeface or font family contains a series of fonts. For instance, Times Bold, Times Italic and Times Roman are actually three fonts, even though people often refer to one entire font family as a font.

A glyph is an individual character of a font. Glyphs are not limited to upper- and lowercase letters. There are glyphs for punctuation, glyphs for special characters such as copyright and trademark symbols and even glyphs that are purely decorative. Most fonts have a set of 265 glyphs. Fonts in the OpenType® format, a format created jointly by Microsoft and Adobe, are cross-platform and can have upwards of 65,000 glyphs.

FONT CATEGORIES

In the same way we organize plants and animals into genus and species, we can organize fonts into categories. The shape of a font's glyphs determines its category. Learning to recognize and identify font categories is an important first step in selecting the right font for the right job. It's also essential in creating harmonious, not discordant,

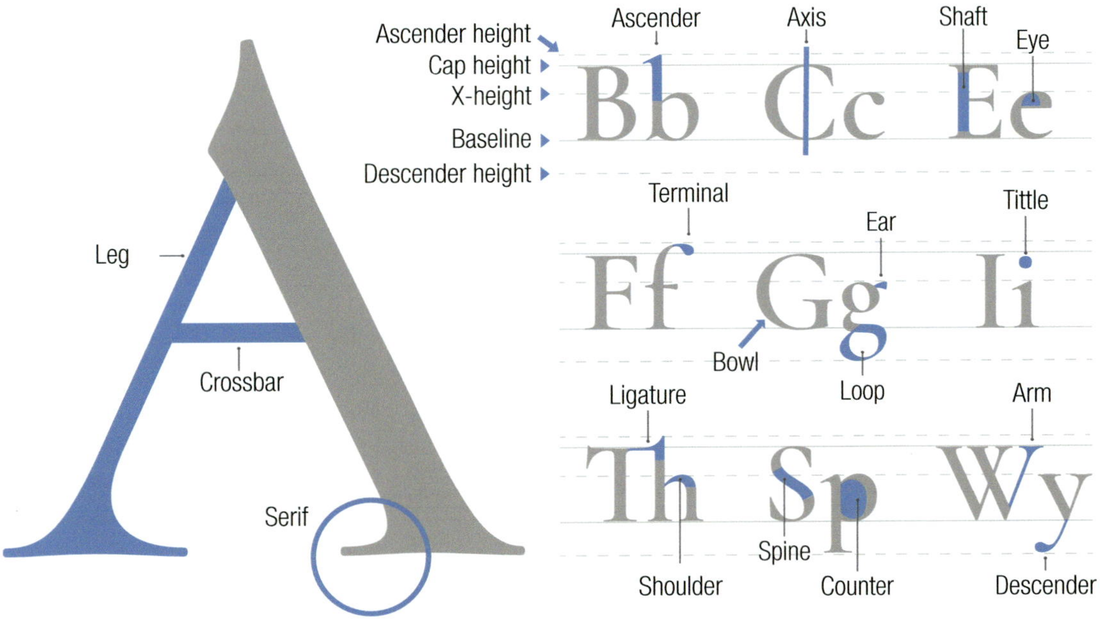

ANATOMY OF *fonts*

Professional designers understand how font characteristics impact font behavior in different design situations. This helps them choose the right font for the job.

We think "anatomy" is apropos given the number of font characteristcs that are named for body parts.

Blend in *and* stand out. Proportional Oldstyle numerals have ascenders and decenders like lowercase letters. This makes them blend in nicely in body copy. They can also be quite beautiful and look well when used in headings or for decorative purposes.

A capital idea. Note the size difference between the standard uppercase letter "I" and the small caps treatment of "CAPS." Small caps tend to fall between the height of the x-height and the ascender. Use them for headings and short copy situations.

A FIELD GUIDE TO BASIC **FONT CATEGORIES**

Depending on the source you consult, you'll find many different font categories. We'll stick to a few of the most common and offer general recommendations for their use.

OLD STYLE & Transitional

Characteristics: Classic and traditional, old style fonts have serifs, little "feet," at the tips of glyphs. Old style serifs are bracketed: They start thick and taper to thin at an angle, creating little triangles. Old style fonts also contain thick stem strokes and thinner hairline strokes, though the difference between the thick and thin is not extreme. Old style fonts often have diagonal stress, which means that a line intersecting the thinnest parts of O-shaped glyphs is diagonal.

Transitional fonts evolved from old style and share many of the same characteristics. The biggest difference is that the diagonal stress is missing or not as prominent in transitional fonts.

Because they are so similar, throughout this text we refer to both types as simply old style.

Note Goudy Old Style's diagonal stress (left) compared to the vertical stress of the transitional font Baskerville (right).

BEST USES:

For print body copy, old style fonts are very readable. Larger bolder versions can work for headlines. But old style's hairline strokes and tapered serifs can get lost when reversed.

Serifs and fine strokes can also get lost on screens of all sizes. Onscreen, old style fonts are best when big and bold in headlines or other short bits of copy.

SANS SERIF

Grotesque
Humanist
Geometric

Characteristics: Contemporary in style, sans serif (French for "without serif") fonts have no serifs. Variations of sans serif fonts include Grotesque (strokes have uniform thickness), Humanist (variations in stroke thickness) and Geometric (letterforms have geometric shapes). For simplicity, we refer to all forms as sans serif.

BEST USES:

In print and onscreen, carefully chosen sans serif fonts can be used for everything from body copy to cutlines. Humanist forms, with their stroke thickness variations, are the most readable of the sans serif fonts. Geometric and grotesque variations are best used in headlines and short copy situations.

Most sans serif fonts reverse very well.

Among the most readable onscreen fonts are Open Sans, Lato, Trebuchet and Arial. Their larger x-heights and open letterforms add to their online readablity. Bigger, bolder versions make excellent headings and subheadings.

Script

Characteristics: If the type style looks like it belongs on a wedding invitation, it's most likely a script font. Script fonts tend toward formality and often resemble old-fashioned penmanship. Like cursive writing, the glyphs in script fonts tend to be connected on the downstroke. Script fonts can be difficult to read, though some are more readable than others.

BEST USES: Because of readability and legibility issues, script fonts are best limited to small amounts of copy in both print and screen applications. Individual characters of script fonts make interesting decorative elements in watermarks and logos. They also make beautiful drop caps.

Decorative

Characteristics: The characteristics of decorative fonts widely vary. They can resemble hand lettering, vintage type, grunge type or whimsical lettering. Consider these examples:

Quickfox MONAD Cracked BADABOOM
Rotrude Stanley Blackmoor Wilhelm

BEST USES: For all applications, limit decorative font use to headlines, decorative details, ornaments or very small amounts of type. Never use them for reading copy. Reversing depends on the thicknesses of glyph details, and those with fine detail will not reverse well. Many place Blackface fonts, like Blackmoor above, in their own font category. They were used for body copy in the early days of the printing press. Today we find them difficult to read. Treat them like decorative fonts: Use them sparingly and with care.

slab serif

Characteristics: As the name implies, slab serif fonts have uniformly thick, fat serifs. Some slab serif fonts look like a hybrid between an old style font and a sans serif font. The result is sort of a sans serif with fat serifs, if you will.

BEST USES: Slab serif fonts were invented for retail display advertising so they work well in print headlines. Some slab serif fonts can work for body copy, but old style fonts are generally a better choice. Slab serif fonts tend to work a little better in reverse because of their beefier serifs.

Slab serif fonts also work for screen applications but in the same limited way as decorative fonts.

MODERN

Characteristics: Modern fonts have extremely thin serifs, and their stress lies on the vertical, unlike old style's diagonal stress.

BEST USES: Modern fonts convey elegance. They work well for headlines, decorative details or ornaments. They are not a good choice for print or screen reading copy, and reversing them is not a good idea because of their ultra-thin serifs.

font pairings. The ability to categorize fonts comes down to training your eye to see subtleties. It's worth your time to develop this skill.

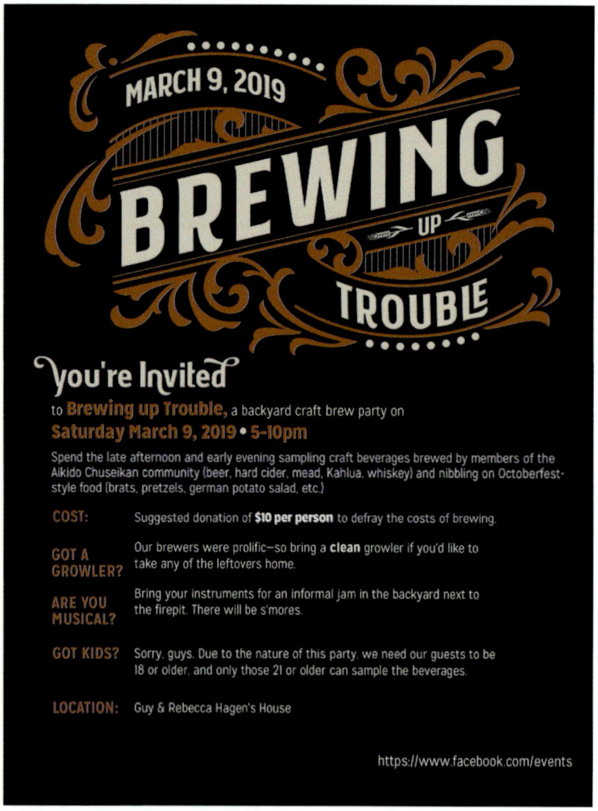

Proper pairings. Ornate decorative headline fonts beg to be matched with a toned-down body font. This condensed sans-serif font fits the bill. Further, its slightly narrower glyph shapes echo the narrower forms of the headline font.

CHOOSING & USING FONTS

Understandably, most graphic designers are like mice in a cheese factory where fonts are concerned. So many fonts! So little time!

Once you discover the big wide world of fonts, it's easy to overdo. But. Please. Resist. This. Urge. Nothing screams "amateur" louder than using too many competing font styles.

Choose one font for your body copy

The No. 1 consideration in choosing a body font for any application is ***readability.*** As we mentioned in a previous chapter, transparent fonts from the old style or sans serif categories are typically the most readable, with sans serif the better choice for screen applications.

We recommend selecting a body font from a larger typeface for all types of design projects. By nature, all the fonts in a typeface get along visually because they're drawn to coordinate with each other. By using fonts from the same typeface, you get both flexibility and a consistent, unified look. For example, the popular web typeface Open Sans contains a "regular" font that is great for body copy. But it also contains bold, italic, semibold and several other variations that can be used for subheadings and captions, or to create emphasis.

Better yet, look for a new class of fonts known as "variable." OpenType Variable Fonts are the equivalent of having an entire typeface condensed into one font. Variable fonts are coded to allow a single font file to render all style variations, mathematically morphing glyphs between different weights and sizes. This allows for virtually infinite typographical choices.

Because variable fonts are a joint project of Google, Microsoft, Apple and Adobe, they work across different computer platforms and web browsers. Plus, loading only one font to your website instead of four or five aids page load times.

It might take a bit of extra effort to find and use this new font format, but it's worth your time to try. The potential benefits are huge.

Choose a second contrasting font for headlines

Generally speaking, if you choose sans serif font for body copy, you can pick a contrasting headline font from almost any category. Think of them as the "basic black" of the font world. They go with everything. Your headline font, then, can be wild and decorative, script and elegant, or sans serif and ultra-hip and still work. Or you could choose a headline font from the same typeface as the body and create your contrast through point size or weight. However you do it, you want the body copy to contrast with the headline.

Old style fonts are also neutral and play nicely with most other fonts. However, sans serif fonts have a reading advantage in onscreen applications. While some old style fonts work onscreen, they do better in print.

Pairing decorative fonts together is almost always a bad idea. They compete with each other. Script fonts have the same problem. Think of decorative fonts and script fonts as the divas of the font world. You just can't put the two of them in the same dressing room.

Modern and slab serif fonts also can present difficulties. Since modern and slab serif fonts are similar in shape to old style fonts, they might not have enough contrasting elements to make them stand out as distinctive from the print body copy. When using modern and slab serif fonts, trust your eyes. If the pairing looks like you've simply made a font error instead of a deliberate design choice then the pairing isn't working. You might be able to make such pairings work if you apply contrast in another way by varying size, weight or color.

No matter which font categories you choose for your onscreen project, make sure you don't choose fonts with a lot of fine detail. Thin strokes and serifs often don't read well on screens. When in doubt, test your choices on different devices. If your design is for the web, consider trying a browser emulator, which lets you view your design on multiple devices and platforms from one application. Don't forget to test-drive any variants of your chosen fonts, too, especially italics. Italicized fonts also may lose legibility onscreen.

WELL MATCHED

Just as there are recommendations for pairing wines with food, there are recommendations for coordinating headline fonts with body fonts. Pairing different weight fonts within the same typeface is a safe bet. Constrasting ornate fonts with sleek fonts is also a good practice. Consider these pairings:

Rockwell Bold
Bembo

Playfair Display
Source Sans Pro Light

Avenir Next Bold
Avenir Next Regular

Cinque Donne
Mission Gothic Light

Oswald
Open Sans Condensed Light

Quicksand
Cormorant Garamond

MOONSHINER
Bell Gothic Light

CHOOSING FONTS *for the Web*

For years, web designers observed with envy the thousands of typefaces print designers could choose from. Traditionally, web designers were limited to using a very small web-safe font set, including fonts like Arial and Times, common to most computers. Designers looking to use more creative fonts resorted to turning type into graphics. This preserved the font appearance but killed search engine readability and made editing difficult.

Fortunately, new coding methods and font formats made a significant portion of the world's font catalog available for use in websites. After addressing hiccups in browser rendering and copyright issues (remember, typefaces and fonts are copyrighted material), font foundries and online font hosting companies now offer a huge range of creative options for web. Designers now have font choices enough to make them giddy—or dizzy—depending on your point of view.

FONT READABILITY

Each of the first three examples demonstrates a "don't." The final example does everything right. See the difference?

This example is typeset using the font Helvetica Neue UltraLight, 12 point

This example uses the smaller x-height font Verlag Book, 12 point

This example is typeset using the geometric sans serif font Century Gothic, 10 point

This example uses the sans serf font PT Sans Regular, 11 point

How to choose a web font

You already know to choose fonts for style, readability and contrast. But as you know, type on paper is not the same as type onscreen. Web typography requires additional consideration. Remember the diagram "Anatomy of Fonts" and the graphic spread "A Field Guide to Basic Font Categories"? Here's how to apply that knowledge.

Select for web readability. Due to the lower pixel density on most computer and mobile device screens, web fonts benefit from slightly heavier details, increased x-heights and humanist rather than geometric shapes. Shafts, crossbars and serifs that are too fine/thin can virtually disappear onscreen. Larger x-heights mean more open counters and space for counters and bowls. This increases legibility of individual glyphs and therefore the readability of words. On the other hand, geometric fonts cut down on readability because all the glyphs look alike. Again, the more legible the glyphs, the easier it is to read the words glyphs form.

Select for scalability. Web fonts need the flexibility of a gymnast. They will be asked to scale up and down to fit huge desktop monitors and tiny mobile device screens. Test-drive your choices to make sure they remain legible and readable across devices.

Consider reading rhythm. The placement of words in lines across a layout creates a visual horizontal path. (Gestalt theory, anyone?) And a font's ascenders and descenders add a vertical rhythm to those lines. Regular rhythm makes easier reading. If the ascenders and descenders are too close together (condensed font) or too far apart (wide font), the reader can experience eye fatigue. Aim for a font width somewhere in the middle.

Web

READING RHYTHM

Ascenders and descenders create reading rhythm. Regular pacing makes easier reading.

Test-drive your font choices and make sure they remain legible and readable across the board. (Helvetica Neue LT Std 57 Condensed 10 point)

Test-drive your font choices and make sure they remain legible and readable across the board. (Helvetica Neue LT Std 55 Roman 10 point)

Test-drive your font choices and make sure they remain legible and readable across the board. (Helvetica Neue LT Std 53 Extended 10 point)

Legibility of glyphs and User Interface.* It's clear that web fonts wear many hats. They set the look and readability of body copy, headlines and cutlines. But they are also key to a website's usability. Think about it. If links and buttons aren't clearly legible, your visitor won't be able to navigate the site. Legibility at small sizes requires clearly differentiated glyphs. If you've ever confused a lowercase letter "l" for the number "1," then you understand the issue. Again, try out font choices in different digital environments and select accordingly.

Final thoughts

As a rule we recommend sans serif fonts for the web, but don't limit yourself. There are serif fonts that work equally well. Just apply these rules to your potential picks and decide which to use from there.

Do we suggest you are restricted to using fonts that meet the letter (bad pun intended) of these selection rules? Of course not. But limit less-legible and less-readable fonts to short copy situations like headlines. Test your selections, preferably across a range of browsers and devices. Trust your eyes to help you make the right choices for your web project.

DIFFERENTIATION FOR USER INTERFACE

Clearly differentiated fonts. Notice how the capital letter "I" and the lowercase letter "l" look identical in the first example. The PT Sans font solves this by adding little tails to the lowercase "l."

In the second example, all the letters in the word "pedagogy" have the same rounded shape. The Franklin Gothic font uses a "two-story" letter "a" and letter "g" to create better differentiation.

Illuminate (Verlag Book)

Illuminate (PT Sans Regular)

Pedagogy (Century Gothic)

Pedagogy (Franklin Gothic Book)

**Adapted from Design by Izo Blog, by Ian Hex. http://www.design-by-izo.com/2011/10/18/what-should-i-look-for-in-a-ui-typeface/*

It's all in the contrast. When typesetting headlines, subheadings and other nonbody copy, make sure you provide clear contrast of size, font style or both. Don't be scared of "too big." The "Bears" title is set at 208 points. A 12-point font is used in the schedule. We're pretty sure that qualifies as clear contrast.

APPLYING ADDITIONAL FONT STYLING

Choosing the right typeface will give you the option of using bold, italic, semibold and other font weight and style variations. You also might have the ability to apply some additional font styling options such as leading, kerning and tracking adjustments to impact your design's readability, visual appeal and communicative value.

Font size

In your typesetting workflow, choose your fonts first, and then choose your font sizes. Layout programs come with default size settings, but don't blindly accept the default size. Actively and deliberately choose sizes appropriate to your unique project, audience and font selection.

When selecting a font size for body copy, choose a size large enough to be easily readable by your intended audience under generally anticipated reading conditions (onscreen, low light, on a billboard at 70 miles per hour, etc.). If your target audience is middle-aged or older, go larger rather than smaller. The older people get the more likely they are to need reading glasses. They'll appreciate bigger fonts. Trust us.

Whatever numerical size you choose, be prepared to adjust. Font size is calculated by measuring the distance from the top of the ascenders to the bottom of the descenders. The length of ascenders and descenders relative to x-height might make some fonts appear smaller and some appear larger. You'll have to learn to trust your judgment on choosing a font size that hits the correct note between mousetype and horsey.

Choose font sizes for headings, cutlines and other nonbody uses based on both readability and contrast. Headings must contrast with body copy, so make them really contrast. A 12-point heading barely contrasts with a 10-point body copy font; a 48-point headline greatly contrasts.

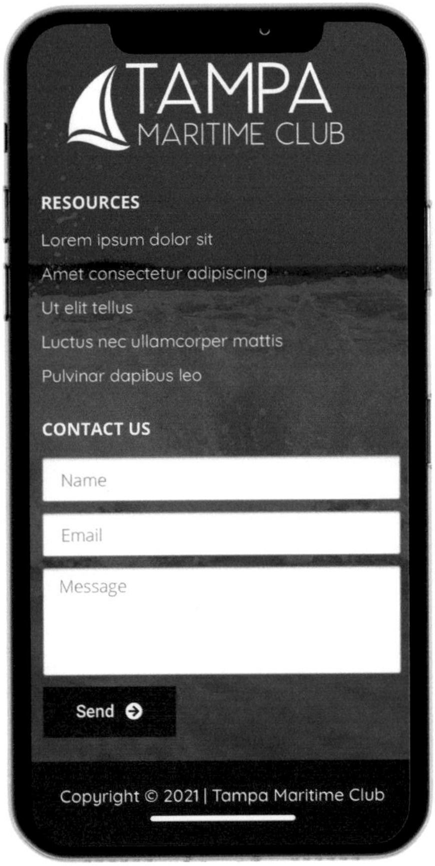

Type that adjusts on the fly. Use fluid typography to ensure that your website text is as readable on smart phone screens as it is on desktop monitors.

Body font sizes for print. While the default font size in many design programs is 12 points, try starting with 10 or 11 points. This size is often sufficiently large for reading, particularly if your body font is a sans serif. Sans serif fonts often have larger x-heights, making them appear larger overall.

Body font sizes for computer and mobile device screens. Modern website designs are responsive—that is, they automatically adjust to the viewing device—and we need font size specifications that adjust as well. Rather than set web font sizes in nonflexible points or pixels, it is better to set font sizes in adjustable "em" or "rem" (root em) units. Another option is to use "vw" (viewport width) units or "vh" (viewport height) units. "Fluid typography" is the official name for this adjustable method of typesetting.

Without wading too far into technical weeds, em and rem are flexible, scalable units which are translated by the browser into pixel values, depending on the font size settings in your design. The baseline size for single em and rem units can be set to any number, but the standard is the equivalent of 16 pixels.

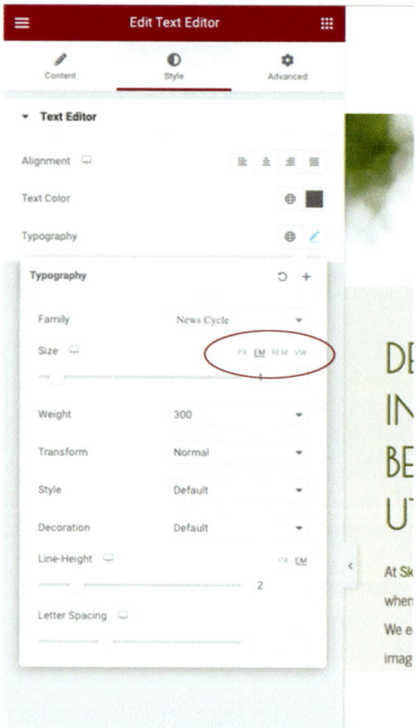

Fluid type units. When you have the opportunity to choose font size units for the web, choose fluid units such as em, rem or vw.

Screenshot used by permission of Elementor, Ltd. https://elementor.com.

Neither the authors nor CRC Press have any affiliation with Elementor, Ltd.

Here is how it works: A designer writes a Cascading Style Sheet (CSS) specification (lines of coded visual instructions for web browsers) that a first-level heading should be rendered as 4rem. With that instruction, a browser will render that heading style four times larger than the baseline size. A specification that a second-level heading should be 2rem would cause that heading to be rendered at two times the baseline. You get the idea.

Viewport units work like em units but, instead of using fixed sizes, they are calculated as a percentage of a viewport. The CSS specification requires a calculation as part of the line of code, as well as some additional upper and lower size limits to prevent onscreen rendering issues. There are potential browser compatibility issues with vw and vh units, too.

Working with em, rem, vw and vh units is a lot more complex than presented here, and full understanding and application requires knowledge of HTML and CSS languages. For now, when you have the opportunity to select your size units, em and rem units are a good choice. They have solid support across browsers. They are flexible enough to not "break" when users zoom in on text in browser windows. This makes em and rem units better for web accessiblity, too.

A good rule of thumb is to use em sizes when specifying margins and paddings, and rem sizes for everything else. Oh, and set your baseline body font to 1 rem.

Font sizes for video. If your typesetting is bound for video, font sizes are best skewed bigger. Web video is likely to be viewed on tiny smart phone screens, and no one watches television from a foot away. Test your font sizes for television by stepping back from your computer and viewing your typesetting from a distance. For smaller screens, use a mobile browser emulator to see what your typesetting looks like on different smart phones and tablets. A baseline font size of 24 pixels is a good place to start.

Optical fonts for special purposes

Some extended typefaces include "optical fonts" that are cut for specific typesetting purposes. Caption fonts are an optical font meant for use in (duh) captions. Caption font glyphs are drawn to facilitate better reading at smaller sizes. Display fonts are designed to showcase font detail and shape at large headline sizes. Display fonts are great for use in poster, newspaper, magazine and advertising design. The general rule is to use a display font if your headline will be 20 points or larger.

Bold & italic type

Both bold type and italic type can create emphasis in short copy situations, such as headings, subheadings or short body copy.

Did we mention short copy situations? Use bolding or italics sparingly. Neither bold nor italic is appropriate for entire pages or long paragraphs of type. Too much italic is hard to read, particularly in digital formats. And too much bold defeats the purpose of having bold at all. When everything is styled to stand out, *nothing* stands out.

We also would like to point out that not all bolds are created equal. Some bold fonts are bolder than others. Sometimes a bigger font size, a different color or a different font altogether provides greater contrast than using just plain bold.

Avoid faux bold and italic. Some non-professional grade software programs include buttons for faux bold and faux italic. You've seen these. They're little squares with "b" or "i" on them. These buttons seem to let you apply bold or italic to any font.

But in truth, these buttons merely stroke or distort letterforms to appear as bold or italic. And using them can have disastrous results in commercial printing. Like crashing-the-printer's-software disastrous. No kidding. You should avoid using these buttons to apply styling.

Go big or go home. Skew larger on typesetting for video. There's a strong possibility your video will be viewed on a tiny smart phone screen. If you're posting to a social media video site, use big bold type to make your video thumbnail stand out among a grid of other thumbnails.

The same is true in webpage building programs. While it probably won't crash your computer, faux styling can cause poor onscreen rendering, especially with italics.

So how do you apply bold and italic? For print, install typefaces with a full range of bold and italic fonts to your computer or page layout programs. Then apply the appropriately styled font to your text using the program's font tools.

For web-based projects, load or activate fonts through your webpage builder or by writing a bit of code. Apply the fonts via your page builder's interface, or by adding specifications to the page's CSS. Avoiding faux bold and italic will save you a boatload of printing and rendering headaches.

But didn't we just say "no" to all caps? Okay, fair. But all caps are fine to use in short copy situations like headlines. Do remember that as font sizes get bigger, line spacing increases automatically. Remember to reduce leading to keep the lines of your headlines visually connected.

IT'S

SPRING

Above: Font *Merova,* 3rem with auto line spacing.

Below: Line spacing adjusted.

IT'S
SPRING

All caps

All caps are an old-school style of emphasis. Type set in all caps cuts down on readability. When we first learn to read, we are taught the shape of each letter and its corresponding sound. We put letters and their sounds together to make words. Over time, our mental process shifts to the point where we recognize shapes of words without the need for scanning and adding up individual characters. But when you capitalize words, they lose the ascenders and descenders that make up their unique shapes. Every word becomes a rectangle, and our brains have to work just a little bit harder to recognize the word.

To add insult to injury, we have come to associate all caps with shouting. And nobody likes to be shouted at.

If you want to use all caps, make sure they don't interfere with your visual communication purpose, including readability.

Spacing

Leading. Pronounced "ledding," leading is the technical term for line spacing. It comes from the days of setting type by hand. Once upon a time, typesetters used a slug of lead to separate each line of type.

Today, your computer calculates leading. Every font size has a corresponding default number (a percentage of the font size) that serves as line spacing. This default number works okay most of the time. However, there are times when you need to adjust it.

When the body copy font has a large x-height, the type on the page or screen can feel heavy and claustrophobic. Increasing the line spacing alleviates this and improves readability. A little extra leading increases readability, too, when the eye must track across a very long line of type, as in wide columns or no columns. Be careful not to overdo additional leading, as too much space also cuts down on flow and readability.

You also can add extra leading for decorative purposes, but only for limited amounts of type. A little extra leading can give the sense of elegance or lightness/airiness if that serves your communication purpose. Just remember to use the technique in moderation to preserve readability and flow.

On the other hand, when creating large headlines, reducing leading is essential. Because leading is mathematically calculated based on font size, as the font size increases, so does the leading—exponentially. For headlines more than one line deep, decrease the leading to bring the lines closer together (i.e., clustering). Beginning designers often overlook this step, leaving headline gaps you could drive a bus through.

Make tracks. Tracking, adjusting letter spacing across a sentence can add visual interest to short bursts of copy. When type is on a curve, extra tracking might be necessary to keep your glyphs from running together along their baselines or cap heights.

Kerning. Manually adjusting the negative space between two characters is called kerning. When uppercase letters have diagonal lines, such as on the capital W, adjacent letters or punctuation might appear too far away, particularly when font sizes are large.

Professional grade design software allows application of two kerning settings: metrics and optics. Usually the default setting, metrics applies the font's built-in kerning settings to instances of that font. The optics setting is best used when your font is not expertly kerned (as in some free fonts) and needs more adjusting. Larger headlines often benefit from optical kerning.

Even with metric or optical kerning applied, you still might need to do some fine-tuning of specific letter pairs. For this purpose, professional layout programs include manual kerning tools.

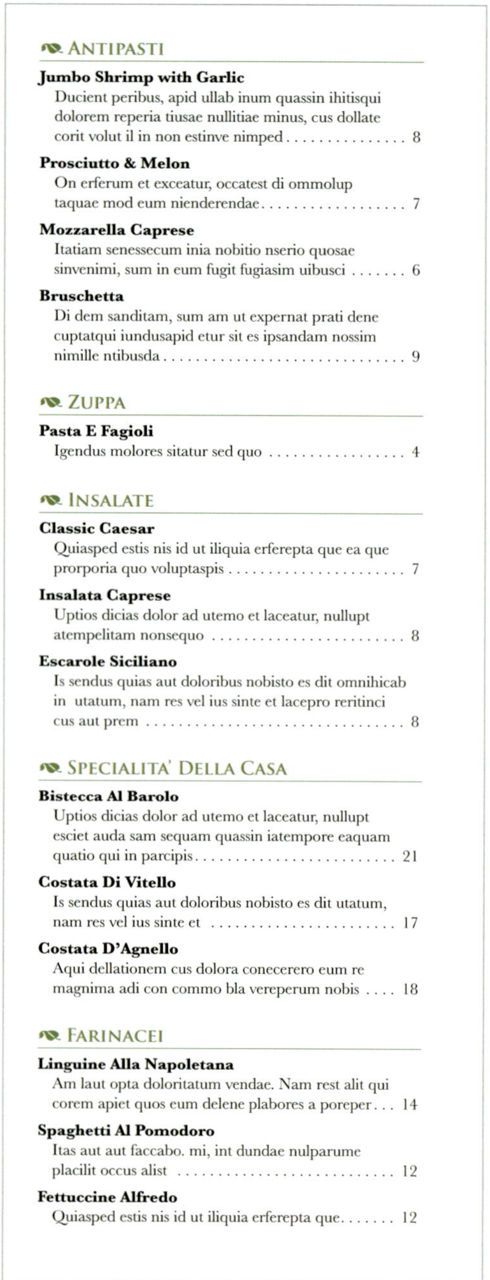
ANTIPASTI

Jumbo Shrimp with Garlic
Ducient peribus, apid ullab inum quassin ihitisqui dolorem reperia tiusae nullitiae minus, cus dollate corit volut il in non estinve nimped 8

Prosciutto & Melon
On erferum et exceatur, occatest di ommolup taquae mod eum nienderendae 7

Mozzarella Caprese
Itatiam senessecum inia nobitio nserio quosae sinvenimi, sum in eum fugit fugiasim uibusci 6

Bruschetta
Di dem sanditam, sum am ut expernat prati dene cuptatqui iundusapid etur sit es ipsandam nossim nimille ntibusda 9

ZUPPA

Pasta E Fagioli
Igendus molores sitatur sed quo 4

INSALATE

Classic Caesar
Quiasped estis nis id ut iliquia erferepta que ea que prorporia quo voluptaspis 7

Insalata Caprese
Uptios dicias dolor ad utemo et laceatur, nullupt atempelitam nonsequo 8

Escarole Siciliano
Is sendus quias aut doloribus nobisto es dit omnihicab in utatum, nam res vel ius sinte et lacepro reritinci cus aut prem 8

SPECIALITA' DELLA CASA

Bistecca Al Barolo
Uptios dicias dolor ad utemo et laceatur, nullupt esciet auda sam sequam quassin iatempore eaquam quatio qui in parcipis 21

Costata Di Vitello
Is sendus quias aut doloribus nobisto es dit utatum, nam res vel ius sinte et 17

Costata D'Agnello
Aqui dellationem cus dolora conecerero eum re magnima adi con commo bla vereperum nobis 18

FARINACEI

Linguine Alla Napoletana
Am laut opta doloritatum vendae. Nam rest alit qui corem apiet quos eum delene plabores a poreper . . . 14

Spaghetti Al Pomodoro
Itas aut aut faccabo. mi, int dundae nulparume placilit occus alist 12

Fettuccine Alfredo
Quiasped estis nis id ut iliquia erferepta que. 12

We'll have the bruschetta. This menu design utilizes different types of font styling such as tabs and tab leaders to create order and organization.

Tracking. Adjusting letter spacing across characters in a sentence or paragraph is called tracking. You also can manipulate tracking for decorative purposes to create tightly packed or loosely spaced words.

Sometimes tracking becomes useful for copyfitting. For example, when you have a widow at the end of a column, decreasing the tracking on that sentence might pull the lone word up to the previous line. Your reader will never notice the difference.

Adjust tracking with care. It's easy to go overboard and end up with squished text. Try to limit tracking adjustments to "-10" or less.

Availability of leading (line spacing), kerning and tracking on the web. You can apply leading (referred to as line spacing in non-print applications), tracking and kerning to web type, too. In the case of line spacing and tracking, web designers write CSS specifications to control how much space appears between glyphs or between lines of copy.

Kerning on the web is generally not needed, but it is possible. It does require a bit more effort, specifically, a little programming/scripting. But it *is* possible.

Tabs & dot leaders

Sometimes, in order to keep things aligned, you need tabs. Use tabs for columns of numbers, too, and pay attention to aligning decimal places. Sometimes tabs space out farther than the eye can travel without some help. In those cases, instead of making readers' eyes do the typographic equivalent of a stunt jump across a Grand Canyon of negative space, dot leaders can function like visual bridges. They assist flow by leading the eye along their line of sight.

TYPESETTING LENGTHY COPY

Page after page of nothing but boring gray words scares people, even when the words are set in a nice readable font. The prospect of slogging through all that reading is discouraging at best. The good news is that there are tactics for carving intimidating text into bite-size pieces.

Paragraph indicators

Paragraphs are traditionally indicated either by a first line indent or by additional leading after each paragraph. Unfortunately, most people use default tabs or an extra hard return to create paragraphs. Visually, these default keystrokes result in spaces that are too large.

For most projects, you set paragraph indents or paragraph space-afters using the specific tools that your layout application provides for those tasks.

For web projects, your best bet is spacing after paragraphs. And again, using double hard returns to achieve this results in too much space. Not to mention it's just plain lazy. Instead, specify a bit of extra bottom margin on your paragraph element in your CSS.

Newsletters utilize many of the same typesetting techniques as newspapers. Graduated headline sizes create hierarchy, and images break up the text-heavy page.

Reproduced by permission of SecurityPoint Media.

How big should the spaces be? Use your best judgment. First line indents should be consistent. They need to be just big enough to communicate their presence and do their visual indicator job, but not big enough to distract. If you choose to indicate paragraphs with the indent, remember the first graph or lead does not indent. Or, if you decide to space between paragraphs, don't overdo the space, but do be consistent.

Still not sure about size? Pay attention to well-styled copy around you. Educate your eye on what pleasing spacing looks like. Then use it in your own design projects.

Headings & subheads

Main headers and subheads also provide a great way to break up blocks of text. When styled for contrast, headings and subheads create a sort of navigational rhythm throughout the design.

Don't let the format fool you. This layout is simply a bulleted list with icons for bullets. Use this approach for presentation decks when the audience has time to peruse the text and visually decode the meaning of the icons. It also works on the web where icons serve as buttons that link to other parts of the website.

Proper spacing for headings and subheads increases readers' understanding, too. Remember to position headers closer to the content they reference (clustering) and farther away from unrelated content.

Additionally, remember that headings and subheads should indicate a hierarchy of content. As you might guess, the bigger the headline, the more important it and its related content become. By graduating the size of subheads, the corresponding copy's importance increases or decreases. Keep track of your levels of headings, along with your own decisions about typesetting them consistently.

Headings are particulaly important in web design. When your headings are "tagged" as such in the code, and those headings include keywords, you've taken critical steps in making your site search-engine friendly.

Bulleted lists

Bulleted lists have earned a bad rap in the last decade, owing to overuse and abuse in presentation decks. They've also been upstaged by the trend in infographic-style layouts. Why use a bullet when you can use an icon?

In defense of the lowly bulleted list, we'd like to point out that you can't beat a bulleted list for delivering information quickly and concisely. They also take up far less space than infographic-style layouts. So don't be so quick to relegate them to the compost pile. If you choose to include a bulleted list in your layout, here are some tips:

- » When the list flows with the body copy, give it the same font styling as the body copy.
- » When the list is in a sidebar, give it font styling that contrasts with the body copy.
- » Consider indenting the entire list for additional impact.
- » Use hanging indents. (Keep reading, we'll explain.)
- » Increase leading or paragraph spacing between bullet items for greater readability.
- » Choose your bullets wisely. Asterisks and hyphens are not decorative bullets.
- » Applying a color from your layout to your bullets visually ties the two together. Plus a pop of color makes for a stronger eye entry point for each item in your list.

Hanging indents. Whether your list is inline or in a separate box, a bulleted list requires a hanging indent. In a hanging indent, the first line of a paragraph "hangs" out—juts out—into the left margin. It's sort of the opposite or reverse of an indent. A hanging indent pushes the organizing numerals or bullets to the left and aligns all the remaining text together along a single axis.

When setting hanging indents, consider adding extra leading between each list item. The extra negative space helps isolate each item and makes it easier to digest the list. This is white space and clustering to the communication rescue.

TRADITIONAL BULLETED LIST

Takes up a lot less space and is great for a quick scan

- **PEOPLE** Pitaquia cum faceped moditi aut mo doluptam doloribus sum ium quo beaquibus eostenime.
- **WORK PRODUCT** Dolor aces es magnis sitatiae cuptatque sus, ommossit explibus inum harum qui quis dit iust lam.
- **PRODUCTIVITY** Escius eaquaspercia nestrup tassini mendem landes aut eaquuntis plignatem sunt mos pro to quo blantiat.
- **SUCCESS** Cumlus quid mo doloresciis eostin etur? Quias.

Same content, different layout. While not as visually sexy as an infographic layout, the traditional bullet list is concise. The bullets (along with bolded text) provide eye entry points for quick scannability.

TAKING A PAGE FROM NEWSPAPER DESIGN

For presenting extensive amounts of type in a digestible format, newspapers rule. Designers of daily broadsheet newspapers manage to lay out five or six text-heavy stories on a single front page each day, with each story clearly delineated in a visual hierarchy. Much of this fantastic feat is accomplished with typesetting. And the best part? These tactics adapt to other types of design, too.

Headings and subheadings effectively break this alumni magazine content into distinct sections for easy scanning and inviting reading.

Story headlines

Headlines are the billboards of newspaper design. A well-styled headline is like a big smack on the nose that says, "Read me!" Newspaper designers are experts at creating interest and visual hierarchy through techniques like page position and font contrast.

Graduated headline sizes also reinforce the idea that some stories are more important than others. The bigger the headline, the more important the story. Headline font sizes vary, but it's unusual to see them set less than 24 points, which means leading adjustments, too, for headlines that run more than one line deep.

Another trick is to choose a condensed font for headlines. Writing news-style headlines can be tricky. They need to be pithy, but keeping them concise can be difficult. Condensed fonts are drawn to be narrower than standard fonts. Since condensed fonts take up less space, they offer an extra bit of wiggle room for copyfitting headlines. You don't need to be a news pro, either, to take advantage of that kind of help.

Columns

We keep going on about columns, but newspapers are set in columns because it's easier for the eye to track back and forth across a few inches as opposed to the width of an entire screen or page. To review, newspapers teach us that about two inches make a good-sized column width—not too wide or too narrow.

In printed newspapers the recommended length for legs of body copy is a minimum of two inches and a maximum of 12. Keeping leg length shorter also applies to news website homepages, where the goal is to introduce multiple stories in the same space. In fact, newspaper homepages often display short excerpts rather than short legs of copy. Once the reader clicks through to get to the full story, the copy is likely to be set in a single column (though rarely a full-screen with column) and length is no longer an issue.

Even if you don't want the look of columns in your document, you can take advantage of the principle of narrower lines of type for the eye to scan by increasing margins and decreasing line length.

Justification

One thing beginning designers should *not* emulate is the full justification of newspaper type. See Chapter 4, Layout Sins.

Technically, justification refers to all forms of copy alignment, including left-justified (flush left with ragged right edge), right-justified (flush right with ragged left edge), centered or fully justified (right and left edges perfectly squared).

The best justification for reading is always left justified (flush left with ragged right). It accommodates natural word spacing and provides easy eye tracking. Poorly handled full justification results in unsightly gaps in copy. Not only does this look awful, it cuts down on readability.

Full justification can be particularly problematic in websites. Well-designed responsive pages adjust in size to fit the viewing device (phone, tablet) or browser window size. It's difficult to control rivers of white space in print when you have total control of the design. Web design never affords you 100 percent control of appearance so you can never guarantee a site viewer won't get rivers.

TYPE: NOT JUST FOR READING ANYMORE

In addition to type tricks that encourage reading to convey information, there are type techniques that set the piece's overall tone and create visual interest. Obviously, any selection from the huge range of decorative fonts can help set mood and tone. But don't discount using more traditional fonts in creative ways. No matter which route you choose, exercise caution when using type creatively.

THIS IS A HEADLINE

This is a "deck," a short summary of the article to come. It is typically found tucked directly under the headline.

This is body copy. Et renimi, nissequi omnis dus nonsedi berunt et voles simus, nihilla nes si in rendam, voluptatquis ex ex estis earit ut harciam id que enim velitat eossunt expedi delita cum re quodi doluptatquid ut vollupt atecta iur, officium quis venitis aut et undes ab incia aliquos et ipsa volupienimil maio tem corum, sundia voluptam vellacitis sinvendebis rese num rerchil imi, volorerae volorum sitaturis mos poresed eium rent. Lorro consequam res alibeatquat faceris cuptum que nis autatinum vel moloria aute velibus et exerio ommolup tatatur si di que voluptiisiti aut quiam dis venda volorum quidunt eati od quam dolum eum etur abor maximax iminvel lorere, conet volessimus atem.

Under the influence. Traditional newspaper typesetting techniques such as narrow columns and the use of "decks" appear in print and digital magazines, newsletters and website designs.

Play with your type. Thoughtful use of font pairing, scale, color and case creates visual interest. Play to the strengths of your fonts.

It is easy to go from type that communicates to type that clutters.

Bold & italic

We've already discussed how bold and italic fonts create emphasis. But bold and italic fonts also have decorative uses. Both type treatments make interesting pull quotes, decks, cutlines, headlines and other short blocks of type.

Small caps

A variation on all caps, small caps are all uppercase letters with a slightly larger first-letter capitalization. Small caps suffer from the same readability issues as all caps and should be used with caution—and only in short copy situations.

Reversed type

Reversed type is light type against a dark background. It's a common technique used in creating headlines, sidebars and other layout elements. Like all caps, it's best used sparingly. Reading a lot of reversed copy may reduce readability or tire the eye.

If you choose to employ reversed type, choose your font carefully. Some fonts lose legibility more than others when set in reverse. Modern fonts, with their ultra-thin horizontals, are notoriously bad in the reversing department. Reversing works best with slightly thicker sans serif fonts, though slab serif, bold versions of old style fonts and some decorative fonts are equally effective.

Initial & drop caps

Those really huge single letters (or words) that appear at the start of the first paragraph are called drop caps and initial caps. Drop caps drop down into several lines of the paragraph. Initial caps sit on the baseline and rise upward well above the line.

Both are excellent ways to create a dynamic eye entry point for your lead. You can set their color and size. You might even set the font to something that contrasts with your body font.

It's best to use only one drop cap per page or story and only at the very beginning. While it is possible to use more than one across a multiple-page spread, don't deploy them in every single paragraph. And if you do use more than one drop cap on a spread, make sure your drop caps don't accidentally spell out something offensive. You laugh, but it can happen.

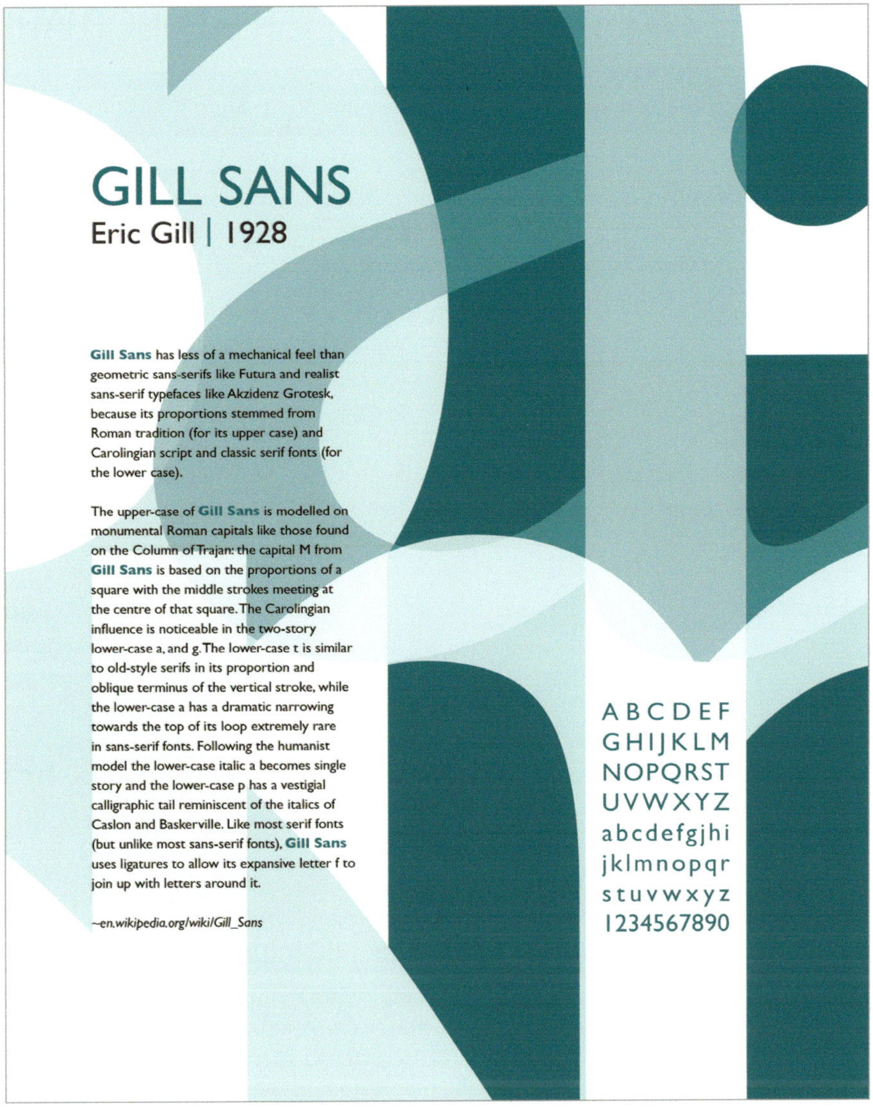

Magazines, websites and other publications are dotted with examples of type used creatively. You'll commonly see logos, navigation, pull quotes and other typographic design details giving life and order to otherwise dull pages.

Letterforms themselves can be interesting with angles and curves that contrast nicely with the rectangular shape of most screens and pages. Creative designers often manipulate the scale and orientation of fonts to turn type into visual focal points in lieu of photos, line art or other graphics. That's when things get really fun.

More than a pretty typeface. Every font has a story that begins with the type designer's vision. Inventing new fonts is a whole industry, while classic typefaces, such as Gill Sans, stand the test of time. Likewise, designing with type is an art form. So let the lines and shapes of letters inspire your layouts. Who needs pictures when letters and words are so beautiful?

TYPESET LIKE A PRO: TYPESETTER’S PUNCTUATION

Glyph	Replace this...	with this...	and code with this.
Quotes	"Straight quotes"	“Smart quotes”	“ ”
Ellipses	. . .	…	…
Em dash	---	—	—
En dash	--	–	–
Prime marks	1’ 3”	1′ 3″	′ ″
Special characters	1/2, 1/4, copyright, registered trademark	½, ¼, ©, ®	½ ¼ © ™
Diacritics	a, n, e, o	â, ñ, é, ö	â ñ é ö

NEXT-LEVEL TYPESETTING: SPECIAL GLYPHS

Although most fonts have 265 characters, that’s a far greater number than the sum of adding up upper- and lowercase letters, numbers and basic punctuation. So what’s up with the other 100-plus characters?

Typesetter’s punctuation and diacritics

If you’re still typing ellipses as “period space period space period space,” you’re doing it wrong. Among those 265 characters are punctuation marks specifically drawn and spaced to match the rest of the glyphs in the font. If you know where to look, you’ll also find a variety of specific punctuation glyphs you may not know exist, even though such glyphs are routinely necessary to produce professional-grade type.

For example, you need smart quotes (curly quotes) for quotations. You need the straight version of quote marks called prime marks for notating inches and feet without writing out the words “inches” and “feet.”

While you need the hyphen to create compound words, you need en dashes (historically the width of a lowercase n) for punctuating such things as the implied "to" in "3–4 weeks." Then you'll need the slightly wider em dash—historically the width of a lowercase m—for dashes used to replace commas, colons and parentheses—when you're trying to be slightly more emphatic.

When you typeset non-English words (and some foreign-born words that have been assimilated into the English lexicon), you'll need diacritics. Diacritics are those small marks above or below a glyph that indicate proper pronunciation. Consider résumé vs. resume, for example. Diacritics are essential when typesetting in languages other than English. Café con leche just isn't the same without the acute accent over the letter "e."

Typesetter's punctuation and diacritics are available in applications for all types of onscreen design, too. Such software provides palettes or menus that allow you to access and insert the character of choice. For web projects, punctuation can also be inserted manually by adding the proper HTML code in the right location.

If you don't think the proper symbols look better than type kluges, we'll give you your money back. Okay, not really. But do check out what proper punctuation looks like and figure out how to use it. Because what you don't know about type can hurt you.

OpenType for print design

OpenType fonts go well beyond the standard 265 characters. Designed to be functional across platforms to work on both Macs and PCs, these fonts can have as many as 65,000 characters. In addition to all the traditional punctuation marks and accent marks, OpenType fonts offer some or all of the following type options:

Ligatures. Ligatures are specially designed letter pairs—a single glyph meant to take the place of two traditional letters. Ligatures were created for certain letter pairs that join awkwardly because of the position of the dot of the "i" or hook of the "f," for example.

Swash alternates. These are just what they sound like: decorative alternatives to traditional italic letterforms. While swash alternates don't work well for body copy, they can be beautiful when used in large decorative headlines, as initial caps or in pull quotes.

Old style figures. Ever notice that normal numbers often look too big and clunky when typed in with the normal flow of text? That's because the height of regular numerals is the same as uppercase letters. Regular numerals have the visual feel of all caps. An alternative is to use old style figures. Old style figures have varying x-heights, ascenders and descenders just like the rest of the letters in a font. Visually, they blend in much better with text.

LIGATURES & SWASH ALTERNATES

Using ligatures is a mark of professional typesetting. Just do it. Using swash alternates on the other hand is like busting out the fancy dinner jacket for a night out. Use them when you need some style. Look for them in the glyphs palette of OpenType fonts.

The girls had difficulty eating the sticky waffles.

The girls had difficulty eating the sticky waffles.

Above: *Mrs Eaves* font with and without ligatures.

Below: Fonts *Redoura, Rennie Mackintosh* and *Paris Pro* with swash alternate glyphs applied.

Serendipity

STYLE & SUBSTANCE

Wonderful

Letters as pictures. Dingbats look like little tiny pictures, but they really are font characters. The logo in this business card design incorporates a scissors glyph. The same glyph repeats in the background.

Dingbats. If you've ever seen a decorative ornament to indicate that you've reached the end of the narrative, you've seen a dingbat. They look like little tiny pictures, but they really are font characters. Many fonts have a few as part of the 265-character set. Typically, OpenType fonts have more of them. Then there are fonts made up of nothing but dingbats.

Because they are technically font characters, you can style dingbats as you would fonts. You can change their size, color and orientation. They can also function as bullets, although, as always, use some discipline. Not all dingbats make good bullets.

Paired with letterforms, dingbats can be logos. Strings of them can become section breaks or borders. Or they can stand alone as artwork.

Still think type is boring? Neither do we. It is perhaps the most important tool in your visual communication toolbox. Use it. Don't abuse it.

TRY THIS

1. Start a "swipe file" of compelling typography and typesetting techniques. Look for anything with interesting type: logos; headline styles from magazines, newspapers and websites; sidebars and infographics; bulleted lists; opening slides from video clips; or interesting product packaging. Look for dingbats, ligatures, swash alternates and other uses of extended character sets, too.

   Assemble your examples in a scrapbook. Annotate your examples with notes on why you like them and why they work. Categorize your selections by style: corporate, kid-friendly, grunge, romantic, extreme, etc.

2. Go to the candy aisle at your grocery store. Look for packages of the following types of candy: Gummy bears, traditional stick chewing gum, a milk chocolate bar, a chocolate bar with additional ingredients such as nuts or caramel and an expensive bar of dark chocolate. Look at the font choices on each package.

   What categories of fonts does your candy-wrapper collection exhibit? Are the font choices appropriate for the target audience? Explain.

Design a candy wrapper for your own favorite candy. Write rationales for your choices.

3. Design a type-only logo for yourself. Use your logo to create your own set of custom business cards and letterhead. Or use your logo as the basis for a new résumé design.
4. Create your one-color typographic self-portrait. Using only glyphs (including numerals and punctuation but not dingbats), create a close-up mug shot of yourself. Size contrast will be important. Direction, in the literal sense of turning glyphs topsy-turvy, also will be important. Otherwise, the rules go out the window since you're not using type to convey narrative information.
5. Research a famous font artist. Write a short history (a paragraph or two) and create a one-page layout using your history as the content. Use only fonts designed by your artist, and use only type in your design. No photos or illustrations allowed.
6. Create a vertically folding restaurant menu with a flat size at 8.5 inches wide by 11 inches high folded to a finished size of 4.25 inches by 11 inches. You'll need to design a cover and a two-page inside spread. A design for the back cover is optional. Begin with some menu copywriting.

   Use typography to convey the kind of restaurant (casual Thai or upscale French, for instance). Create a visual hierarchy and a sense of visual order, too.

   Demonstrate appropriate punctuation marks, paragraph indicators, bulleted lists and hanging indents, tabs and tab leaders, and whatever else is appropriate to your design.

LOGOS + *branding*

WHAT YOU NEED TO KNOW

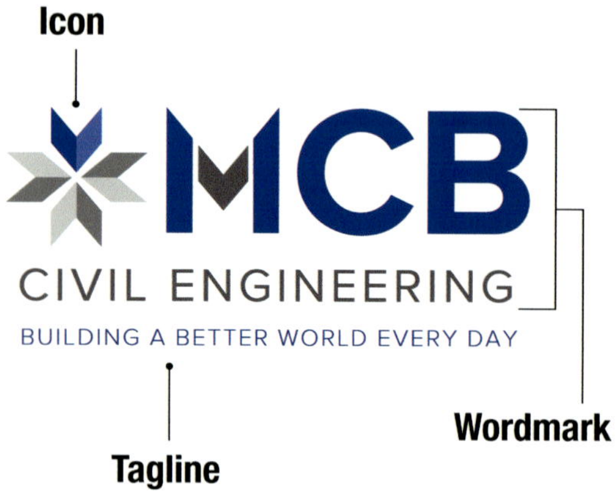

Some of the world's most iconic logos are bare-bones simple. This makes people think that logo design is simple. But in fact, designing logos requires hundreds of hours of brainstorming, sketching, rendering, rejecting and securing approvals. One tiny little picture, or word and picture combination, must encompass the philosophy, activity, spirit and brand promise of an organization. This is why logo design is best left to professionals.

That said, you will have to work with logos in some form. Maybe you've been tasked with providing direction and feedback to a designer-for-hire. Or perhaps budget dictates that you must come up with something on your own. In either case, you need direction. Let's start with some terminology:

Icon. A logo's graphic element is called an icon or symbol. Some logos consist only of an icon.

Wordmark. Many logos include the name of the entity represented. This verbiage is called the wordmark. Some logos consist only of a wordmark.

Combination mark. More often, icons and wordmarks appear in tandem. An icon paired with a wordmark is a combination mark.

Tagline. A tagline is an additional, optional line of text that further explains something about the entity represented by the logo.

Monogram. A monogram is a type of symbol or icon created out of two or three letters. Often the letterforms are intertwined in some fashion.

Enclosure. Logos may include some sort of outer boundary or shape, such as a rectangle, circle or shield. Such boundaries are known as enclosures.

Brand. The terms logo and brand are often used interchangeably, but they are two different things. Communication sage Seth Godin says that your brand represents the "set of expectations, memories, stories and relationships" a consumer has with your organization and its products and services. Your logo is the graphic avatar for the best you hope your brand to be. Logos literally become the part that stands in for the whole, a process called synecdoche. Logos remain the example par excellence of visual synecdoche.

Attibutes of a successful log

Whether you are evaluating the work of a professional designer or trying your hand at your own designs, consider:

Logos should be unique to the subject/product/organization. Avoid anything too generic. If the design in question easily could represent another organization with the same name and a different mission, then go back to the drawing board.

Logos must be scalable. The design needs to be as clear and readable at the size of a postage stamp as it is at the

Marvelous monograms. Letterforms can be beautiful and, used singly or in multiples, they make interesting logo options. Pair your glyphs with basic shapes and a dash of gestalt for nearly infinite icon and logo possiblities. Be wary of traditional monograms (upper left), however. They can be unreadable and often have fine details that make them poor for logo applications.

You've got personality. The right icon adds personality to a logo. Successful designs use fonts with design features that coordinate with the icon's attributes.

Versatility is essential. Creating your logo in different color ways and orientations (stacked, horizontal) ensures your logo is outfitted for every occasion. Reversed out logos are particularly useful against photo backgrounds like the one on the book cover below.

size of an outdoor board. Avoid fine lines and details that disappear when a logo is reduced in size. If a logo uses more than one font, make sure both fonts are readable even when the logo is small.

Simple means versatile. Logos must be flexible. A complex illustrated logo might look great on outdoor signage, but what if you want to embroider the logo on polo shirts? Complex designs are costly, and sometimes impossible, to render in certain media. If you must have a complex logo, consider creating a simplified version as well.

Limit the number of colors. If the brand requires consistent color, limit the number of colors used in the logo. Choosing one or two "spot" colors, or one color plus black is a good option. Spot colors are pre-established printing ink colors. Choosing them is similar to picking a paint color from swatches at a home improvement store. Because spot colors come "out of the can," they are consistent.

Make sure the logo can be rendered in one color only. Sometimes printing requirements or logo placement dictate that a logo appears in all black or all white ("reversed-out" in design terminology). All black and all white logos tend to fare far better than full-color logos against busy photo backgrounds, for example.

Logos are mini layouts. Composition matters. Consider the overall balance of the various elements, as well as alignment, movement and unity. Make sure fonts contrast with each other and font parts contrast with backgrounds. Give thought to the overall shape. A strongly horizontal logo design might work well in a website header but appear tiny when squished into the icon/logo block on a social media site. Create stacked (vertical) and horizontal versions for maximum flexibility.

Set up final files as vector files with fonts "outlined." The only scalable file format is vector so make sure you get vector versions of the finished logo. Vector filenames end with the extension .eps or .svg. Photos are bitmap images that can't be scaled without loss of resolution. Never use a photo in a logo because photos lose resolution when scaled.

Also make sure to convert fonts to graphics via an "outline fonts" function. This prevents your logo font from being accidentally replaced by something ugly, like Courier, when you share your logo with others.

Avoiding amateur hour

The best way to avoid getting stuck with a crummy logo is to hire a professional designer. Seriously.

That said, if you must do this on your own, purchase and learn to use a vector graphic program. This is not optional. Logos *must* be rendered in vector formats in order to be scalable.

Remember the layout sins from Chapter 4? Here come the logo sins:

Using the font-du-jour. A few fonts get done to death each decade. Some fonts were so overused they've become synonymous with time periods. Some recent grossly overused fonts include Lobster, Papyrus, Copperplate Gothic and Scriptina. In general, avoid fonts that came installed on your computer. There are thousands of fonts out there for minimal cost. Or better, hire a font designer to create somethine new.

Clip art as icon. If you must add a graphic, don't use clip art. Instead try a simple shape paired with an interesting letterform. Or consider a decorative dingbat or type ornament as a graphic. But use care in your selection. A smiley face dingbat is no better than smiley face clip art.

Application of type effects. Professional logo designers generally avoid quick filters for bevels, embossing, glass, chrome, glowing, warping and drop shadows. You should avoid them, too. A very popular search engine had a beveled, glass-effect-with-drop-shadow logo once. Back in the *1990s.* It had an exclamation point, too. For the record, don't add exclamation points either.

Too much. Amateurs try to cram too much in their logos. Too many fonts, too many colors, ugly clip art or other graphics used together create visual bedlam. This is bad when the logo stands alone, and it only gets worse on application. A super-busy logo on top of a super-busy background image might just give your reader a migraine.

Too literal, too obvious. The amateur approach to designing a logo for a home builder is to put a roof over the builder's name. A professional designer uses client interviews and research to find inspiration beyond the obvious.

It's just a logo. What could possibly go wrong? A lot, judging from the number of awful logos out there. Choosing overused fonts like Zapfino (sorry, Luigi!) **(1)**, using bad clipart **(2)**, typsetting with competing fonts and applying bad type effects **(3 & 4)** are sure ways to make your design look amateurish.

1

2

3

4

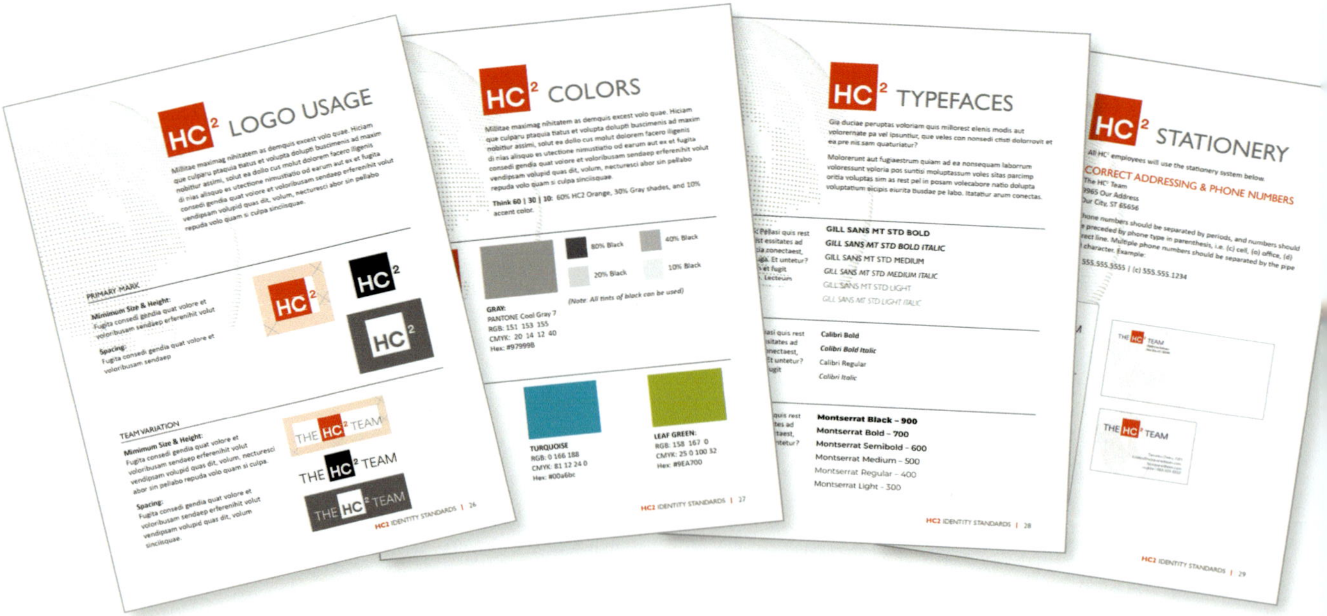

About brand standards, you must know the rules, and you may not break them. Think of an organization's official brand standards as the visual equivalent of a text-based style guide. A brand's standards guide or manual codifies the rules for where, when, and how the brand's visual material and assets may be configured and deployed—and by whom. Standards cover such things as the logo (icon, wordmark, combination mark, monogram, tagline), official colors (digital and print spaces), designated typefaces (fonts, weights, sizes) and associated graphics and images.

BRAND STANDARDS

The key to using logos as part of brand building is to use them consistently. To that end, many organizations create a set of brand standards. The most basic brand standards include a systematic listing of the logos available for use, the colorways in which they may appear as well as size, position and spacing requirements.

Maintaining brand consistency requires more than just slapping a logo on all print and digital collateral. Standards also include:

» A full slate of colors and color builds

» A list of fonts including weights, sizes and usage

» Layouts for stationery and other collateral

» Examples of imagery and graphic elements

» Sets of icons

» Social media graphics

» Reference designs showing proper logo usage

Increasingly, standards are moving beyond graphics and including content such as brand story, positioning, vision and values, personality, messaging and even tone of voice.

For the web, an additional set of standards called a "design system" comes into play. Design systems are similar to brand standards, but also include specifications for links, buttons, icons, animations and other types of motion and interactivity. We discuss these in Chapter 13: Designing for the Web.

CHAPTER 8

COLOR BASICS

CHOOSING & USING COLOR

Ask children about their favorite colors, and you get instant exuberant responses: "Red!" "Blue!" People just respond to color. We select or reject everything from clothes to cars based on what colors say to us.

In this chapter we talk about how designers harness the power of color to grab our attention, organize visual flow and evoke emotion. We also talk about finding color inspiration from culture, history and nature, as well as on the color wheel. But translating inspiration into effective design requires some understanding of color technologies. We cover that, too, along with some tips for designing with color.

THE POWER OF COLOR: IMPACT, ORGANIZATION & EMOTION

Color is a powerful compositional tool

Color is eye-catching. It makes you look. Picture a black and white poster with one pop of color—a hat, for instance—in bright pink. That bright pink immediately becomes a focal point. Part of the attention-getting power is the principle of contrast at work. But a color's shade and intensity also play a role in attracting interest, whether as eye entry point, contrast, wow factor or all of the above.

If color captures attention, you can use color to keep drawing the eye's attention over and over again for flow through your design. The eye will follow color around your composition like a dog follows the cook in the kitchen.

Color organizes

Imagine you're in an airport terminal. You see a large group of people wearing red T-shirts. Either they're all part of the same group or it's a freakish coincidental convergence of red T-shirt lovers. Our money is on the group thing.

Color can sort and cluster to indicate what goes with what. That's the principle behind color-coding systems, such as electrical wiring and mall parking lots. This is some potent design mojo if you think about it.

Color evokes emotion

Humans respond physiologically to color. For example, interior designers have long recommended painting walls blue for a calming effect. That said, most of the emotional muscle we attach to color is learned.

Imagine watching athletes emerging on a playing field. The local crowd will cheer enthusiastically at the sight of the home team's colors. When the opponent's colors hit the field, cue the crickets.

The bottom line? Designers must be tactical about choosing and employing color. Some lucky people seem to be born with good color sense. For others, just trying to match two socks is a challenge. Fortunately, there is help.

HOW TO CHOOSE COLOR

A color palette is a set of colors you choose for your project. When creating color palettes:

1. Choose a main color that sets the tone for the layout
2. Choose a supporting color that contrasts with and complements the main color
3. Choose as many additional accent colors as needed for your specific project. A good rule of thumb is to pick the minimum number of colors you actually need. Three or four total colors is a good number to start. Make sure your full palette includes a range of light, middle and dark tones.

Color is evocative. The colors in this website are drawn from pizza ingredients and are intended to make you hungry. We say, "Please pass the grated parmesan."

Design by Rebecca and Guy Hagen. Reproduced by permission of the Tampa Bay Pizza Company and Tucker/Hall, Inc.

Color question No. 1: Does the client have exisiting brand colors? If so, what are they? Request color builds or spot colors for print projects and color builds for screen projects before you design too far down the wrong technicolor rabbit hole.

I'm one of those people who can't match socks. So how do I know which colors to use?

A number of factors come into play when selecting specific colors for your layout. Remember the research and brainstorming discussed in Chapter 2? Project objective, audience, the need to coordinate with existing design work, budget and final format all impact color choices.

Budget & project format. To determine whether your palette needs two colors or 10, consider your project budget and format. Full color is generally the no-extra-cost default for web, television, video and screens. But if your project is destined for print, extra color can add cost. Can you afford full color process printing plus additional ink colors if you need an exact match for a brand color? If your final format is marketing swag such as spot-printed water bottles, shopping bags or T-shirts, does your budget allow for printing six colors? Two colors? One color? No need to spend time picking ten colors when you only need two.

Working with brand colors. If your project must match an existing brand, or your client has requested a specific color, your palette might already be chosen for you. Some brand color palettes contain only one or two logo colors. Others have a substantial selection of additional supporting and coordinating colors. Simply having a set of brand colors may or may not answer your color selection needs. There are many examples of good design projects that display brand color only in the logo. In any case, brand colors offer a quick answer to "which color?"

Project objective & audience. Design objective and audience might be the strongest influencers of color choice. An informational layout such as the minutes of a meeting is not likely to need a main color, secondary color and a set of six accent colors. On the other hand, an infographic-heavy presentation deck might need an extensive palette of distinct contrasting colors.

For layouts intended to establish brand positioning or motivate viewers to action, select color for emotional impact and symbolism. Calm, stable, solid blue makes a better choice for an attorney's website than hot pink or chartreuse. Promotional materials for a gym might incorporate strong, dark or energetic colors such as reds, golds, blacks and charcoal grays.

Be wary, however, about what you think you know about color. Color "meaning" is learned and can change based on the age, gender and culture of your target audience.

Color symbolism & learned meaning

Color & Culture. The sighted and those who aren't colorblind read symbolic meanings into color. Let's do a quick word match-up to test that theory. Pair each word in the first column with the color that best represents that word:

1. Anger	A. Green
2. Growth	B. Blue
3. Earthy	C. Yellow
4. Trustworthy	D. Brown
5. Happy	E. Red

If you were born and/or reared in the United States, you probably had no difficulty pairing red with anger, green with growth, yellow with happiness and so on. However, if you asked people from other parts of the world to do this matching exercise, you might get different results. The meanings people attach to colors depend on their cultures.

In U.S. culture, for example, white can symbolize purity, such as a white wedding dress, a custom that began as a way to communicate the bride's virginity. But in China, brides often wear red, a color that symbolizes good fortune. The thought of a red wedding dress is a little shocking in the United States because we associate red dresses with, well, something else. On the other hand, in numbers of Pacific Rim cultures, white is the color of mourning while Americans and Europeans connect black with mourning.

So it's important to consider the audience when communicating with color.

It's also important to consider context. The same color can symbolize multiple things within the same culture depending on the circumstance. In the United States, green can be a fresh, cool, natural, environmentally friendly and healthy color. But "hospital green" has negative associations with sickness and cold impersonal institutions. Green also can connote envy.

Does this mean you should not use green as the main color when creating a social media site promoting a community garden? Of course not. But do not to take the symbolic meaning of color for granted.

Color & History. Like clothing styles, color styles come and go. If someone you know has an old pink-tiled bathroom, you know what we're talking about. Knowing a little bit about the history of color trends can help you choose (or avoid) time- and era-evocative colors for your projects.

Here comes the bride. In India, red is the traditional color for bridal attire, representing new beginnings, passion and prosperity. Red also represents the Hindu goddess Durga, who symbolizes new beginnings and feminine power. No white dresses here. In India, white is for funeral attire.

Mother Nature has great color sense. If a color pairing occurs in nature, it's a good bet the pairing will look good in your layout. Sliced peaches and background foliage inspired the color palette for this magazine spread.

For example, Rebecca dates herself by admitting she had an elementary-age bedroom sporting a burnt orange chenille bedspread, stylized "daisy" curtains in shades of yellow, orange and green, and a gigantic foot-shaped green shag rug. If you don't get the joke, we'll tell you that burnt orange, avocado green, harvest gold and brown are classic early 1970s colors.

Every decade has a color palette or two. Pink, black and turquoise still evoke the 1950s. Neon brights bring to mind the 1980s.

In fact, color designers are currently deciding what colors will be trendy two years from now. So if you're plugged in to the industry, you might even be able to choose color for your designs based on the future.

Pulling color from your project assets

Another way to select main and supporting colors for your project is to look closely at your project's visual assets. Photos, illustrations, animations and video each come with built-in colors. Dominant colors should suggest a color scheme to you. As a bonus, there is a compositional benefit to this color selection approach. Repeating the colors found in imagery in other parts of your layout creates pleasing visual unity.

Color from nature

If you are still having a hard time putting colors together, take a cue from Mother Nature. Colors that appear together naturally can make pleasing palettes. You might not consider putting bright orange, deep green and deep blue-violet together on your own. But on a bird of paradise plant, these colors come together in a vibrant color scheme.

A color palette can contain one color or many. When building out larger color palettes, the best tool in your design toolbox is something you probably learned about in grade school: color theory.

BUILDING PALETTES USING COLOR THEORY

In the canon of color knowledge, Sir Isaac Newton of falling-apple-equals-gravity fame also gets credit for discovering the color spectrum by playing with prisms. Color is light. White light is the mixture of all colors of the spectrum visible to the human eye. Black is an absence of color.

THE TRADITIONAL COLOR WHEEL

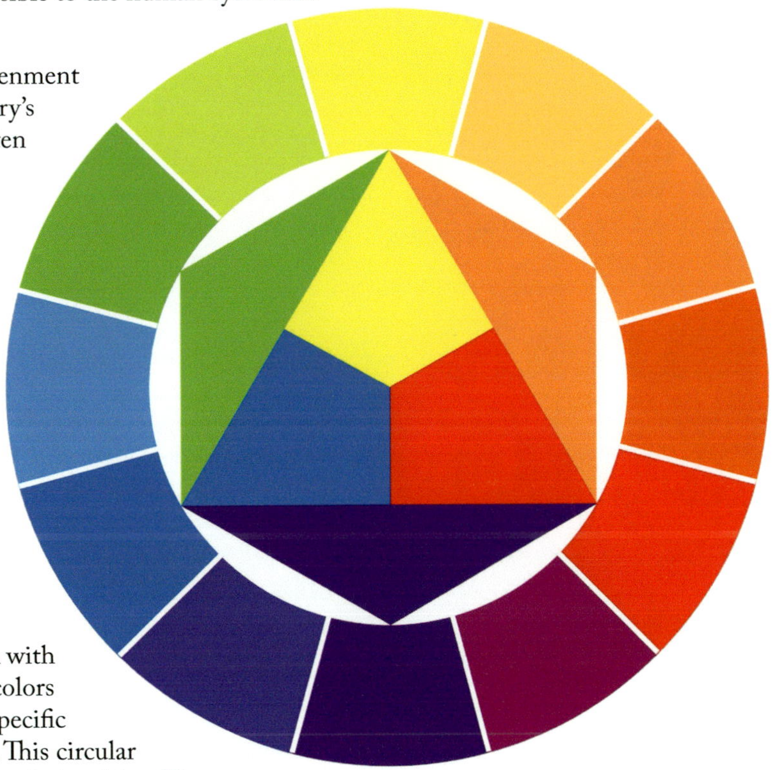

Now let's skip ahead from the Enlightenment to Modernism. In the early 20th century's Bauhaus school of design, Johannes Itten taught his students techniques for achieving color contrast, including pairing color complements, dark with light values and warm with cool shades, among others.

Fast-forward again, and we're still working with color theory. But now we're applying it to color on digital displays. Before you nod off over color science and theory, let's move on to practical color knowledge. *Ergo*, the color wheel.

The color wheel

The color wheel is like an analog clock with three primary colors, three secondary colors and six tertiary colors arranged in 12 specific positions in the order of the spectrum. This circular arrangement creates a diagram of color relationships. If you understand these working color relationships you can use them to build color palettes.

"Christmas, kings & blue jeans." If you can remember that phrase, you can remember the three primary colors and their complements.

COLORFUL RELATIONSHIPS

All colors on the color wheel come from various combinations of three primary colors: red, blue and yellow. The resulting relationships (i.e., relative positions on the color wheel) provide the basis for harmonious color palettes. For example, colors opposite each other on the wheel are called "complementary colors."

Primary + Primary = Secondary

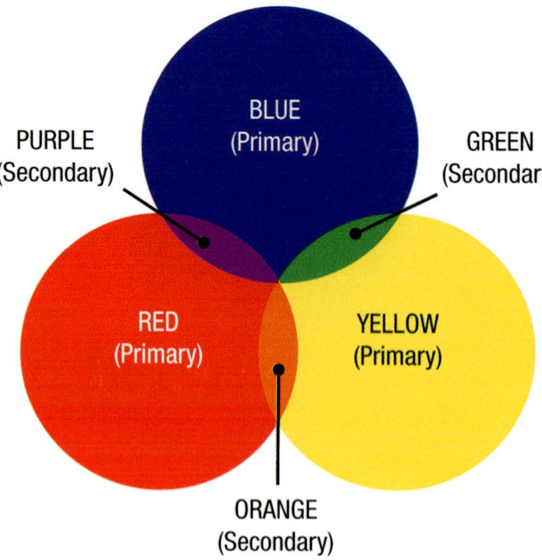

Primary + Secondary = Tertiary

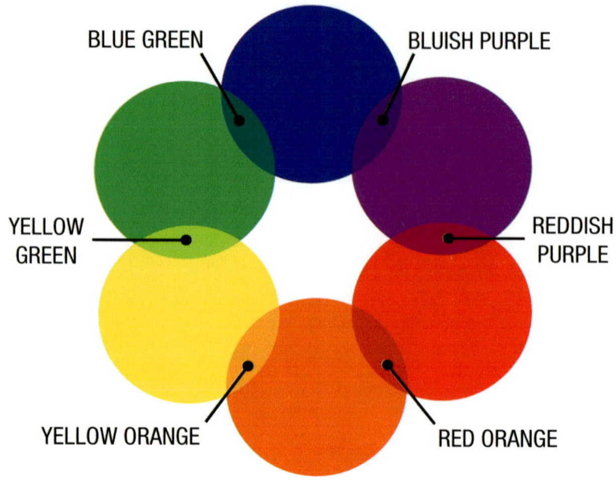

Christmas colors are red (primary) and green (complementary). The king's royal colors are yellow (primary) and purple (complementary). And blue (primary) jeans typically are stitched with orange (complementary) thread. All six colors have relationships to each other defined by their positions on the color wheel. Designers can use these relationships to build color palettes for all types of design projects.

Color relationships

Primary colors. Using the clock analogy, the primary colors yellow, blue and red appear four hours apart at, say, noon, 4 and 8, respectively, to form a triangle.

Secondary & complementary color. Next we can build the secondary colors by mixing two primary colors at a time. Mixing yellow and blue produces green. Mixing blue and red makes purple. Mixing red with yellow makes—you got it—orange.

Notice how each secondary color appears on the wheel directly opposite the primary color it complements. Per "Christmas, kings and blue jeans," green lies opposite red, purple lies opposite yellow and orange lies opposite blue.

The point is that color complements found at opposite sides of the color wheel indeed do "complement" each other visually. Opposites attract, as they say, to make attractive pairs.

Tertiary colors. Mix a primary color with the closest secondary color on the wheel to get those subtler "in between" tertiary colors.

Triads. Although the primary colors are blue, red and yellow, other triplets of color from the color wheel also can make pleasing color palettes. Form any triangle four hours apart on the color wheel to locate a viable color-scheme triplet.

Analogous color. Additionally, mixing colors next to each other on the wheel produces "in between" colors. Side-by-side colors on the wheel are related because they contain some of the colors sitting next to them. We call that analogous color.

Color temperature. The notion of warm and cool colors reveals another property of the color wheel: One side is warm, and the other side is cool. Obviously, the red-orange-yellow side is warm, and the green-blue-purple side is cool. Maybe not so obviously, you can warm up a cool color by adding a little red, orange or yellow. Or you can cool down a warm color by adding a little green, blue or purple. That's part of how contrasting color works. Notice how each opposite, thus contrasting, color pair on the wheel includes both a warm and a cool color.

Another good thing to know about warm and cool colors is that when used in layouts, warm colors appear to come forward and cool colors recede. This concept can be helpful when you're trying to emphasize or de-emphasize elements in your layout.

In sum, the color wheel can inspire and help you expand your project's color palette. But we're not done with color theory and the color wheel yet. Next up, we'll talk about the properties of color.

APPLYING THE COLOR WHEEL

These colorful logo options draw their palettes from color wheel relationships.

Analogous

Complementary

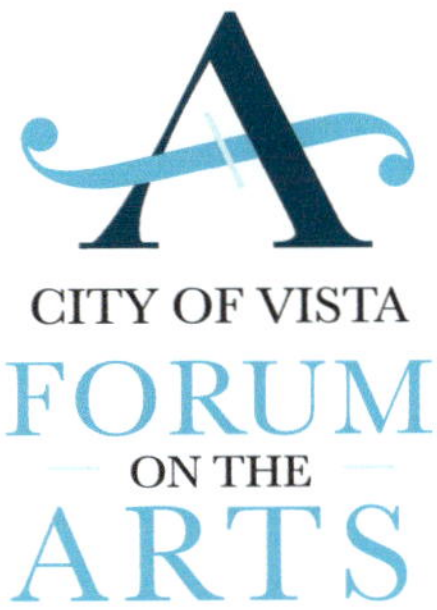

Monochromatic

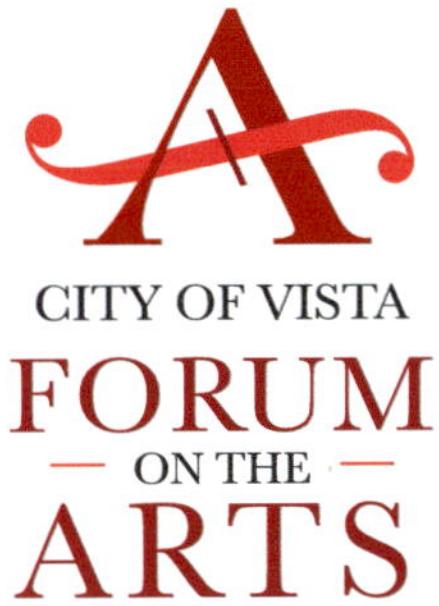

Shades

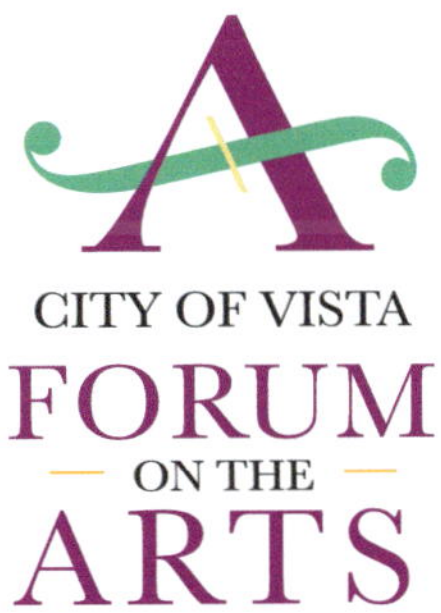

Triad

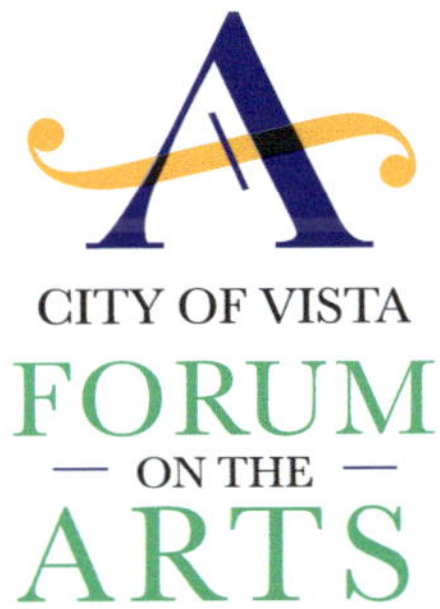

Split Complement

Building a pleasing palette. Orange and green, both secondary colors on the color wheel, appear in this layout's background image. Adding a third color—purple—completes the triad of secondary colors.

COLOR PROPERTIES

It might have occurred to you that working with 12 colors, even with a multitude of gradient colors in between, is pretty limiting. Like trying to paint the Sistine Chapel ceiling with a 24-count box of crayons limiting.

The good news is, if we extend the color wheel in a different direction we exponentially increase our color options. To color, we add the concepts of value and saturation.

Hue, value & saturation

Hue. When we talk about color by name, for example "blue" or "orange," what we're really referencing is hue. Generally, hue refers to the purest, undiluted form of a color. Each hue corresponds to a unique wavelength on Newton's light spectrum.

Value (Tint & Shade). Take any hue, say red, and add some white to it. The resulting color is pink. Take the same red, add black to it and now you get burgundy. Adding white to any hue produces a tint of that hue. Adding black produces a shade of that hue. You can add as much black or white to your hue as you like, approaching total white and total black. Extrapolate this process to each hue on the color wheel. Suddenly your color options have blown far past that little 24-count crayon box.

Saturation. Referring to the brilliance or intensity of the hue, saturation describes how pale or strong the color appears. The level of hue saturation is defined relative to its relationship to neutral gray. The closer the hue is to gray, the less saturated it is. In the world of fine art, artists desaturate colors by adding other colors to them. Mixing in a bit of a color's complement is one way to desaturate. In the world of digital design, desaturation is about the subtraction of light.

COLOR PROPERTIES

Color has properties which, when applied, add variety and visual interest to your layouts. Hue answers the question "what color?" Value is the lightness or darkness of the hue. Saturation refers to the amount or intensity of the hue.

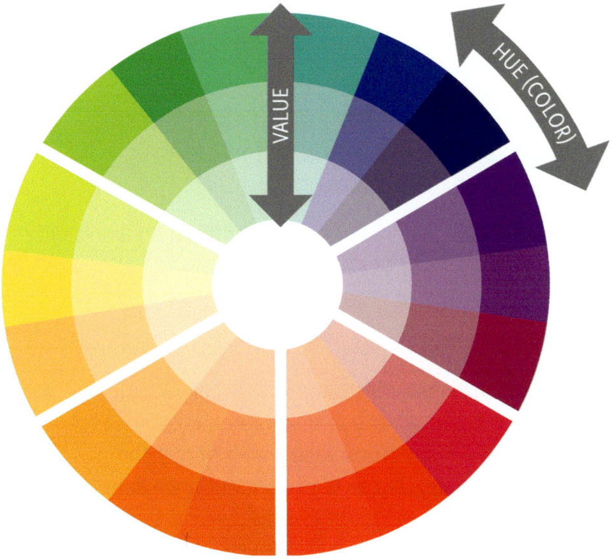

Color properties do more than provide a bigger box of crayons. They give us more options to pair colors for our communication purposes.

Color properties at work

Monochromatic color schemes. A monochromatic color palette is just what it sounds like—one color is used throughout the layout. But adding tints and shades of a single hue can keep this from being blah. Place a lightly tinted blue logo over a background of the same blue with a different tint and you have a watermark effect. Shades of the same color can make interesting icons for apps, presentation decks or websites. On the utilitarian side of design, changing the color of a web navigation link to a different color tint can indicate which page a site visitor is on.

Tints & shades create contrast. Despite the fact that complementary colors are supposed to, uh, complement, each other, when used side-by-side at full saturation they are migraine-inducing. When pairing complements, use a tint or shade of one of the colors. This provides needed saturation contrast while still providing the increased vibrancy of a complementary pair.

Readability requires good contrast, too, and the rule of thumb says stick with dark-on-light or light-on-dark color combos. Tints and shades give you lighter and darker color options for both fonts and backgrounds to optimize readability.

Increasing or decreasing saturation changes mood. Like tints and shades, increased or decreased saturation can add valuable contrast to layouts. Or shift saturation to create emphasis. If all elements of a layout are desaturated (pushed towards grayscale) save for one element left in full color, the element in full saturated color becomes the instant focal point.

COLORBLIND DESIGN

Accessible design accounts for colorblindness, a set of conditions affecting 5–10 percent of people.

TYPES: Red–green colorblindness includes deuteranomaly (green looks like red), protanomaly (red looks like green) and protanopia and deuteranopia (green and red are indistinguishable).

With tritanomaly and tritanopia, the following pairs become difficult to discern as separate colors: blue–green, purple–red, yellow–red and yellow–pink. Tritanopia also makes colors seem duller.

Monochromacy is complete colorblindness, meaning the inability to see color beyond grayscale.

TIPS: Chapter 5's Mini Art School provides tips for colorblind-accessible design:

Contrast: Use light/dark value to pair colors, and choose images for contrast. Or pair a saturated color with a diluted pastel—saturated yellow with barely-there pink, for example. Deploy high-contrast grayscale for monochromacy.

Shape/Form: For troublesome color combinations like red and green, employ shape or form as a color design booster. A minus sign inside a red stop button and a plus sign inside a green start button represent classic examples.

Texture & Pattern: Use texture and pattern to aid in differentiating difficult color pairs. In a bar chart, for example, blue bars might sport diagonal stripes and green bars, verticals.

But don't overdo it. A busy design won't work for anybody.

TOGGLE: Best practices invite users to toggle among color combos specifically designed for red–green, Tritan and monochromacy.

TEST: Your design software likely has a built-in function to mimic colorblindness. If not, the web offers varieties of such tests.

Color shifts. The diagram at the top shows how color shifts for people with colorblindness. The bottom images show how this story teaser appears to a person with protanopia, making red and green indistinguishable.

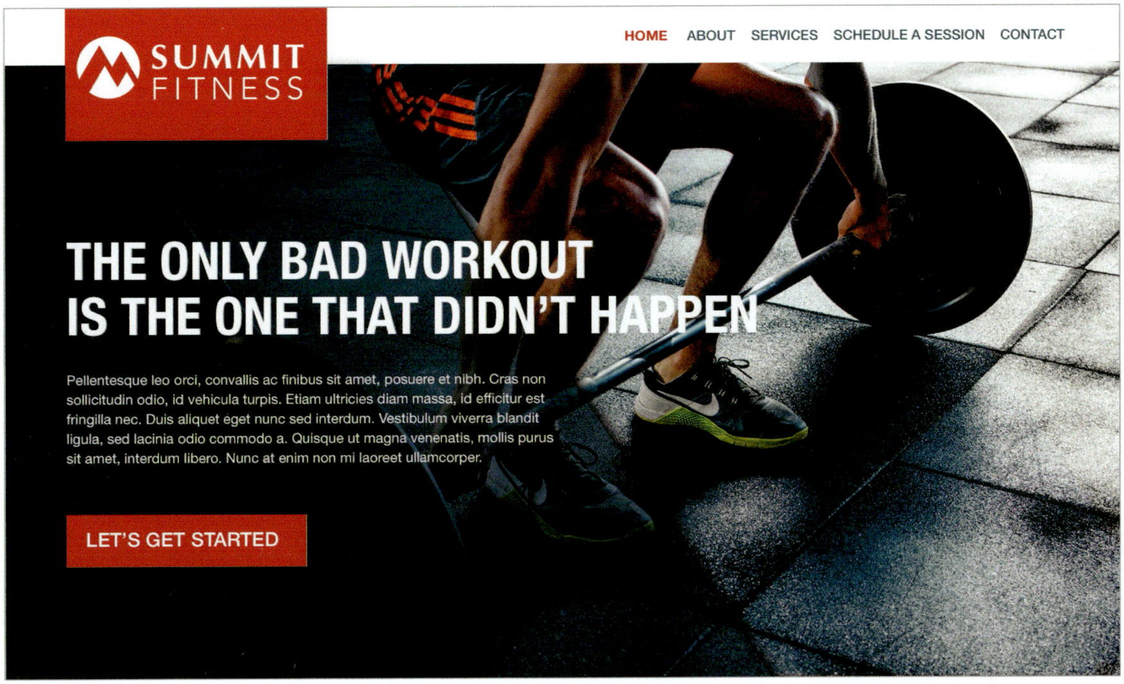

To saturate, or not to saturate. The desaturated background image gives a masculine, gritty feel to this fitness training website. The background contrasts nicely with the saturated red in the logo color, allowing the pops of red to be the stars of the layout.

Generation of mood and atmosphere is a more interesting use of increased and decreased saturation. Desaturated color creates a somber, grungy or vintage feel, while fully saturated color evokes brightness and energy. Oversaturation can feel otherworldly and dreamlike. Filmmakers are masters at pairing different saturation levels with color casting to evoke everything from gritty, dystopian futures and vintage dramas to life on Mars. These same techniques, along with their emotional punch, work if applied to other types of design as well.

The color wheel has had tremendous staying power—you should be so lucky to be active at 300 years of age—but artists who use it primarily work with pigmented media such as pastels, pencils and paint. Today, we use computers to paint with light. So some color theory for this century is in order.

ADDITIVE & SUBTRACTIVE COLOR

To recap, you know that color (hue) is basically light at a specific wavelength. White is the presence of all color. Black is the absence of all color. Arranging colors in a circle in the order they appear on the spectrum creates a color wheel. Mixing different colors on the wheel creates additional colors (hues). With us so far?

Additive and subtractive color models relate to the idea of color mixing. If you learned about the color wheel in grade school, you

Subtractive Color Model

Additive Color Model

likely were told that mixing complementary colors produces neutral gray. (Somehow Rebecca always managed to get some unappealing shade of greenish brown.) If you mixed all three of your primary colors, you got black.

The traditional painter-centric color wheel you learned in school is based on a "subtractive" color model. In the subtractive color model, all paint colors mixed together make black. Calling this subtractive seems counterintuitive until you remember that color is the eye perceiving reflected light. When you mix all the paint colors together, you block all light from reflecting off your design surface, whether that's a canvas or paper. So, you are subtracting *light*.

When you design for screens, you use an "additive" color model. Instead of mixing paints, you mix light. And as you already know, all the color wavelengths together make white (light).

You might notice something a little weird about the primary colors in the additive color diagram. In the additive model, the primaries are red, blue and *green*. As you can imagine, that changes the color wheel a smidge. Okay. A big smidge. But the color wheel still works the same way. You just adapt to the idea of different set of analogous colors, triads and complements. Who knew that in the screen universe the complement of red is turquoise and that red + green = yellow?

Additive and subtractive color models each have a place in contemporary design. The additive model translates into what designers call RGB color space for red, green and blue. The subtractive model more closely relates to the CMYK color space. Designers use CMYK space for print projects. Cyan (blue-ish), magenta (red-ish) and yellow correspond with the three primary colors. The "K" in CMYK stands for "key," which refers to black.

SCREEN COLOR: RGB COLOR SPACE

Designers who prepare layouts and graphics for viewing on monitors work in RGB space. To complicate things, there are different flavors of RGB each with a different gamut. A gamut is a subset, or range, of all possible colors. The human eye can see only a fraction of existing color. An even smaller subset of visible colors reproduces on screen or in print. We specify a color space in our design software to ensure we design with colors that can be reproduced in the final product.

Two of the most common gamuts in use today are sRGB and Adobe RGB. Most applications default to sRGB. Adobe RGB offers a slightly wider gamut, but is not as widely supported across capture and viewing devices.

Once you set the color space for a layout, new content you create in that layout adheres to that color space. Imported images and video inherit color space from the original capture device. If you work with broadcast-quality video, Rec. 709 is the standard camera encoding color space for HDTV, with a similar gamut to sRGB. More recently, the video community has started to move towards DCI P3 color. DCI P3, which stands for Digital Cinema Initiative, is a wide range gamut used in movie-quality film. But as the quality of all screen types improves, P3 color might be adopted more broadly.

Syncing color spaces is important, and we'll return to this shortly. But for now, we will simply refer to screen color space as RGB space.

THE RGB COLOR WHEEL

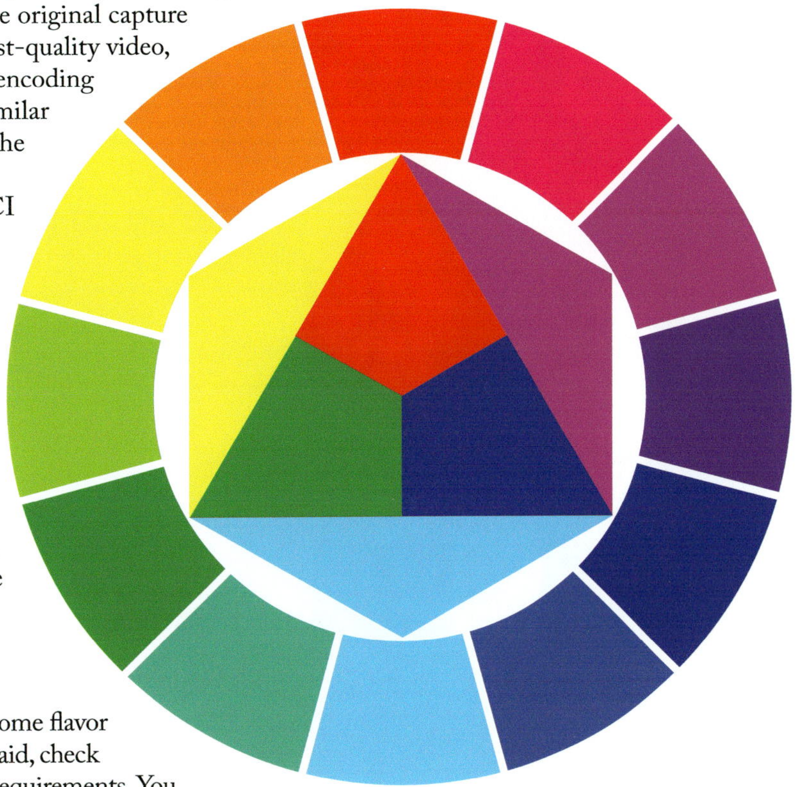

Working with RGB color

For most of us, most of the time, some flavor of RGB is your best choice. That said, check your project specs for color space requirements. You might have to convert imported images and video clips to your working color space to ensure color consistency throughout editing and output.

For headings, backgrounds or other design elements, specify those colors by a set of numbers, known as a "color build," unique to each color. The saturation, or "intensity," of red, green and blue light along with their various combinations determines the color build. It's a little like having a dimmer switch for each of the overlapping RGB colors. Simultaneously turning the three dimmer switches produces different colors.

For any onscreen color, the red, green and blue in RGB each has a numerical value between 0 and 255, whether a color is 0 (meaning off) or 255 (meaning fully on). Black, for example, would be 000 000 000 (or just 000), indicating that red, green and blue are all off. White, for example, would be 255 255 255, meaning red, green and blue are each at full intensity.

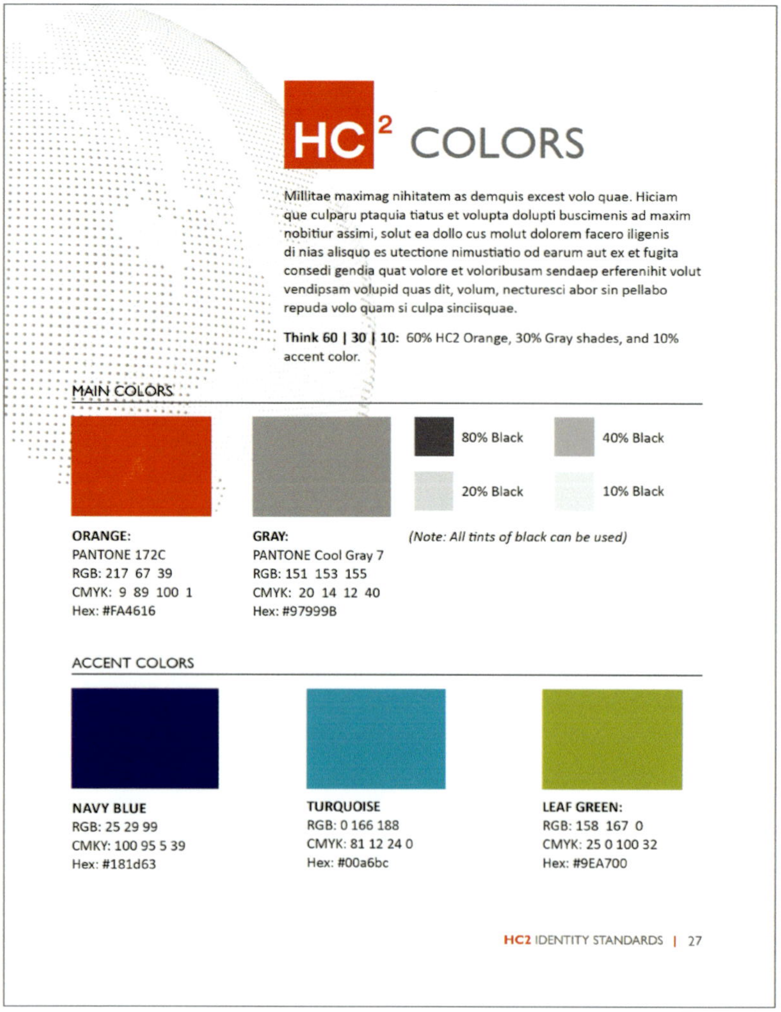

HC² COLORS

Millitae maximag nihitatem as demquis excest volo quae. Hiciam que culparu ptaquia tiatus et volupta dolupti buscimenis ad maxim nobitiur assimi, solut ea dollo cus molut dolorem facero iligenis di nias alisquo es utectione nimustiatio od earum aut ex et fugita consedi gendia quat volore et voloribusam sendaep erferenihit volut vendipsam volupid quas dit, volum, necturesci abor sin pellabo repuda volo quam si culpa sinciisquae.

Think 60 | 30 | 10: 60% HC2 Orange, 30% Gray shades, and 10% accent color.

MAIN COLORS

80% Black

40% Black

20% Black

10% Black

ORANGE:
PANTONE 172C
RGB: 217 67 39
CMYK: 9 89 100 1
Hex: #FA4616

GRAY:
PANTONE Cool Gray 7
RGB: 151 153 155
CMYK: 20 14 12 40
Hex: #97999B

(Note: All tints of black can be used)

ACCENT COLORS

NAVY BLUE
RGB: 25 29 99
CMKY: 100 95 5 39
Hex: #181d63

TURQUOISE
RGB: 0 166 188
CMYK: 81 12 24 0
Hex: #00a6bc

LEAF GREEN:
RGB: 158 167 0
CMYK: 25 0 100 32
Hex: #9EA700

HC2 IDENTITY STANDARDS | 27

The right color. Organizations use brand standards to ensure everyone preparing graphics uses the correct colors.

Hexadecimal code

Since specifying nine numbers for any and every color is unwieldy, a system called the hexadecimal code mathematically converts these nine numbers into as few as three or as many as six numbers and/or letters. Let's skip the math here. Just know that designers specify web colors by their corresponding combinations of numbers/letters in the hexadecimal system.

For example, HC² Human Capital's colors are orange and gray. But not just any orange and gray. The company specifies its hexadecimal web colors as #FA4616 green and #97999B gray.

RGBa

The next iteration of web color specification is RGBa. As you know, the RGB stands for red, green and blue. But what about the "a"?

The "a" stands for alpha channel, which controls transparency, or whether we can see *through* a screen color to view an image or text. RGBa lets web designers create transparency effects via code.

RGBa rules are expressed in Cascading Style Sheets (CSS) using the same numeric system as basic RGB. For example, rgba (255, 0, 0, 0.6) produces a saturated red with a 60 percent transparency (.6 = 60%).

Because RGBa is not fully supported across older browsers, designers who take advantage of it should provide a backup color build.

COLOR FOR PRINT: CMYK COLOR SPACE

Print designers work in CMYK color space. They prepare all graphics and layouts in CMYK mode to correspond with commercial printing technology. The most common technology printers use to apply inks to paper is called 4-color process (also referred to as full-color, built color or process color) because just four ink colors—cyan, magenta, yellow and black—are combined to build any color.

In 4-color printing, instead of mixing ink colors beforehand, printers use four separate plates to build colors on the paper. Commercial printers separate the colors designed on a document and put each color onto its own C, M, Y or K printing plate. The technique is called color separation. Printers apply the appropriate ink color to each of the four plates and apply each one to paper, one on top of the next.

Setting up a document for commercial printing

When you set up a document for CMYK printing, you must save your document and related graphics in CMYK mode. You also need to specify colors within your software program using CMYK builds. CMYK builds are a series of digit pairs that indicate the percentages of each C, M, Y and K that make up a color. Most graphic design software applications provide a space for you to specify a build or provide some sort of swatch palette that will generate the proper build for you.

Watch for "out of gamut" warnings when choosing color from swatch palettes. Your computer screen can display many more colors than printers are capable of recreating with ink. An out-of-gamut warning signals that you've chosen a color that won't reproduce accurately in print.

Four-color process printing is not your only option, however. Documents can be printed using only one, two or three inks. This process is called spot color printing.

Spot color printing

Instead of trying to build a particular color with CMYK, designers can choose premixed colors from a swatch book. Sometimes called matched color, spot color is like picking out paint colors from hardware store paint chips. Pantone created the PANTONE MATCHING SYSTEM®,

Cyan

Cyan + Magenta

Cyan + Magenta + Yellow

Cyan + Magenta + Yellow + Black

4-color process. In 4-color process printing, cyan, magenta, yellow and black inks are layered to create the final image.

sometimes referred to as PMS® Colors, the world's most commonly used color-matching system for solid colors.

When printing with spot colors, printers create a plate for each spot color the designer has specified. If the job uses two spot colors, only two plates are needed. Three colors require three plates.

Setting up a document to use spot colors. If you use one or more spot colors in your document, you must load those colors into your color palette from a preset library. These libraries generally come preinstalled with professional-grade design software applications. If you don't specify the spot color in your color palette, your printer will print your document as process color instead. This may result in a more expensive print job. It also might mean that you won't get the exact color you chose from the swatch book.

Achieving accurate color is always difficult, and the consistency of spot inks is one of the most compelling reasons to use them. Consistent color is essential when creating and communicating brand identity. Going back to HC2's orange and gray logo, HC2 would prefer always to print its logo using matched PANTONE® colors: PANTONE 172 orange and PANTONE Cool Gray 7.

Another option is to use the 4-color process version of your selected spot color. For each PANTONE solid color, there is a corresponding "color build." For example, use corresponding tint builds C=9, M=89, Y=100 K-1 for HC2 orange, and C=20, M=14, Y=12, K-40 for cool gray. Be aware, however, that CMYK builds don't precisely match their spot color counterparts. They come close, but no banana.

Choosing spot color. When print designers choose spot colors, they use a chip chart such as this Color Bridge® fan from Pantone. The PANTONE MATCHING SYSTEM® is the world's most commonly used color-matching system for solid colors.

THAT'S NOT THE COLOR I CHOSE. WHAT HAPPENED?

We've all experienced this: The layout, the typesetting and the color were brilliant. But something awful happened after pressing "print." The saturated orange turned nasty pink. The pure blue came out blue-green. Or perhaps the colors you carefully curated for a website—which looked great on your laptop—looked a little dingy when viewed on the client's desktop monitor.

Color matching from device to device is one of the most difficult challenges designers face. Unfortunately, there is no easy solution. However, best practices can help.

A phenomenon so common, it's an internet meme. 1) This highly-saturated yellow and green ginkgo leaf image looked great onscreen. **2)** But it turned blue-green when converted to CMYK for print. A photo-editing gamut preview grayed-out all the yellows, confirming those colors were out of gamut and would not print. **3)** Once converted to the narrower gamut for printing, the image lost much of its original luster.

Screen color vs. printed color

Discrepancies between screen color and print color are related to working color spaces. We design with light on screens (RGB mode), but output printed projects with paper and ink (CMYK mode). To make a long story short, your printouts don't match what you see onscreen because your screen is displaying French but your printer is only capable of printing in Portuguese.

When you design for print, make sure your document is set for CMYK to match the space of the output device, and convert any graphics to CMYK space as well.

With digital projects, set your layout color space to sRGB or to the specific space your project requires. Convert your graphics to the same color space before output to final format.

These actions will help, but not completely resolve, color inconsistency. Simply put, you can control your output, but you can't control the settings on viewing devices of your audience. People adjust their monitors to their own preferences. In addition, each monitor renders color a little differently. To see for yourself, the next time you visit a home electronics store take a look at the wall of television screens. The color variations astonish.

But before you totally give up on having any control over the appearance of color, there is one more thing to do. Calibration is the process of getting each of your devices speaking French. It is part of an overall process called color management.

Color management. Color management is the formal term for getting your color to match properly across devices, from scanners to digital

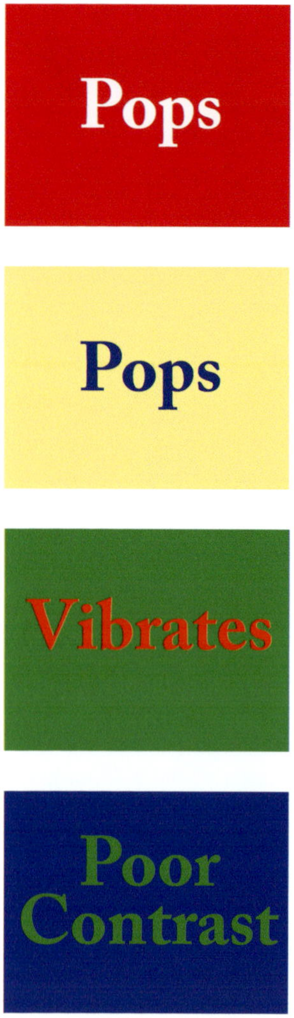

Visibility & readability. Pair colors with care, especially when placing colored text on colored backgrounds. Color pairings lacking contrast result in illegible copy.

cameras to computer screens to printers. Some aspects of this process can be handled by making adjustments at the device level, through software or through the system settings on your computer. Your computer screen, for example, can be calibrated to match the settings of any output device, including your personal printer or a commercial printer.

A more in-depth way to manage color involves applying color profiles to images and layouts. These profiles allow for more accurate—though not necessarily completely accurate—color translation from device to device. The International Color Consortium (ICC) created some of the most commonly used color profiles, but there are other color profiles out there, some industry-specific.

The ICC has profiles for almost any application, whether you're working in electronic-screen RGB space or printing-with-ink CMYK space.

That concludes the tech portion of this basic color lesson. We'll leave you with a few tips on using color in your layouts.

WORDS OF COLOR DESIGN WISDOM

» **Make your color palette work for your communication purpose.** Begin with a big reminder of the brand's visual identity, the design's communication objective and the message's target audience. Don't work at cross-purposes.

» **Design for visibility & readability.** While readability means readers can read it easily, visibility means viewers can see it clearly. Either way, you need contrast. The rule of thumb says stick with dark-on-light or light-on-dark color combos. In terms of readability and visibility, mostly think value. Light type on a dark background pops, although we've warned you about reversing. Dark type on a light background pops. But dark-on-dark and light-on-light both lack contrast, thus visibility and readability.

» **Avoid gray backgrounds for copy.** Generally, gray makes a lousy background color for copy, unless the gray is very dark or very light relative to the value of the type. Mid-tone grays don't provide enough contrast to support readable typographic information.

» **Most colors pair well with neutrals.** If color wheel pairings confuse you, consider pairing any color on the wheel with one of these neutrals: black, white, navy, gray, brown, beige or olive green. But beware, despite the terminology, some neutrals can have warm, cool or even slight color casts that can impact color harmony.

» **Beware of pairing fully saturated complements.** Pairing complements can make for loud color palettes. To compensate, pair complements at different levels of saturation, one pale, the other deep. And use them in disproportionate quantity. For example, if your layout uses a lot of blue, accent with a small amount of orange. Using split complements (pairing a color with the two colors next to its complement) is another good option.

» **Use splashes of color for visual emphasis.** Judicious splashes of color are like cosmetic makeup. Maybe a purple scarf (or a red ball cap) is all you need to perk up the look. A few well-chosen spots of color can highlight focal points as well as draw the eye around the layout.

Using less saturated tints of spot color to highlight larger areas of the composition is another way to design with color. For example, instead of using saturated orange as spot color, you might opt for diluting that orange down to a soft peach color and spreading it over a bigger area. You even can place sheer tints, of pale peach for example, over dark type without disrupting readability—if you're careful.

Like little stepping stones. The eye follows the red in this layout from the flag at the top, through the headline and down to the tags in the lower right.

TRY THIS

1. Collect printed pieces in which color is a crucial element of the design. You can collect ads or stories from magazines and newspapers. Collect rack brochures, direct mail pieces, take-out menus, candy wrappers, shopping bags, fast-food wrappers—anything printed.

   Write a short paragraph about each describing why the designer chose that color for that piece. Is the color about history? Emotion? Culture? Does the color wheel play a role in selection of the main or supporting colors?

2. Choose a brand and compare the reproduction of color in its visual branding across devices: smartphone, tablet, desktop/laptop, color printout from the web, commercially printed piece. Describe differences you see.
3. Find three pictures demonstrating different cultural meanings for the same color. For example, find three pictures each using the color red to communicate a different symbolic message.
4. Imagine you must brand a new restaurant. Name the restaurant. Then go outside to find a color palette inspired by nature. Take some photos of your color inspiration. Use your design software's color functions to match your nature-inspired palette.
5. You've been hired as the art director for a new musical play set in the 1990s. Suggest a historical color palette for the production's overall design, and justify your recommendation with some graphic evidence.

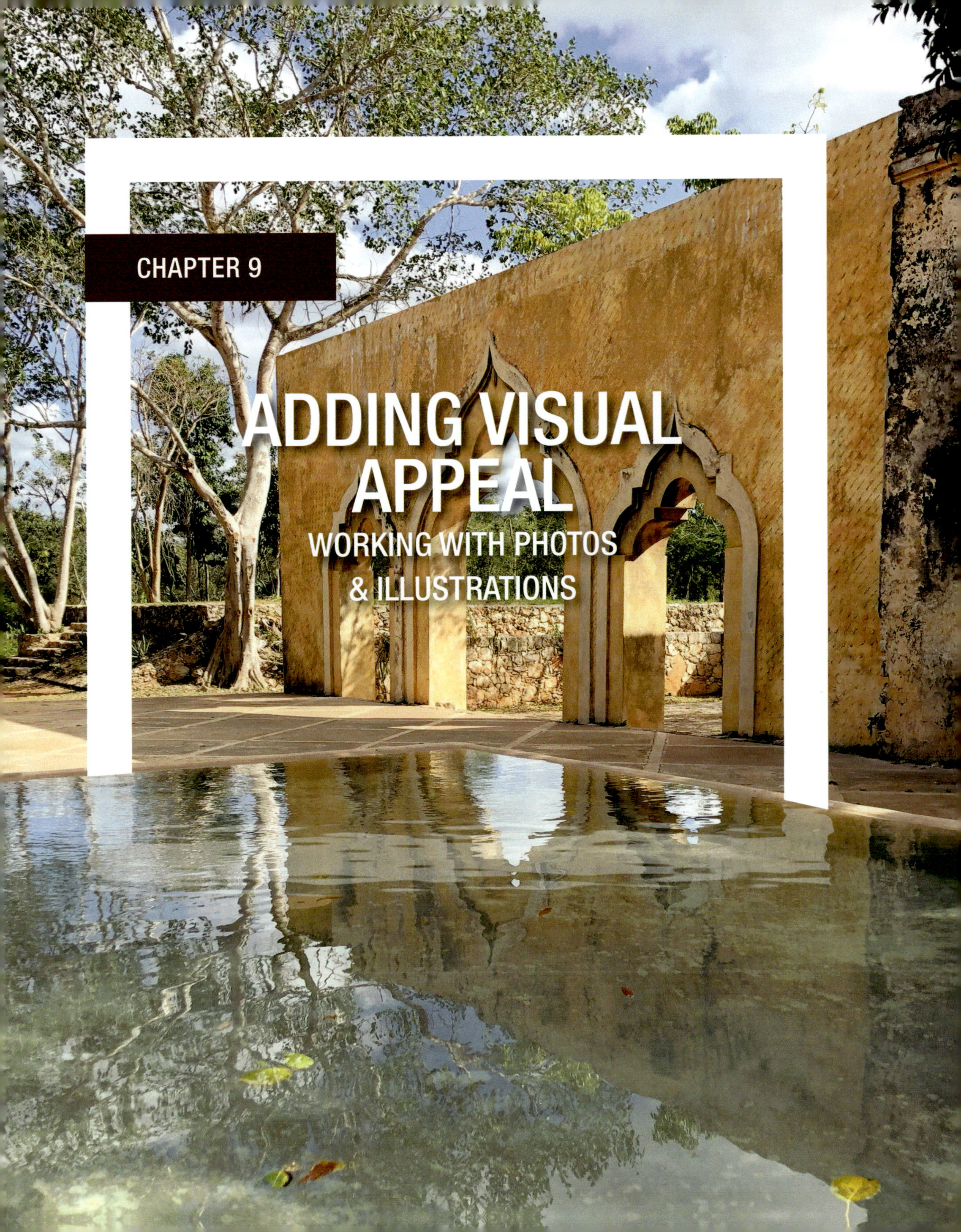

CHAPTER 9

ADDING VISUAL APPEAL

WORKING WITH PHOTOS & ILLUSTRATIONS

Tonal range. Choose photos that display a range of dark and light colors. Photos that lack tonal range may appear flat and lifeless.

While it's certainly possible to create readable print and online materials without the use of images, most of us prefer pictures to accompany our reading material. In fact, when it comes to communication, visuals are just as important as type.

Images—photos, illustrations, infographics—set tone, add interest, provide additional information and visually break up intimidating blocks of type. The right image can add color, texture, line and movement to your layouts. The use of images adds eye entry points and communicates visual hierarchy. Images help create rhythm to assist flow, thus providing your readers with much-needed direction, i.e., where do I start, where do I go next and where is the end?

When choosing the right images for your particular project, you'll need to consider a range of factors from image content to image quality.

IMAGE CONTENT

Of course you should choose your photos and illustrations to fit the overall tone of the piece you're producing. Tone, obviously, is determined by what you or the boss wants to project and, more importantly, what will resonate with your audience. You just don't put pictures of circus clowns on the front of an investment-banking brochure.

Say, for example, you really are choosing images for an investment-banking brochure. You might have a selection of appropriately serious-looking photos of people in suits shaking hands or conversing with other people in suits. How do you pick the best suits from the bunch?

Image quality

One of the first and easiest things you can do to whittle your photo selections is to throw out the technically defective images. This is the photo equivalent of weeding out résumés by tossing out those with typos. Scrap any photos that are out of focus, that lack good tonal range (value and grayscale) and that lack proper resolution (more about this shortly). Despite the availability of photo-correcting software, it's still best to start with a good-quality photo that needs little to no correction. Some things can be fixed. Others, like lack of focus and resolution, cannot.

Clear subject

Read any book on what makes a good photo, and you'll learn that simple subjects are best. In a simple photo, its subject is clear. Don't leave your reader wondering.

If you're shooting new photos, remove distracting objects from the composition's background. If moving items is not possible (or is inappropriate, as in news-gathering), reframe the shot so the distracting items aren't visible. Avoid photos in which background objects such as trees or lampposts appear to grow out of people's heads. In order to eliminate distraction, consider shallow depth of field, in which the subject remains in focus while the background goes out of focus.

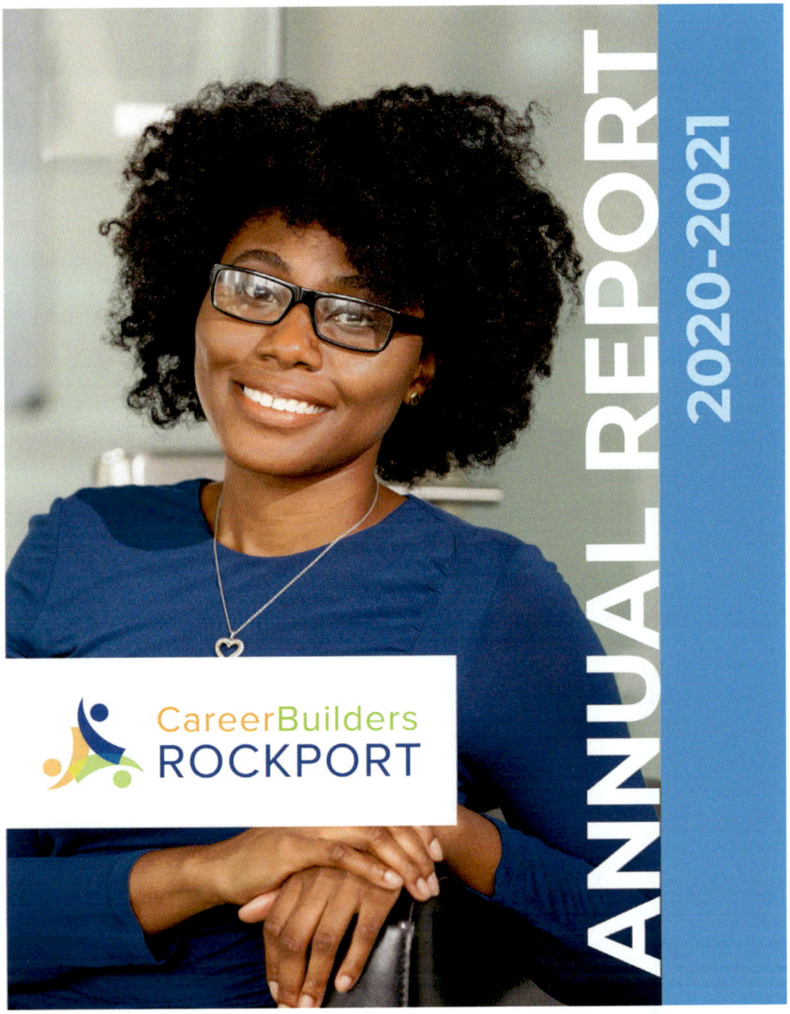

You can't go wrong with simple. Photos with clear, simple subjects are always good choices. Photos of people's faces are particularly engaging.

Photos of people doing things are more interesting than photos of people standing around. The "grip-and-grin" shot—a picture of one person giving an award of some sort to another—is about as dull as it gets. A much better approach would be to show the award winner engaged in the activity for which she won that award. Equally dull is the "police line-up" image, which consists of a group of people (board members, committee members, team members) all lined up against the wall. Again, it's much more powerful and interesting to show these people in action and in context. If you must photograph the group, at the very least vary the heights of your subjects. Some people seated plus some people standing makes better composition.

Bottom line? People *always* make good subjects for photos. Particularly engaging are photos of people looking right at the camera. While such photos may or may not be appropriate for

Choose images with good composition. Well composed images can serve as the backbone of strong layouts. Atmospheric lighting (above left) is eye-catching. Close cropping (above left) transforms ordinary subjects into abstract shapes and textures. Natural line (bottom) can direct the viewer's eye.

journalistic applications, they are powerful in advertising, marketing and public relations materials. Don't forget to consider the diversity of people you represent in your photos as well as the diversity of people in your audience. Ethically speaking, gone are the days when white men symbolically stood for everyone. Tactically speaking, you want your audience to identify with your photos.

A well-composed photo

Technical qualities aren't the only considerations for judging a "good" photo. A boring subject in perfect focus saved as a 300 dpi TIF image is still a lousy image. To qualify as a good photo—one that will be a compelling addition to your project—the photo also needs to be well composed.

Professional photographers know that the most interesting photos share some characteristics:

Asymmetrical balance and the rule of thirds. Centered photos are boring. Asymmetrical balance makes interesting shots, and using the rule of thirds is the quickest way to compose for asymmetry. Imagine the shot as a 3 × 3 grid, then position the focal point on one of the resulting four gridline intersections.

Tight cropping. Images that fill the frame communicate in no uncertain terms what the subject matter is about, and they also crowd out background distraction. Extreme tight crops and close-ups are particularly interesting, as they force us to look at the subject in a new way.

Natural lines to create movement. As in all visual communication, you want to control the eye's movement and flow through a photograph.

Interesting light. We've already touched on good tonal range. Playing with interesting highlights and shadows also results in compelling atmospheric images.

RESOLUTION, FILE FORMAT & SIZE

Even the most well-composed, compelling image is useless if it lacks the size, resolution and format appropriate to your chosen output. Images that are too small or lack resolution will appear pixelated and fuzzy in the final product.

Interesting asymmetry. The photographer perfectly positioned the photo's subject at the lower right rule of thirds intersection. This created an interesting asymmetrical background as well as nice negative space for titles, tags and copy.

File formats

Images can be saved in a number of different formats, each with different properties, suitable for different purposes.

Web and screen file formats. For web, the most common file formats are JPG (Joint Photographic Experts Group), PNG (Portable Network Graphic) or GIF (Graphics Interchange Format). JPGs are best for photos, PNG files are the choice for illustrations and logos, and GIFs work for simple animations and some small icons.

COMMON **FILE FORMATS** AND THEIR USES

	FORMATS FOR PRINT	FORMATS FOR SCREEN
Encapsulated PostScript (EPS)	File format of most vector graphic files rendered through mathematical calculation, not pixel-by-pixel. Can be resized without loss of resolution. Best for logos, word art. Required for "duotone" images where *only* two spot colors can be used	
Graphics Interchange Format (GIF)		Best format for web icons and animations. Supports transparency
Joint Photographic Experts Group (JPG)	Can be used for print pieces, but not recommended. Lossy format means poorer print resolution	Excellent for publishing photos on the web. Use a photo-editing program to optimize and save at 72 ppi. Should not be used for video
Tagged Image File (TIF)	Best format for saving photos for commercial print purposes	Good format for still images intended for video. Supports layers
Portable Network Graphics (PNG)		Best for web logos and illustrations. Also a good format for video stills and animations. Renders gradients well and supports a higher degree of transparency (drop shadows). Note, only PNG-24 offers full transparency support
Scalable Vector Graphics (SVG)		Vector graphics format for web. Excellent for basic shapes, charts and graphs. Works well in responsive websites
WebP		Provides superior compression for web graphics while maintaining image quality. A conversion tool is needed to turn JPG and PNG files into WebP files

It's important to note that PNG files and GIF files will both support transparency. JPGs do not. Transparency by definition means "see-through." In the case of web graphics, transparency is essentially the ability to make certain color groups "invisible." If you've ever tried to put a logo in JPG format on top of a colored background and discovered that your logo has a white box around it, you've encountered lack of transparency. By creating your web graphic in the correct software application and saving as a PNG or PNG-24 image, you can eliminate the white box.

WebP files are the new kid on the graphics format block. Google created the WebP format to minimize the size of web graphics without losing image quality. WebP files also support transparency. The drawback of this file format is that it requires a special tool or application to convert JPGs and PNGs to WebP.

Print file formats. JPGs are great for the web, but you should avoid them for print. The JPG is a "lossy" format, which means that each time you open or manipulate a JPG, it loses data. For print purposes, your best choice will be TIF (Tagged Image File). TIF images are larger in file size and do not lose data. So choose TIF for print purposes.

Yet another file type for printing, EPS (Encapsulated Postscript) is used for some specific kinds of images. Vector graphics, usually illustrations, are saved in EPS format. Photographs styled with limited color palettes, such as monotone and duotone, are also saved in this format. EPS format is typically used for logos and, like GIF and PNG, supports transparency.

Those pesky white boxes. Placing graphics on non-white backgrounds can result in ugly white boxes around your graphics. Prevent this problem in your layouts for screens by saving your graphics in the proper format. **(A)** JPGs do not support transparency and will always give you white boxes around logos and silhouetted (cut-out) images. **(B)** PNG files *do* support transparency, but PNGs are not all created equal. If your image has a drop-shadow, you must save in the higher resolution PNG-24 format **(D)** or you will find yourself right back in ugly white box mode **(C)**.

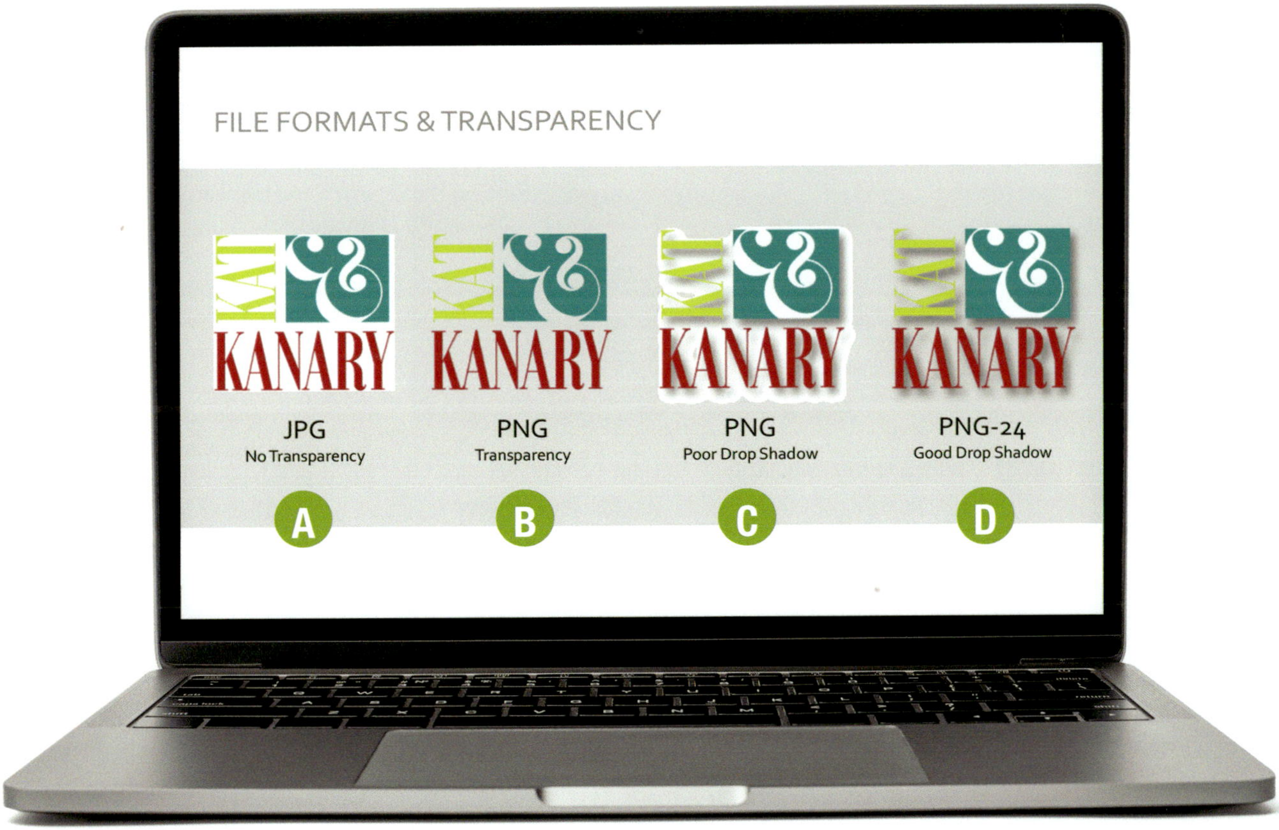

Size & resolution

One of the most confusing things to grasp when working with digital images is the relationship between image resolution—usually expressed in dots per inch (dpi) or more accurately pixels per inch (ppi)—file size and physical image size. Take, for example, two images:

One image is 300 dpi at 1 × 1 inch with a file size of 263K.

The other is 72 dpi at 4.16 × 4.16 inches with a file size of 263K.

Image 2: 300 dpi, 1 x 1 inch, **263K**

Which is high resolution? Despite the fact one image is 72 dpi and the other 300 dpi, the file sizes are the same, and both could be used as high-res images.

Making Image 1 high-resolution (300 dpi) without losing file size would result in an image with a physical size of 1 × 1 inch, the same as Image 2.

If your print project specs call for a 300 dpi image, which of these files is appropriate for use?

If you guessed that the 300 dpi image is the only print-appropriate image, you would be incorrect. Even though the resolution and dimensions are different, the file size (263K) is the same. Most crucial to determining image usability is the file size.

Using photo-editing software, you can take any image and change its size and resolution, including our "low-res" example listed here. But what you need to look at is what happens to the file size when you make the change. As a rule, you want the file size to stay the same or get smaller. If you make your changes and your file size gets bigger (sampling-up), your photo quality will drop (the image gets pixelated and fuzzy).

When you sample up, you are asking your software to add more pixels to the

HD monitors. High pixel density monitors make images look much sharper by squeezing in more pixels per inch than regular monitors. Images need twice the traditional resolution to look their best on HD monitors.

image, increasing both physical and file size. Software does a crummy job of this, and the result is a fuzzy image. Software does a better job of "down-sampling" (when your file size goes down). In this case, the software is choosing existing pixels to throw out, rather than having to create new ones.

In short, when evaluating an image, look at its dimensions, file size and original resolution. If both resolution and dimensions can be changed to what you need without an increase in the file size, you're golden.

Resolution for print & screen

As you've likely figured out, one resolution does not fit all. While your end product dictates file format, it also dictates optimal image resolution. For high-end printing such as magazines, brochures and annual reports, optimal image resolution usually comes close to 300 dpi, so most designers simply use 300 dpi for all images destined for print. Graphics for the newspaper are the exception. Newspapers require a 200 dpi because of the presses involved and the nature of newsprint. Additional dots per inch on an absorbent paper like newsprint produce muddy images.

For screen graphics, lower resolution is required. Traditionally, images for the web have been saved at a low resolution of 72 ppi. On standard flat screens, low-resolution images look great. Plus the smaller ppi images load more quickly, holding the attention of

STILL GRAPHICS FOR VIDEO

When putting together videos, you expect to work with video clips (crazy, we know). That said, there's plenty of room for still images in video production. Broadcast news employs still images and infographics in newscasts. Still graphics show up in title slides, lower thirds and program promos. And what documentary would be complete without panning and zooming in on vintage photos?

Between bars. Match the aspect ratio of your still images to your video format to avoid photos "between bars."

However, if you prepare images for video the same way you do for print or web, you'll be in for some surprises and disappointments. Computer monitors are significantly sharper and show more color than television screens. Plus, different video formats use different aspect ratios. The dimensions for a clip on a video-sharing site differ from those of an HDTV promo trailer, and none of those match the dimensions of a photo right out of the camera. If you've ever tried to drop a still photo into a video and gotten funky black boxes on the top or sides of your image, you understand the implications.

Output determines format. To prevent still images in video from becoming a distorted mess, first consider the end product, in this case, the final video. You need to determine the dimensions of the final video and make your graphic fill or fit within that space. Things would be much easier if there were a standard size for all video. But you know what they say about things being easy. To find the size you need, ask the professional producing the final video. We recommend such a consultation for most larger scale video projects. For smaller do-it-yourself videos destined for sharing sites, search online for the correct dimensions. Video parameters for common video-sharing sites are not difficult to find.

Proper set-up solves issues. Video pros who work with still images recommend that you create your new document first, then import or "place" your chosen assets (images, logos, etc.) into the document. This allows you to set appropriate film and video document parameters at the outset, such as file sizes and formats, pixel aspect ratios and color spaces. A big benefit of "create document first, place image second" is that professional-grade photo programs automatically adjust the visual appearance of imported photos to compensate for the difference between camera and video pixel aspect ratios.

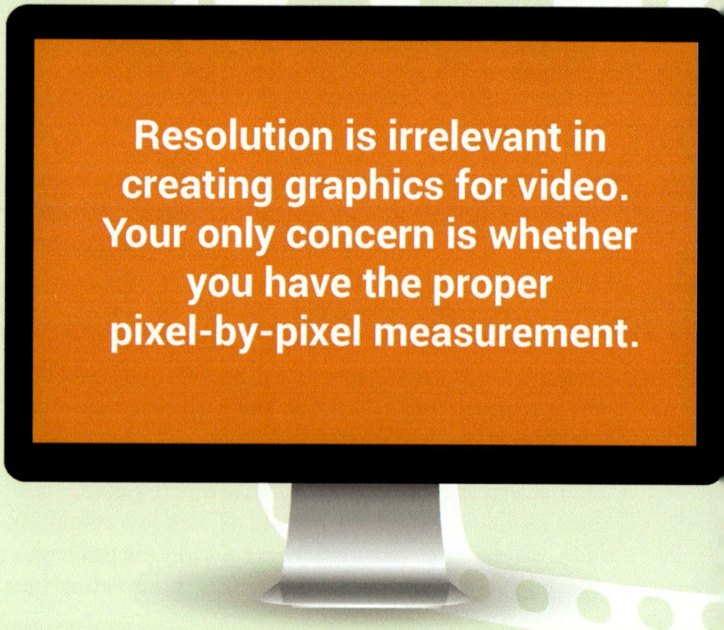

Computer square pixels (1:1)

HDV 1080i non-square pixels (1.33:1)

Go pro. Use professional-grade photo-editing programs to automatically adjust the visual appearance of imported photos. They automatically compensate for the difference between camera, computer and video pixel aspect ratios. Because no one likes stretched duck.

Another benefit is that grids and guides for live area and title safe area might be automatically generated. (For a review of grids and live area, revisit Chapter 6.) Such a feature saves you some math—and time.

What resolution? Surprisingly, the answer here is, "Who cares?" Resolution—the concept of pixels—or points-per-inch—is irrelevant in creating graphics for video. Your only concern is whether you have the proper pixel-by-pixel measurement. For example, if you'd like to create a full-screen still image for your video, and the video dimensions are 1280 pixels × 720 pixels, then your image needs to be at least 1280 pixels × 720 pixels. Getting your image to fit likely requires scaling (downsizing only, please) and/or cropping.

Keep in mind that if you want to use panning or zooming effects on your image (a.k.a., the "Ken Burns Effect"), you'll need an image larger than the screen size. Don't forget about aspect ratio, and make sure your larger image stays in proportion to the screen size.

What color space? Recall Chapter 8's discussion on color space? While it's not a perfect match for video color, set your document to use RGB color space. RGB gives you the greatest range of color (referred to as gamut) for your completed image. Some colors on the far edges of the RGB color space don't work well in video, particularly on television screens. If your software provides the option to set a color space based on final video format, take advantage of it. You'll get better color results in your end product.

What image format? Once you finalize your image or graphic, save it in a format compatible with importing into a video-editing program. The best formats for saving images for video aren't what you might expect. While JPG is great for web, its lossy format makes it a poor choice for video. PNG files, on the other hand, are acceptable for importing into video.

Although other formats work, a TIF image remains the best option. TIF images do not lose data, and they support layers if created in a graphics program that uses layers. Elements created on separate layers may be edited independently of each other. If you created a color block on one layer and a slide title on another layer, you have the option of animating them separately—making each fade in one at a time, for example—once imported into the video-editing program.

Adobe Photoshop® CC product screen shot(s) reprinted with permission from Adobe Systems Incorporated.

SMALL BUT MIGHTY!

Huge file sizes mean slow load times for websites. This is bad for both your visitors and your search engine optimization (SEO). To ensure your graphics don't load at the speed of smell, do a little groundwork. Start by resizing your graphics to the appropriate dimensions. Next, for bitmap (raster) images, change the resolution to 72 ppi. In addition:

Choose the right format for the job:

» Use JPG or WebP for general photos and screenshots

» Use GIF for small animations

» Use PNG if you need images with high detail and high resolutions

» Use vector images (SVG) whenever possible alongside your PNGs and JPGs

Use an application to further optimize your graphics. The optimizing process lets you find the sweet spot between image quality and lowest file size. This requires a bit of experimenting to find the best settings for each format. If your application and file format offer these options, you should:

» Reduce the bit-depth to a smaller color palette. GIF images, for example, can be reduced down from 256 colors

» Use lossy compression where possible

» Remove any unneeded image metadata

» Use an external compression program and CDN (Content Delivery Network) in conjunction with your webhosting

impatient readers and making search engines happy.

High pixel density monitors used in the latest mobile devices changed the web graphics game. High pixel density monitors squeeze in more pixels per inch than regular monitors, making images look much sharper. Images need twice the traditional resolution to look their best. For example, an image 150 × 200 pixels at 72 ppi would need to be 300 × 400 pixels at 72 ppi to look good on a high pixel density monitor. One way designers and developers address this issue is to create two versions of the same graphic, one twice the size of the other. The site is coded to detect the monitor type and call the appropriate version of the graphic to load.

When dealing with graphics at larger file sizes, use a graphics program to optimize images. Optimizing is the process of reducing file size by selectively removing data from an image while preserving visual quality. When optimizing, aim for a balance between best visual quality and smallest file size.

CHOOSING MORE THAN ONE PHOTO

In many instances, such as websites, brochures, feature news and magazine stories, you might find that you need more than one image. When choosing multiple images for your project, first eliminate any poor quality images from consideration. Next, look

at your potential images with an eye towards contrast. (Remember the element of contrast from mini art school?) While there are many types of contrast, in this case, the contrast you should look for is contrast in image content.

Think about pairing establishing shots, which are wider in scope and content, with detail shots, which are typically closer to the subject and more tightly cropped. For example, an image showing the width of the Grand Canyon is an establishing shot. A close-up image of a rabbit on the canyon rim is a detail shot.

Pairing establishing shots with a detail shots increases your storytelling power. The establishing shot sets the stage: time, location and action. The detail shot provides additional information, and by nature of close cropping, puts your reader "inside" the story.

If your project requires more than two images, the same process applies. You should weed out poor quality images first, then make your remaining selections based on content contrast.

Establishing and detail shots. When your layout calls for more than one image, consider pairing an establishing shot like the temple view at top with a detail shot like the image of the flower market. The contrast of subject makes for a more interesting layout.

A little cosmetic photo retouching is common. But retouching that results in false or misleading communication will get you in serious trouble. Rebecca is old, but not old enough to have played Chinese Checkers with her grandmother Joyce (standing in the back row), despite what the bottom photo shows.

ETHICS OF SHOOTING & EDITING

To be clear from the start, shooting images for documentary and news purposes is very different than shooting images for commercial or political purposes. Documentary or news photography, however artful or evocative, strictly adheres to the principles of truth, accuracy, fairness and balance. Such principles are necessary to maintain viewer trust that such images are factual and reality-based. Photos staged for advertising, publicity and marketing purposes, not so much. Differences between photojournalism and commercial photography persist after the images have been shot, too.

If you've played with photo-editing software, then you know there are all kinds of things you can do to alter photos—from turning them into watercolor paintings to removing an inch or two from your subject's buns and thighs. It is certainly true that most, if not all, images of professional models are digitally retouched. We are greeted daily by photographic images that have added effects for visual interest. However, let codes of professional conduct, if not your personal integrity, guide your decisions about the ethics of altering photographs. Fear of unemployment and lawsuits can be persuasive forms of conscience, too.

If the photo represents news, regardless of format or context, restrict photo-editing to only those techniques you could accomplish in a traditional darkroom. This limits your editing to cropping, overall value adjustments and dodging and burning (lightening or darkening specific areas in an image). For news photos, edits other than darkroom-based techniques run the risk of altering or negating the truth of the image. That rule applies to media relations folks on the public relations side of the news business, too.

Formal rules are looser in non-news contexts when the photo merely sets tone or delivers a message in advertising, public relations and marketing materials. However, be aware that truth reigns here, as well, according to the Federal Trade Commission and the Supreme Court. Professional ethics say you should avoid puffery, photos that seem to exaggerate commercial claims. But the law prohibits false, misleading and deceptive commercial claims, including those implied by photos. Proceed with caution in taking artistic license when altering photography.

DIVERSITY AS CRAFT EXCELLENCE

Diversity. We live in a wonderfully diverse world. Successful design reflects and respects this asset.

While we're talking about professional conduct and ethics, this is an appropriate time to remind you of your responsibility to rise above the lowest common denominator when it comes to doing the right thing. Journalism, advertising and public relations all define diversity as part of craft excellence. Just look at those professional codes of conduct again. First, you have an ethical responsibility to deploy images free of stereotypes, whether based on gender, race, ethnicity, sexuality, religion, nationality, age, disability, class or any other kind of physical, social or cultural difference. "Everyone else does it" is no excuse. You're better than that. But accidental harm is no excuse, either. Symbolic annihilation refers to images that injure via symbolic messages about individuals or groups of people. Second, sometimes the problem has less to do with what actually appears in your image and instead has more to do with what does not appear in your image. Ask yourself who or what is missing from the images in your design work. Learn to look critically at images with an eye toward mitigating prejudice

and ignorance. Plus, working against the grain by avoiding visual stereotypes can offer the added benefit of capturing people's attention, as well as surprising and delighting them, with something unexpected. Sad but true.

Stock image saves the day. Hmmm. Don't have a selection of seafood, coarse salt, silverplated cutlery and a beautiful slate display board on hand to photograph? Digital stock to the rescue!

WHERE TO GET PHOTOS

To lay photographers tempted to shoot their own photos, we say—as diplomatically as possible—don't. You might be a mobile camera magician, but that doesn't qualify you as a pro.

On the other hand, many graphic designers take up photography in the interest of being able to shoot exactly what is needed at a moment's notice. Journalists also have the know-how to handle both mobile and traditional cameras.

If you are still inclined to try your hand at photography, familiarize yourself with the appropriate file formats and resolutions needed for design work and learn how to set them on your camera. Also educate yourself on what makes a good photograph (re-reading this chapter is a good start).

Digital stock

If photography is not your thing, consider buying images from digital stock sites. There are scores out there, and their inventory is immense. Fees vary from free to upwards of thousands of dollars for high-res high-quality images with restrictions. You can purchase single images or subscriptions that allow multiple downloads over a given timeframe. In addition to photos, many stock sites also offer vector illustrations, video clips and stock animation.

Comp Images. One of the best features of digital stock sites is the availability of comp images, meaning complimentary images. Comp images are lower-resolution versions of stock images available for free. They give you the chance to test-drive one or more images in a design so you can decide what you like before you buy. Often, comp images are watermarked with the name of the stock site to prevent people from using the images without paying.

Royalty-free and rights-managed images. At the point you do have to cough up some cash, you usually have the option of purchasing images royalty-free or rights-managed. Royalty-free images are typically cheaper, but the drawback is that you don't get exclusive use of the image. You could choose a splendid image for your project only to discover another organization in town is using the same image for its project. We've seen it happen.

Comp images. The trade show image in this newsletter is a digital stock comp image. Comps are free, low-resolution watermarked sample images. Designers use them to test images in layouts before committing to purchasing a high-res, watermark-free version.

Using rights-managed images solves this issue. However, rights-managed images are more expensive than their royalty-free counterparts. You may find yourself paying once to use the image for one project then paying again later if you want to use the same image for another project. While you don't want to pay for rights-managed images you'll never use, good planning suggests thinking about how, for example, a photo you use for an expensive brochure might also create some continuity if you use it for your next website update as well as in this year's annual report.

No matter where you get stock, or what type of stock you get, be prepared to agree to various restrictions. Stock sites have restrictions on reselling images and may have limits on alterations, types of use and frequency of use. When purchasing and using stock images, do read the fine print.

Working with photographers

If you have sufficient budget and time, hiring a professional photographer to take custom photos is the best possible scenario.

Depending on the project, you'll want to find a photographer who has experience in the type of photography you need. Portrait, landscape, product, catalog and food photography each require a different eye and, often, different equipment. Freelance photojournalists and documentary photographers, bound by stricter ethical constraints than commerical photographers, also vary widely in skill sets. So find someone with the expertise you need.

You could check a local directory, but finding your photographer by word-of-mouth is safer. Ask colleagues and friends in the business for recommendations.

When you do find a photographer, be prepared to discuss a number of things up front. Specifically, everyone will need to be clear on the timetable and the actual deliverables. You may want a high-res copy of every image, but the photographer may want to give you only a set of retouched images. From the beginning, make sure everyone is on the same page.

If a commercial photo shoot involves people, make sure all the models (professional or otherwise) sign photo release forms. Whether news or commercial photography, in the case of minors, parents or guardians do have to sign consent for underage photo subjects. Photographers often have their own release forms. You'll want to have a form of your own for your specific project.

You'll have a better chance of getting the best photos if you arm the photographer with all the necessary project knowledge. Are you producing images for print or web? What is the overall feel you are shooting for? A good photographer will ask you many of the same questions you asked the boss at the start of the project. Be prepared to give concrete, detailed answers.

Show the photographer a rough or comp mock-up of the design. This visual will help the photographer plan and frame the shots, including, for example, such things as vertical versus horizontal formats or left- versus right-facing content.

Keep in mind that photographers are creatives, too. Give them as much information as you can then step back and let them work. But don't be shy about providing feedback when necessary.

WHERE NOT TO GET PHOTOS

Why go to a photographer or digital stock site when there are billions of images out there on countless web galleries? Two reasons. One, as we've already discussed, web images might not have enough resolution for your particular needs. Two, and more importantly, it's illegal.

Copyright law in the United States protects ownership of creative works (art, the written word, music, photography) from the moment of creation, with or without notice of copyright. Because something is posted to the internet doesn't mean it's free for the taking. To pull an image (or text, or anything) off someone's website and use it without permission is essentially stealing. Depending on the circumstances and severity, a person can be charged with a felony for engaging in this sort of practice. Transcendent of the fear of legal action, ripping off other people's creative work generates bad karma.

Unless the owner of an image explicitly states that the image is available to all for any use, do not assume you can use it without arranging for permission. If you find a must-have image on the web, track down the owner and get written permission to use the image before you proceed.

Stealing graphics off the web is illegal. There are two really good reasons not to steal graphics from the web: Optimized web graphics likely will lack the resolution you need, and it's illegal.

All photographers, whether amateur or professional, own the creative rights to their work. Get photographs through proper channels and provide credit where credit is due.

ALTERNATIVES TO PHOTOS

Maybe you're on a tight timetable, maybe you have a really low budget or maybe it's the particular concept, but sometimes a photo just isn't the right thing.

As we've already noted, you still need something to break up lots of text. The good news is that illustrations, clip art and text-based elements such as pull quotes are solid alternatives to photos.

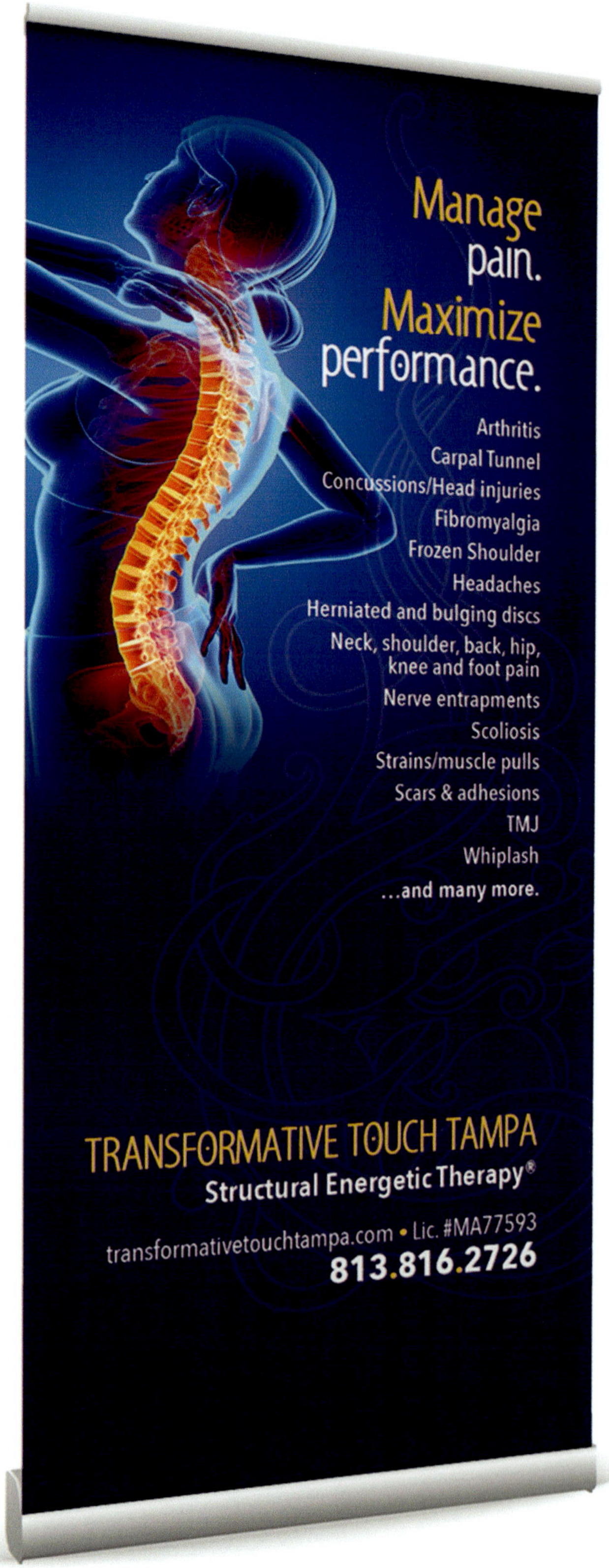

Illustrations

Under no circumstances should you think of illustrations as second-rate substitutes for photos. On the contrary, illustrations are often the best choice, if not the only choice, for a design project.

Illustration gives form to the imaginary. Say, for example, you are writing a story about fire-breathing dragons. Let's say you want to find a photo to accompany your story. Good luck with that. For hundreds of years, illustrators have been giving visual form to people, places and things found only in the imagination. Fiction (for both adults and children) is full of wonderful illustrations that bring everything from fairies to flying monkeys to life.

Illustration isn't just for the fantastic. Architects, landscape designers and interior designers sell concepts to clients through the use of renderings. An essential part of designer–client communication, a rendering allows the designer to show the client their interpretation of the project and provides a basis for any feedback prior to the start of a project. It's far easier to provide an illustration of what the fountain, walkways and shrubbery will look like than it is to explain it verbally.

Illustration for sensitive subject matter. Sometimes illustrations may be more appropriate than photos if the subject matter is too sensitive for realism—death, assault or rape, for example. Caricatures can be used to illustrate stories about public figures such as celebrities or politicians, especially when the story is commentary, satire or feature news. Political

Illustration gives form to the imagination. From the human spine curving along the copy to the dragon-shaped watermark, this layout employs illustration to show viewers what no photo could.

Banner image used by permission of Transformative Touch Tampa.

cartoons are another example of this type of illustration.

Illustration to show change over time. While photos capture a single moment in time, illustration has the power to show change over time. Attorneys use illustration for this purpose. Consider a court case involving a traffic accident. Evidence might include still photos taken before, during or after the accident, but the still photos can't convey a sense of motion or timing. For this, attorneys hire illustrators to create illustrations showing a simplified layout of the street and position of the vehicles involved. Arrows, time stamps and other devices are used to add the information still photos can't provide.

Photo effects. Photo-editing software can turn ordinary photos into interesting images. The miniaturized look on this book cover was created using a filter that mimics the look of tilt-shift photography.

Illustration to evoke history. Before photography, illustration was the method of choice to record both day-to-day life and special events. Egyptian hieroglyphics, the Bayeux Tapestry, Native American petroglyphs and 1970s-era graffiti each has a distinct illustrative style and color palette. By echoing historic illustration styles in contemporary design work, it is possible to evoke a specific sense of time and place.

Using photo-editing tools, you can turn a simple photograph into an illustration. If your skill isn't up to the illustration task, hire a professional illustrator or search digital stock sites for art you can purchase.

Video & multimedia components

The popularity of video-sharing sites on the web leaves no doubt that the democratization of design has hit video production as well. Websites are just as likely to include video clips and animation as they are photos and illustrations. Video and animation make excellent focal points because they include the eye-catching element of motion.

Some extra planning is required if you want motion elements to carry the same compositional punch as still images in your project. If your clip is a slideshow, each image in the sequence should coordinate with the overall layout in terms of color, shape or content.

Traditional video clips also must work with your layout. You should choose a title slide that provides a good tease for the video content and coordinates with your other layout elements. Quality, style and speed of video and animation transitions also impact your layout. Video that is choppy and animation transitions that are too fast or slow can be distracting. Like a poor quality photograph, poor quality video and animation bring down the quality of the whole project.

Type as image. Letterforms are so interesting they can take the place of images in layouts.

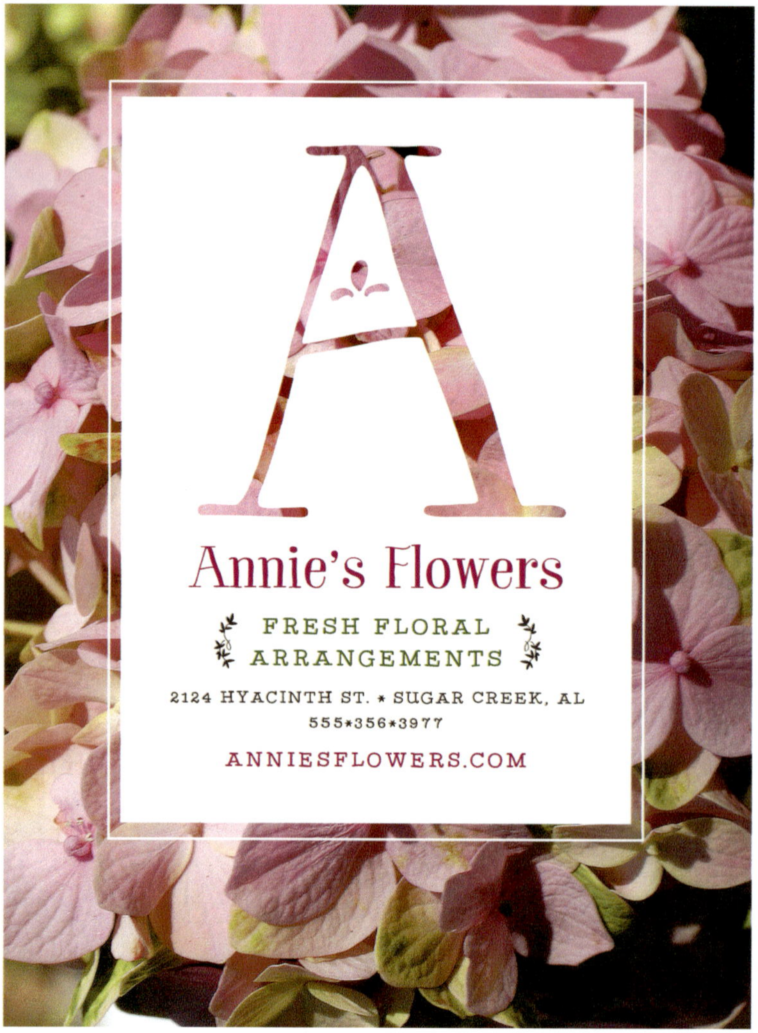

Type as image

Maybe, for whatever reason, you have been reduced to choosing between a poor photo and a cheesy piece of clip art for your project. Trust your judgment and skip both. Instead plan for creative type to do the job of adding visual interest to your long copy.

Letterforms are interesting. For most of us, the last time we really looked at individual letters was in kindergarten. When we learned to read, we were taught to recognize each letterform in upper- and lowercase and to associate each letterform with a particular sound. Once we trained our brains to equate the shape with the sound, and letter pairings with the sound and meaning of words, conscious thought regarding the shapes of letters fell off our radar screens.

In the name of good design, we'd like you to rewind and

reconsider letterforms. As design elements, letterforms are fantastic. Set alone, or as individual words, letterforms can have the same compositional impact as photos. Letterforms have curves. They have negative space. They have line. And of course, they can have color. Set large and in color, the right letterforms can turn a basic headline into the focal point for any layout. Individual decorative characters can be used as watermarks. Repeated decorative characters add background texture.

Highlighting a QUIRKY QUOTE IS A GOOD WAY TO entice readers to READ ALL YOUR copy.

We discussed some of the more traditional uses of type in Chapter 7 on typesetting. But there are a couple of type treatments more closely related to image and illustration that we'll discuss here: pull quotes and rendered type.

Pull quotes. A pull quote (also called a lift-out or callout) does exactly what its name implies—it pulls a quote from the copy for the purpose of highlighting it. Choosing a particularly interesting, compelling or quirky quote is a good way to entice readers to read all your copy.

You often box a pull quote. Because a quote is relatively short, you significantly increase the font size so that it will pop off the page to read as a graphic element or visual. If you're feeling really wild and crazy, you might replace your standard quotation marks with decorative ones. If the source of the quotation is as eye-catching as the quotation, provide an attribution line.

Some design tips for creating pull quotes include:

- Don't forget to include margins outside and inside the box. Don't cheat your margins!
- When adding color to pull quotes, there are options. The whole quote can be in color, or you might put your color in the box's background (the fill) or the box's outline or border (stroke). If you choose a background color, make sure the text is set in a color that contrasts with the background color.
- Use a hanging indent to pull the first quotation mark outside the margin bounding the text box. Set your second and subsequent lines to align with the first letter after the first quotation mark.

Rendered type. Rendered type is a character, word or string of words that has been filled with an image, or otherwise transformed using photo-editing software. Rendered type is commonly seen in magazines, newspaper features, posters, websites, video, television and movie title sequences. The technique allows you to create type that

looks like it was made out of polished brass, stamped in rusty metal or even chiseled out of stone.

Rendered type. For some really interesting effects, try filling your letterforms with an image. Or use image-editing software to make your type look like polished chrome, needlework or skywriting.

To summarize what you've learned about adding visual appeal with photos and illustrations, be selective in terms of quality. Choose the appropriate resolution, file format and size, too. If photos aren't an option, don't discount using illustrations, clip art, video and decorative type for visual impact. Remember the lessons of mini art school when you compose and place any kind of visuals. If you hire outside help, treat photographers and illustrators with the professional respect they deserve. And when it comes to altering photos or paying for your visuals, do the right thing to ensure a clean conscience.

Maybe, however, your design is begging for something more. Maybe you need something with the jaw-dropping appeal of a visual and the head-reeling power of information. For that kind of one-two punch, you're talking infographics, which we cover in the next chapter.

TRY THIS

1. Find an example of a printed piece with a photo that does not work (poor quality, inappropriate subject, whatever). Visit a digital stock site and find a suitable replacement image. Redesign the piece using your new image. Explain why the photo you chose is a better solution to the design problem.

2. Brainstorm photo options for the following situations. Create a set of thumbnail sketches for each scenario. Use two or more images in each sketch.

    a. A feature story on a famous artist for the leisure section of a broadsheet newspaper. The artist is opening a show at a local venue in the coming week.

b. A trifold brochure for a small independent bookstore. This piece needs to have some "shelf-life." In other words, the brochure content cannot be time-sensitive.

c. A website homepage for the bookstore in letter b.

d. A 24 × 36-inch poster for an upcoming Latin Jazz Festival.

3. Collect several advertisements relating to the following topics:

a. Luxury goods (watches, perfume, jewelry, expensive cars)

b. Baby products

c. Clothing for teens and tweens

d. Sporting goods/athletics

Compare and contrast the photo treatments. Consider compositional techniques, color use and alterations applied using photo-

Pulling out all the stops. By combining interesting images, illustration, decorative type and rendered type, you can create rich textural compositions.

editing software. Choose one of the topics and create two ads of your own: one in a style consistent with convention and one using an entirely different style. Use digital stock imagery and the photo-editing software of your choice for this assignment.

4. Visit the websites of two mainstream magazines: one publication for general audiences and one targeted to a particular group (The Advocate, Bust, Latina Magazine, Essence, etc.). Compare and contrast the use of imagery throughout both magazines. What are the similarities, differences? Take the ad you designed in exercise 3, or an ad from another exercise, and redesign it to better reflect diverse audiences.

5. Design a website landing page for a travel desination you would like to visit. Do a little research and write some copy that sells your chosen location as the perfect getaway spot (or camping location, hiking destination, foodie paradise, etc.).

   Search free digital stock sites for images. How many images will you need? Which ones will you choose? Justify your selections, and create your layout using your selected images along with your text.

Cut it out! Please pay as you go, whether you rely on stock illustrations and photos or you hire a professional for custom work.

Postcards reproduced by permission of USF Department of Women's, Gender and Sexuality Studies.

CHAPTER 10

INFOGRAPHICS

MAXIMUM INFORMATION IN MIMIMUM SPACE

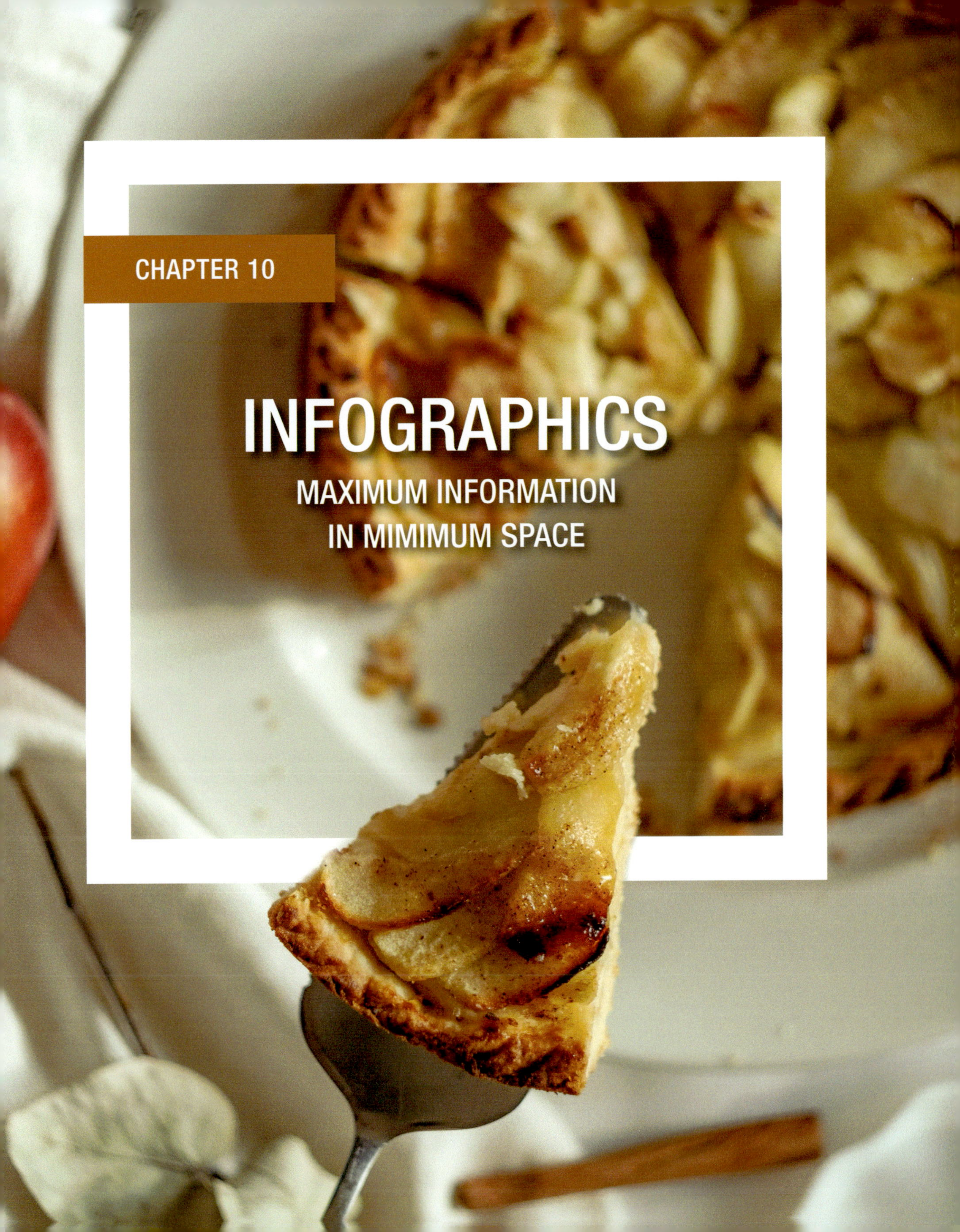

Here in the 21st century, people want quick, handy chunks of visual communication via smart phones and tablets as well as traditional electronic screens and printed material. We scan for pictures and headlines that pique our interest. We may or may not read further. There may or may not be anything further to read. We may be moving so fast that we need to absorb it at a glance or miss it altogether.

Enter infographics, as in graphically delivered information. From news organizations to NGOs, virtually everyone is using infographics to tell deeper, broader, evolving stories faster than text or raw data alone.

THE ART OF CUTTING TO THE CHASE

Sometimes an infographic tells the story faster and better than words. Consider this example:

A recent poll showed that 20 percent of the residents in Precinct A voted for candidate Smith, 10 percent voted for candidate Jones, 65 percent voted for candidate Doe, and 5 percent voted for write-in candidate Anderson.

Or we could go this route:

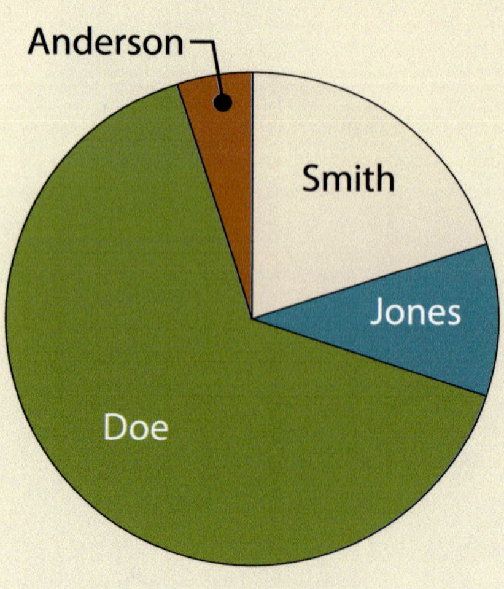

Before sharing best practices for the use and design of such things as maps, bar charts, fever graphs and timelines, we'd like to talk a little about the evolution of infographics.

A TERSE HISTORY OF INFOGRAPHICS

USA Today usually gets credit for popularizing modern infographics. And colorful charts and graphs remain hallmarks of USA Today's design for busy readers. But people were using graphics to deliver information well before the 1982 origins of USA Today.

The earliest humans on the planet shared information in pictures carved and painted on rocks and caves, not to mention tattooed on bodies. All over the globe, ancient peoples documented themselves and the world around them in pictographs from Japanese Kanji derived from Chinese ideographs to Egyptian hieroglyphics.

At the 1900 Paris Exposition, W.E.B. Dubois, civil rights activist and a founder of U.S. sociology, curated 60 hand-drawn hand-colored infographics as part of "The Exhibit for American Negroes." The visualized statistics narrated the status of formerly enslaved Africans and their descendants in the U.S., from population distribution maps to bar charts of land ownership. Influenced by the au courant art nouveau style, the series historicizes anti-racism, as well as today's on-trend infographic usage.

More recently, NASA's Pioneer 10 and 11 interstellar

space probes, launched in 1972 and 1973, carry information-rich diagrams. Just in case we're not alone. No joke.

In modern history, infographics evolved to include sound and motion while working in the TV business. With the great web migration, infographics reinvented themselves as interactive. Infographics went 3D in step with the proliferation of video games. Color graphics, sound effects, animation, 3D perspective and interactivity all working together exponentially increased the communications capability of infographics. When social media platforms arguably became the ultimate source of quickly scannable information, infographics use exploded. Everyone wanted—needed—a chart to prove their point.

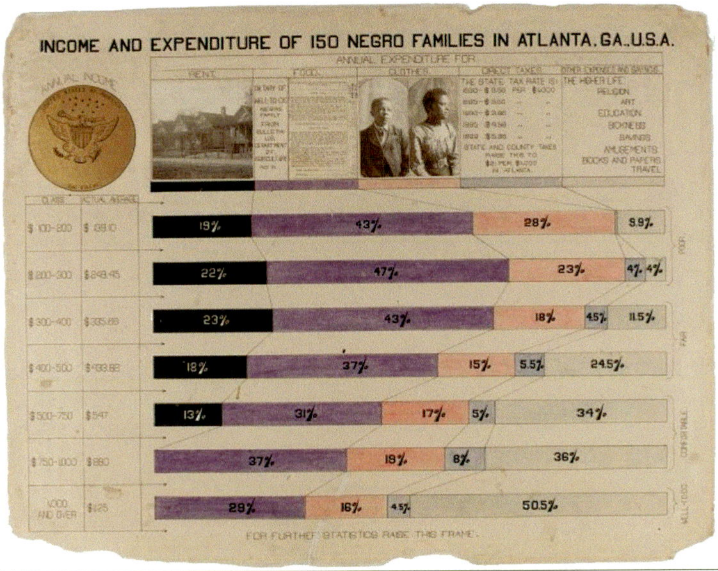

WHAT EXACTLY IS AN INFOGRAPHIC?

The popularity of infographic use resulted in the rise of services offering "do-it-yourself infographics" templates. Naturally, a matching set of articles about what infographics are and how they are used grew in tandem. Do an online search for "what is an infographic," and you'll find scattershot definitions and muddy terminology.

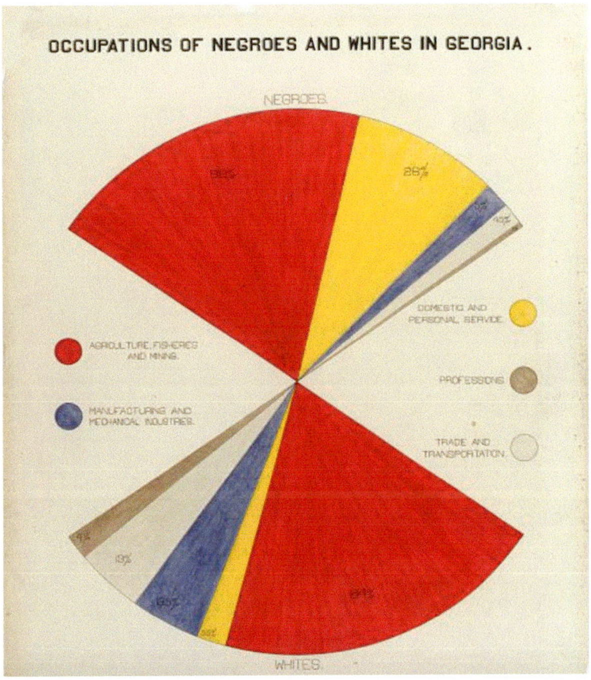

A history lesson. For the 1900 Paris Exposition, W.E.B. DuBois curated an exhibit to graphically represent the African American experience using data visualizations. Produced by hand, the images are as much art as social science.

U.S. Library of Congress, loc.gov

People today call any layout with illustrations, colorful boxed content, icons, large stand-alone numbers and possibly a chart an infographic. Trained graphic designers understand the difference between true infographics and text styled as infographics. But non-professional infographics users need

IS IT AN *Infographic*

e whole layout **IS NOT** an 'ographic. It is a *layout* (poster, er, handout, social media aphic) that includes infographics it.

e stand-alone figure **IS NOT** an 'ographic. It's just a really big ımber with its own cutline. It's ɔre akin to a pull quote than an 'ographic.

e horizontal bar graph **IS** an 'ographic. It is a *chart* based on ɔtted numerical data and shows lative percentages of people lled.

e fact box **IS NOT** infographic. ‹e the stand-alone figure, it's ɔre pull quote than infographic.

hile it might look like a simple dinal list, this ranking **IS an** fographic. The items are listed order of popularity. The listing der shows relationship.

education, starting with a better set of definitions. In deference to those professionals who are far more versed in the history, use, and types of infographics, we propose the following:

Infographic. A visual representation of information or numerical data that demonstrates a relationship among the individual parts. Infographics come in many forms: charts, maps, sequences, diagrams and others. The distinction lies in the presentation of *relationships.*

Data visualization. Mapping numerical data in graphical form. Charts such as bar, fever, scatter and pie are data visualizations. Location maps based on points of latitude and longitude are also data visualizations. All data visualizations are infographics. But not all infographics are data visualizations.

Infographics layout. A single layout such as a poster, social media post, website or flyer that includes one or more infographics.

Digital storytelling and multimedia journalism. An in-depth study of a topic presented through multiple media types including infographics, narrative (story), video, animation and still image. These are most commonly used in journalism (multimedia journalism), but can be found in magazines and websites.

Infographic-style layout. A layout that mimics the design of an infographic layout through use of icons, large stand-alone figures, colorful boxed content and other visuals but does not include a true infographic based on presentation of relationship or numerical data.

YOU MIGHT NEED AN INFOGRAPHIC IF...

Infographics are an excellent tool for your designer's toolbox, but they aren't perfect for every situation. They are best used when:

» You need to communicate quickly.

» A verbal or written account is too complicated—or tedious—for comprehension.

» Your audience can't hear or read well—or at all.

I WANT AN INFOGRAPHIC FOR MY LAYOUT. WHERE DO I GET ONE?

Despite their complicated appearance, many types of charts and graphs are easily generated using common word processing, spreadsheet or presentation deck applications. For more advanced needs, or instances when you need more control over your colors or formats, programs designed specifically for creating charts and graphs are available. There

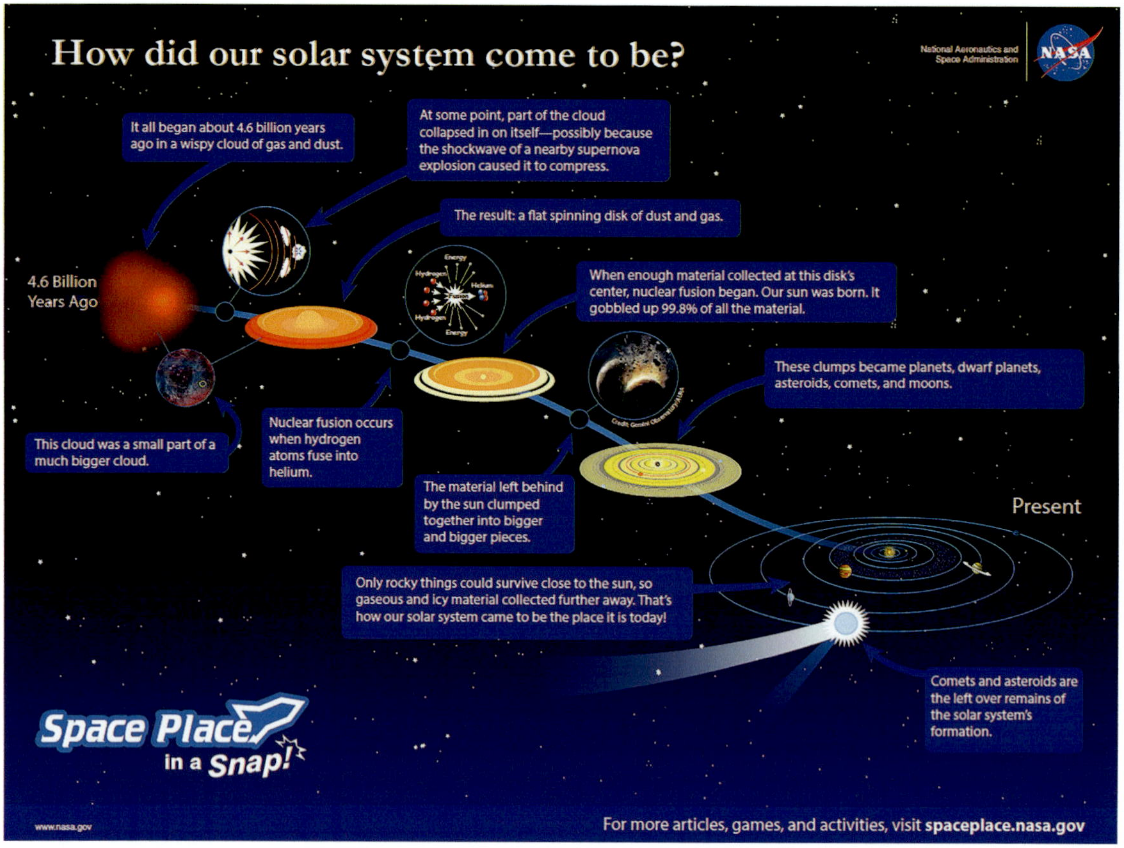

No spontaneous generation here. Infographics are commonly generated by plugging numerical data into software. But they also can be custom-rendered using graphic design applications. This might be your only option if you need a highly specialized infographic like a diagram.

U.S National Aeronautics and Space Administration, spaceplace.nasa.gov

are also online services for creating infographics. Some are free, and others are subscription-based.

Infographics also can be drawn from scratch using graphic design software. This might be your only option if you need a highly specialized infographic like a diagram.

If your layout is web-based, then plug-ins, widgets and shared code snippets can populate your site with some types of charts and graphs. Embedding maps is perhaps the most common example of this practice.

Dynamically generated infographics

To take the concept of the embedded web infographic further, some graphics automatically update themselves as new data are collected and added to the source. Your website can display the results of an informal poll even as the numbers are still being collected, for example. Other websites with content to share might offer code snippets, plug-ins or widgets. You might add code to your site to

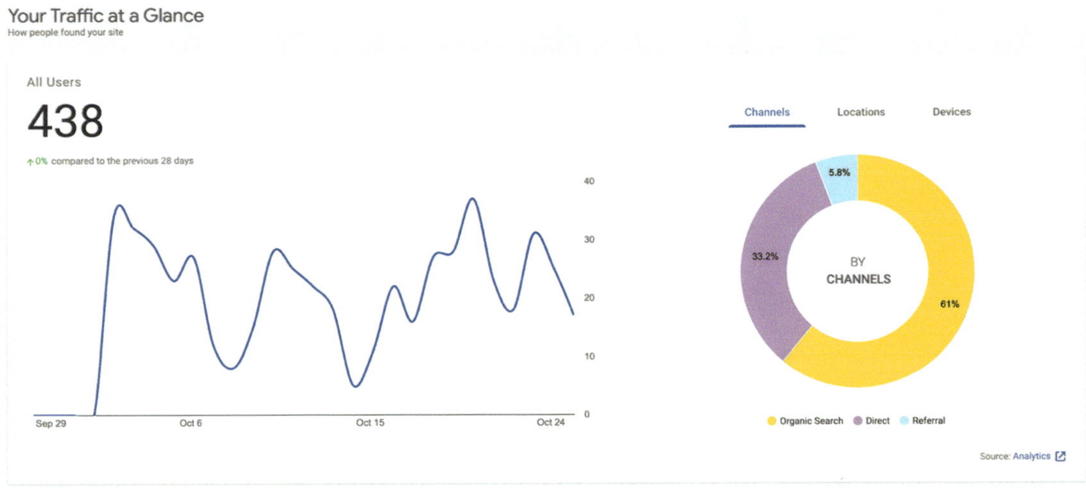

display the week's highest-grossing movies or perhaps updated weather information.

Some infographic needs can't be met with preexisting shared code. In these cases, web developers can code solutions for mining, assembling and displaying the desired data. A wealth of existing data on the Internet can be tapped to create all types of infographics. Or a developer can help you collect entirely new data. What if, for example, the local college web team developed and posted an interactive campus map accessible via a website or mobile device? Imagine the instant ability to report, avoid and dispatch repairs to dangerous walkways, burned-out light bulbs and buildings in/accessible to wheelchairs.

_Semi_spontaneous generation here. These site visitation charts are automatically generated in the dashboard of a website. An installed plug-in allows Google to track site visits and present the data in an easily understandable infographic.

Google and Google Analytics™ service are trademarks of Google LLC, and this book is not endorsed by or affiliated with Google in any way.

DESIGNING YOUR OWN INFOGRAPHICS

Everything we've covered in previous chapters will serve you well in designing and evaluating infographics, starting with research, brainstorming and thumbnail sketches. You'll also use what you know about grids and layouts, along with the elements and principles of design, including Gestalt. Your knowledge of color, typography, photos and illustrations applies here, too.

A word to the wise as you incorporate infographics into your layouts: Test before you launch. Never just assume folks understand your infographic. Allow us to share a cautionary tale. In 2004, Hurricane Charley devastated a completely unprepared Port Charlotte, Fla. In a research project shortly thereafter, a University of South Florida graduate student discovered two facts: One, people living in Port Charlotte misinterpreted the hurricane maps that weather forecasters

PARTS OF AN *Infographic*

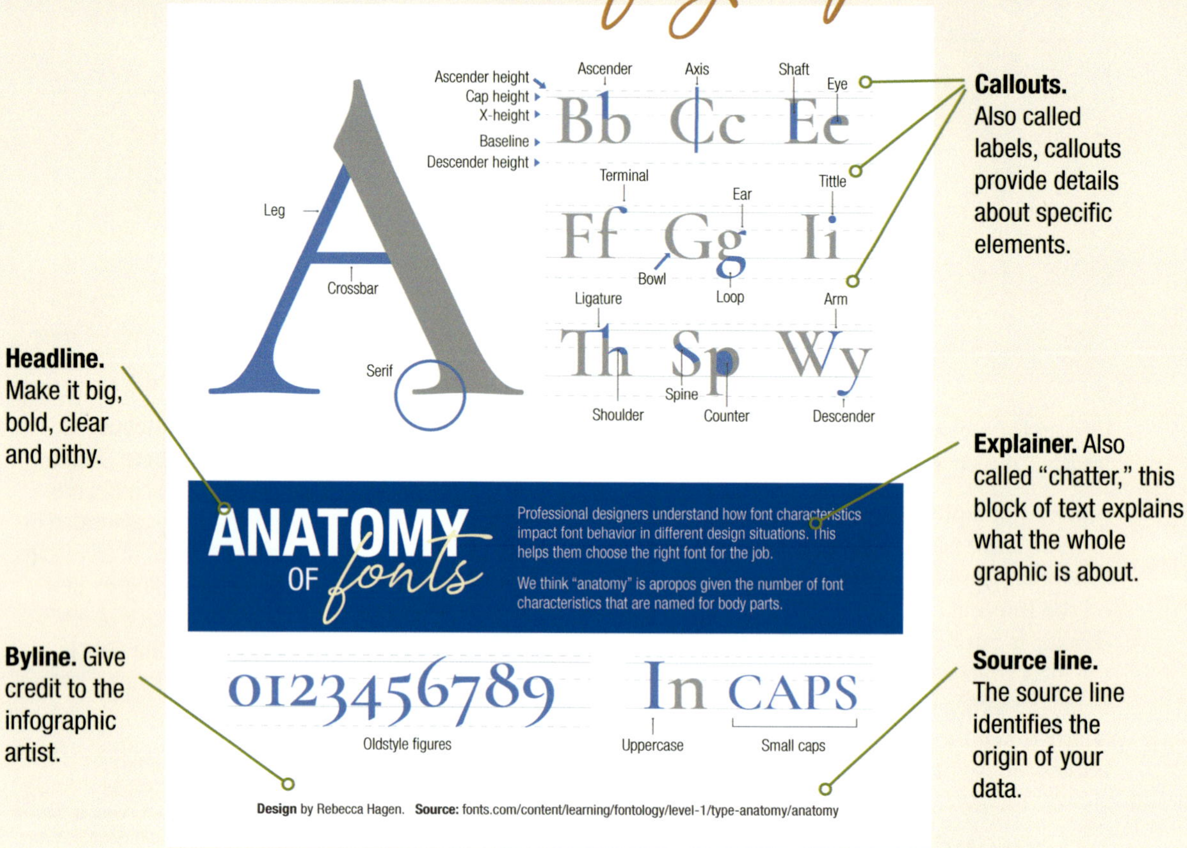

use to predict the uncertain paths of storms. Study participants did not understand what the maps were supposed to communicate. Two, those widely used hurricane maps had never been audience-tested for comprehension, although scientists intended the maps to save lives. Sobering.

While accounting for audiences and employing the basics of good design, start by choosing the right infographic for your communication purpose and available data. Sometimes your topic offers clues to suggest a certain kind of infographic is suitable. For example, dates imply a timeline. References to geographic areas such as neighborhoods, floor plans or precincts hint at maps.

A number of best practices apply to specific types of infographics. Some best practices are universal. We cover both here, starting with general tips and ending with more specific advice.

Design tips for all types of infographics

Infographics must be able to stand alone. This is perhaps the most important thing to remember when designing any type of infographic. If people are scanners searching for interesting things to look at, then the infographic might be the only thing the viewer sees. Infographics shouldn't rely on information buried somewhere else.

Thoroughly research your topic before you begin. It does make sense to understand the material you're attempting to illustrate. You won't be able to facilitate others' understanding if you don't get it, either.

Use a grid to organize and structure your infographic. Think of your infographic as a design within a design. The same rules for good layouts work for specific graphics and infographics, too. As in larger layouts, a grid provides order and organization for the various parts

Break it down, visually. The inside spread of this quad-fold brochure presents a 10-step process for going solar in a visually interesting way.

Design by Rebecca Hagen. Reproduced by permission of SECO Energy.

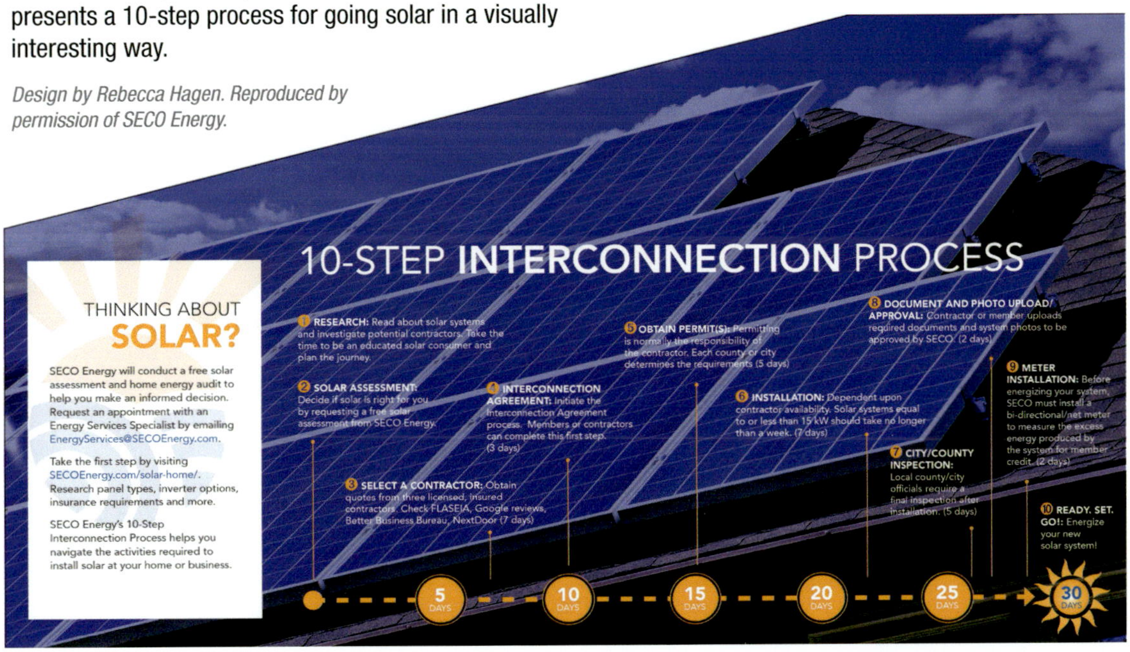

of your layout, such as explainers and callouts. Aligning elements to a grid provides cohesion and unity, and it will help your reader understand the flow of the graphic.

Group things. As you create your graphic elements, be sure to cluster related items, and leave ample negative space between items to prevent confusion. Employ proximity. Remember, clustering is good, and clutter is bad.

Choose a design scheme compatible with the overall design. Think colors, fonts and other design details. If you're creating an infographic for an existing website or serial publication, there might be a style guide that specifies the look of design elements. If there is no style guide, you're hired. You get the job. Create a style guide in order to maintain similarity and unity.

Use care if your graphic must appear in black and white. Color is one of your greatest allies, providing organization and way-finding for viewers. If you can't use color for your infographic, be clever with grayscale. But each gray should vary from the last one by at least 20 percent, or else the eye has a hard time telling them apart. Or consider using distinct

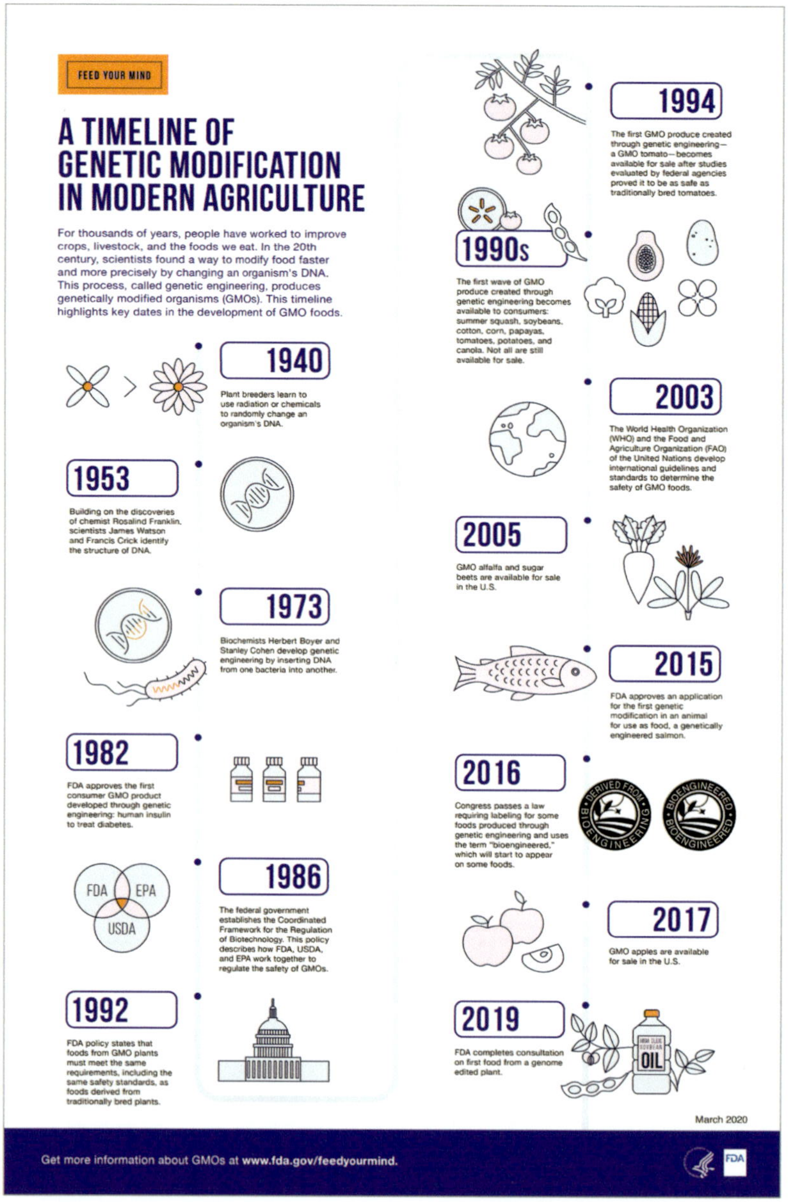

Quality control. It's tough to find a timeline generator that produces a quality infographic. For complex infographics like timelines and diagrams, the best approach might be a custom design. This timeline is consistent in use of fonts, colors, shapes, illustration and underlying grid to create an easy-to-understand and visually pleasing layout.

U.S. Food and Drug Administration, fda.gov

Don't forget unity. Whether you're creating true infographics or simply infographic-style layouts like this one, choose a color scheme for your charts, graphs and icons that coordinates with your overall design scheme.

Design by Rebecca Hagen. Reprinted by permission, Florida Maritime Partnership.

patterns or textures instead. This is a good practice even when you are working with full color. Use of pattern and texture helps the colorblind differentiate data points in your charts.

Stick to one color. Speaking of color, unless you have a data-driven reason to use more than one color in a chart, use just one. Do use the unifying power of color to group data sets, such as all items in the same year, or all members of the same demographic. Applying candy colors randomly creates a visual mess.

Give credit where credit is due. Attribute. Cite. This goes for the source of your data and the source of any photos or illustrations you use.

Minimize ornamentation. You're shooting for a clean comprehensible infographic. Cutesy backgrounds and other embellishments can detract from your message. Easy does it.

Keep the writing tight. Keep headlines and titles short. If possible, explain your subject and purpose in six words or less. For explainers and label text, keep your writing concise and in the third person. Use action verbs.

Design tips for specific types of infographics

Pie charts. Pie charts are intended to show parts of a whole. The full circle represents 100 percent. So don't forget to indicate what

INFOGRAPHIC *Ethics*

As with all public communication, there are ethical guidelines to follow when creating infographics. Here we cover a few of the biggies:

Can you spell plagiarism and copyright? Never reproduce someone else's graphic without permission. And after you get permission, you must credit your source. Usually graphics sources are noted in the lower left corner. Same goes for attributing the sources of your information.

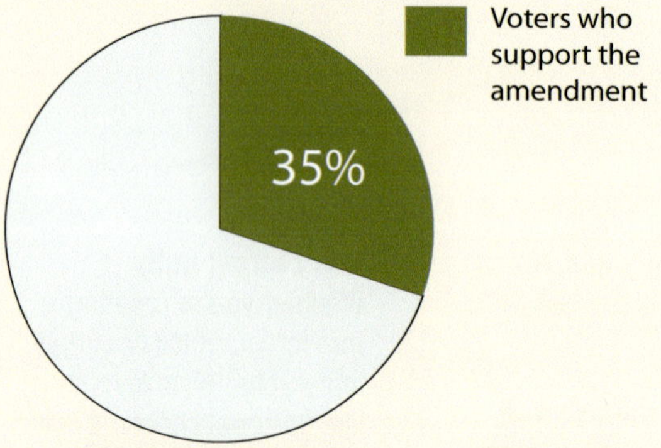

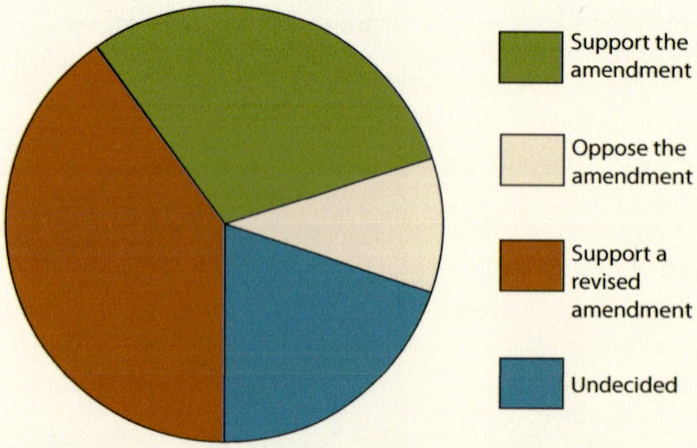

Who supports the amendment? Each pie chart above contains accurate data. Yet each chart tells a completely different story. Poorly executed charts can be downright misleading. In this case, plotting cherry-picked numbers creates a false impression.

Stick with the facts, please. It should go without saying that guessing at or making up information to fill in the blanks of an infographic is a career-ending blunder. But we'll say it anyway: In infographics, the word is "information," not "fiction." Keep it factual from credible sources you can corroborate and attribute. If you have holes in your information, work harder at your research to fill in the blanks. Or drop the graphic.

Speaking of filling in the blanks with credible sources, do be critical about the sources of data. Who pays the research bills? What are the agendas of your sources and their funding arms? Perpetual skepticism is not simply an occupational hazard of the information business. It's a prerequisite. That fact segues to the ways so-called objective numbers can mislead.

Statistics (and people) can be shifty. There are two big ways you can get in trouble when using numerical data: 1) The numbers are flawed to begin with. 2) Your presentation of the numbers is questionable or misleading. Avoid both.

If you didn't collect the data for your infographic, put on that skeptical hat. Track down the original study to give it the once over. If you're clueless about stats, enlist the expertise of someone with a clue.

Even if the original data are good, your graphical representation of the data might not be. Some common ways to ruin perfectly good stats include:

- Cherrypicking numbers to prove your point
- Failing to adjust money for economic inflation (or deflation)
- Inflating the significance of large numbers if they represent a small percentage of the whole (or vice versa)
- Specious comparisons (like comparing apples and oranges)

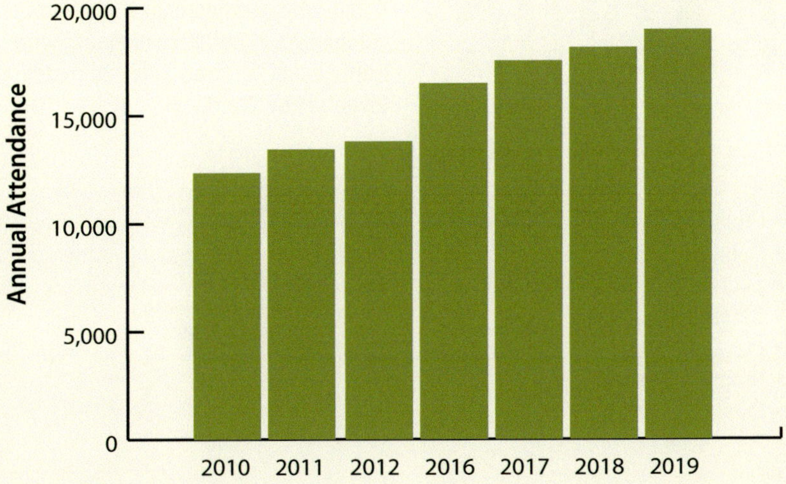

Missing something? This bar chart gives the impression of consistent annual attendance increases. But the chart doesn't actually include data for the years 2013–2015. For all we know, attendance dropped sharply in those three years.

And there are others. So if you don't know what you're doing in the research and quantification department, partner with someone who does.

On the other hand, don't be one of those wimpy math-phobic communication types. Don't let numbers intimidate you. Read a book. Sign up for a class. Take an expert to lunch.

Being ethical also means accounting for diversity. Account for the diversity of your infographic audience. People respond best when you invite them to identify with your visual messages. Beyond being inclusive, stay alert for images and text that are inaccurate, inappropriate, unfair or injurious.

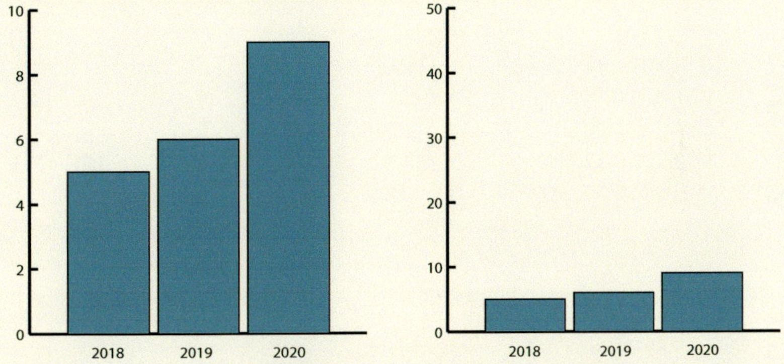

Battle axes. Both bar charts show exactly the same data, but the example at right uses a much wider range in the value axis. This makes the differences between the values in the left chart seem much greater than they appear in the right chart.

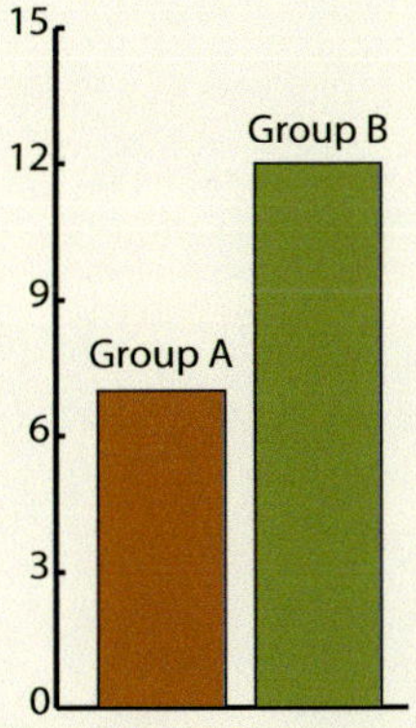

Does this chart make my data look fat? Same data. Same axis values. Different *chart shape.* The shorter chart shape minimizes the difference between the values of Group A and Group B.

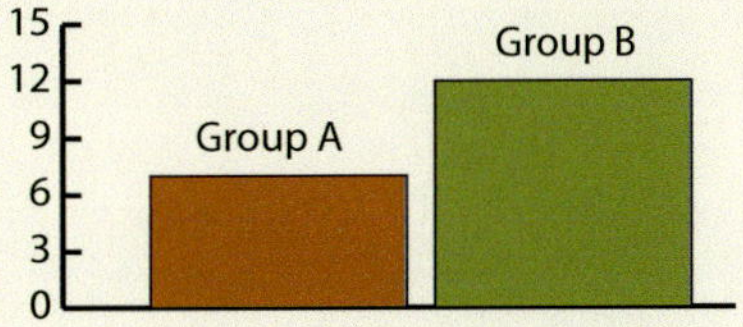

INFOGRAPHIC *Types*

A self-consciously ironic, though not exhaustive, infographic about infographics. Purity is not required. Mix and match. Or invent a new form.

DESCRIPTION | TYPES | EXAMPLES

EASY TO CREATE

COMPARATIVES

Text-based comparative infographics highlight relationships across terms by such things as rank, order, timing or outcome.

- Rankings
- Ratings
- Scores
- Before-After
- Pro-Con
- Problem-Solution
- Compare-Contrast
- For-Against
- Outline

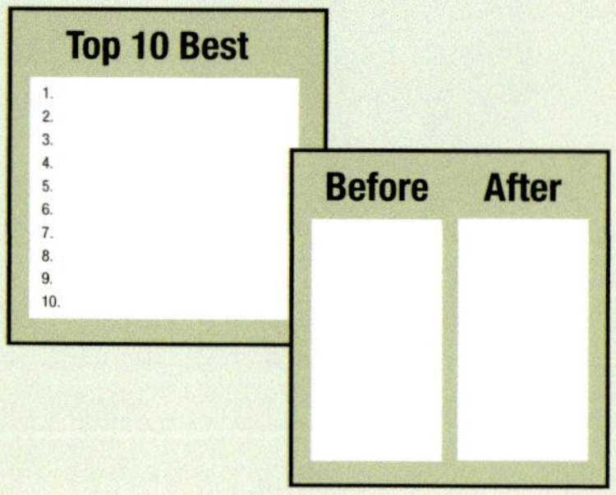

CHARTS & GRAPHS

A mainstay of business communication and easily created from spreadsheets, charts and graphs visualize numerical data.

- Pie
- Bar
- Stacked Bar
- Fever
- Scatter
- Area

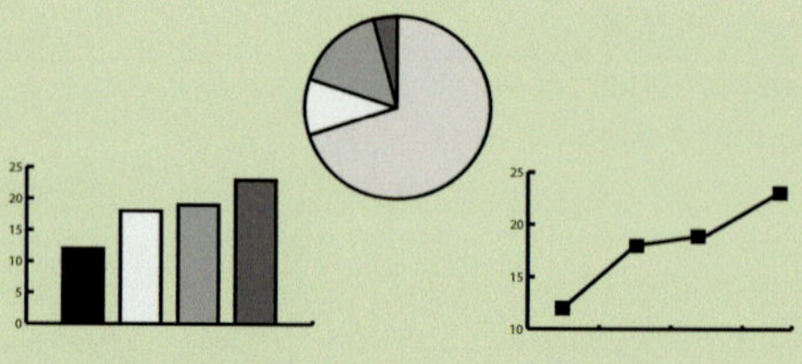

SEQUENCES

Sequences show a step-by-step progression using words, images or a combination of both.

- Demo
- Instruction
- Timeline
- Flowchart

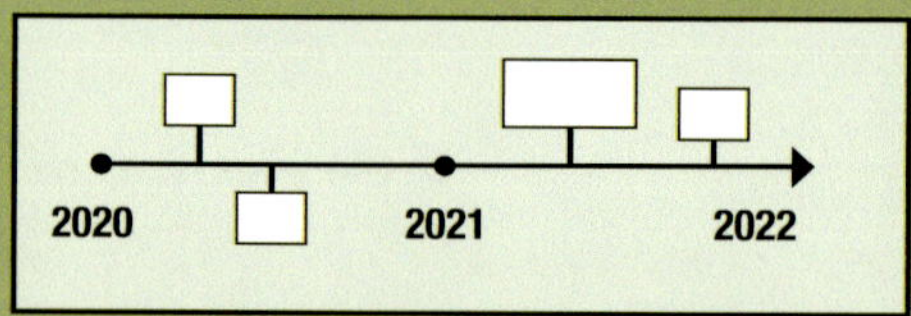

MAPS

"X" may mark the spot, but maps can also show geological features or data distribution.

- Location
- Geological
- Data/Statistical

DIAGRAMS

Diagrams come in a range of formats and vary greatly in complexity.

- Cutaway
- Schematic
- Network
- Cluster
- Venn
- Circular
- Pyramid
- Tree
- Explanatory

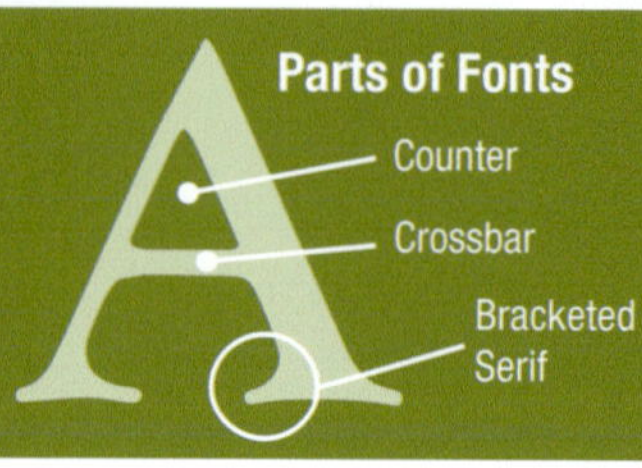

DIFFICULT TO CREATE

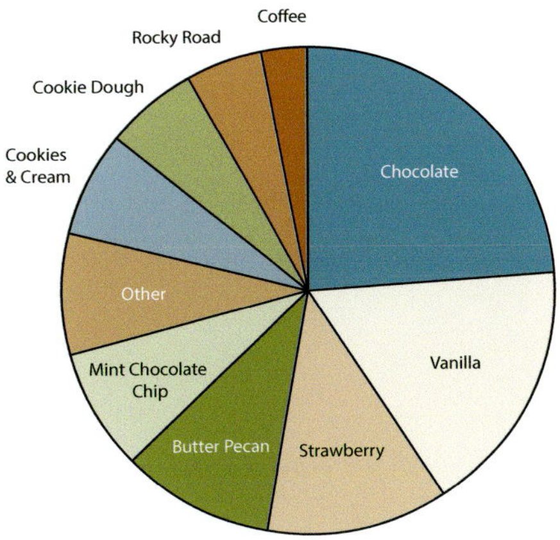

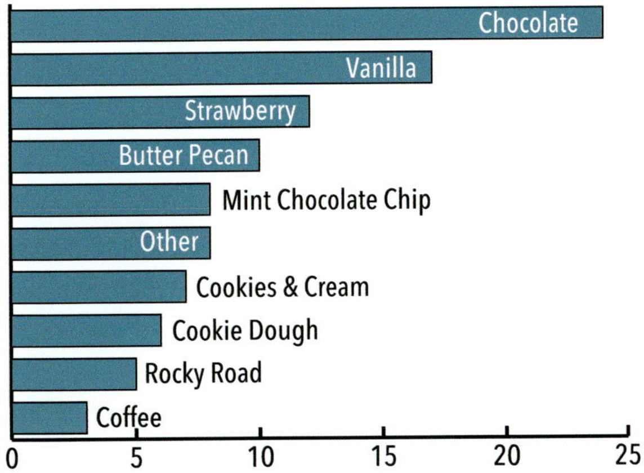

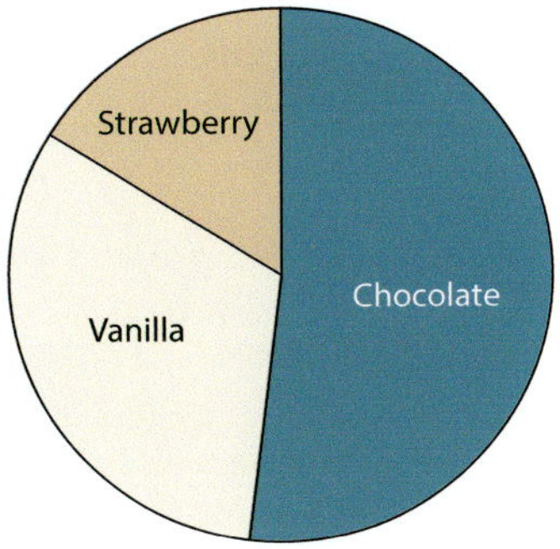

Easy as pie? Pie charts are popular but not always the best way to show comparison. If your pie needs more than five slices, or multiple small slices, go with a bar chart instead. Bars are easier to read at a glance.

If you must pie, keep it *flat.* 3D extrusions, like the example at bottom left, look interesting but make it harder to discern the actual value of the slices.

the "whole" is. This ain't no mystery. Then slice your pie portions accurately. Finally, make sure your slice percentages add up to 100 percent. If they don't someone will notice. 100 percent guaranteed.

Pie charts work best when the number of data points (pie segments) is small, say five or less. Any more than that and the segment relationships are harder to distinguish. If you have more than five data points, a bar chart will do a better job of displaying them.

Likewise, keep your pie charts 2D. Three-dimensional charts might look fun, but they make it harder to discern the actual value assigned to each slice.

Fever charts. Known for their spikes and valleys, fever charts are good for showing change over time. A background grid helps readers quickly grasp the trends. Remember algebra, slope and "rise over run"? Didn't think so. But you do need to know that the Y-axis equals the rise going up and down vertically. What are you measuring? The Stock Market? Rainfall? Daily traffic? That's your Y. The X-axis is always time or "run," running left (from the past) to right (into the future). In 3D, the Z-axis pushes out towards the viewer.

PARTS OF A *Map*

Maps are a common infographic form. There are several types, including locator maps, geological maps and statistical maps.

Reproduced by permission of Tucker/Hall.

Pointer box. Pointer boxes highlight key map details.

Compass. A compass establishes direction. When possible, keep the top of your map pointing north.

Reference points. Reference points are identifiable landmarks to orient map users. They can be structures, streets or other identifiers.

Inset (not pictured). An inset is an enlarged detail of a small section of the map.

Scale. The scale defines distance.

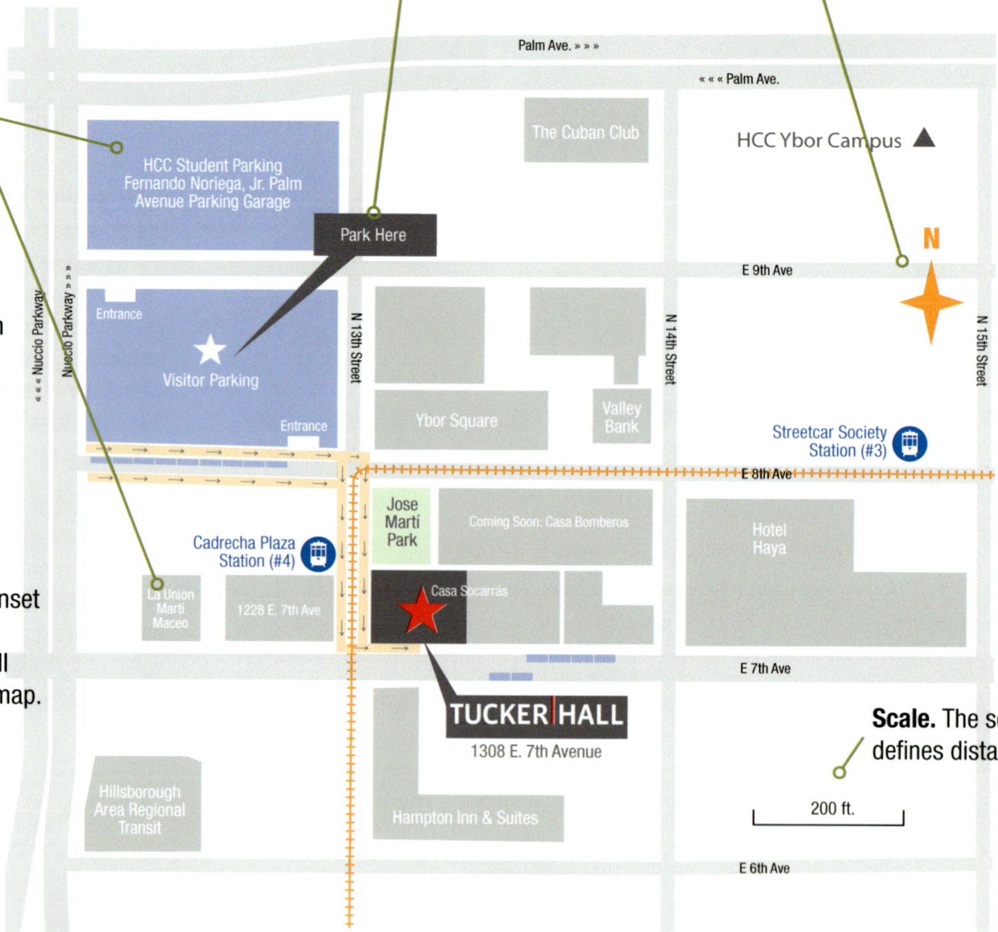

Key. The key defines symbols and other reference markers.

LOCATION & PARKING

Tucker/Hall is located in the Casa Socarras building, 1308 E. 7th Avenue in Ybor City.

Parking is available in municipal parking garages and on the street. The TECO Line Streetcar system runs along 13th Street and has a stop near the Tucker/Hall offices between East 7th and East 8th Avenues.

TUCKER/HALL | 813 228-0652 | WWW.TUCKERHALL.COM

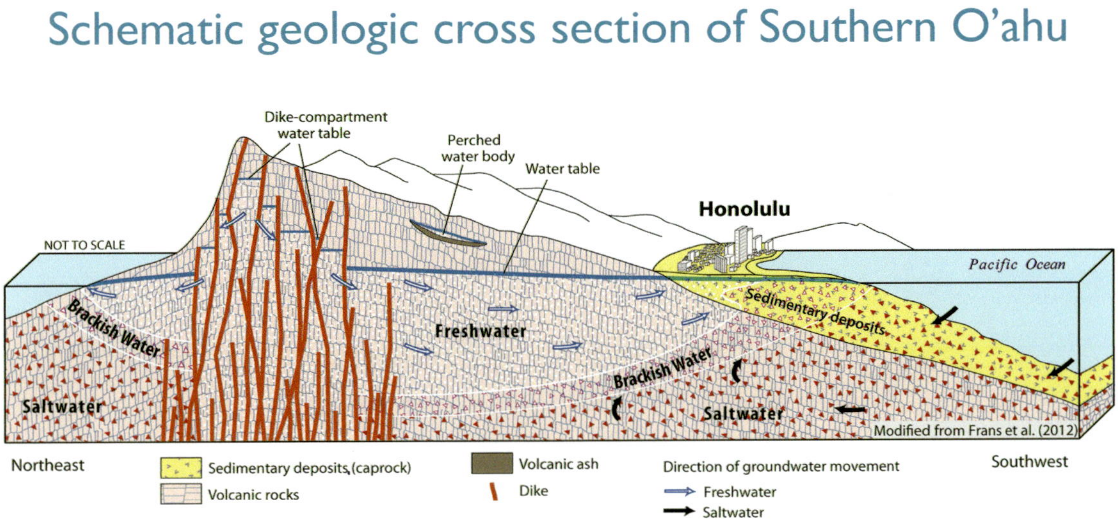

Bar charts. Bar charts are good for comparing things. Generally, use horizontal bars—unless there's a time element involved, for example data over a span of years. If your bar chart shows change over time, revert back to the idea of time as horizontal "run" going left to right, and lay in your bars as vertical blocks and towers. In either case, label each bar with the actual number it represents. Once again, a grid in the background helps clarify relationships visually.

Timelines. Timelines are excellent for sharing history, providing context, demonstrating cause and effect, etc. The rules say it's good practice to limit a timeline to 10–20 items or "frames." The best timelines are visually to scale or proportional to the time range they represent, which suggests enlisting the help of a grid again. Or think in terms of the timeline-equivalent of a measuring tape segmenting and parsing out your particular units of time. If your timeline includes giant gaps, a list format might be a better choice.

Maps. Maps show location. But they also show topographical data or distribution of data points. In any case, put your map on a grid and eliminate unnecessary details, called "map fat." Streamline and simplify. Be sure to include a scale showing distance. Include a legend as needed and directional indicators (at least North, if not all four directions), and indicate reference points for your reader.

Diagrams. These are the most complex of the graphic styles and usually require real artistic skill to execute. They can illustrate everything from the geologic layers of the Earth to how to put together a big box store chest of drawers. Diagrams and illustrations are best kept simple. Again, the rules for good composition will help

Diagrams. Diagrams such as this cutaway rank among the most complex infographics. They typically are drawn with illustration tools or 3D modeling tools.

This USGS diagram does the job. However, we are inclined to ding the designer for the unappealing color palette.

USGS.gov. Public domain image.

you set up strong diagrams and illustrations. Give them focal points, as well as rhythm and flow.

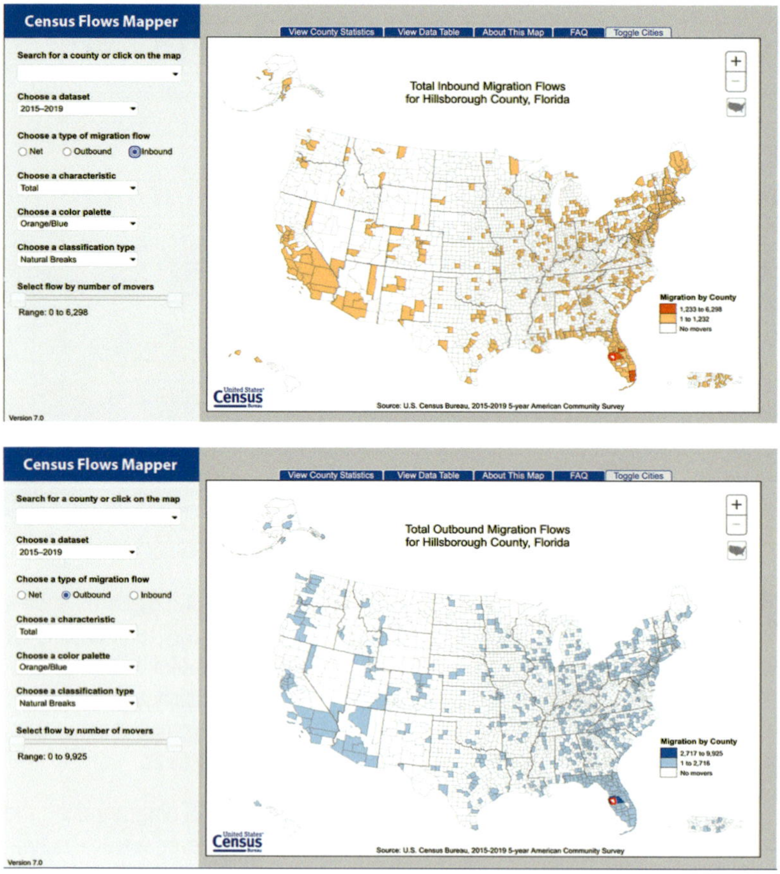

New chart on click. Interactive infographics change on input from the user. The map at top shows inbound migration for Hillsborough County, Florida, 2015 to 2019. Changing settings in the left side panel results in a new map (bottom) showing outbound migration for the same period.

United States Census Bureau Census Flows Mapper, www.census.gov

INTERACTIVE INFOGRAPHICS

The methods for generating infographics and the means for collecting data have changed. But so have infographics themselves. Charts and graphs were once largely static visuals printed in hardcopy. But today, digital interactive infographics are so embedded in our daily lives that we don't give them a second thought.

If you have a cell phone, you've most likely typed your zip code into a mapping tool and gotten the location of the pizza place nearest you. Or perhaps you've used a GPS (Global Positioning System) to find the fastest route through morning traffic.

The good news is it doesn't require a Ph.D. in computer science to make simple interactive infographics. If you're looking to create a map that shows the population density of a region over time, with a slider that morphs your map decade-by-decade, you're going to find an online tool for that.

So when you're brainstorming infographics, don't forget to concept for interactivity. No need to go wild, but take advantage where available and appropriate to your project's objectives. Remember to plan for accessiblity, too.

MULTIMEDIA JOURNALISM, DIGITAL STORYTELLING

These days, infographics rarely appear solo. One or more charts are typically cohabitate—ofttimes loudly—in the same layout. Newsrooms created the original graphics packages, which reported news or feature stories using multiple types of graphics all working together. A focal illustration or lead graphic generally anchors these multimodal stories, supported by related smaller graphs, charts, timelines, rankings, etc.

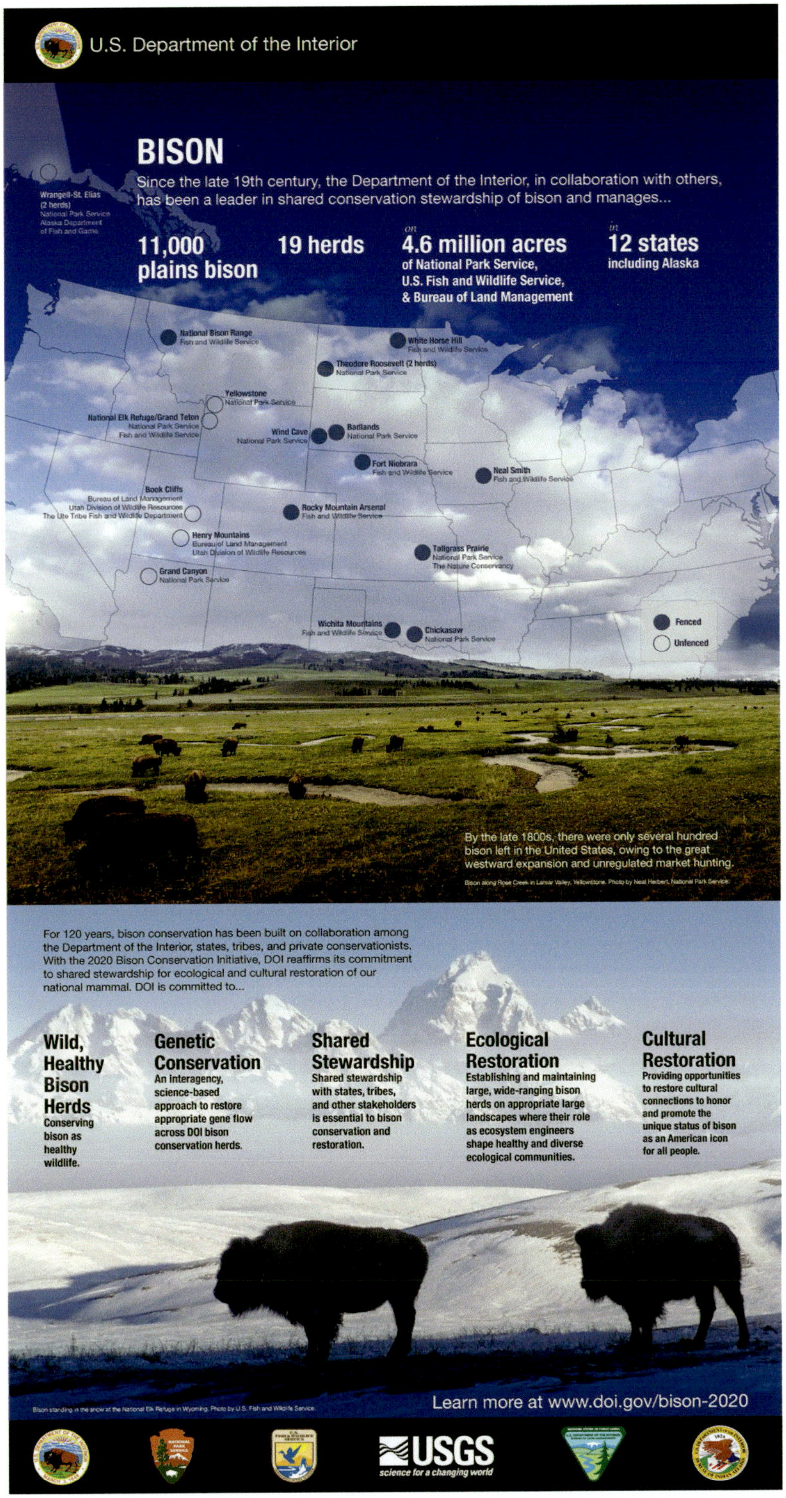

Maximizing media. Digital storytelling makes use of a wide range of media types to tell engaging stories. Media types include but are not limited to text, video, audio, animations and infographics. This story on bison herds in the United States appears on the U.S. Geological Survey website.

United States Department of the Interior, US Geological Survey, www.usgs.gov

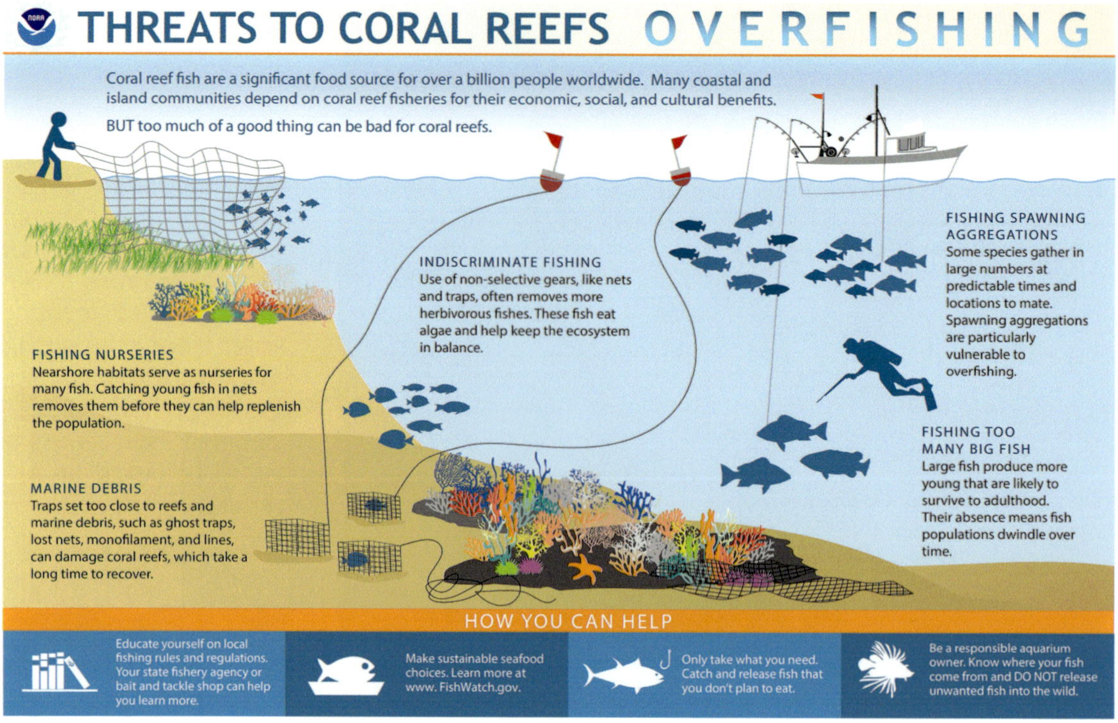

Just to illustrate the point. Sometimes you're better off hiring an illustrator. Credit the unacknowledged illustrator for the above visual story's consistent style and easy-to-scan flow from one topic to the next. Deceptively simple drawings literally illustrate below-the-surface facts.

U.S. National Oceanic and Atmospheric Administration, oceanservice.noaa.gov

No longer bound by printed formats, multimedia journalism and digital storytelling include animations, interactive infographics, video, slideshows and narrative or ambient audio tracks.

Consider a diagram showing the flow of air through a heating, ventilation and air conditioning (HVAC) system. In print, we would use arrows and ordinal numbers to signify directional and sequential flow. But with the help of high-end animation, we would simulate 3D perspective and mimic the effect of a theme-park ride through the ductwork.

In addition to typographic explainers, audio could add the recorded sound of the airflow. Voiceover narration could add yet more information and help accommodate the visually impaired.

The combination of well-crafted story, photos and infographics makes one-stop-shopping of visual appeal, in-depth information and at-a-glance comprehension.

We have a few recommendations about multimedia journalism and digital storytelling:

1. Don't avoid multimedia journalism and digital storytelling because you're not in the news business. Digital storytelling can be effective

and useful in any communication context, including PR, advertising and social media, in the public and private sectors alike.

2. Plan, plan, plan. Without serious coordination, visual stories can result in information overload. Executing successful multimodal stories requires significant preparation and cooperation. This might mean enlisting the help of photographers, illustrators, animators, researchers and writers, not to mention web designers and developers.

   Most anyone can create simple charts and graphs. Effective multimodal storytelling is generally the product of professional team effort.

3. Lumping multiple charts together with a lot of boxed text and some colorful icons does not equal an infographic, much less an infographics package.

Like all visual communication, the best infographics provide accurate information simply. Practice that, and you can't go wrong.

TRY THIS

1. Design an infographic bio for yourself. First imagine a real-world use for it, such as putting it on a social media page or adding it to your resumé. Then design it accordingly.

2. Following the rules for map design, execute a floor plan of one room in your home or office. Try desiging a flat map with a standard design program. Alternatively, find an online service and make an *isometric map* like the example on the next page.

3. Find a news story presented through multimedia journalism. Deconstruct the story. What are the text and visual components? What types of individual infographics are used? What data were needed to create the visuals and what was the data source? Create a diagram of the news story using your findings to create labels.

4. Design an interactive timeline demonstrating the history of infographics using an online infographics tool. Remember research comes first. No cheating.

5. Put your hands on some credible research statistics (we like the U.S. Bureau of Labor Statistics at http://www.bls.gov/). Using the research project's findings, thumbnail a visual story for the web. Execute one statistical graph or chart from your package.

Got game? Isometric drawing gives maps a 3D appearance. The gaming industry popularized this map style—think simulated cities and fantasy battle maps. Okay. Gotta go. Rebecca's 13th level half-orc barbarian Tyrevüld Goatsniffer has a guild raid starting in 10 minutes.

Map and map elements by Rebecca Hagen, created via Inkarnate.com.

Shangri-Layout
WhyteSpaece Keep
Valley of Visual Balance
The Kerning Pairs
Gestalt Wizard's Tower
River of Justified Text
Creative Idea Desert
Ledding Mine
Mystic of the Missing Margins
Fearsome Forest of Visual Clutter
Em-dash Ent
Comic Sans Troll Bridge
Fountain of Useless Client Feedback
Dingbat Cave
Blackletter Bay
Bog of Clipart Goblins
N
W
E
S
The SS Garamond

CHAPTER 11

STORYBOARDING

PLANNING VISUAL STORYTELLING

Before we leave off talking about visuals—photos, illustrations and infographics—let's cover storyboarding, too. Storyboards lay out the visual stories of planned video and film, including the animated sorts. Computer games begin as storyboards. Today's computer-generated imagery (CGI) also begins with "previsualization" storyboards. In most cases, then, storyboarding involves representing moving pictures and sound with still pictures and type.

A storyboard visualizes the entire project in the form of individual scenes, shots or screens. A concept storyboard distills the project down to the minimum number of views necessary to tell the story. A production storyboard or a shooting storyboard provides more detailed information for a production crew.

Up, up and away! Even though drone footage and traditional video share many shots, techniques and transitions, drones are more vertically liberated. Pushes, pans, chases and tracking shots—not to mention turns, rolls and orbits—go epic with drones.

If you're planning to produce video or film of some kind, you will enlist preproduction, production and postproduction assistance from professionals. But you still may find yourself concepting a storyboard for a TV commercial or spot, a public service announcement (PSA), a corporate video, a video news release (VNR) or even an animated web ad. Sometimes a feature news film package also benefits from a storyboard.

Whatever the project or your role in the process, this chapter gives you some of the basics of storyboarding.

GETTING STARTED

Once you have a storyboard project, you have to think about how to tell the story shot-by-shot. Much of what we've covered in earlier chapters comes to bear in storyboarding. You begin with research and brainstorming for a concept. You account for format and aspect ratio, and you experiment with visual composition using thumbnail sketches.

The elements of design—space, line, shape, size, texture, value—become your tools for telling visual stories. As you'll see, the principles of design, including focal point, contrast, balance,

movement, rhythm and unity, also become important storyboarding tools.

You don't have to be an accomplished illustrator to create a storyboard, either. You can indicate your ideas with rough drawing and stick figures, just as you would with thumbnail sketches. Or you can use, mix and match stock images, whether photography or line art. If you fancy yourself a photographer, you might grab a camera or phone.

Our point is that you already have a fairly large visual toolbox for dramatic storyboarding. So take advantage of it. Your eyes, however, continue to be the most useful tool in your toolbox. As to acquiring new tools for storyboarding, below we provide some necessities regarding:

- » Framing the Shot
- » Perspective
- » POV
- » Camera Angle
- » Movement
- » Continuity
- » Transitions
- » Lighting
- » Type
- » Audio

Storyboards, from thumbnail sketch to screen grab. As a student, filmmaker Sarah Wilson first sketched her ideas before committing her cast and crew to the week of shooting and editing it took to produce her award-winning short film "Rhapsody." In the sequence shown here, the POV is omniscient. Notice how the first shot of this scene in the final film demonstrates a low-angle shot from below, as well as a canted camera angle producing a dynamically tilted horizon line.

"Rhapsody" storyboards and screen captures reproduced by permission of Sarah Wilson.

FRAMING THE SHOT

Your direction for how to frame a scene within the four corners of the visual screen is called framing the shot. Common shots include variations on the close-up, medium, full and long shot. Other frames

A VISUAL GLOSSARY OF WAYS TO **FRAME** THE SHOT

Extreme Close-up

Medium Close-up

Full Close-up

Wide Close-up

Close Shot

Medium Close Shot

Medium Shot

Medium Full Shot

Full Shot

Long Shot

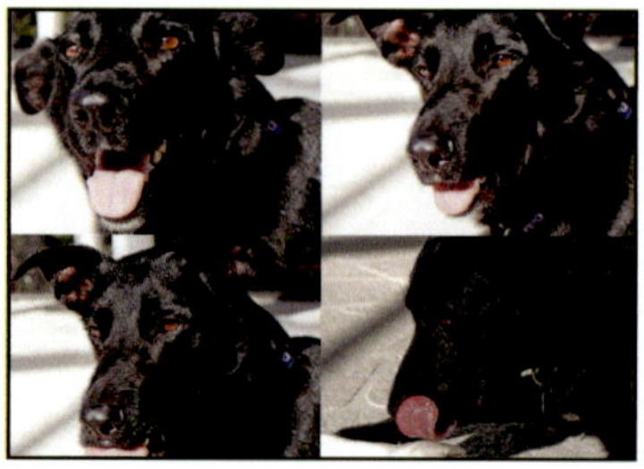
Montage

Split-screen

include the split-screen and montage. Drone cameras make bird's-eye frames accessible.

An establishing shot orients viewers to the visual scene in order to avoid confusion before proceeding with the story.

Advertising giant David Ogilvy reminded would-be advertisers to make the product the hero. A beauty shot frames an object or product to show off its best visual features, as if it were a movie star. "All right, Mr. DeMille, I'm ready for my close-up," said the aging film star Gloria Swanson playing an aging film star in the 1950 film "Sunset Boulevard."

The farther the transparent "fourth wall" of the screen lies from the focal point of the shot, the more impersonal the symbolic tone. As the fourth wall moves closer to the focal point, the audience feels increasingly intimate with the focal point, whether it's a person or a thing.

Establishing shots orient viewers. In the first frame, a third-person POV establishes the scene: a conversation. Subsequent frames then alternate between the two characters' first-person POVs.

Reproduced by permission of Willow Payne.

PERSPECTIVE

Perspective becomes especially important in film and video, thus in storyboarding, too. If framing refers to how the shot crops the viewer's visual field, perspective refers to how deeply the viewer sees into the shot.

Where the horizon line sits in the composition communicates distance for the viewer. Atmospheric perspective via value as well as linear perspective via flowing sightline and vanishing point also help establish the scale of distance. Speaking of scale, perspective by relative size of objects in the shot can enrich the sense of distance, such as framing a sweeping vista in the background with two human figures in the foreground. And remember that depth of field refers to what in the shot remains in focus and what goes out of focus, whether foreground, midground, background or some combination.

More than communicating literal spatial distance in the narrative, perspective also communicates a sense of emotional distance or,

Perspective done four ways. 1) The "horizon line" in the upper third of the frame indicates distance. 2) The road's "linear vanishing point" also communicates distance. 3) The car's large "relative size" says nearby; the buildings' small sizes say faraway. 4) "Atmospheric perspective" is achieved by using light color value to make the skyline seem to recede into the background while the car's dark value feels closer to the viewer.

Reproduced by permission of Willow Payne.

conversely, intimacy. Perspective also may communicate symbolic meanings such as a sense of freedom from wide-open spaces versus the tension and anxiety of oppressive low-ceiling closed spaces. Yet a small close space also might seem warm and sheltering while a vast sky or plain may send a lonesome message about human frailty.

POV

Perspective also leads to considering the camera's point of view or POV. If you think about the camera (or the screen) as an eye that looks, you need to think about whose eye is supposed to be doing the looking. While the viewing audience is always the implied eye, you can nudge the audience to identify with different points of view in the story.

Do you want the audience to remain an invisible omniscient third-person eye observing the story?

Or do you want the audience to participate in the story by seeing with the same eye as the protagonist? For example, both protagonist and audience, through the camera lens or screen, might look the villain in the eye in a visual stare-down.

Or should the audience see as the villain sees, while sneaking up to peer over an unsuspecting shoulder?

If two people onscreen are to have a conversation, you probably need to provide a third-person establishing shot of the two people framed together if you are going to alternate back and forth between the two characters' first-person POVs.

Sometimes you want the viewer to ignore the fourth wall in order to participate in an admittedly one-way conversation with an onscreen personality who maybe offers a how-to, reads the news, sells a product or runs a yoga class. Think of intimate confessions to the camera in reality TV and social media.

In short, plan the POV.

CAMERA ANGLE

Planning the camera's angle also relates to POV and perspective. In addition to shooting straight on or level, there are other ways to position the camera's angle for effect. A canted or tilted camera angle creates a sense of unease by tilting the horizon line and upsetting the viewer's visual equilibrium.

Framing the shot from above, as if the camera were looking down on the focal point, can make the focal point seem small, communicating symbolic insignificance and powerlessness. Shooting the focal point from below can have the opposite effect, communicating the focal point's larger size and power. Extreme versions include the crane or bird's-eye shot and the ground or worm's-eye shot. Such angles also can make for a comic effect because they tend to distort the proportions of the focal point. So be careful. Hard news, assumed to be objective, would avoid special effects angles.

You don't always have to shoot from the front, either. You may decide to shoot from behind, from the side or at a 45-degree angle. Mix it up, but do it with a visual communication purpose compatible with your subject matter and tone.

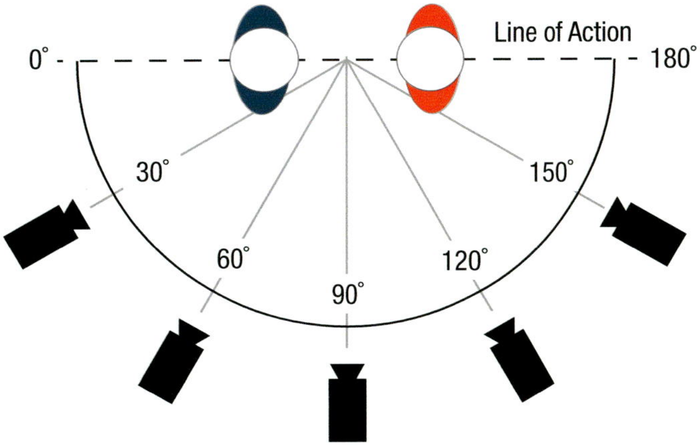

The 180-degree line of action. To avoid disorienting viewers, the 180-degree rule cautions against crossing the imaginary line of action intersecting two characters—unless you have a narrative purpose for doing so.

The 30-degree rule. This rule says any change of camera angle relative to the focal point should represent at least 30 degrees of change. Anything less reads as an editing error or the amateur hour.

Camera angles. Use camera angle to help tell your visual story. Starting in the upper left, these frames demo shooting from the side, from below, from above and, last, from behind at a wide angle.

Reproduced by permission of Willow Payne.

MOVEMENT

The design principle of movement shifts from being implied in stop-action pictures to being literal in live-action ones. Storyboarding movement shots involves knowing another vocabulary.

For example, a pan or panning indicates a stationary camera that sweeps across the scene. The effect is that of turning your head to look around. In a truck,

Zoom. First the establishing shot (this can't be good). Next the push into the scene for a close-up (not a happy camper).

Reproduced by permission of Willow Payne.

usually accomplished with a camera on a dolly, the camera trucks sideways across the scene. The effect is like rubbernecking from a moving car. A tilt is a vertical up-and-down pan.

Handheld refers to the cameraperson holding the camera as she or he walks or runs through the scene—resulting in a bumpy visual ride. This can increase realism, as in breaking news footage, but can be difficult to watch for long periods of time. The steadicam is a kind of harness the cameraperson wears to hold the camera steady as she or he shoots a handheld scene.

In a tracking shot, a stationary camera tracks along with a moving focal point. Think of the classic 1967 Patterson Bigfoot film tracking a tall hairy arm-swinging two-legged creature looking right at the camera as it walks off into the woods. Hoax or not, it's a memorable example of a tracking shot.

Push shots push into the scene. In a zoom, a stationary camera pushes into the scene by using the lens to zoom in on the focal point. In a dolly shot, the camera itself, positioned on a dolly, moves or pushes toward the focal point. A rack-focus uses a stationary camera to shift a scene's focal point simply by refocusing from one object to another.

Drone cameras revolutionized "movement" with maneuvers that only a drone aircraft can perform outside of computer-generated images. Think helix rotations and tilt orbits, for example. Video and film movement like chases and flybys, which used to seem like special effects, can go epic with a drone—higher, faster, tighter, smoother—in the most inaccessible places. A licensed drone pilot also renders superfluous the bulky equipment setups for truck, dolly and crane shots. And why hire full-size aircraft if a drone can do a better job capturing the same aerial footage? Even steadicam shots get slicker with a drone.

As is often the case, purity here is not required. You might achieve several effects at once. The infamous Bigfoot tracking shot is obviously handheld. We've seen movie scenes in which the camera pans and zooms from atop a trucking dolly.

CONTINUITY

Unity is critical when you're telling one story using many shots. Each shot must build on the previous one and prepare for the next. That makes for narrative continuity. Does the visual story hold together as one cohesive narrative from beginning to end and from shot to shot? Are the POV and chronology clear to avoid confusing the audience? Is the dramatic or comedic timing impeccable?

Think of your storyboard as having an obvious beginning, middle and end. Make each pull its visual storytelling workload. Beginnings should capture attention immediately—no warm-up necessary—and establish the relevant W's. Middles do exposition and drama. That's the convey information and evoke emotions part. Endings put closure on the tale or ask for the sale. Advertising always ends with a call to action, whether explicit or implicit.

Speaking of advertising, timing takes on special significance if you only have 10, 15 or 30 seconds of exposition. You can't storyboard a :60 or even a :12 if you only have :10. Short-format web video runs about 2 minutes, a bit more for a news package and a bit less for a news clip.

Regardless of the type of project, make

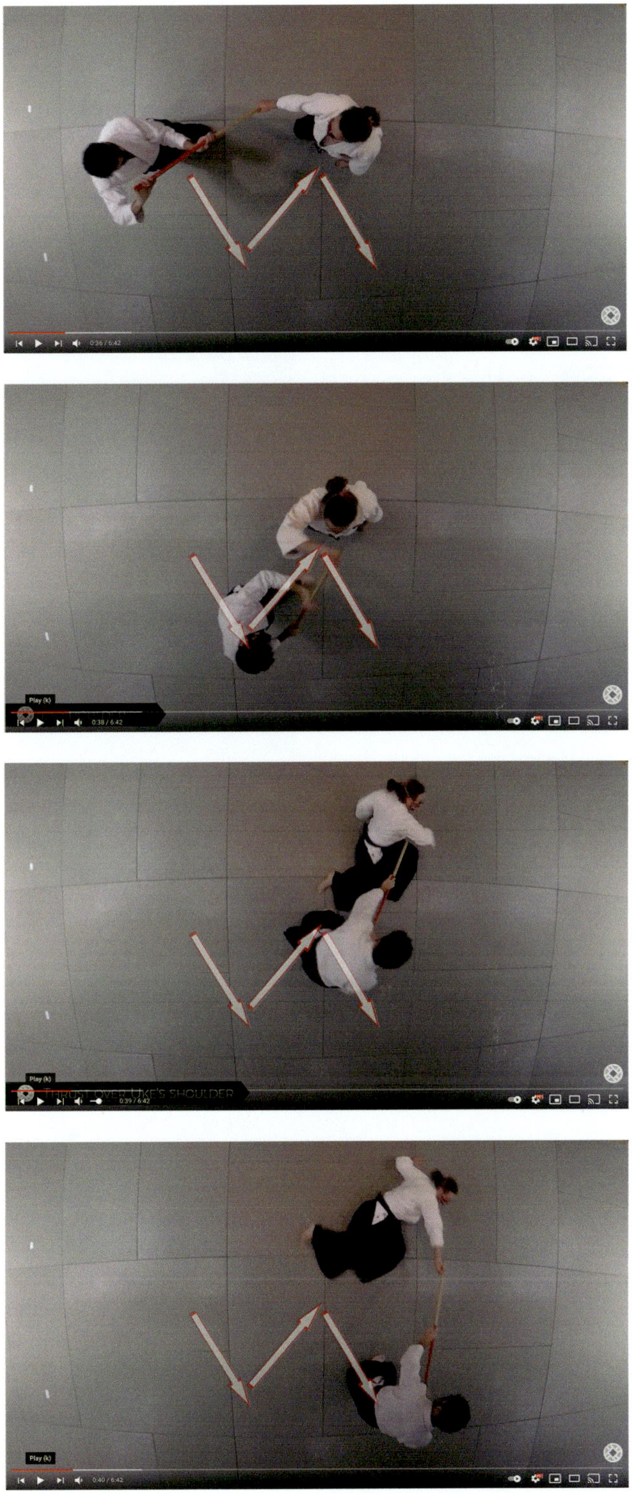

Master class in action choreography. A good fight scene, like a good dance performance, requires planning, which can involve storyboarding a series of steps. Literally.

Video stills used by permission of Aikido Chuseikan.

Let's grind it out over coffee. Use your storyboard to serve up the project vision in as much detail as possible from camera direction to ambient audio. In this sequence, a cut-in close-up of a cup of java transitions from the establishing shot of the scene's coffee shop location caught from above.

sure your storyboard is doable given your time constraints. Where appropriate, indicate the timing of shots on the storyboard, use a stopwatch to test your timing and make sure your math is accurate.

TRANSITIONS

In film and video, part of continuity is transitioning or segueing between shots and scenes. The most common type of transition is the simple cut from one shot to the next, such as cutting from an establishing shot of two actors conversing to a close-up of one of the actors speaking.

A cutaway "cuts away" from the main action by inserting something else going on simultaneously in the scene. If the scene shows two arguing people standing beside a car stopped on the side of the road, inserting a shot of the dog's head poked out the car window watching the argument is a cutaway. A shot of cars whizzing past the arguing people would be a cutaway, too.

A cut-in or insert "cuts in" or "inserts" a close-up shot of something significant to the meaning of the scene. In the scene of two people arguing beside a car stopped on the side of the road, inserting a shot of the flat tire on the stopped car would be a cut-in underscoring the reason for the stopped car and ensuing argument.

You have to be careful with cutting so the viewer can keep up with the chronology of events. Some kinds of transitions are helpful for indicating different events occurring simultaneously, perhaps even in different locations, or, conversely, flashbacks in time. But, again, make sure the viewer is keeping up.

The wipe, the dissolve and the fade each transitions between shots in the manner their names imply. These transitions, while time-honored in the hands of professionals, may come off as cheesy or kitschy if you're not careful, however.

LIGHTING

In storyboarding, you can use light and shadow for dramatic effect. Here the principle of contrast comes into play.

A key light is the main or key light source in the shot, whether natural or artificial. Fill light supplements the key light by filling in unwanted shadows for less contrast. Backlight is a light source used to highlight the focal point from behind to give it contrast and dimension. Most shots require a combination of all three light sources to produce what viewers would perceive as a natural or realistic effect.

For additional drama, you might consider the amount and direction of light. Soft light or high key evens out the shadows to decrease harsh contrasts. It makes people and products look more attractive. ("I'm ready for my close-up.") Hard light or low key emphasizes shadows, thus contrast, including shadows on people's faces—an interesting if less-than-flattering effect.

A key light shining directly from above (overlighting) or from below (underlighting) can form sinister shadows, especially on people's faces. Backlighting can make a focal point appear angelic with a halo effect or make the focal point appear powerful or significant (think backlit grand stage entrances of silhouetted superheroes, rock stars or pro wrestlers). Side lighting casts long shadows and increases the sense of three-dimensional space, as opposed to the flattening effect of soft light.

3-Point Lighting. Key light is the main light source illuminating your subject. Back light and fill light weave in with the key light to even out harsh shadows.

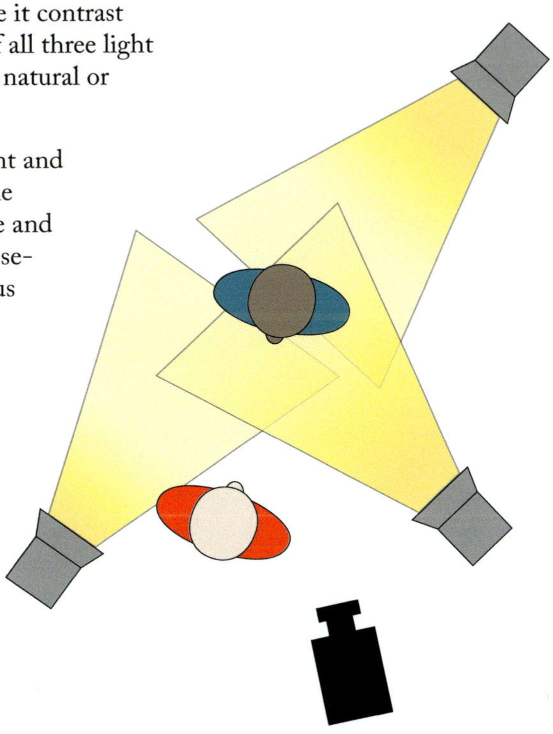

Lower third. In TV business lingo, "lower third" refers to supers, which mostly appear somewhere in the lower third of the screen.

Remember the rule of thirds? And foreground, midground and background? Foreground, at the bottom of the screen, appears closer than mid- or background. Hence, supers get the lower third.

The lower third super might be copy or an image like a logo. It can be static or a crawl. But it must be visible and readable, especially if overlaid on moving images.

As you storyboard, think about how you might cast light as a supporting actor in your story. All these effects work for inanimate objects, too, as well as infographics. A side light on a pie chart gives it shadow and dimension. Go easy, though. Like a backlit superhero, overly dramatic lighting not only might seem cartoonlike when that isn't your intent but also might distract viewers from your visual communication purpose.

TYPE

Last we move on to dealing with words and sounds, whether onscreen or off and whether part of the show or merely behind-the-camera direction.

As for onscreen type, a super is any type or graphic superimposed over a picture. A crawl is moving type running—or crawling—across the screen. You see this on cable news channels or when your area comes under a severe weather alert.

When you super, design for typographic readability and legibility, whether the super is static or animated. Contrast, thus color and value, are crucial, whether you reverse or not. And when positioning your type, remember to keep it within the prescribed title-safe area.

AUDIO

In a chapter about storyboarding in a book about visual communication, audio becomes the proverbial elephant in the room. Hello—sound? If your storyboard project includes audio, you obviously have to represent it visually on the storyboard by using textual direction.

Using a script setup, type your audio direction to correspond with visuals. Make your intent abundantly clear, including who is speaking when.

Also specify direction for things such as music, sound effects (SFX) or visual effects (FX). An off-screen voice, narrator or announcer (ANNCR) is called a voiceover, indicated as VO. Background music is called a music bed or track.

As far as dialogue goes, nothing is more difficult to write well. And nothing is worse than stilted unnatural repartee. So fair warning. We advise amateurs to develop concepts that avoid multiple characters engaged in dialogue, especially in extended conversations, which provide little visual interest anyway. "Show, don't tell."

On the other hand, don't shortchange audio because you've become a visual communicator. Audio—ear candy—can make or break your visual story. Think creatively and include the details on your storyboard.

Provide direction for audio. Audio—ear candy—can make or break your visual story. Think creatively and include the details on your storyboard.

AFTER THE STORYBOARD

After the storyboard and before the actual production shoot, there may be an in-between stage that cheaply simulates what the storyboard might look like as live action. This generally is done using software to cut together rough approximations of the shots. It might be accomplished with stock, archived or homemade footage or stills that come as near as possible to the storyboard's visuals. Or you might use animated illustrations or cartoons.

If you're a beginner, focus on generating a killer concept. No amount of money can make a bad concept look good.

These kinds of preproduction pieces have been called spec cuts, videomatics, animatics and ripomatics. They tend to be more impressive, thus persuasive, when you're presenting your storyboard to the conceptually challenged or to the person holding the purse strings. But, lest we wax creative snobbery, speculative cuts also can be helpful as narrative, shot and timing trials before you start spending big bucks on production.

And that leads us, at last, to some final advice concerning production budgets: KISS (Keep it simple, stupid). Video production is expensive, and film, even more so. Hollywood director Cecil B. DeMille developed a reputation for visual spectacle using elaborate productions and, as the expression goes, casts of thousands. But he had the financial backing of the Hollywood studio system. We're guessing you work with more modest budgets.

If you're a beginner, focus on generating a killer concept. No amount of money can make a bad concept look good. The best concepts are usually the most parsimonious anyway. Don't script for two warm bodies when one will do. Don't storyboard an on-location shoot if you can get away with a studio shoot. Don't storyboard multiple sets if one is sufficient. And don't storyboard more shots than necessary. If it isn't vital to advancing the story, cut it.

Be smart, have fun, and, as they say, "Break a leg."

TRY THIS

1. Develop a concept for a short educational video on storyboarding. Then execute a storyboard for your concept.

2. Storyboard a favorite scene from a favorite film or series. Account for:

    » Framing

    » Perspective

    » POV

    » Camera Angle

    » Movement

    » Continuity

    » Transitions

    » Lighting

    » Type

    » Audio

    How does each contribute to the narrative?

3. Storyboard a TV commercial currently running. Account for:

    » Framing

    » Perspective

    » POV

    » Camera Angle

    » Movement

    » Continuity

    » Transitions

    » Lighting

    » Type

    » Audio

    How does each contribute to the narrative?

4. Remember the Patterson Bigfoot film? Let's get silly to make a serious point. Choose three of the following and storyboard a few conceptual frames for each:

    » A music video starring Bigfoot

    » A televised interview with Bigfoot

- A selfie tour of the best locations to see and be seen by Sasquatch hunters
- A wildlife cinematic extravaganza on Bigfoot in its natural habitat
- A sports highlights-style review of Bigfoot engaging in extreme snow sports. Don't forget the drone shots.
- An infomercial teaming up Patterson and Bigfoot to sell product
- A corporate training video using Bigfoot as the spokesmodel
- A PSA of some kind using Bigfoot as the spokes—ahem—person. This is definitely a use-your-imagination no-holds-barred exercise. Don't forget that "experts" believe the Patterson Bigfoot is female

5. Storyboard a new :15 TV spot for a commercial consumer product currently in your kitchen, pantry, laundry room or bathroom. Start with a unique selling proposition (USP) or claim about the product. Then develop a concept. You know the rest of the drill by now.

CHAPTER 12

DESIGN FOR SOCIAL MEDIA

…BUT NOT REALLY. WORKING WITH MULTIMEDIA ASSETS

Our readers used to ask, "Why is there no chapter on designing social media pages in your book?" Our answer? Because you don't *design* your own social media pages. You do, however, customize preexisting social media templates with images, video clips, animations and apps that you *can* design. It's the same with presentation decks and websites that use templates. So this chapter is not about designing social media *pages*. It's about how to design the assets used in customizing different types of digital communication.

WHERE TO BEGIN?

Visit any social media page or website and you'll encounter many different types of media on the same page. A single layout might combine type, image, audio, video and infographics, not to mention forms, polls and even games. All this must be available to active "users" on their desktop computers, laptops, smart phones, tablets and TVs.

Multimedia: The early years. When actor Clara Bow made silent films in the 1920s, "intertitle" cards allowed moviegoers to read the dialog on screen. Live musicians provided musical accompaniment from the theater's orchestra pit.

Photo by Bain News Service - This image is available from the United States Library of Congress.

Beginning designers can get overwhelmed by the multimedia options out there. Plus, the myriad of multimedia-building *tools* available can be equally discouraging. But don't give up just yet. For the novice digital communicator, here are some things to keep in mind.

First, multimedia design can be implemented in degrees. A simple animated hero image might be all you need to enhance an otherwise static website. Graphic designers create online virtual worlds where audiences participate in massively multiuser online role-playing games (MMORPG), but as a beginner you don't need to start there. We suggest working your way down the bunny hill before you try to ski Dead Man's Peak.

Second, digital multimedia means multisensory, which translates into a richer user experience. It allows for communication via sound and touch in addition to sight. Users swipe, click, pinch and tap their way through all sorts of digital content. Implementing some sort of multimedia into your project is well worth your time. (No such thing as smell-o-vision yet, but maybe that's a good thing.)

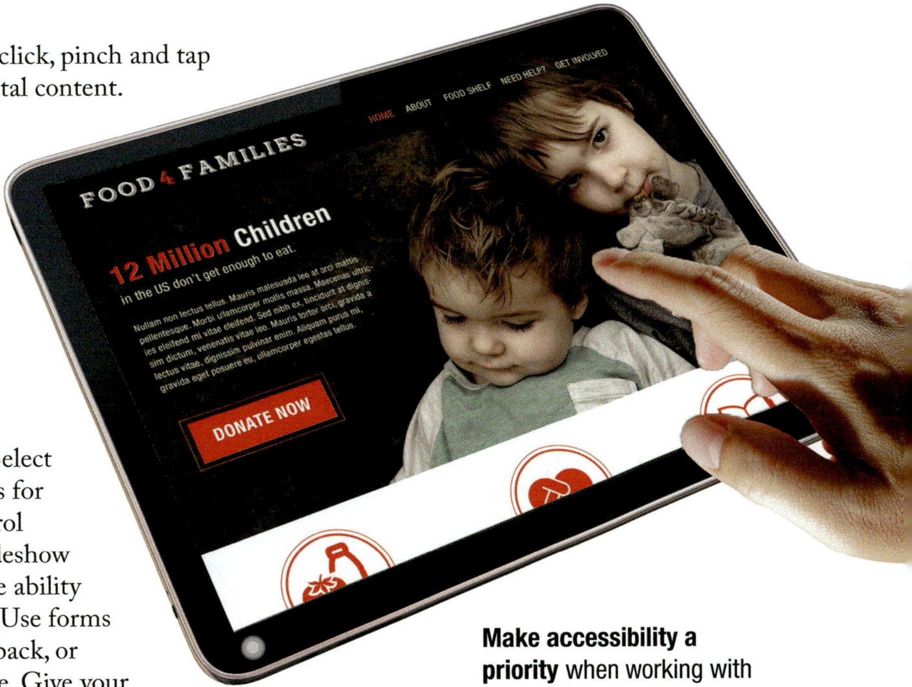

Make accessibility a priority when working with multimedia components. This website uses large, bold buttons and adjustable font sizes to make the site navigable for visually impaired visitors.

Third, restraint is a virtue, and user control is appreciated. One animated GIF in one paragraph is (arguably) cute. One in every paragraph is decidedly *not* cute. Select the right multimedia components for your purposes. Do give user control where appropriate (video and slideshow controls come to mind). Offer the ability to search and sort when you can. Use forms and commenting to capture feedback, or start a dialogue where appropriate. Give your visitor a multisensory experience, not sensory overload.

Finally, offering a multisensory experience is great. But be aware that not all users have the same abilities. From the outset, you should design not only multiple ways for your users to interact with your content but also alternative ways your users are able to access content. How will you accommodate, for example, the deaf community? Or folks with limited hand dexterity or the visually impaired? These are front-end planning issues.

Complex multimedia asset creation remains best left to professionals. However, simple multimedia production tools exist for the non-professional. Many are available for free online or come preinstalled on your computer or mobile device. Just know that not all mobile and tablet devices support all web-based applications and proceed accordingly.

A DESIGN SPEED BUMP

Hold up. Before you sit down at your computer to take that new video-editing software for a spin, remember to step away from the computer for planning.

Get the specs

Before you start creating assets, figure out which elements you can customize. Then find the correct specifications for those elements. Such specs include but are not limited to pixel-by-pixel dimensions, file size and file format. Social media sites, for example, have recommended resolution and pixel-by-pixel dimensions for avatars, logos, header images, post images and ad sizes. Video sharing sites might only accept video rendered in certain formats. And even though social media sites are forgiving about photo uploads (they tend to resize or crop your images to fit preset spaces), there might be limits on maximum file size. Design your asset to fit the specs. You don't want to spend 4 hours photo-editing your face on the body of a T-Rex to use as a background image only to discover your efforts unusable due to incorrect format or file size.

Finally, be aware that recommended sizes for all types of social media graphics seem to change every time the wind blows. Check for specification updates at the start of each new project.

Thumbnails, storyboards & site maps

If you are working on a complex custom project such as a clickable interactive commercial or a big online investigative story with text, photos, footage and interactive infographics, then you need more planning than just looking up specs. You'll need to brainstorm concept, design and organization.

Rough sketch some thumbnail layouts that imagine how all your content might go together. For slideshows, video and animation, use storyboarding techniques to nail beginnings, middles and ends, along with transitions, pacing and timing. And for multi-page web projects, site-map content relationships along with user flow via intuitive links and navigation.

Better yet, to maximize creative synergy, do the preliminary noodling with the whole team sitting in the same meeting—in which case you'll need the big whiteboard, virtual or face-to-face.

WORKING WITH IMAGES

In the attention-grabbing department, images win hands down. But still images are—you know—still. Turned into slideshows or placed in interactive image galleries, however, even still images become engaging multimedia components.

Sorting, cropping and editing photos need to happen before you begin assembling your slideshow or image gallery. We already covered the rules for dealing with photos in "Chapter 9: Adding Visual Appeal." Those best practices apply here. Plus, always work on a *copy* of the original photo; save and protect the original to be available for another day. Don't forget to optimize. Large image file sizes slow down page loads, so choose the best file format for your graphic. When possible try to keep the final file size less than 200K or better, 100K.

Image galleries. Free and inexpensive image gallery plug-ins exist for displaying your photos on websites and blogs. The masonry-style gallery above serves as a visual menu for a graphic design portfolio.

Captions, cutlines, descriptions & tags

Not all visuals require captioning. But news contexts probably do. In any case, captions, as well as image descriptions and tags, provide a place for keywords. And well-chosen keywords boost search engine rankings. We'll discuss this more in Chapter 13 on web design.

More importantly, captions, descriptions and "alt" tags are essential to web accessibility. Screen readers use them to channel site content to visitors with vision and hearing challenges.

In addition to having a narrative beginning, middle and end, three rules apply to captions: One, make the caption/cutline "go with" the image. Oh, yes, we have seen it go the other way. Two, don't state the obvious. A photo of a black dog doesn't need a cutline that reads, "This is a black dog." Instead, supplement the obvious, such as "Duke, a 6-year-old rescue lab/shepherd mix with exemplary manners, loves children." Three, do cover what's not obvious but relevant, such as a photo's Ws. Clearly identify who, what, when and where. And don't forget to fact-check and proof. Also be kind and credit the photographers.

Image galleries

Image galleries are common on websites. Some social media platforms are *nothing but* galleries of user-uploaded imagery. Galleries allow the user to scan many images at once; interactive galleries add sort and search capabilities to suit individual needs and interests. Such galleries

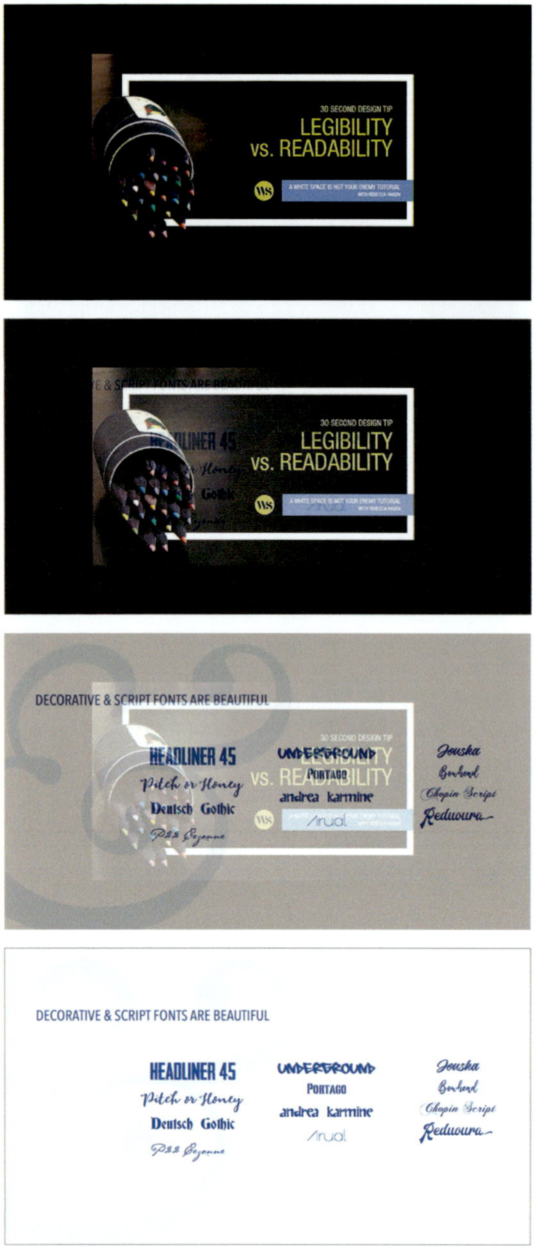

Smooth & steady. Slide transitions should not outshine your actual slides. Pick one simple transition style and stick with it. We recommend cross-dissolve (above) as opposed to exploding and twirling out of control.

Adobe Premier Rush CC screen shot(s) reprinted with permission from Adobe Systems Incorporated.

are adept at displaying creative portfolios, sharing organizational event photos and, of course, selling products.

Some photo-editing programs have the ability to generate web-ready image galleries from your selected images. All you have to do is upload the files to your web server.

Photo-sharing websites offer similar options. Signup is typically free, and once you have an account you upload your images. You can organize images into galleries and then put a link on your main website to your galleries. If you prefer to embed your galleries in your own website, photo-sharing sites offer plug-ins, widgets or code snippets that make this possible. Plug-ins and widgets allow photos stored on the photo-sharing site to display where you want them.

Slideshows

Slideshows have the visual impact of photos with the added bonus of eye-catching movement. Slides as entertainment date back to "magic lantern" shows of the 17th century. These entertainments featured images painted on glass slides and projected on a wall via a candle-powered lamp. Contemporary slide presentations include rotating images in website headers, mini digital slideshows embedded in websites and slide decks for business presentations. No lamps required.

Design tips for slideshows. Before you begin, consider the content of your images, along with transitions and user controls. For a simple set of images intended to add interest to a web banner or content area, choose quality images united by a theme (color, subject, etc.) with similar orientation.

Select compelling imagery. If the opening slide isn't interesting, visitors might not click through all your slides. Using compelling imagery and copy on the cover slide and throughout keeps viewers watching. Make your selections first, then crop, edit, resize, optimize and save to single folder before assembling your slideshow.

If you're providing information, make sure we can *read* the information. Slide captions deliver information about images, but beware readability issues. Design your slides with enough contrast for easy text readability. This example comes up short in this regard.

Telling a story? Use a storyboard. If your slideshow is intended to tell a story or includes a narrative, use a storyboard to organize the storyline and assist with image selection. Select quality photos with tight, medium and wide angles for variety.

Slide transitions. You have a ton of options, but simple is best. We recommend cuts and fades (cross-dissolve), and unless you have a clear design reason for doing so, use one transition type throughout.

Pacing. Whether slow and measured or fast and frenetic, the duration of your images and the speed of transitions set an overall tone for your slideshow. If you expect viewers to absorb and appreciate your slideshow content, give them enough time to do so.

To loop or not to loop. You can set a slideshow to loop continuously or a particular number of times before stopping. If your slideshow will be used as webpage header, then a subtle continuous loop might be appropriate. If your slideshow is intended to tell a story, letting it play through once is sufficient. Do provide user controls on story slideshows. Viewers appreciate access to buttons that start, stop, rewind, pause as well as adjust volume.

Would your story benefit from audio? Begin by assessing whether you have a story that supports both audio and visuals. Audio and photos should supplement and complement each other, the same as captions/cutlines. Time audio and visuals to "go with" each other. Use storyboards to maintain narrative continuity.

Tools for recording audio are easy to come by and easy to use. Most slideshow programs allow audio recording as part of the application. If you are recording audio separately, edit and save your audio track before adding it to your slideshow. Remember that a 2-minute audio slideshow begins to stretch the limit of user tolerance, so don't ramble. Keep your storytelling compact.

Slideshows are a simple way to tell concise, effective stories with audio and visuals. But if you want more from sound and pictures let's talk about video.

VIDEO CLIPS

Video runs the gamut from carefully orchestrated multiple-camera commercials to cell-phone-recorded clips posted on video-sharing websites. In between the complex and the amateur, video types include interviews and monologues, short events and activity clips, tutorials and others.

Simple video-editing software is as commonplace as slideshow-making tools, and non-professionals can create good quality clips.

WORKING WITH AUDIO

Audio might seem off-topic in a discussion about visual communication. But audio plays a role in multimedia. Audio is the narration or natural (nat) or ambient (ambi) sound on captured video. It's the background track or bed in web and DVD projects. Short audio clips as sound effects or SFX signal action, such as the sound of a button being pressed or email being sent. Audio can highlight what's important. It also reinforces tone and mood.

Back in the heyday of radio, great audio was "theater of the mind." That continues to be the way you should think about audio production. But if you find yourself unable to enlist an audio pro, stick to the basics. In general:

1. Use ambient audio sparingly, especially for trigger sounds like button clicks. A little goes a long way.
2. Background music should enhance the overall tone and message of the project. It should not be expected to set the tone by itself.
3. Give your user controls, preferably start, stop, pause and volume. We've all been blown out of our chairs by a web soundtrack that was a big surprise, too loud or both.
4. When the audio is narration, an interview or some other situation where clarity is crucial, capture the highest quality audio possible. Use the best microphone you can—which might not be the one on your digital recorder, video camera or smart phone. Your audience is more likely to forgive a poor quality image than an inaudible soundtrack.

Can you hear it? Audio is a powerful multimedia component. Try to imagine the sounds that would accompany this image.

Where to get audio

Ambient sounds and music as well as trigger sounds like button clicks are available for purchase from digital stock sites. Many websites offer free sounds and music. Be aware, however, that free downloads might come with restrictions or attribution requirements. Make sure you respect both.

You don't *design* video, you compose, shoot and edit it, although in some cases it might be art-directed. Like shooting photography, if the stakes are high, shooting video and film is best left to professionals. Nevertheless, if it's you or *nada,* follow these shooting and editing tips for beginners:

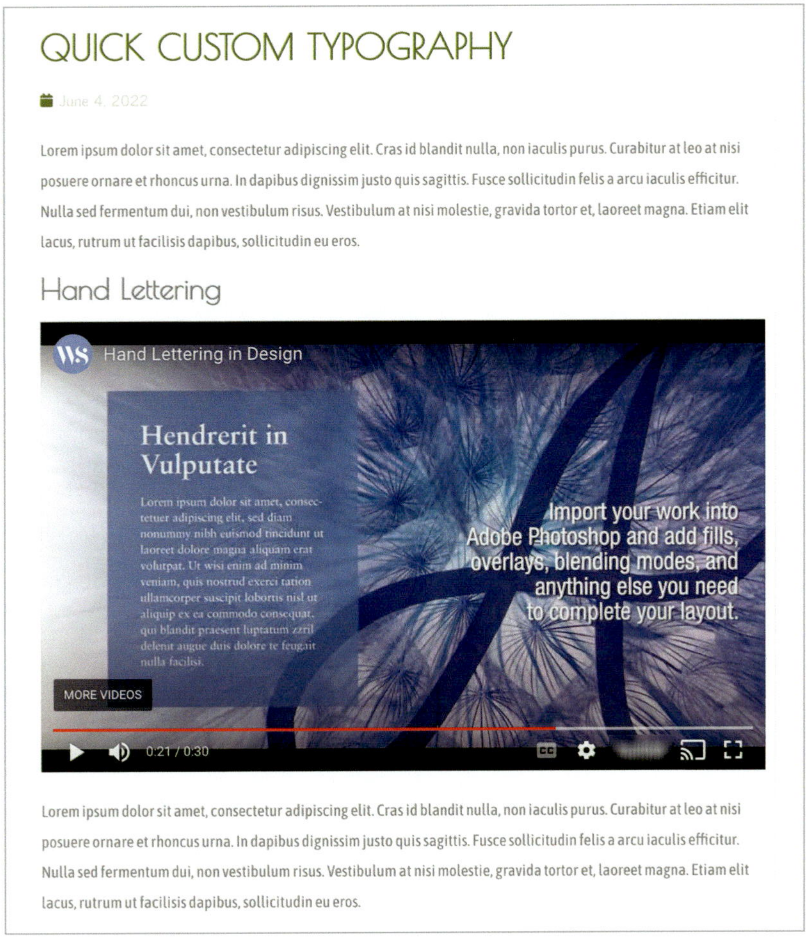

In control. If your project includes video and audio clips, give your audience access to the controls where appropriate. At the very least, provide volume control and start and stop buttons.

Choose landscape, portrait or square

Now that video cameras are standard equipment on smart phones, everyone is a videographer. Unlike traditional video cameras, smart phones can shoot vertically as well as horizontally. Choose your orientation based on your end usage. Consider:

» Horizontal formats are the most familiar. Since human vision tracks horizontally (think peripheral vision), horizontal video feels more natural. This makes it a better choice for longer videos.

» Professional videographers shoot horizontal video. People filming themselves for social media posts often shoot vertical. If you want your video to look professional, shoot like a professional.

» Social media is more friendly towards vertical and square video, so if your end destination is social media, consider using vertical or square videos there.

» Not all video players support vertical video. Check specs before loading or your viewers might find themselves watching your video sideways.

» When in doubt, shoot horizontal. It's easier to crop a horizontal video to vertical or square than the other way around. Even better, frame your horizontal video with the ability to crop as needed.

Portrait or landscape? Smart phone cameras shoot both vertically and horizontally. Choose orientation based on your end usage. When in doubt, shoot horizontal. Your videos look more professional in landscape orientation.

That means keeping important subject matter closer to the center of the frame and leaving "margins" of less important content to the sides.

General shooting tips:

- Steady your camera with a tripod or other solid surface. Camera shake gets very old very quickly.
- Shoot in a location with bright, even lighting. Avoid harsh high-contrast lighting and backlighting, along with what you might believe are special lighting effects.
- When possible, shoot some test footage to check blocking, sound and light.
- Shoot more video than you think you'll need, at least 10–15 seconds for each shot you want to capture. You can always cut extra material, but you can't magically insert file footage no one ever shot. (B roll is file, secondary or archival footage used as visual fill or for creating transitions between clips.)
- Capture a variety of angles for each scene: tight close-up, medium, full, wide and long. Think about establishing shots versus detail/ beauty shots.
- Avoid zooming and panning. Cutting from scene to scene is actually more natural.
- Compose your shots. Use the rule of thirds as your guide and place your focal point accordingly.

» Don't talk while shooting. The microphone might pick up your voice. Heavy breathers off-screen can be a problem, too.

When shooting interviews & monologues (talking heads):

» Shoot in a quiet location.

» Select your talking head wisely. Not everyone appears interesting and engaging (or articulate) on-camera.

» Test footage… Better safe than sorry.

When editing video:

» Begin with the best quality video possible, i.e., uncompressed raw footage.

» Make sure you have good usable audio, too. "Audio is half the picture," as they say.

» Select simple transitions—cuts and fades. Pick one transition style and stick to it. Attention should be on the video, not on the transitions.

» Try to keep overall video duration short. In multimedia contexts, viewers can drop out in seconds, and most casual online video viewers only hang around for 2–3 minutes.

» Don't forget title and credit slides (if needed) and a poster frame. A poster frame is an image that serves as the icon for your final video. A poster frame can be a still image captured from the video or a graphic created in another program. Title slides and poster frames are excellent opportunities for branding. If your final video is being shared on a video-sharing site, create a final frame with links to your other videos you've posted to generate website traffic.

» When adding text to slides, style for contrast and readability. Heavier sans serif fonts at larger sizes generally work well. Make sure to keep all text within the title-safe boundary.

Microphones are more sensitive than you think. If you don't want the sounds of the kids, the pets or Uncle Eddie and his bag of potato chips to be part of your audio track, make sure you clear the room before you start recording.

Video encoding

After editing, encoding is the next step in making a video. Many file formats exist, and choosing the right one takes a little research. Video-sharing sites, for example, often post file size and format requirements. Meanwhile, different software and hardware brands peddle their unique file formats.

When choosing a file format, try to avoid those that are exclusive to particular devices, platforms or software applications. You want your video to be viewable by the greatest number of people. MPEG-4 (Motion Pictures Expert Group), or MP4 for short, is the most popular video file format for the web (at the time of this printing, anyway). MP4 is friendly across platforms and supported by the most popular web browsers.

In addition to file format, you'll also need to pay attention to aspect ratio, which refers to screen frame proportions, and final file size, which also includes modes of compression. Video files are huge and must be compressed before packed into files for transport. So compression and file size matter not only for uploading and downloading but also for storage space. Wherever your video is being housed or hosted, once again, a few minutes' research on the specs can save your—ahem—"project" at deadline time. Stay within uploading parameters. Quick downloading is critical, too, if you want your viewer to stay tuned long enough to see your clip.

That's all folks! Title slides and poster frames are excellent opportunities for branding. If your final video is being shared on a video-sharing site, create a final frame with links to your other videos you've posted to generate website traffic.

Adobe Premier Rush CC screen shot(s) reprinted with permission from Adobe Systems Incorporated.

Speaking of viewers, don't forget they need access to a video player of some sort for viewing. Fortunately, most modern browsers support common video formats. And if you come across a format your browser does not support, plug-ins are generally free and easy to find and install.

An excellent way to bypass many browser and video format incompatibilities is to post your video on a video-sharing site. Most video-sharing sites will provide a bit of code allowing you to embed the clip on your own

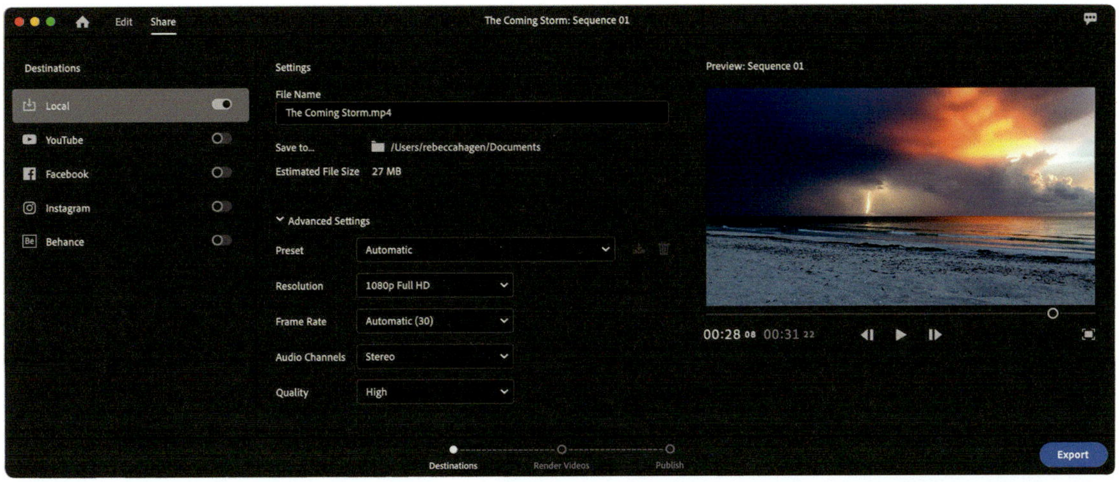

website. A minor drawback of this method is that the video-sharing site might require you to include its branding on your video clip.

Once viewers find your video, waiting for the whole clip to download, as in "progressive" video delivery, can be a real drag unless the clip is short and sweet. "Streaming" video is advisable for longer videos. But you would hire professionals for those longer videos anyway.

Shooting & editing video not your bag?

The same sites that offer stock images also offer stock video clips. Stock might not work for your situation. But if using stock saves time and money, check it out.

ANIMATION

Animation is having a moment. Once a form of entertainment for children, animation is everywhere from expressive avatars on your smart phone to spectacular CGI effects in blockbuster movies. Even the lowly animated GIF (anyone remember the mailbox GIF announcing that "you have mail"?) has returned, and is often found punctuating segments of blog posts.

It's about time

Interestingly, *time,* not motion, differentiates animation from other graphics. Elements appear, disappear and change shape at different points along a timeline. Pacing and transitions aren't issues when designing for print or even when designing static websites. But in animation and video, pacing and transitioning impact the overall feel,

File formats for video. MP4 remains a popular format for video destined for the web. Look for it in your video application export or share settings.

Adobe Premier Rush CC screen shot(s) reprinted with permission from Adobe Systems Incorporated.

Twice the motion. This animated title sequence drops in and unfolds one letter at a time as the video rolls in the background.

Adobe AfterEffects CC screen shot(s) reprinted with permission from Adobe Systems Incorporated.

thus message, of the piece. A quick pace and sharp transitions give intensity and edge. Subtle, gradual changes are more soothing.

We're way beyond mice, anvils & flying toasters

Things have changed greatly since a certain mouse piloted a steamboat back in 1928. And yet, animation still works on the same principle as the original hand-drawn version. A series of images, each one slightly different from the last, is flashed in rapid succession giving the illusion of movement. Where traditional animators drew 30 images to create 1 second of animation, today computers do the heavy lifting.

A testament to the growth of the medium, the animation field now includes several specialties including 3D computer, 2D vector-based, stop motion, traditional animation and motion graphics (moving text, logos and basic illustrations). The forms range in complexity. Animation used to create full-length feature films and found in sophisticated interactive websites remains the bailiwick of highly skilled pros. More accessible animation, such as transitioning in presentation slides, is generated by the presentation program itself. Since designing highly complex forms of animation is outside the scope of this book, we focus primarily on motion graphics.

If you're inclined to try your hand at motion graphics, affordable programs and courses are out there. The learning curve for animation software is steeper than most but not insurmountable. The average person can create simple animated logos, video title sequences, banner ads and animated website

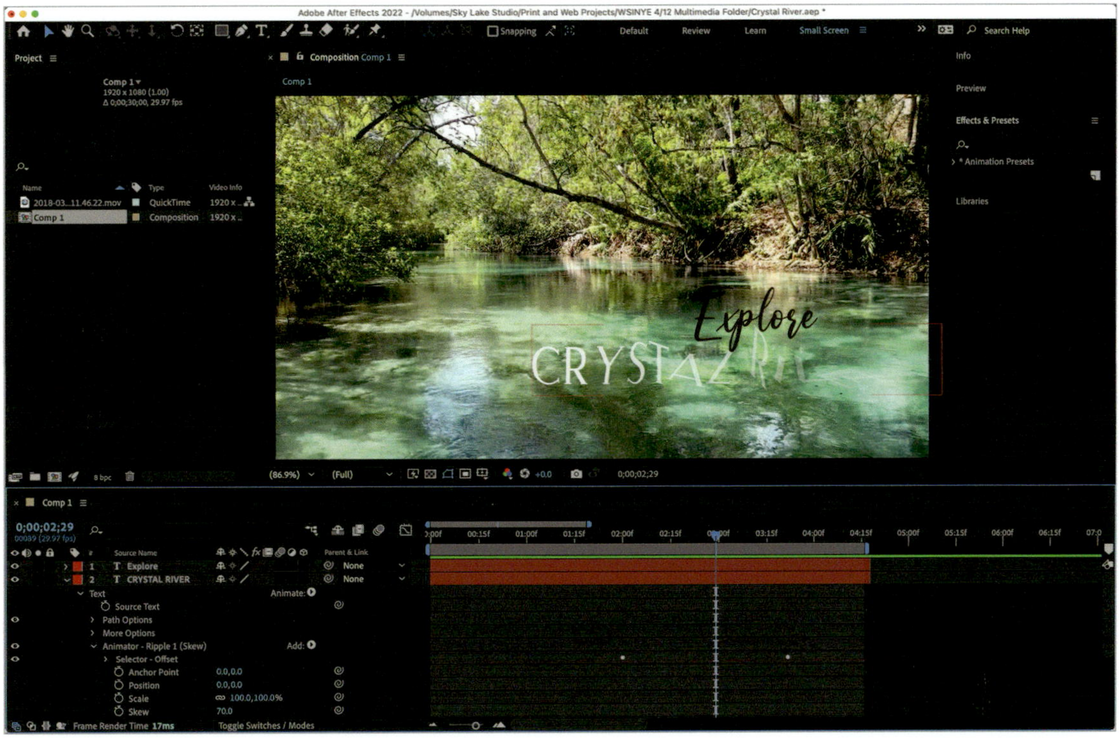

Space & Time. In animation, objects move through space over time. Animation programs include a timeline, seen here. "Events" happen at points along the timeline. In this screen grab, the gray bars represent the duration of the animation. The inverted blue triangle and faint line indicate "you are here" in the sequence. The preview window shows what the animation looks like at a given point in the animated sequence.

Adobe AfterEffects CC screen shot(s) reprinted with permission from Adobe Systems Incorporated.

components without an advanced degree in motion design.

That said, when quality is crucial and the project is important, hire a professional animator. You won't be sorry.

When to use animation

Well-executed, well-placed animation can be a communications powerhouse. Use it when you want to:

Capture attention. Even a small amount of movement captures attention, so use it where you want to draw the eye. Animation draws the eye to web and social media advertising, the start of the layout (animated headers, banners and hero images) and important content (calls-to-action, buttons, pull-quotes) within the layout.

Direct eye movement. Objects proceeding along a path of motion draw the viewer's eye along that path toward your selected destination. Remember that movement is one of the principles of well-composed design. With animation, movement is literal.

Enhance understanding. Adding animation to infographics can enhance viewer understanding. Think adding a row of animated arrows to a proposed traffic flow map. Animations added to buttons on hover, on click or after completion of an action (like sending a form) help users understand that they successfully completed a desired task.

Set a tone. And, as noted earlier in this chapter, purposeful pacing, transitions and even animation style evoke emotion. Is the style of animation grungy, vintage, anime, highly complex or super simple? Do the colors evoke response? Is the pacing slow and deliberate or rapid and intense?

Lottie animations. Lottie files, named for Charlotte Reiniger, a German pioneer of silhouette animation, are high-quality, scalable animations with small file sizes due to their JSON (JavaScript Object Notation) file format. Excellent for web use due to their fast load times, Lottie files can be found online for purchase or for free. See this animation in action on the White Space website: https://whitespacedesignbook.com.

Animation by Annie Theriault, lottiefiles.com.

Keep in mind that restraint is a good thing. Adding a little animation to a layout can help break through all the visual clutter viewers suffer every day. But don't let your animation add to visual clutter. Use animation with a purpose. Don't use animation just for the sake of using it.

Where do I get animation files?

Add animation files to the list of graphics available on stock sites. Alternatively, you can build your own animations using online animation tools, though be aware that some of these tools are subscription-based. As always, pay attention to file formats and image quality. You get what you pay for, and no animation is better than crappy animation.

Motion graphic animations, such as video title slides and website button actions, come built into many layout applications. Smart phones come with animated emojis, avatars and animated GIFs. All you have to do is plug, play and hit "send."

Tips for creating motion graphics

As always, we recommend planning first, computer second. Begin with brainstorming and sketching. Collect specifications required for your end usage including file size, format and duration. The longer and more complex the animation, the greater the file size. So be aware of file size limitations—server, application or project-imposed.

Use storyboards to plan your animation. Arrows and other directional devices can signal the movements along with the relationships of shapes and type. Each sketch on the storyboard can describe the contents of a key frame, as well as—uh-huh—audio.

Assemble & organize your assets. Experienced animators recommend that you assemble all project assets before you start, and organize the content in folders. Even seemingly simple animations can have multiple moving parts, so create folders for images, video clips, logos, illustrations, music and audio files. Keep them in the same folder as your main project file. You will thank yourself later when you don't have to spend 45 minutes trying to find a missing logo while on deadline.

Design considerations. Motion graphics are graphics like any other, so anything you learned in "Chapter 5: Mini Art School" applies here. However, we now add time and literal movement to the design pot. In addition to practicing good composition techniques, be sure to:

Animate like you're telling a story. Good stories have a beginning, a peak of action and a conclusion, so give your animation an opening, a highlight and a resolution. And remember to keep all types of movement on-brand.

Keep it simple. Too many flying, swirling, twirling, blinking, bouncing or flashing elements are just sensory overload. Not to mention potentially seizure-inducing. No joke. Remember that when everything is moving, nothing stands out.

Keep it short. Always assume your audience is busy, bored or in a hurry. Don't belabor your visual point longer than necessary. That is, unless you expect us to read copy, in which case you need to hold content onscreen long enough for us to do so.

Keep text readable & legible. The things you learned in Chapter 7 on type also apply here. Choose fonts for their style and feel, but also for screen legibility. Sans serif fonts are almost always going to be good choices. Create

Animating logos. Animating logos requires brand consistency in color, font and shape, but also motion and sound. Exuberant motion and music are better suited to athletic logos than public library logos.

Make your own app. Anyone can build a simple app using an online app-builder. We discuss designing interfaces in Chapter 13.

background contrast with color and value. Consider blurring image and video backgrounds for better text legibility.

Stay on brand/message. Like other branded graphics, motion graphics use carefully curated color, fonts, shapes and imagery to convey information about the organization. But motion graphics also convey information through the *behavior* of graphic elements. Consider a logo for a children's party planner. An on-brand appropriate animation behavior might involve transforming the wordmark into a set of balloons that float off the top of the screen. The tone of the animation changes greatly if, instead of floating, the balloons pop with a bang or speed around losing air making rude noises.

Branding applies to audio, too. Short single sounds, single or multiple musical notes, music clips or ambient sound can register as everything from cheerful to ominous and everything in between. Choose sound that supports your message and employ with restraint. Consider pairing the occurrence of sound with the movement on screen. The Versare logo animation on the previous page triggers a "click" sound when the quotation mark finally drops into its final position.

"Easing" does it. Easing is an effect that makes objects in motion slow a bit before coming to a stop. It lends a more natural feel to the motion and makes the animation look professional. Easing and other advanced techniques are worth learning. We recommend additional reading on the subject.

Final words of advice

Make your decision to use animation a conscious one that serves the objective of your project. Use restraint. And setting GIFs to infinitely loop is obnoxious.

APPS & PLUG-INS & WIDGETS, OH MY!

Perhaps the most exciting thing about multimedia is the opportunity it provides to engage the audience fully. For advertisers, interactivity is a luxury only dreamed of just a generation ago. Each element we've discussed thus far allows for some interactivity, be it the pause, play and volume controls on a video clip or the ability to browse photos in an online photo gallery. And don't forget the banner ad's click-through (cha-ching).

Fortunately, you don't need to be a web or application developer to include interactive multimedia components in your screen layouts. Plug-ins, widgets and apps make it possible for non-developers to add a wide range of interactive components with ease.

Applications (Apps)

Applications, commonly referred to as "apps," are programs designed to run on a computer, tablet, smart phone, website or social media site. Large complex applications such as word-processing programs have been available on computers for decades. Since the introduction of smart phones and tablets, professional and amateur programmers have been adding to the slate of apps for those devices, too. Some common examples of apps include calendars, mileage trackers, restaurant finders and, of course, games.

Some companies and organizations build custom apps to supplement websites. This makes sense as interaction with the smaller touchscreens of handheld devices is different from that of websites. A specifically designed app can provide the smart phone or tablet owner with a much better user experience.

Building highly complex "native" apps (apps built for specific operating systems and sold in app stores) is still largely the realm of professional designers and developers. However, you can find do-it-yourself app-building programs online. Anyone can create a simple app, such as a walking tour of an historic neighborhood, with minimal or no knowledge of code.

Plug-ins & widgets

A plug-in is code that gives a browser or website additional functionality. For example, when a website automatically

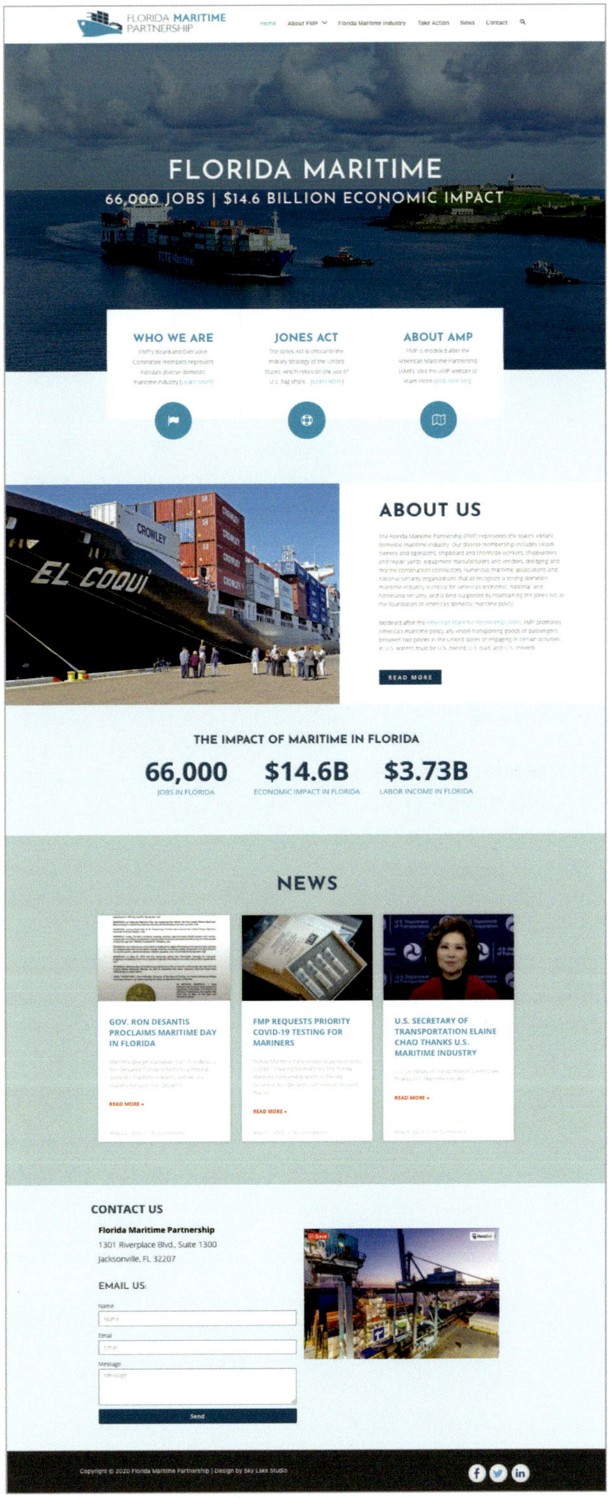

Widgets for functionality. The Florida Maritime Partnership website uses a page-builder plug-in with widgets for an animated counter, news feed and contact form.

Reproduced by permission of Tucker/Hall and the Florida Maritime Partnership.

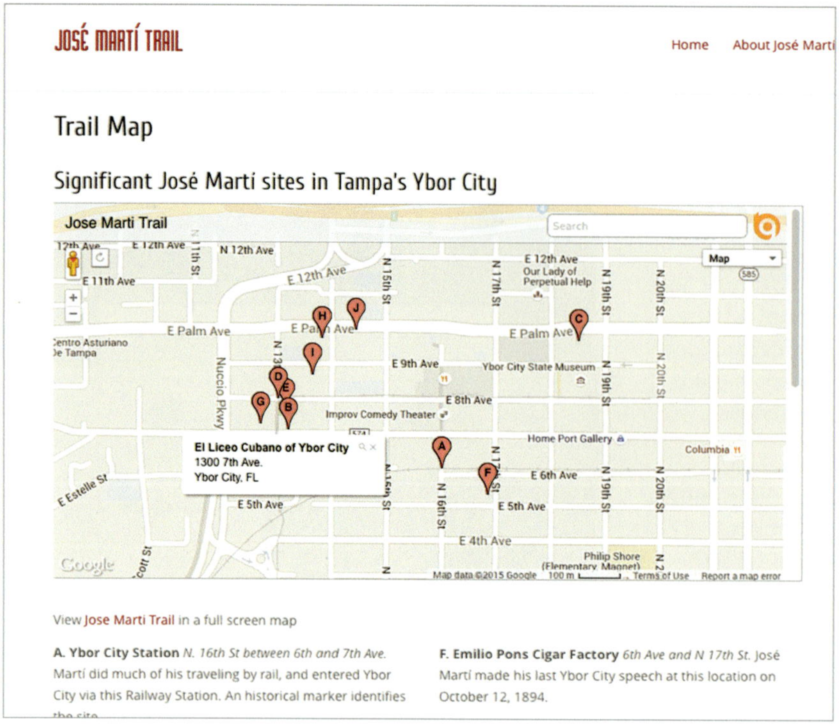

Interactive map widget. This interactive map of locations on the José Martí Trail was generated by a free online map-generating service. A snippet of code provided by the service then embedded in the website creates a live map with clickable pins.

displays the most recent posts from a separate blog, a plug-in is at work.

Available plug-ins can do everything from filtering spam or viruses to allowing game playing or viewing different media types. They are easily added to sites or browsers via an installation program or by copying and pasting code in the right location.

Plug-ins commonly work behind the scenes and often are invisible on the front end. However, if a plug-in requires input from a user, or needs to physically display some sort of content on a page, then a widget is needed.

While the terms plug-in and widget are often used interchangeably, they are two different things. Widgets are the visible expression of the existence of a plug-in. For example, imagine you want to measure social media activity on a specific page and display the results in a sidebar. An installed plug-in will track the activity, but the widget is what displays the results. Widgets are also required to gather user input, as in online forms. All widgets require a plug-in, but not all plug-ins have a widget.

Widgets can display local weather, list upcoming events, play video and slideshows and even map the nearest pizza places.

The availability of thousands of plug-ins and widgets exponentially increases your ability to add interactivity to your projects.

Where do I get plug-ins, widgets & apps?

The short answer: Search online. Most plug-in or widget code can be had for free or for minimal cost. Often all that is required is a code cut-and-paste. Oh, and sometimes a credit to the developer is needed, too. Don't forget to check, and provide credit where credit is due.

When searching for and installing plug-ins and widgets, pay attention to online reviews. Since these mini programs can be created by anyone, quality is all over the board. Some are not regularly updated. And many are not "supported," meaning if something goes wonky, you're on your own to fix it.

Another thing to look for is whether a plug-in or widget comes with an editable Cascading Style Sheet (CSS). Style sheets dictate the way design features like fonts and colors display onscreen. If you can access a style sheet, you can tweak the appearance of a plug-in to better match your overall layout.

As mentioned, apps tend to be more complex, and building them requires the skills of a developer. However, if your organization needs a strong unique presence on tablets or smart phones, hiring a developer to create a custom app might be worth the investment.

DIGITAL STORYTELLING

The most recent iteration of the slideshow is digital storytelling. Digital storytelling tools, usually in the form of an app or an online builder, allow you to create a media form that is a cross between a single-page website and a slide presentation deck. Using these tools, you can pair images, video, audio, transitions and animation with narrative to create a full multi-sensory experience.

For the end user, scrolling down the page (some call this type of design "scrollytelling"), reveals text and triggers both animations and transitions. The more you scroll, the more story appears. The final story can be shared via URL or embedded in social media or webpages.

Digital storytelling lends itself particularly well to conveying stories with emotional and experiential impact. Such stories might

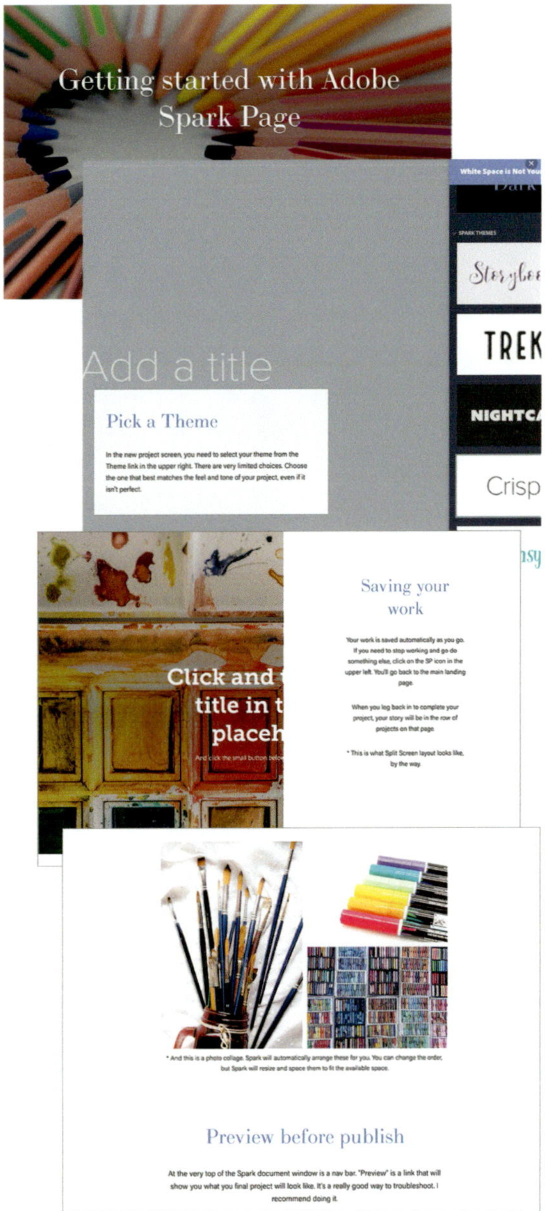

Quick, compact & compelling. Digital storytelling tools marry traditional linear slides with the rich media capabilities of single-page websites. Rebecca created this set of instructions using an online digital storytelling application.

Adobe Express screen shot(s) reprinted with permission from Adobe Systems Incorporated.

SOCIAL MEDIA ETHICS FOR VISUAL COMMUNICATORS

Social media represent an ethical obstacle course for visual communicators. It doesn't help that the speed with which we communicate often preempts clear-headed decision-making about posting and reposting combinations of visuals and type. The advice below on professional ethics could help you avoid tripping over your professional social media.

Transparent doesn't just mean see-through. Disclose your sponsors, particularly when you receive compensation for your reviews. This blog post begins with a disclaimer and offers a link to a full advertising disclosure policy.

Know your code. Your professional association's code of ethics stands as your backstop for ethical conduct on social media. If you're not familiar with it, introduce yourself.

Do no harm. Posting on social media can harm the reputations of not only disreputable public figures but also innocent private citizens. Beyond libel and slander, the spectrum of possible harms is long and growing from inviting individual harassment to inciting mass violence, not to mention willfully deceiving and defrauding. The best way to avoid harm? Stick to facts and the truth.

Defend truth & fairness. And respect. And civility. Go back to the communicator's ethical basics: Is the image or information truthful, an accurate representation of fact? Is it fair to and respectful of the parties involved? The answer should be yes to all of the above.

Respect ownership. If you don't have the owner's permission to use an image, then don't. Even if someone else already posted it without permission, you still need permission. Beyond ethics, you could find yourself in legal trouble if you don't respect others' property. We covered this in Chapter 9 on photos.

Don't be a manipulator. And don't be manipulated into sharing deepfakes, which are visuals altered to fool people. Here we're mostly but not exclusively referring to altered photos meant to represent objective reality. Educate yourself on the varieties of image fakery, from splicing and resampling to blurring, cropping and retouching—all the things you can do with photo-editing software. Learn how to spot inconsistencies in such forgeries to avoid passing them on. Revisit Chapter 9 on the ethics of shooting and editing images, as well as Chapter 10 on the ethics of manipulating visual information such as infographics.

Disclose your sponsors. Who influences the social media influencers? That would be the folks paying for your good opinion, i.e., sponsors, advertisers and employers. And maybe family members who benefit from your endorsement. Best practices require transparency. You are ethically bound to be forthcoming about financial and filial relationships influencing what you post in professional contexts. The U.S. Federal Trade Commission agrees.

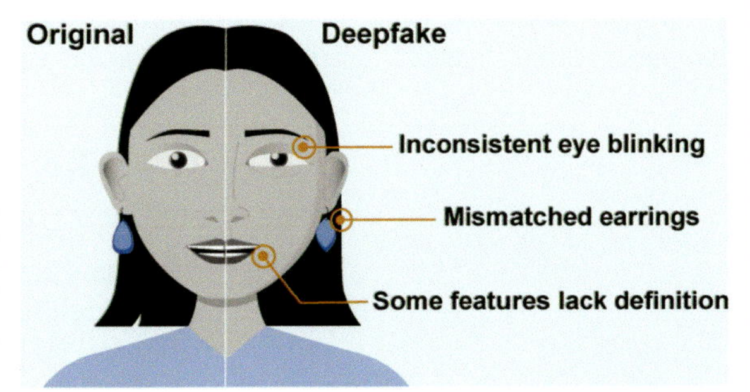

Anonymous (re)posting is not truthful. If it's anonymous, you should be suspicious. Follow the money. Scrutinize your sources, corroborate them, and attribute your information. Don't be guilty of purveying falsehoods and half-truths. Anonymity is only ethical when a journalist is protecting a whistleblowing source.

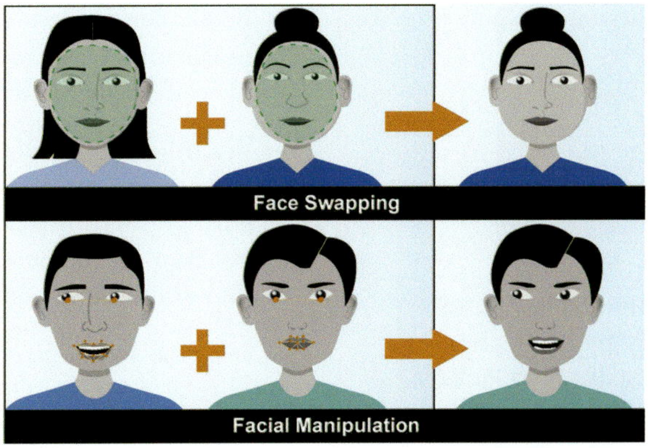

Protect people's privacy. Privacy protection is not just about data breaches, although there is that. On social media, you have a responsibility to know the difference between public information suitable for broadcasting and individuals' private information that you have no right to share.

Fact-check & correct. Fact-checking is not as routine as it once was and still ought to be. You can avoid a lot of trouble by checking your facts before you blast them through your digital bullhorn. On the other hand, no one is perfect. If you make a mistake, own it. Publish the correction. Be generous with apologies.

Curate & moderate. Be thoughtful about what you post to protect your credibility and avoid harm to others. Be a good moderator, as well, in facilitating the exchange of ideas. Expressing divergent opinions can be civil. Be courteous beyond reproach, even when you vehemently disagree on righteous principle.

Defer to the policy. If your organization doesn't have a social media policy, then it's on you to get one. Write a policy that lays out the rules. Update the policy when new concerns arise.

The socially responsible visual communicator will be guided by professional ethics. But even that standard might not be high enough. Our advice is to ask yourself whether it's going to keep you up at night or if it's likely to come back to haunt you.

Learn to spot the deepfakes. This pair of infographics from the U.S. Government Accountability Office provides tips on identifying deepfake videos and images.

Illustrations courtesy of the U.S. Government Accountability Office, gao.gov include public affairs issues, environmental issues, human interest stories and social justice topics.

MULTIMEDIA JOURNALISM

Multimedia journalism has a lot in common with digital storytelling. But think of multimedia journalism as a more sophisticated version of digital storytelling. It utilizes many of the same digital assets, but expands storytelling beyond linear presentation. A multimedia story includes several segments, and each segment explores a *different* aspect of a story using the media best suited to the telling. Media forms include text, image, video, audio, motion graphics and infographics. The result is interactive, immersive, in-depth reporting of stories that readers can explore in a nonlinear fashion.

Traditionally, journalists published these extended reporting efforts in special sections of the newspaper. A main story anchored the piece, with photos, infographics and smaller related stories rounding out the package. When newspapers went online, journalists adopted the new digital tools and added them to the mix.

Multimedia stories (image opposite). Traditional multimedia stories appeared in print newspapers and magazines where infographics and photography enhanced storytelling capabilities. When news delivery spread to websites, other forms of digital interaction such as video, audio and animation became essential parts of the storytelling toolbox.

Imagine an online multimedia story devoted to the human heart. The centerpiece might be a high-end 3D animation of the inner workings of the heart providing something like a virtual ride through the pulmonary system. We could enhance the online experience with sound effects and narration.

Other interactive features and links would layer additional information. Users might click to learn more about platelets, heart chambers, red blood cells, etc., or even how to read an electrocardiogram (EKG) or become a cardiologist. Users might take a quiz to test their knowledge of or calculate their risks for heart disease. Maybe users entertain themselves competing in a heart health game that pits exercise and eating habits against genetics. How about chatting in real time with a medical expert? Anyone want to upload personal stories, share medical resources or add data to a map? You get the idea.

Multimedia storytelling is not limited to journalists. Any public or private sector organization can leverage the power of multimedia storytelling for their own communications purposes. What *is* required is a team of professionals skilled in writing, research, photography, illustration, motion graphics and infographic design. It also requires research, planning and a battery of thumbnail sketches, storyboards, site maps and wireframes. True multimedia stories can take months to bring to fruition.

Should you find yourself part of a team creating an interactive multimedia experience, here are some things to consider:

- » Not every story or subject lends itself to full multimedia treatment. Make sure you have a deep, interesting and multifaceted topic to work with.
- » Choose the best multimedia elements for your particular content. If you don't have a good candidate for a talking-head expert or spokesperson, don't plan to include a video interview. Do consider all your media options, including infographics.
- » Elect one medium to tell the main story, and let the other media play supporting roles. Think in terms of creating a content focal point.
- » Decide on an overall look and feel. Then choose design elements that support that look and feel.
- » Make the interface intuitive. Make buttons look like buttons, and make them easy to find and use. Same goes for links.

» Don't let the technology get in the way of the information or the story. The technology should be "invisible" to the user.

New technologies can and do inspire designers and visual communicators. But there's an old aphorism about the shortsightedness of designing the whole living room around the coffee table.

TRY THIS

1. Research a few social media sites. Find out what types of assets you can upload and determine the correct file sizes and formats. Prepare and optimize graphics for three different social media site headers/banners that reflect your personality.
2. Visit the website of a large news organization. Look for examples of multimedia storytelling. Which multimedia elements are employed? Write a brief critique.
3. Locate some simple logos or design one yourself. Storyboard three options for animating your favorite. Render your best sketch using the animation tool of your choice.
4. Find a website or online magazine that accepts animated banner ads. What are the specs and requirements for file size, format, duration, etc.? Spend some time exploring the animated banner ads on this site. What animation techniques are being used?
5. Visit a site that sells video and audio clips or animations. What formats do they come in? What styles and genres are available? Find some clips you like. Brainstorm ways of using them in a website and create a wireframe demonstrating your ideas.
6. Produce a digital story that documents reality. Story ideas to consider include a visual oral history of your oldest living family member, the status of adoptions at your local animal shelter or the hidden story of a nearby nature preserve. Maybe attending and documenting a public event, such as a quilt show, or a political rally is more your speed.

CHAPTER 13

DESIGNING FOR THE WEB

STARRING ON THE SMALL SCREEN

Technological innovation has long driven design adaptation. But in recent decades, the internet has been steering the innovation steamroller.

If you choose a communications career, working with websites to capture attention, control eye flow, convey information and evoke emotion is a given. But web design departs from graphic design in substantial ways. Unlike print, websites are nonlinear and dynamic. Their designs must adapt across screen sizes and orientations. Website success depends on effective interface design as well as novel content in a variety of media. The design process—planning, sketching, prototyping and testing—is more technical, too. It really does take a village.

Not your parent's website design. Today's websites must adapt across screen sizes and orientations. Over 60% of website traffic comes from mobile devices.

Raymond James Gasparilla Festival of the Arts website reproduced by permission of Gasparilla Festival of the Arts, Inc. and Raymond James Financial, Inc.

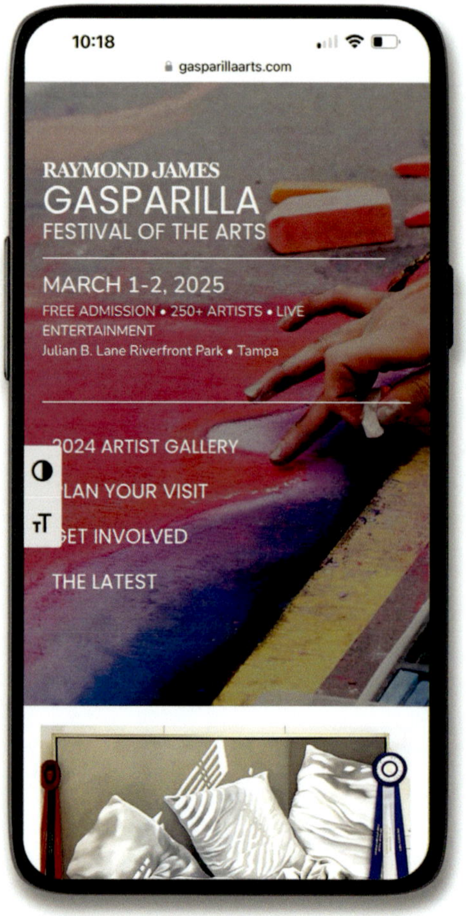

Bear with us as we lean into the wonk in this culminating chapter. Let's begin with some ways you might work with websites:

Working with an existing website. Sooner rather than later you'll need to update text and images on a site that already exists. You might provide content to a web administrator who loads updates for you. Handing your assets to the expert to upload is a good idea if your site was custom-coded by a third-party design/development team.

If you can make your own changes, a Content Management System (CMS) is likely under the hood of your site. A CMS is an internet-based site-building and management application that dynamically generates pages from a database. With a CMS, you upload content such as text, image and video to the database via a word processing-like interface. Although no coding is required to use a CMS, do yourself a solid by acquiring basic knowledge of Hypertext Markup Language (HTML) and Cascading Style Sheets (CSS).

Creating a site using a website builder. A website builder is a subscription-based online tool for creating websites using preset templates. Once you set up your account, a "wizard" (an interface guiding users step by step) takes you through the setup process, including selecting your template. The template establishes page structure, content areas, colors and font choices for the site. You just add content to the spaces provided; no coding is needed.

Is this a cheap, fast way to launch a website? Yes. Is it flawless? Not even close. Website builder interfaces are not always as easy to use as advertised. Available templates can be limiting. You might be out of luck if you want a special countdown feature or a specific display for team member bios but your template doesn't offer it.

Before going the website builder route, research the service and available templates. If you find the features you need and a design you love all in one template, then by all means, proceed. If you prefer more control over your site design, consider CMS tools, or hire a professional designer.

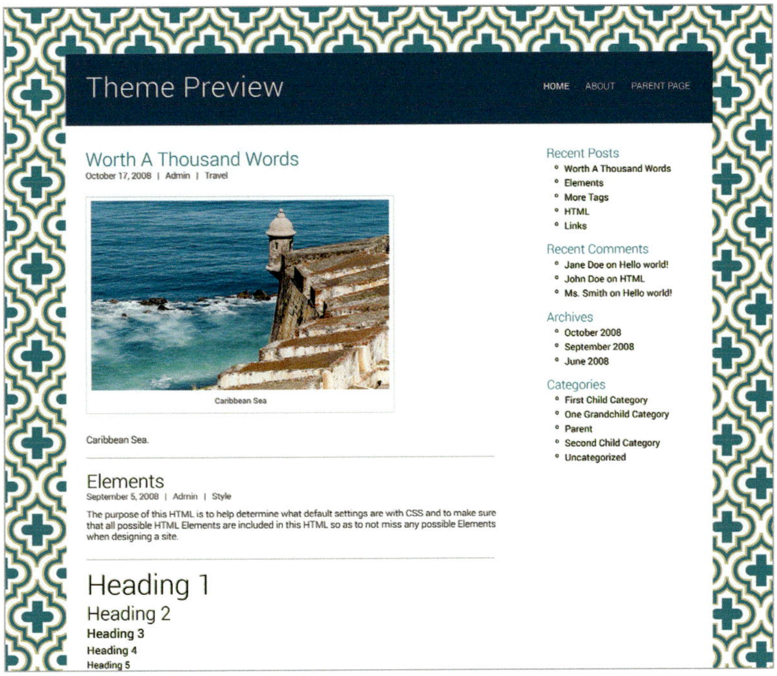

Building a site using a CMS. Content Management Systems are available via cloud-based subscriptions or software you can install onto your own hosting. CMS sites are built using a set of files that generate individual page parts, such as headers, footers and content areas.

A "theme" delivers a packaged set of files that once installed dictate how the parts go together and what they look like once assembled. Most themes are highly editable, and many have simple no-coding-experience-needed interfaces that let you make changes. At a minimum, themes allow you to change color palettes and font choices, and add your own images. Some themes have drag-and-drop interfaces that allow you to reposition content blocks.

More advanced themes might accommodate third-party plug-ins for custom features. Beware, however. Plug-ins can raise issues. You might have trouble finding that perfect plug-in without spending a lot of money on subscriptions. Too many plug-ins on your site increase the chance of site glitches and conflicts between plug-ins.

But, if you have coding skills and your particular installation gives you access to the code, you can customize themes any way you choose.

Working with a web designer &/or developer to create a custom site with custom functionality. Work with pros if you need a bespoke look and feel, have extensive quantities of content or require highly specialized site tools. You also might need a pro if high search rankings are crucial to your site's success. Search Engine Optimization (SEO) requires professional planning and implementation.

Try before you buy. When searching for a blog or CMS theme, check out theme previews and demo sites. They provide a sneak peek at font styling, color palettes and layouts available with the theme package. You can find thousands of themes out there for free download or for purchase. Premium (meaning *not* free) themes not only come with better features but also often provide tech support.

HOW THE WEB WORKS

Ever wonder how your computer can pull so much data from servers all over the world? Here's a 5-second explanation of how the World Wide Web works:

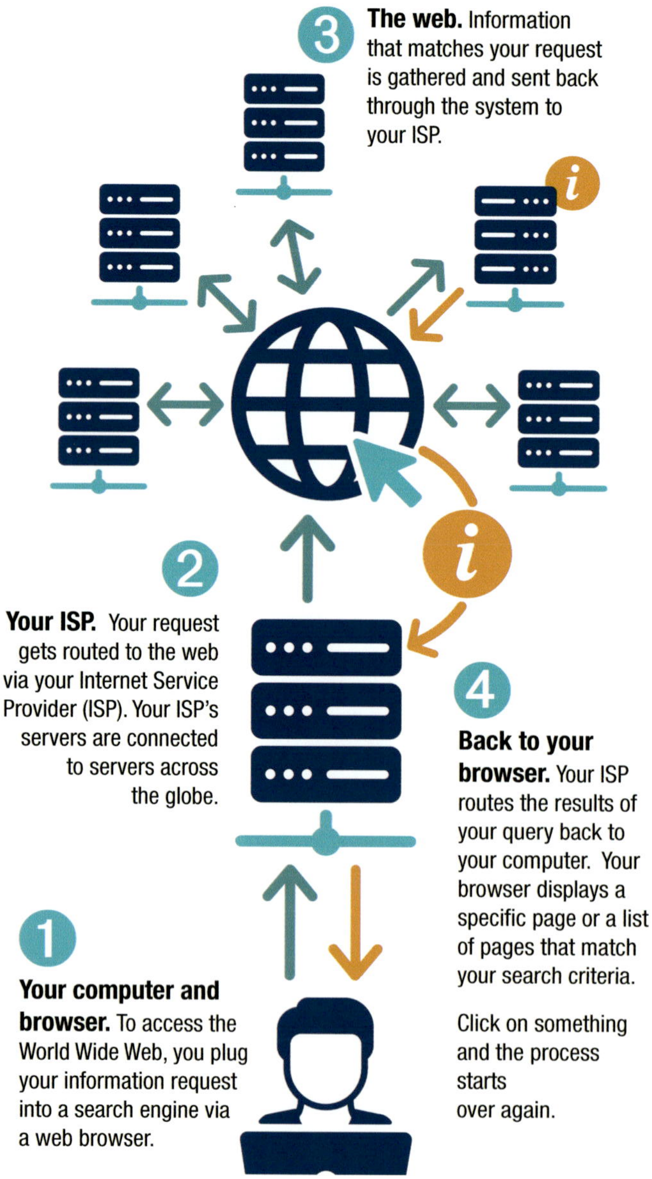

HOW THE WEB WORKS (THE 5-SECOND VERSION)

Web design requires you to understand how the files you create show up on the computer screens of your viewers. If you know how the web works, you can troubleshoot why your content is not showing up properly…or not at all.

Accessing existing websites. To access the web, you need three things: a computer or other internet-capable device, a web browser and an Internet Service Provider (ISP) or wireless network. When you type an information request (a keyword or search term) or a specific address (Uniform Resource Locator or URL) and hit enter, your request is sent to your ISP. In turn, your ISP sends the request to the World Wide Web portion of the internet. Information on the network that matches your information request gets sent back through your ISP. Your browser displays either the page you requested by URL or a list of potential pages that meet your search criteria.

Server space/web hosting. To house and maintain a site on the web, you need server space, also called web hosting. Think of server space as your site's paid parking space on the web. If you are designing a site for a large company, that company may provide hosting on its own internal servers. If you are not working with a private server, you can buy space from any number of web host providers. Professional web designers select web hosting packages based on the requirements of the website to be built. Requirements to consider include the amount of storage space, speed, stability, security tools, underlying hardware and software, and other features such as site backups and availability of email accounts.

By default, the name of your server plus the name of the directory assigned by your host become your site URL. Your host also gives you a string of numbers called an IP address that represents the location of your site on the web. To continue the parking space analogy, your IP number is like your parking space number. But nobody wants a URL that reads www.awesomewebhosting.com/~ilovekumquats, or worse, 65.97.106.162. This is where domain names come in.

Domain names. A domain name is a custom URL you purchase through a domain name registrar. Think of the domain name as a personalized "reserved" sign that replaces the number identifying your parking space. Domain names are chosen to reflect the content of the website they represent.

XYZgraphicdesign.com is easier to remember than an IP address, and it says something about what the organization does. The most common and desired domain suffix is ".com" for commercial. But hundreds of others exist. The suffix ".net" was intended for personal webpages, ".org" for groups and organizations, ".gov" for government and ".edu" for education.

Once you purchase a domain name, you then access your domain registration to enter your host provider's Domain Name Server (DNS) or enter the host's IP address into an "A record." "A" stands for address. Either action "points" the domain name to your web host, and subsequently your webpages. Thus, when a person puts your custom domain name into a browser, the browser locates the domain name at your registrar, and the registrar redirects the browser to your website. When set up properly, your website shows up in that person's browser window.

File Transfer Protocol (FTP). The final piece in this process is the mechanism that parks your pages and content into your server space. If your website uses a content management system or a site-builder, the uploading mechanism is baked into the software, sort of like a self-driving car. Posting and publishing happen on pressing "publish." Uploading via CMS is sufficient most of the time.

Occasionally, however, you need to access the host directly, perhaps to upload multiple files at once or resolve a website error. Manually accessing your host requires another kind of software called File Transfer Protocol (FTP). Often you get FTP access through your web-hosting dashboard. You can also download standalone FTP programs. These programs are inexpensive (often

In the late '90s, website-building exploded, and so did the demand for unique domain names ending in .com. In short order, easy to spell and remember .com names became as rare as common sense in Congress.

Out of necessity, the Internet Corporation for Assigned Names and Numbers (ICANN) released additional sets of domain extensions. Use of original domain extensions like .com, .net and .org lend an air of trustworthiness to your website, but we think there is some creativity to be employed with the newer extensions. Consider:

braggadoc.io

conleche.cafe

bayouzyde.co

indigo.blue

flashcu.be

catchthered.dot

whenpigs.fly

inwiththe.new

* If *ilovekumquats.com* is already taken, we might consider *kumquat.love* instead.

free) and come with instructions for connecting the software to your web host. Once connected, uploading files is usually as simple as dragging and dropping.

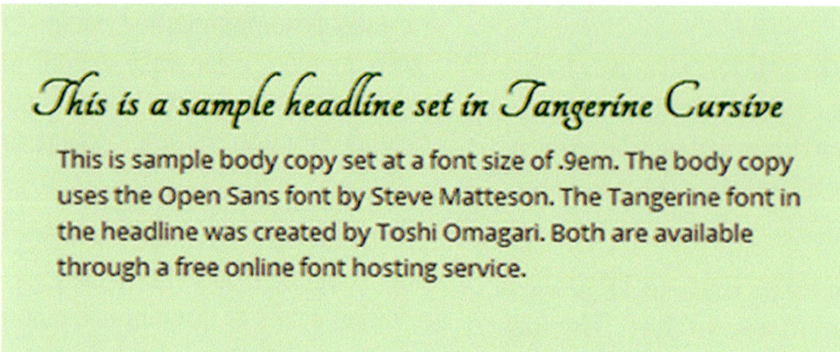

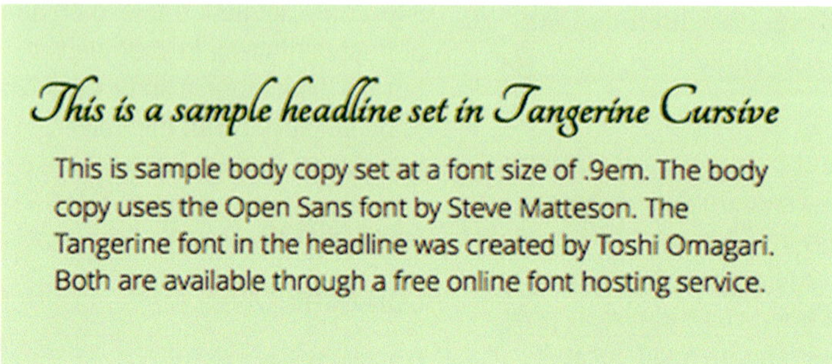

No, you don't need to get your eyes checked. Despite access to the exact same page code and style sheet, each browser renders fonts differently. Look closely at the line breaks, font size and overall height of the copy blocks. These subtle differences are enough to cause a layout to break on one browser or another.

HOW WEB DESIGN DIFFERS FROM OTHER TYPES OF DESIGN

In Chapter 1, you learned that good design is good design, regardless the medium. The end product must capture attention, control the eye's movement, convey information and evoke emotion. To achieve these ends, web design needs a focal point, visual hierarchy, balance, rhythm and flow. But web design is not without unique opportunities and challenges:

You don't have 100 percent control over your layout's onscreen appearance. Print designers know what they'll get back when they send their files to the printer. Not so for the web designer. Any layout created for the screen will look slightly different to every person who views it. For this, blame both hardware and software. In our color chapter, we discussed the issue of color-shifting on different monitors. What is more, different browsers render fonts and spacing differently, thereby also changing the design's appearance.

The wrong resolution impacts more than image appearance. In previous chapters, we discussed the appropriate image resolutions for print and screen. Unlike the high-resolution requirements of print, the web is about low-resolution images. On the web, smaller asset file sizes load faster, provide better user experience and even improve search engine results. When it comes to your web assets, *aim for the lowest resolution you can achieve while retaining image quality and integrity.* Optimizing, a process we described in Chapter 9, means getting each image to the smallest file size that still supports good image quality.

Your layout is built on an incredible shrinking (or expanding) canvas. Today's websites are more likely to be viewed on a smart phone than on a 27-inch monitor. Or on a 15-inch laptop. Or on a tablet. For your site to look good on all devices, you must plan for layout flexibility.

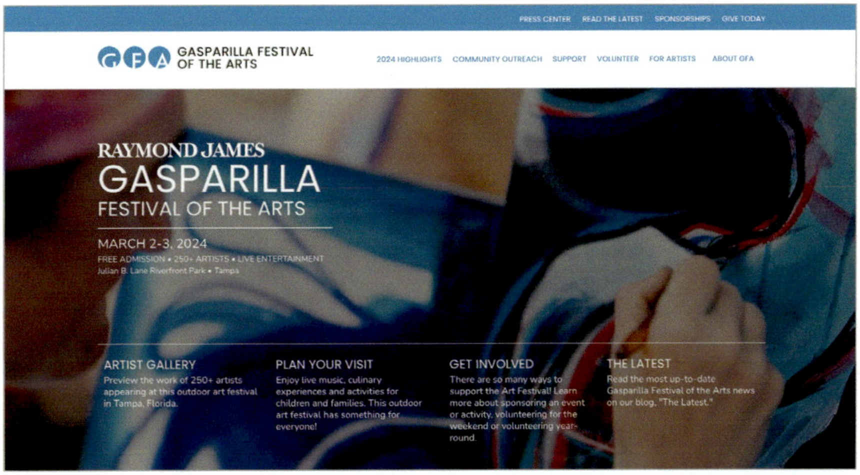

This is not a hero image. The "hero image" on this website isn't an image at all, it's a looping video. The video runs in the background while the text floats consistently over the top. Video, audio and animation make the web a multi-sensory experience.

Raymond James Gasparilla Festival of the Arts website reproduced by permission of Gasparilla Festival of the Arts, Inc. and Raymond James Financial, Inc.

Websites are nonlinear. Multi-page websites are nonlinear. Viewers can jump to any point in a website at any time, and things still need to make sense when viewers arrive. Viewers also need a clear path to get back to wherever they came from, or to find their next destination in the site. Design concepts of hierarchy, repetition and unity become crucial to site navigability and usability.

The web can be a multi-sensory experience. Websites allow for the addition of multimedia components such as animation, video and audio, creating richer multi-sensory experiences. This means entering a whole new world of video and audio formats as well as browser compatibility issues.

The web is interactive. As you read the web, it reads you back. As we click, our choices are recorded and come back to us in the form of messages like, "Those who purchased this item also bought…" With a click we can control the template of our online music service. We can add our own words and images to blogs, forums and social media sites. Websites are expected to be interactive and dynamic. Web design creates the framework that orders and organizes, despite constantly changing and ofttimes user-generated content.

THAT'S ALL GREAT. BUT HOW DO I DESIGN ONE?

Because websites are complex combinations of type, visuals and interactivity, the best ones result from the joint efforts of designers, web developers, writers and web usability experts. Whether you're designing on your own, editing an existing site or working with a team to build something new, you should understand the design conventions and processes involved in creating a good website.

But before we dive into website-building specifics, let's talk about building essentials for all websites. Let's talk about web accessibility and inclusivity.

WEB ACCESSIBILITY & INCLUSIVITY

The web is for everyone. But too often web design fails to work for people with divergent visual, auditory, cognitive, neurological, physical and/or speech abilities. Universal design refers to designing access to spaces and places, products, services, experiences and information communication technologies to accommodate the widest possible range of disabilities and abilities. Web accessibility refers to design that makes the web accessible for as many people as possible.

> "The power of the web is in its universality. **Access by everyone** regardless of disability is an essential impact."
>
> *~Tim Berners-Lee*

Accessible design is so important that the U.S. Department of Justice (DOJ) identifies websites and mobile apps as "places of public accommodation" that must be accessible to people with disabilities. The mandate covers websites for, or funded by, state and local governments as well as websites for businesses.

Section 508 of the Rehabilitation Act of 1973 contains compliance requirements, effectively a checklist for web accessibility. In 2017, the Americans with Disabilities Act (ADA) staff incorporated Web Content Accessibility Guidelines (WCAG) 2.0 into Section 508. WCAG, a product of the Word Wide Web Consortium (W3C), is the industry standard for website accessibility.

More than following a checklist for a particular disability, inclusive web design considers the environment and circumstances in which people interact with technology. One need not have a disability to struggle viewing a smart phone screen in poor light. People with cold or allergy congestion might have difficulty hearing website audio. And don't forget that not all impediments to website usability originate with a human. Not everyone has the most recent smart phone or 24/7 access to blazing-fast internet.

Inclusive design crafts solutions to situations that might exclude people. As you might guess, when we design for accessibility, we automatically increase inclusivity. As a bonus, inclusive design tends to increase website audience reach and participation. Below we recommend user experience (UX) best practices along with a dash of Gestalt theory as a recipe for inclusive design.

Prioritize people. Never forget that your website has human users who visit to accomplish tasks. Splashy animation, color gradients and crazy font choices become deficits rather than assets if they make your website hard to use.

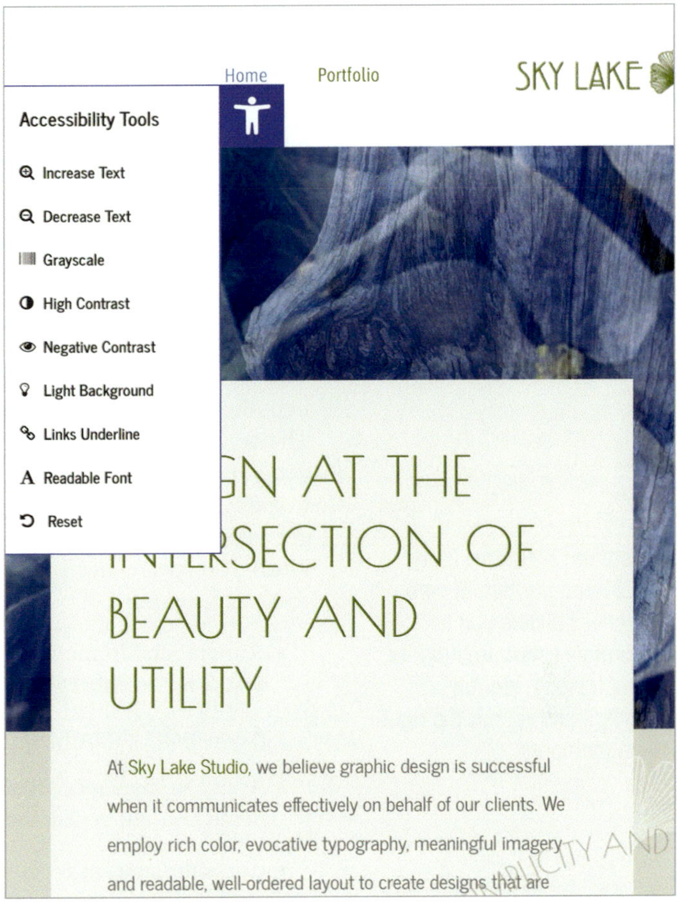

User control increases web inclusivity. A website plug-in allows site visitors to change features such as overall color contrast, font style, font size and how hyperlinks appear to improve readability.

- **Keep design simple.** We keep preaching "keep it simple." Only include website features that add value.
- **Be consistent.** If one hyperlink is styled in color, bolded and underlined then all hyperlinks should be similarly styled. Consistency and similarity make learning a website's rules of interaction easier. And nothing makes website visitors happier than easy-to-use.
- **Provide equitable experience.** Consider the tasks your website or app is intended to complete, and design multiple ways to complete them. Adding transcripts to video clips for the hearing impaired is a good example.
- **When preparing content, consider all types of learners.** Some people learn best by reading. Others learn by watching and doing. Ensure your site has multiple kinds of content for all kinds of learners.
- **Give users control.** Let site visitors control their experiences by providing the ability to change features such as site orientation, contrast, font and font size, degree of magnification, language and volume.

Now that we've planted the "web is for everyone" idea, we can move on to the specifics of building that accessible, inclusive site you need. It's a four-step process: planning, sketching, prototyping and assembling.

PLANNING

Remember way back in Chapter 2, we wrote, "Step away from your computer for research and brainstorming." Not the most glamorous part of the design process, planning begins with meeting with stakeholders and generating a creative brief. As important as timetable, budget, and color palettes are, your site visitors' needs and wants are more important. These, along with the organization's objectives, dictate the size, shape and scope of your website project.

The importance of objectives

To illustrate how objectives impact your website project, consider a hypothetical organization that wants a membership-based website. The organization's objectives include selling memberships and generating income. Your site's users have other objectives: to be able to easily join, pay for and manage their membership online and then get value from interacting as a member with the website. Now what kinds of software and applications will be required to manage all these expectations?

Objective: Website! Early, considered crafting of web objectives allows you to accurately estimate budgets, select hosting, identify software and recruit the right team members.

- » A membership management tool with signup forms and account access for member users
- » A payment gateway to pay for memberships online
- » A way to manage content available to members, maybe even with tiered content access for increasing levels of membership
- » Communications tools such as newsletters and membership notifications, among others

Website image reproduced by permission of the C.G. Jung Library of Tampa Bay.

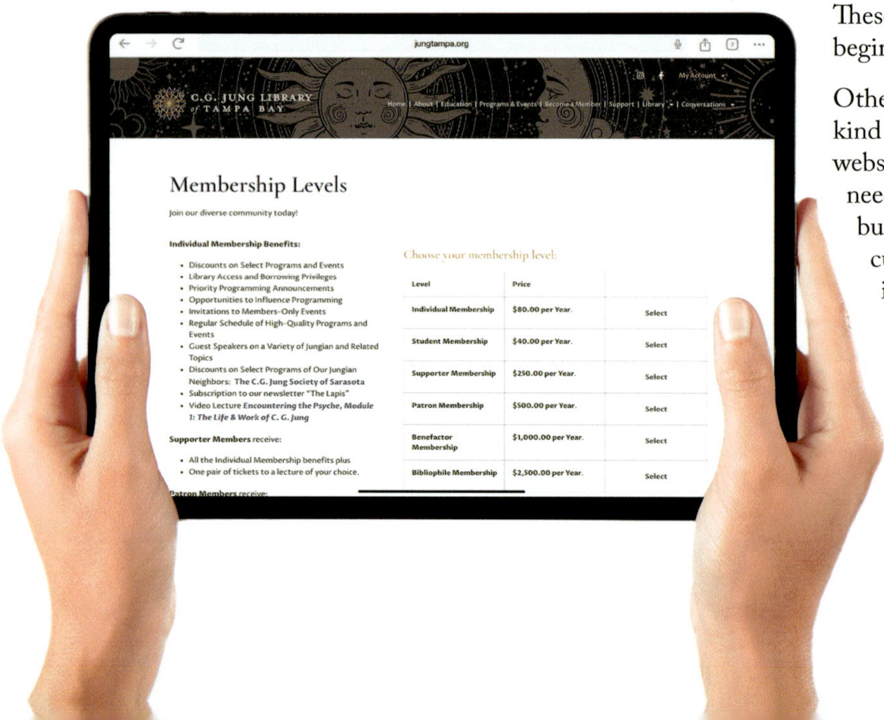

These minimal objectives are just the beginning.

Other considerations include the kind of hosting platform best for the website. Can you meet the project's needs with an online website builder? Or is this a ground-up custom code job? Maybe a CMS installed on a private hosting account or internal server is sufficient. How much site traffic can you expect? Do you need extra site security?

Answers to these questions impact budget and staffing, too. Should you hire a web

A	B	C	D	E	F	G	H
	GFA Website Navigation						
	Festival Information	**Info for Artists**	**Community Outreach**	**Supporters**	**Artist Gallery**	**About GFA**	**The Latest**
	The Basics	Event Info	Overview & Initiatives	Support the Organization	2022 Artist Gallery	Mission	
	Festival Map & Program	Application & Rules	Scholastic Showcase Overview	Sponsors	2022 Emerging Artists Gallery	Festival History	
	Parking & Transportation	Emerging Artists Program	Local Artists Spotlight Overview - split into 2 pieces (LAS & Live Art)	Community Partners	2022 Local Artists Spotlight Gallery	Press Center	
	Food & Drink	Jurors	GFA Collegiate Scholarship	Collectors Krewe		Award Winners	
	Live Entertainment	Where to Stay	Permanent Art	Volunteers		Volunteers	
	Interactive Experiences					Festival Committee	
	TBBCA Chalk Walk					Board of Directors	
	Children's Activities					Recognition	
	Emerging Artists						
	Local Artist Spotlight						
	Scholastic Showcase						
	VIP Experience						
	The Showcase						
	Merchandise						

We love a good grid structure. Use a spreadsheet to track your audit data. In this example, the column headings represent the main navigation items. Listings under each column indentify either subpages or content blocks on that page.

developer? Who will maintain the site and server? Who will provide ongoing content? Who will manage customer service?

Website success depends on selecting and deploying the right combination of platform, applications, custom coding, plug-ins and other tools. Your stated objectives might touch on these topics, but to get all the answers before you find yourself backtracking and frustrated, consider depth interviews or a questionnaire with your constituents. You can find a questionnaire example on the book's website, whitespacedesignbook.com.

Once you've collected the best answers to the right questions, you're ready to conduct an audit and create a site inventory.

Site audits & inventories

Whether you're designing a new site or redesigning an existing one, you need to organize your content in a meaningful way. Content includes text, images, video clips, animations, forms and other assets too numerous to list here. Grouping content into pages and subsections will make it searchable and usable. But you can't meaningfully organize your content until you know what you need to organize.

For a redesign, audit the website's content. Look at every page with an eye toward content form, quantity and quality. Consider whether the existing content is effective as well as who manages it and how. Create a spreadsheet with each page as a primary heading. Under each heading, list the content segments that appear on that page. Make notes about each piece of content, starting with purpose. Is it evergreen or in need of regular updates? Consider the type of content: Blog? White paper? Tutorial video? Is the content dynamically generated from a third-party source? Who is responsible for updates? Is the content well-written? And, key of course, is it useful to the site visitor?

Inventory *everything.* Your inventory should include a wide range of website assets including but not limited to text, logos, headlines, taglines, video clips, mission statements, minutes, press releases, quotes and tutorials. If it can go on a page, include it in your inventory.

Review site structure as well. Is navigation logical and functional? Are there gaps in menus? Does the content flow logically on each page? Are there wayfinding tools, such as breadcrumb trails? Is there a clear relationship between and among pages?

Don't be daunted by the auditing. The resulting inventory will make your job much easier. You'll have a clear picture of the site's good, bad, ugly and missing in action. Plus, the audit process lays the foundation for your content strategy and website design system, both described later in this chapter.

If you're constructing a website from scratch, revisit the creative brief. Then create a content list using the site's objectives and anticipated user needs as your guide. Include headers, body copy, image captions/cutlines, general messaging, calls to action, product or service descriptions, product images, video clips, blog posts, contact forms… You get the idea.

Most likely, some keyword-rich copywriting will be in order. But consider other sources for website content. Your boss or client might have brochures, fact sheets, spec sheets, catalogs, annual reports, newsletters, internal memos or other documents with content that could be repurposed for the website. Record your created and collected content in a spreadsheet, or use the digital file organization method of your choice.

A final word of advice: Designate a "keeper of the content." You will appreciate having a single, well-informed source of information on the type, quality and location of all your site assets.

At this point, you're equipped to create a high-level brief and formal inventory for the team. Your brief should reveal any gaps in your content or things that need revisiting. Assign individuals to address those issues, and hire third-party programmers or other content creators as needed. A Gantt chart or online project management tool is helpful at this stage to keep everyone on track to meet your deliverables deadlines.

SKETCHING

So far we've talked at length about website design without actually talking about *design*. Traditionally, sitemaps and wireframes were the first visual renderings of a webpage

design. We introduced both concepts back in Chapter 2. But the times, as the song goes, they are a-changing.

From "responsive design" to "mobile first"

The reality of web access on computers, phones, tablets and TVs spurred web designers to build flexible fluid websites. Appropriately called "responsive websites," these designs adjusted to fit the screen size of any viewing device. Designers and developers coded assets in such a way that they could scale—change size and orientation—without losing quality.

It was the right solution, but it was far from perfect. Some website assets scaled poorly. Others didn't scale at all. Interactive elements such as navigation menus and pop-up windows obscured key content on tiny smart phone screens. Some types of videos, animation and graphics simply didn't function on smaller screens. To prevent glitches, many designers opted to hide multimedia elements from view on mobile devices.

In 2011 interface designer Luke Wroblewski advocated for across-the-board—or, rather, across-the-screen—quality in web experience. Wroblewski believed that viewing a site on a smart phone should not be a watered-down version of viewing the same site on a desktop computer. He thought web design should be about designing *experiences,* not just presenting attractive visuals. To ensure a quality

Almost, but not quite. Responsive design attempted to address the multiple screen size issue by making site designs fluid. Unfortunately, some types of web content reacted badly to fluidity. Note that the website on the smart phone shows a static image in lieu of the homepage video. The horizontal video was too small to be viewed on the small screen.

This page and opposite: *Raymond James Gasparilla Festival of the Arts website, logo and other images used by permission of Gasparilla Festival of the Arts, Inc. and Raymond James Financial, Inc.*

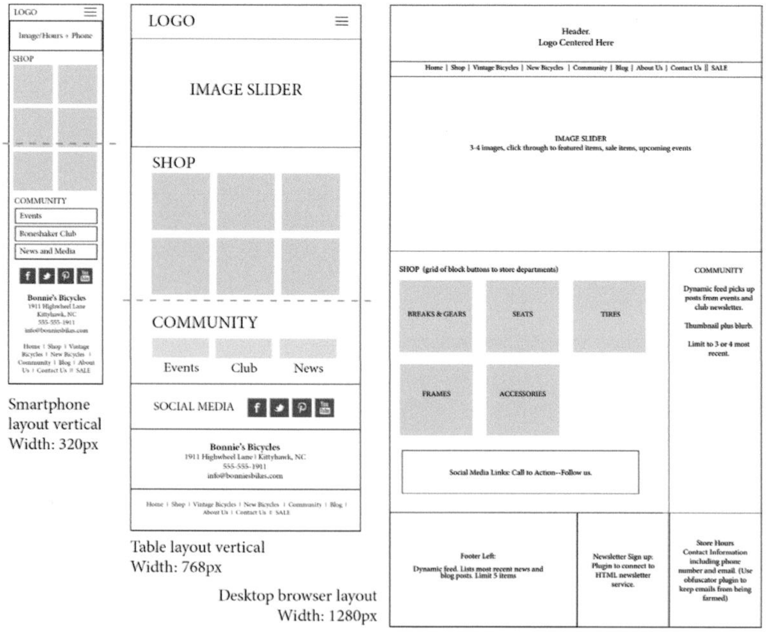

No longer the best tool for the job. Static wireframe sketches fail to capture the interactivity and motion inherent in modern web designs. Not to mention they only display one screen layout at a time. To show a client how the site design would work on a smart phone, tablet and desktop, you need three sets of sketches for each page in your site.

experience for everyone, then, Wroblewski argued that web designers should design for the small screen first, then scale up for larger screens. Wroblewski's approach became known as "mobile first."

To wireframe or not to wireframe

This brave new world of mobile-first, experience-centric design bumped the wireframe to the B-list of web design tools. Traditional static wireframes fail to capture the essential interactions and fluidity of responsive websites. Additionally, each page planned for your site requires a wireframe. To account for smart phone and tablet layouts triples the number of wireframes. That, friends, is *a lot* of sketches. Not to mention that by focusing on design elements, wireframes undermine user-centricity. Color, alignment, size and positioning of elements become distractions when the true emphasis needs to be user needs such as site function and desired content. As they say, pretty is as pretty does. It's important to make sure your website design *does.*

Yes, people in the industry still use wireframes. But what the industry needs are tools that focus attention on the order, organization and utility of content that isn't static but rather dynamic and interactive.

Information architecture

Information Architecture (IA) is the practice of organizing, structuring and labeling website pages and content for maximum findability and usability. Audits and inventories collect and account for content. Architecture creates categories and labels to arrange that content.

Teasing labels out of your content. Since we interact with labeled and sorted information every day, categorizing content seems easy. The most common sorting methods we learned in primary school: alphabetical or numerical (membership lists), location (maps), time (event calendars), category (clothing websites), hierarchy (ratings) and others.

But sorting isn't always obvious. Consider three socks: one red, one purple and one striped blue and purple. We could fold them under one group labeled "socks," or two groups called "solid socks" and "striped socks." But then what happens if we introduce a green and pink argyle sock?

To avoid sock-sorting dilemmas necessitates well-defined labels with distinct parameters. To return to the sock drawer, the labels "socks," "solid socks" and "patterned socks" indicate ways we can categorize. Where did those labels come from? In this case, from the sock pile itself. In the case of a website design, label cues come from your collected pile of content, as well as the objectives of the organization (or your boss or client) and the needs of your website users. Your audit and inventory provide an in-depth

view of your content. Your creative brief lists the website owner's goals, and hopefully users', too.

If you find your information on desired user outcomes lacking, consider conducting some user experience (UX) research. True UX research can be complicated, time-consuming and expensive. If this is not in your budget, do some informal research instead. Talk to people who are involved with the organization. Interview people who have visited the current website, if one exists, about their experiences. You might be surprised to find that your users' top reason for visiting is to find your hours of operation, not to read your scintillating blog posts.

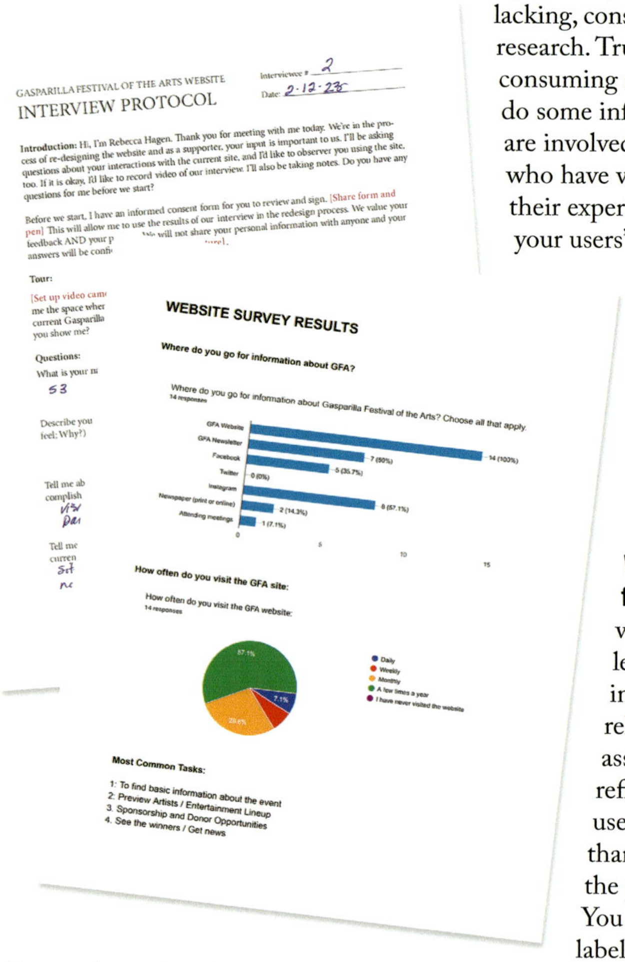

Bottom line? Topics deemed important lend themselves to becoming labels. If the boss or client lists "increase membership" as a primary goal, and users indicate that "learn about membership" is important, making a membership-related label is a no-brainer.

What if my web project already has labels from a previous version of the site? If you're working on a redesign, the current site's top-level navigation consists of the labels chosen in the last design. Rather than automatically reheating those choices, look to your newly assembled inventory. Ask yourself if the labels reflect the desired outcomes of the clients and users. Observe if some labels house more content than others. All this might clue you in to where the previous design team placed content emphasis. You might surmise the need for more or fewer labels to balance out content distribution.

Research need not be expensive to be useful. Formal user experience research can be expensive and time-consuming. If UX research is not in your budget you can still gather important information with simple surveys and informal interviews.

If you're working on a brand-new design, and you're not drawing label inspiration from your content, users and boss or client, there is always card sorting. Don't scoff.

Card sorting. In the days before the internet, teachers assigning reports instructed students to write each bit of researched information with a reference on a 3 × 5 index card. Sorting the cards by topic and rearranging the cards by importance, students outlined their reports. The same process works for outlining information architecture. Or you can do it on a computer. We prefer sticky notes and a group effort.

Open card sorting for scratch-made projects. First things first: Record each piece of content from your proposed site inventory on an individual sticky note or card. "Mission statement" or "contact us form" will do. They need not be detailed. Put all your notes in a pile and shuffle them. Assemble a small group of your stakeholders and ask each person to grab a stack. Direct group members to sort the notecards into categories that make sense. After the initial sort, arrange the stacks into side-by-side columns. Instruct the group to review and revise until everyone is satisfied. Keep blank notecards and markers handy so your group can create appropriate labels for the columns.

Definitely old school, but it works. Card sorting is an effective way to order and organize your site content from the user's perspective.

Closed card sorting for redesign projects. Closed card sorting follows the same steps as open sorting, except you already have a website with structure and content. Create your cards, and lay them out in the order they currently appear. Ask your group to rethink and reorder the content in a way that seems logical. Use blank cards and markers to rename labels or create new ones.

Whether you use open or closed sorting, your top-level labels become the core menu items in your main navigation. Each card under that menu item represents a subpage, or a single element of content on a page named for that menu item. The labels and cards provide the foundation for your first official sketch: a sitemap.

Sitemap & navigation

Part of the UX toolkit, a sitemap visually diagrams the outline of a site's pages and their relationships to one another. Also called an information architecture diagram, a sitemap can help you come up with the best, most logical site structure for your needs. Your sitemap also helps get stakeholder buy-in.

Begin with your site's main navigation. Since it functions as the primary gateway getting your site's visitors from point A to point B, take the time to get it right.

Once you've nailed the main navigation labels, a.k.a. main menu items, you're ready to arrange the content labels. Revisit the content-organizing methods we've already covered as you organize your content items under each label. If you're unsure how to organize, think "most to least important." Otherwise go for utility and trust common sense. For instance, content labels referring to a process suggest an ordered list of steps. Similarly, logic dictates that logout buttons or links to elsewhere ought to go last in a content list.

With navigation and ordered labels organized, now step back to look at the big picture. Look for overly long or short content lists. Long lists are not only off-putting but also more difficult to wrap our brains around. Literally. Working memory can only handle about 5-9 pieces of information at once, says Miller's Law. And making decisions gets harder with more choices, says Hick's Law. Both suggest a better user experience by keeping the number of labels lower and lengths of lists shorter.

Just keep consolidating and rearranging until you have a well-balanced concise site with logical order and organization. Then with those choices, create your sitemap infographic. Oh, yeah! Sitemaps and architecture diagrams are infographics.

A site map serves as an infographic of the pages and their relationships in your website. This diagram makes it easy to see if you've gone overboard with your navigation and violated Miller's Law. Or Hick's Law. Or both.

Sketching & rendering a sitemap. To sketch your sitemap infographic, draw some boxes, one for each of your main navigation labels and content segments. Arrange them in your order. Did you forget anything? Did you remember to plan a link for the homepage? Maybe you need a separate menu for member or administrative logins. If you solicit donations, consider locating your donation button perpetually in the top right of the homepage.

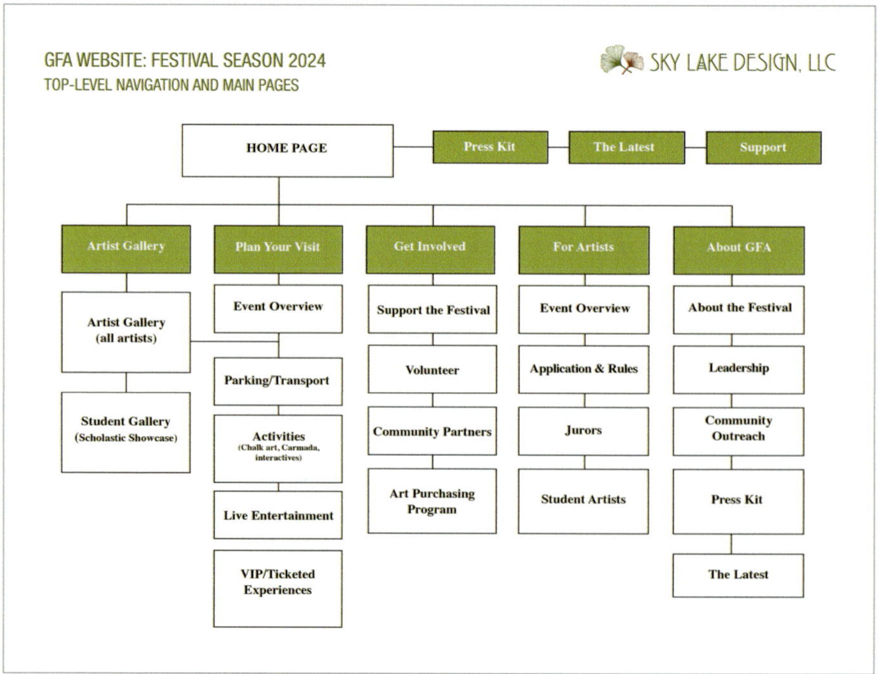

Call on your design expertise. Draw on shape, color and Gestalt Theory to add additional meaning to your sitemap. Use one color for content boxes representing pages. Use a different color for off-site links. Use different shapes to represent the sub-menu for social media links. Use spacing to show relationships by grouping things together that go together. Add direction arrows to show linking relationships between pages.

What you've created is a flow chart, reflecting the idea that visitors don't travel through pages sequentially but have the option of going in different directions from any given point.

Show it to your team. Show it to the boss or client. Get feedback. Adjust accordingly.

With your site architecture mapped, you're ready to drill down to page level to consider content priority.

Content priority guides. In 2012, content strategist Drew Clemens came up with content priority guides to direct the placement of website content based on priority or importance.

Content priority guides use simple sketches to lay out web content and elements vertically from most important to least important with layout boundaries drawn tall and narrow like smart phone screens.

Objective driven, your website's content priority guides ask you to establish the goal or goals for each webpage. Then you list content necessary to achieve those goals. Add in the content segments, top to bottom, in priority order—sans navigation since it's on every page anyway. These resulting preliminary sketches are called top-level guides.

Second-level guides include more detail. Include the purpose or intent of each bit of content. Add notes about functionality. For example, if a blog feed is part of a homepage priority guide, the second-level guide might indicate updates monthly.

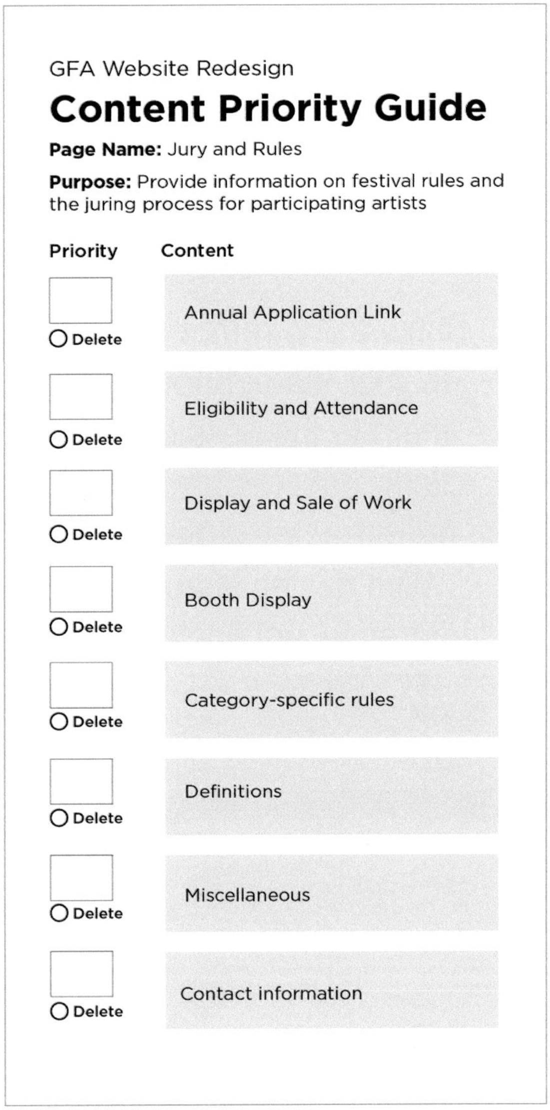

A top-level priority guide identifies your page goal, and the content necessary to achieve those goals. Content is placed in order from most important to least important. The narrow structure mimics the size and shape of mobile phone screens.

HTML wireframes. Yeah. We know. Ten minutes ago we said the wireframe is going the way of phone booths and paper roadmaps. But unlike traditional wireframes, HTML wireframes are built online, using your second-level content priority guides as your first-pass blueprints. The designs remain low-fidelity, restricted to basic fonts, a black and white color palette and gray boxes indicating content areas.

Because these wireframes are viewed in a browser, you can demonstrate how placeholder content reacts to changing browser environments. This means you can show how your single, vertical list of content components adjusts to wider tablet and desktop screens. You can navigate through your content via hyperlinks or scrolling for a more realistic web experience. Previewing the HTML wireframe in different browsers helps identify potential structural issues early on. Try doing that with a paper wireframe.

> Show the wireframes to your team. Show them to the boss or client. **Get feedback. Adjust accordingly.** Web design is an iterative, not linear, process.

In addition, building HTML wireframes jumpstarts the site-building process. While you aren't adding style elements yet, you can build the underlying code for site headers, navigation, footers and any other page structure.

Again, show the wireframes to your team. Show them to the boss or client. Get feedback. Adjust accordingly. Web design is an iterative, not linear, process.

Whew! You've audited, inventoried, sorted, labeled and prioritized your content. You organized that content into pages and created a sitemap demonstrating the site visitor's path through it. Next, you need to determine the best way to visually present your content in each section of the website. Now we're talking about crafting user interfaces and building prototypes.

USER INTERFACE & PROTOTYPING

If we've learned anything about digital design, it's that we can't keep reinventing the design process each time some new internet-capable device captures everyone's imagination. We need a design framework capable of adapting to rapid changes in internet technology.

Design systems

Modern web design is anchored in design systems. These are collections of modular, reusable, functional elements that allow web teams to rapidly build visually unified and experientially consistent websites, apps and other digital products. Component libraries form the core of design systems, but fully developed systems also include brand identity standards and style guides from coding to visuals and copywriting voice and tone. Google's Material Design System is perhaps the best-known example.

It's never too early in the web-building process to establish your own design system, and based on your earlier planning activities, you already have a head start on brand identity. However, assembling a library of components requires a bit more work. And maybe a methodology. Web designer Brad Frost created a popular modular web design methodology based on molecular chemistry. It's called atomic design.

Atomic design. In case you need a refresher, atoms are basic building blocks of the universe. Atoms group up into components called molecules, and different kinds of molecules group up in particular ways to function as complex organisms. You can see where this is going for modular web design systems, right?

In Frost's atomic design, the smallest units, called "atoms," include basics like buttons, icons, labels and form fields (inputs for online forms), among others. A label like "Subscribe" paired with a form field collecting a viewer's name and email address plus a live button becomes a "subscribe" molecule.

Molecules working together form an organism. A form field molecule for the website's page headers paired with a menu molecule and an image icon might become the header for the membership page.

Frost notes the chemistry analogy in atomic design reaches its limit after atoms, molecules, and organisms. So the final two elements in atomic design are templates and pages. Templates, as you'll recall, provide structure, in this case to give order and organize organisms, creating multi-functional components. Pages, the final stage of the methodology, organize templates into layouts and display content.

Atomic design is not the only modular methodology out there, but it's a good one. The modular approach has benefits, regardless of the flavor you choose. Modular design provides an easy-to-understand structure the whole design team can follow. It creates a shared language that ensures all members of your team—including your boss or client—are discussing the same thing.

And modules you build, even if they don't follow atomic design structure, all become items in your design system's component library.

ATOMIC DESIGN

Atomic design is a type of design system that combines bare bones web "atoms" into functional "molecules" and "organisms" that can be reused throughout a website. Building sites this way facilitates visual and functional consistency across all pages in the design.

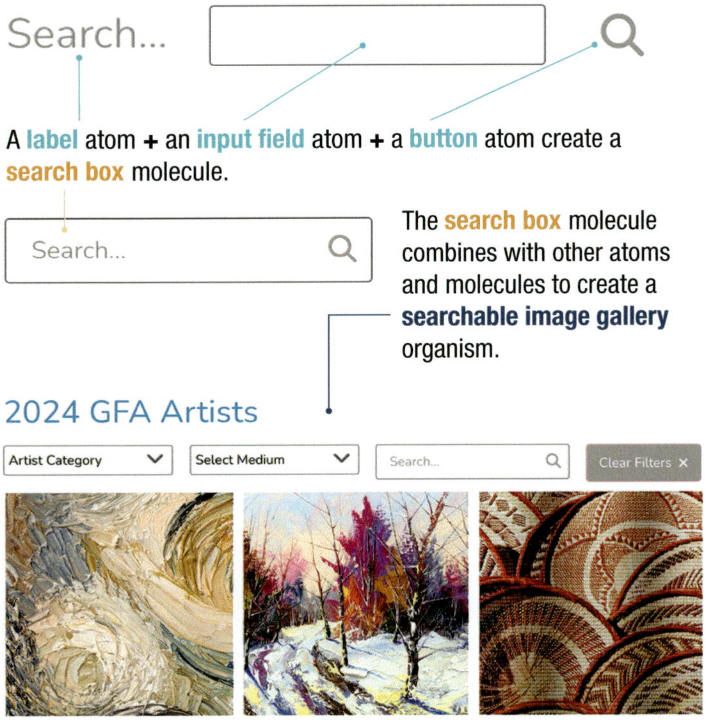

PATTERNS AT WORK

Using common Interface "patterns" keeps your websites user-friendly. If you've been paying attention, you'll notice that many of these patterns are remarkably similar to the page layouts outlined in Chapter 6's "Layout ideas you can swipe."

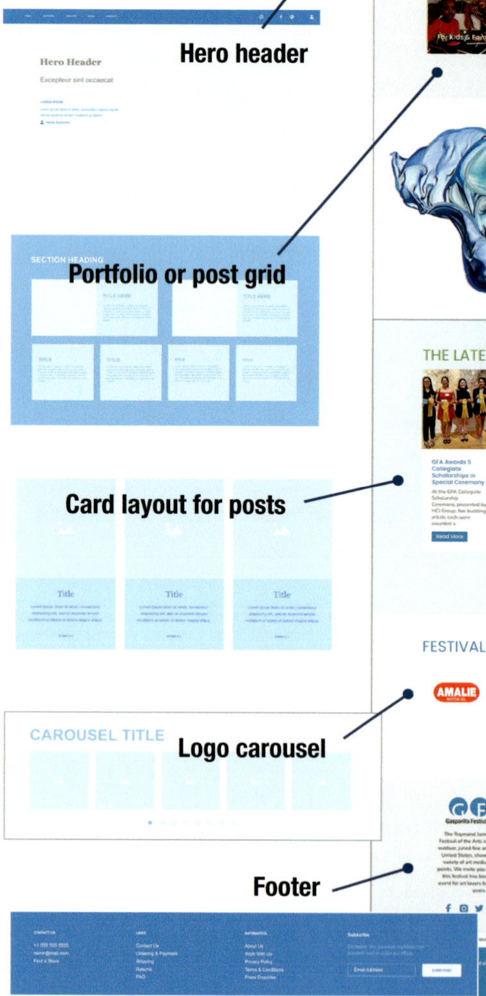

Borrowing items from your own library maintains visual consistency and streamlines future design projects. But before you get too excited about snapping together website atoms like plastic building blocks, we're not finished. We still need to introduce you to User Interface Patterns (UI), which are web components crafted and vetted by professionals.

User Interface (UI) & design patterns

We've been tossing around the terms "interface" and "interface design." Let's agree on some definitions.

Often confused with UX (user experience), UI (user interface) refers to the *mechanics* of interaction as opposed to the *experience* of interaction. UI designers create the bits, bobs and doohickeys that allow a user to interact with a device. While UX and UI are not the same, they are closely linked.

The buttons on a blender are an interface for turning the appliance on and off. If it's a fancy blender, the buttons adjust speed and other settings. If the interface elements, in this case the blender buttons, are too small, poorly placed or badly labeled, the product is difficult to use. Frustration ensues. (We didn't really want that smoothie anyway.) So it's in the best interest of UX, specifically our desire for a smoothie, that the blender UI be well designed.

Translated for the web, UI design becomes the process of putting content and components (atoms, molecules, organisms and templates) together in a way that makes it easy for the site visitor to access content and achieve goals. For 30 years, web designers and UI specialists have been concocting, testing and refining a thousand ways to effectively deliver and make usable every type of content you can imagine.

The most effective design patterns exist in online pattern libraries which are free-to-use collections of visual tactics created by web professionals to address usability needs. Many patterns are now self-explanatory. Most people understand how tabs, radio buttons, color swatches and image galleries work without having to ask. Using known patterns in your website improves usability. Visitors don't have to spend time learning a new interface.

Review your inventory, your content priority guides, sitemap and wireframes for clues about patterns you'll need for your particular content and user goals. A commerce website, for example, needs patterns for arranging products, accessing product details and completing purchases. UI patterns exist for all these activities. Ultimately, you'll make your own set of reusable patterns and add them to the component library of your design system.

PATTERNS FOR MOBILE

Smart phone web browsing necessitated the creation of interface patterns specifically for small screens. Consider these pattern examples. How are they similar to their desktop counterparts? How are they different? Why?

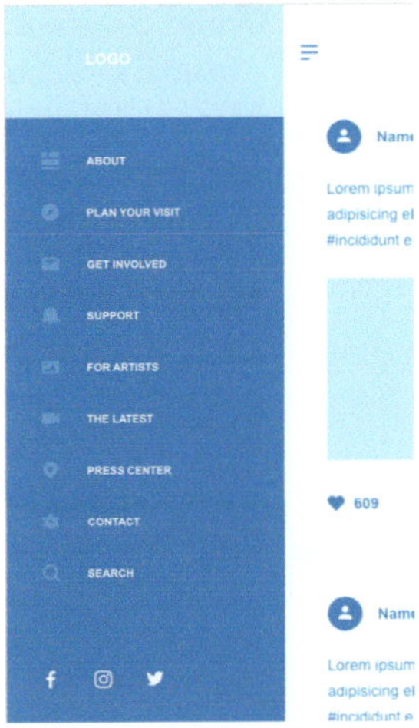

Mobile menu pattern

Account form pattern

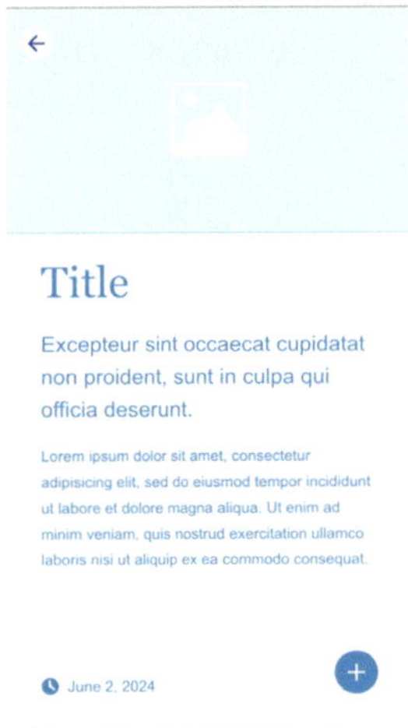

Single post pattern

UI patterns are tweakable to match your site's visual brand and voice. The next step, then, involves a first-go at styling your patterns, sort of like coming up with design chips, swatches and idea boards but done digitally.

Building buy-in, one pattern at a time

Earlier in this chapter we discussed the limitations of using static wireframes and mockups to demonstrate dynamic content. Rather than serving a full buffet of printed web mockups, imagine a digital sampler flight of style tiles.

Opposite page: *Raymond James Gasparilla Festival of the Arts website design reproduced by permission of Gasparilla Festival of the Arts, Inc. and Raymond James Financial, Inc.*

Style Tiles. Invented by designer Samantha Warren, Style Tiles apply brand colors and fonts to a set of conceptual website components (atoms, molecules) to demonstrate how the brand will play on the web. Warren likens Style Tiles to paint chips and fabric swatches interior designers show their clients. Style Tiles are built on a webpage to demonstrate interaction and accurately represent fonts and colors.

Elemental collages. When you want to show the boss or client more than just heading stylings and mouse-over effects, create an elemental collage. It's exactly what it sounds like: a digital collage of rendered web design elements meant to be shared and explored as dynamic demonstrations. Perhaps you have some interesting ideas for a button animation or a way to arrange a grid of thumbnails. The boss or client sees concrete, colorful movement towards the final design, while the design team gains flexibility as they work towards the best design solutions.

Add your boss- or client-reviewed and approved patterns, including CSS styles and any other required coding, to the component library portion of your design system. Include agreed-upon style decisions, such as heading treatments and button styling, in your design system as well.

Style Tiles are more specific than a mood board, but less formal than a full mockup. Designers use them to present a sampler platter of colors, textures, fonts and other elements for client review and feedback.

The Style Tile below was created with a template by @Samanthatoy, http://www.styletil.es

Creating a prototype

A website prototype combines the big-picture view of a flat plan, the live website capabilities of an HTML wireframe and a full-color mockup. It's a complex, interactive demo of all or at least significant portions of your website.

Prototyping tools. Online prototyping applications are a must for rapid prototype building. These tools include UI kits with nearly every conceivable pattern, making page layout a matter of dragging, dropping and style application. By applying styles from your established design system, and adding links, mouse-over effects and other functionality, it's possible to make a prototype that closely resembles your intended design.

In addition to providing the client with a funtional website preview, prototypes help identify design issues that might not be apparent in paper sketches, HTML wireframes and Style Tiles. As working models, prototypes minimize the potential to misinterpret how features and functions actually work. So they provide better feedback to members of the web team and the boss or client.

But before you can show your boss or client the prototype, you have to build it. That means figuring out how to arrange the atoms, organisms, modules and templates you've identified and designed to make your content usable.

How do I know where to put stuff? The web edition.

In Chapter 3 we outlined a formula for positioning the parts of a layout. You learned to establish margins and grids, before placing headings, images and text for logical eye movement and flow. Web prototype layout follows suit, but instead you'll drop UI pattern blocks representing your chosen content molecules, organisms and templates into a page structure. You have four essential regions of a webpage layout to work with: canvas, page identification, navigation tools, content area.

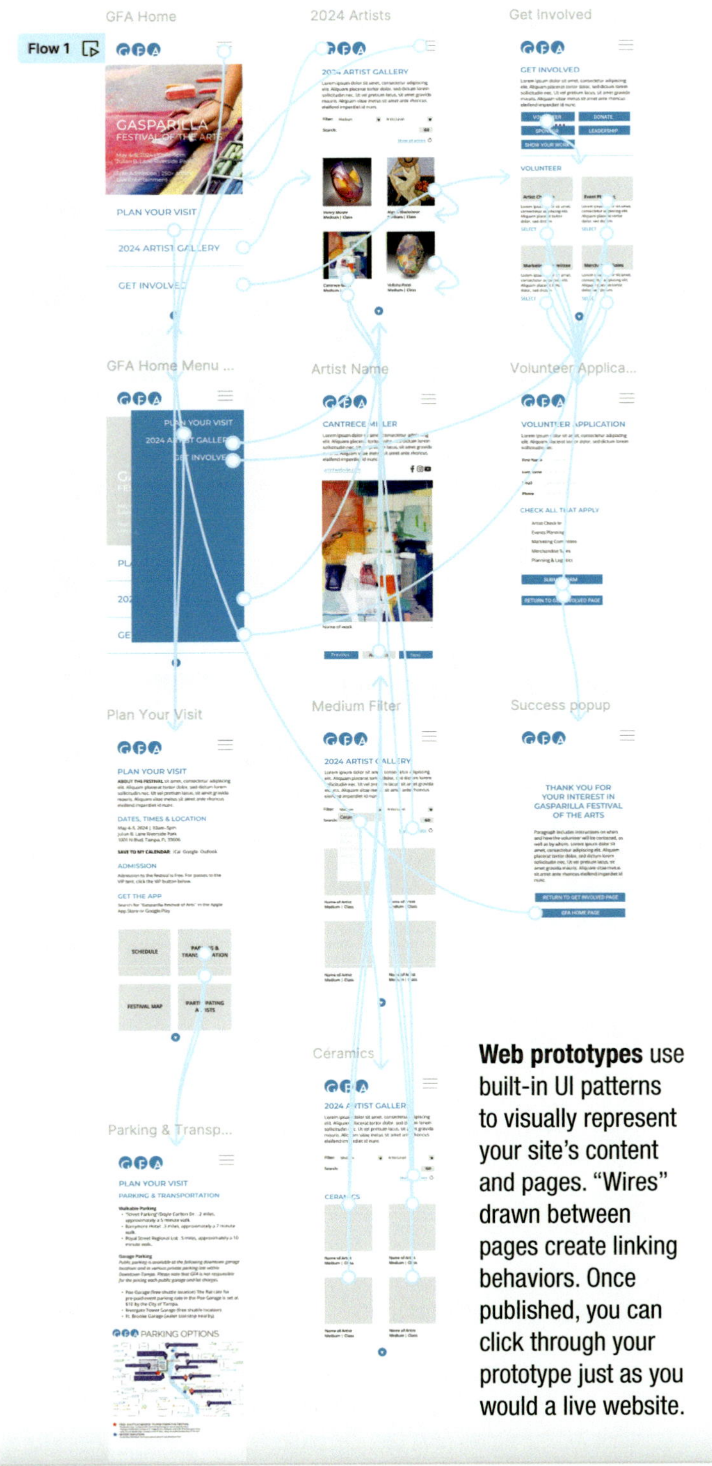

Web prototypes use built-in UI patterns to visually represent your site's content and pages. "Wires" drawn between pages create linking behaviors. Once published, you can click through your prototype just as you would a live website.

BUILD IT BETTER

Using UI patterns pushes your web design in a positive direction, but it's still possible to tank your design by making poor content and styling choices. Here are some tips for making all parts of your website functional and attractive:

1. **Canvas.** If you choose a full-width canvas, consider "boxing" your content to prevent text boxes from widening past the point of comfortable readability.

2. **Page identification.** This "hero header" identifies this website via a logo, relevant image, large centered headline and tagline.

   » Always position the logo in the top left and link it to the home page. Clearly differentiate the logo. Don't let it blend in.

   » Select a compelling image or video for your hero. It takes up a lot of screen, so position other content nearby so your site visitor knows where to go next. This hero includes a row of cards with links.

3. **Navigation.** Style your navigation to strike a balance between in-your-face and shy wallflower. It's not the focal point, but it needs to be visible to be usable.

   » Position navigation in familiar locations. For desktop, choose the top for horizontal navigation and the left for vertical navigation. Experts lack consensus on position of mobile menus, but top right makes sense. It's where site users naturally look for it.

   » Build using fluid font sizes to ensure readability on all devices

   » Make your links look clickable. Add mouseovers, underlines, button-style treatments. Just don't make them look like plain text. This site uses a different font for the navigation and a different color for the active link, i.e., the page you are currently viewing.

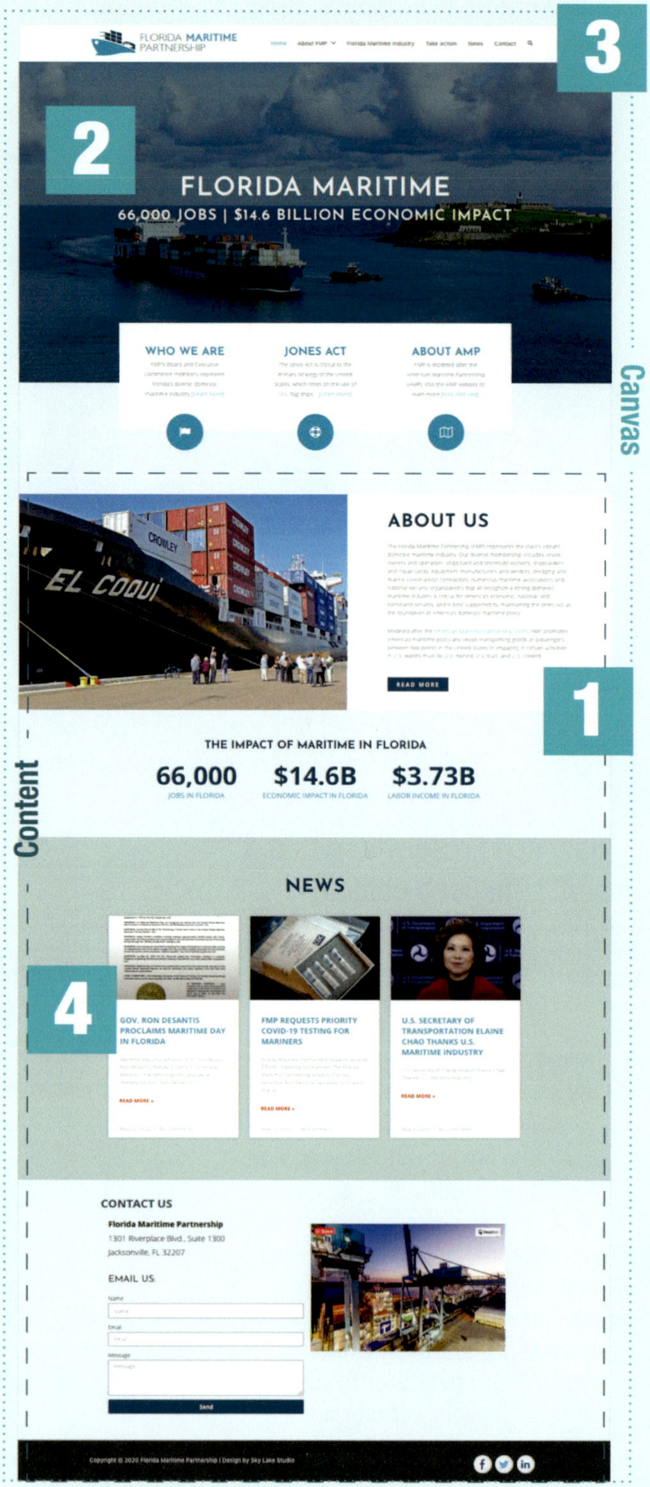

» Give your navigation ample padding. That's web design lingo for white space. And while you're at it, make sure your links have enough contrast. Dark links on a white background work well here.

» For lengthy pages, add navigation tools such as back-to-top buttons, or previous/next links for post series and gallery items.

4. **Content.** The part of the canvas not occupied by page identification and navigation is the content area. Some split the content area into a main column, a sidebar or two and a footer, but it's all content to us. You already know a lot about arranging content from "Chapter 6: Layout" and the Gestalt Laws from Chapter 5. Here are a few more tips:

» Balance the overall use of images, text and white space on the canvas. White space is particularly useful for visually separating chunks of content.

» Employ page hierarchy with most important to least important content positioning, along with graduated headline sizes.

» Make your text blocks a comfortable read with good contrast and plenty of white space. The "About Us" block demonstrates this.

» If using icons, make them visually consistent.

» When possible, use information-carrying images rather than decorative images.

» Eliminate visual clutter. Clean and simple layouts not only are visually appealing, they also enhance usability and accessiblility.

Website design reproduced by permission of Tucker/Hall and the Florida Maritime Parntership.

Canvas. Start your prototype layout by formatting your canvas, which refers to the rectangular digital page upon which you will create your website masterpiece. Because responsive webpages don't have single fixed layout widths, you can choose to allow your content to stretch the width of the full browser. Or you can contain it with maximum and minimum widths. Containing—or boxing—your content prevents your copy from stretching into long difficult-to-read lines of text spanning the width of the screen. Allowing some elements to stretch to full width is a style decision. Setting up grids with rows and columns creates consistency within your pages and across your entire website. Don't forget to include margins, coded in ems or percentages for fluidity, and keep them consistent throughout your prototype pages. If you haven't already added these settings to your design system, do it now. You'll use them on repeat thoughout the prototyping process.

Page identification. The name of your website, your organization, your logo, or a combo thereof comprise your page identification molecule or organism. Place page identification somewhere near the top of the page canvas, preferably at center top or top left. On *every* page in your prototype. This element functions as a key part of a site's main navigation. The site name or logo should always take the site visitor to the homepage on click. Speaking of navigation…

Site navigation. It serves as your prototype's table of contents. Primary navigation, i.e., the main menu, goes at the top of the page canvas. Paired with page identification and other molecules, the main menu becomes a header template. Because mobile screens lack room for multiple navigation links, designers and developers collapsed traditional navigation into single-button mini menus. The most common mini menu style is the "hamburger": three horizontal lines that look like a slice of something between two pieces of bread. Place hamburger menus at the top of the page as well. On *every* page in your prototype.

Lengthy and complex pages might require additional navigation menus or navigation aids.

Visitors reading a lengthy blog post appreciate a "back to top" button at the end. The usability of an e-commerce site with thousands of products improves with page-by-page navigation at the end of search results.

If you use more than one navigation structure in your prototype, make sure to include a copy of each template in your design system.

Content. Finally. Content is the reason we're all here. It occupies the most webpage real estate, and there are more types of content and content patterns than we can itemize. If you created content priority guides for each of your pages, use them to place your content molecules and templates in order of importance from most at the top to least at the bottom. Also, consider site-user end goals. If your content area contains a meaningful pitch for a donation along with an emotionally moving photo or video, make sure there's a "donate now" button nearby. As you place your modules and templates, don't forget that responsive websites shuffle page content. Make sure you know the order in which your content will appear on all types of devices.

Finally, don't forget to make space for content molecules, organisms and templates that might not have made your priority list. Where's your search box? Don't you need a footer with contact information, copyright information, disclaimers or additional navigation? Better account for those accessibility tools, too.

If you are still not clear on how to arrange your content, review "Chapter 5: Mini Art School" and "Chapter 6: Layout" for best practices. The infographic on page 256 demonstrates several design best practices to help guide your layout choices.

Share your published prototype with your team and the boss or client. Consider doing some usability testing by asking reviewers to complete tasks with your prototype, such as finding specific content or making a purchase. This is a terrific way to do the equivalent of safety inspections for interface malfunctions before final assembly. Hardhats and goggles not required.

ASSEMBLY

You did the heavy lifting of creating an inventory, crafting information architecture, prioritizing content and building both stylistic and comprehensive prototypes. This is the point when some assembly is actually required.

So far all our web-building activities apply to all types of websites. At the assembly stage, however, methods diverge.

UX LAWS AND THEORIES

UX Laws describe how humans interact with interfaces. These laws offer concrete clues on how to design for maximum usability. You've met Miller's Law and Hick's Law before. Here are a few more.

Fitts' Law. The size of and distance to a target impacts task completion time. The clickable target (the button) is big enough to hit easily and snugs up to the call-to-action.

Miller's Law: Working memory can only handle about 5–9 pieces of information at once and…

Hick's Law: Making decisions gets harder with more choices, says Hick's Law. Limiting menu choices to six satisfies both laws.

Serial Position Effect. Users remember the first and the last items in a group. This menu places commonly used "search" and "contact us" items first and last in the list.

Jakob's Law. Users prefer that all websites they use function in the same way. This footer uses a familiar layout as does the sign-up form.

Aesthetic Usability Effect. Users have more tolerance for minor usability issues if the product (website) design is clean and aesthetically pleasing. White space is legit.

Professional developers. If pro developers are building your site, and they have been active members of the design team, they should already have what they need for a final site buildout. If not, provide the developers with access to all documentation including your creative brief, inventory, information architecture diagram, content priority guides, HTML wireframes, design system with component library, prototypes and anything else that speaks to the look, feel, presentation and usability of your content. Be on hand to assist and answer questions.

CMS. If your site is CMS-based, it's time to select a theme. CMS sites are built using a set of files that generate individual page parts, including headers and content areas. A theme is a packaged set of coded files installed in your CMS that dictate how the files come together as a page. Themes are highly editable and let you style fonts, colors, backgrounds and other elements to align with your design standards. A no-coding-required dashboard interface makes site styling simple.

EYE TRACKING

In the mid-1990s, the Nielsen Norman Group began conducting web-reading eye-tracking studies. Their findings, which hold true today, tell us that:

» Web readers scan for usable content rather than read in depth

» Text, not graphics, draws the eye

» Users focus attention on the left

» Users skip anything that looks like an ad

These heat maps illustrate typical eye movements.

F Pattern

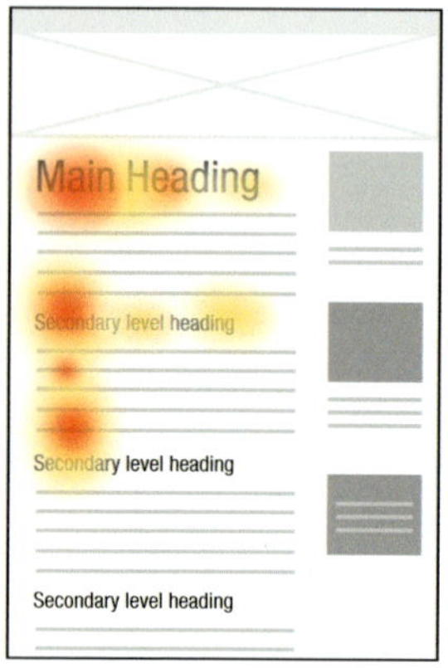

Layer Cake Pattern

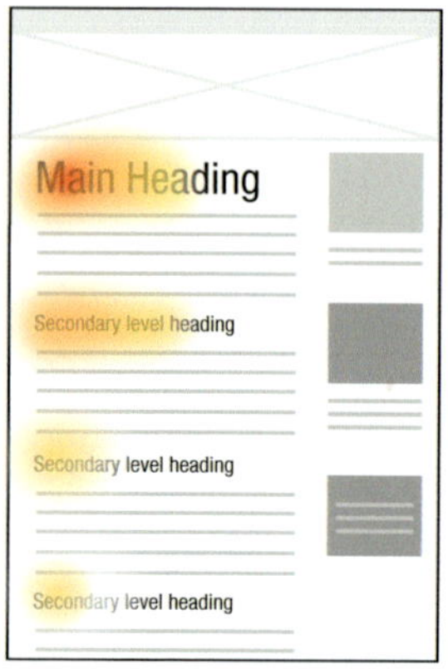

Configuring your content into your chosen UI patterns requires widget installation. Widgets, as you should recall from "Chapter 12: Design for Social Media," are mini-applications that add specific functions to your website. Widgets require little or no coding skills to install and can be customized to match your design system specifications. The Gasparilla Festival of the Arts homepage uses widgets for a hero video, a grid of content squares, a blog feed, a logo carousel and a newsletter sign-up form.

Search engine optimization (SEO)

If you collected keywords and brand messaging during your audit and inventory, now is the time to put them to work. Search engine optimization is the process of formatting your front-end web content and back-end code to land your site high on search engine results pages (SERPs).

SEO starts with identifying words and phrases relevant to your website topic. Keywords such as "art," "art festival" and "art show" are logical choices for an art festival website. Create a unique set of words for each page you want to rank highly. Work keywords into the HTML code for your page titles, headings, hyperlinks, alt tags (alternative text for page images or objects), captions and descriptions. Ideally, your domain name will include your keywords, too. SEO plug-ins make short work of this task. If your site is built on a CMS, take advantage of plug-ins and other built-in SEO tools.

On the front end, repeat your keywords throughout using natural phrasing. Balancing SEO with good copywriting requires finesse.

Non-word-related formatting impacts SEO, too, including site load speeds, originality of content, frequency of content updates and whether your site is mobile-friendly. In truth, SEO is complex and search engine algorithms consider more factors than we describe here. Consult an SEO expert if your website must rank.

Final flight check

Recruit people from inside and outside the team to thoroughly review the website before launch. Astronauts and pilots don't launch without flight checks, and neither should you. Use the checklist in the sidebar. Assign specific reviewing tasks—spelling, links, design consistency, brand continuity—to ensure the whole site is thoroughly vetted. Establish a procedure for making edits. Once the site has been cleared for launch, schedule it for evening or weekend hours. Slow traffic periods mean fewer visitor eyes on anything that might go sideways during launch.

Content strategy & site maintenance

For the record, launching a website does not mean done and done. Websites need regular maintenance to keep search engines happy and site visitors engaged. Regularly updating your website with new content on the front end along with code, theme or plug-in updates on the backend, is good for site security and discourages hacking. Develop a content strategy to keep your content fresh, and assign one or more content creators. Use your organization's goals and visitors' interests to schedule content uploads. Consider blog posts, videos, podcasts, live events, sales, book or product reviews, etc., to keep your site appealing and visitors engrossed.

Don't forget to review your site for needed updates to your hosting, site code, themes, plug-ins and widgets. Browsers update frequently, as do CMS systems and other services needed to run your site. Changes to hosting and browsers can have a cascading effect through your entire site, causing features to stop working or entire sites to fail. Check under the hood at least once a month to keep things running smoothly.

Well done, You, for hanging in there through the long and longer of website design. This might be the most important chapter in the book for today's communications pros. Web design certainly requires all the know-how you acquired in earlier chapters. Employ your designer's good eye and your communicator's sense of goals and audience, don't shy from getting expert assistance and you'll be good to go. Flight Control, we are ready for liftoff.

WS WEBSITE DESIGN PRE-LAUNCH CHECKLIST

- ☐ Check your spelling. No, really. Check all your spelling. Especially in your headlines and captions.
- ☐ Delete any remaining dummy/placeholder content
- ☐ Make sure all links work correctly
- ☐ Test your forms
- ☐ Test for problems with different browsers
- ☐ Check your website on mobile devices
- ☐ Set your site icon/favicon
- ☐ Create a custom 404 page (page not found) with useful links back to home page or other location
- ☐ Set up 301 redirects if needed for page URLs from your old site that don't exist in the new site.
- ☐ Activate SSL certificate and enable HTTPS
- ☐ Set SEO titles and meta descriptions
- ☐ Set up web analytics
- ☐ Submit your site's XML sitemap to search engines. An XML sitemap is a specially formatted list of your site's pages that helps search engines effectively crawl your site
- ☐ If your site uses a CMS, consider setting up an email service to keep emails from being sent through your web host. This helps prevent your emails from being tagged as SPAM
- ☐ Make sure your site is legally compliant. Set up legal pages (e.g. privacy policy) as needed
- ☐ Test your site's speed and optimize your site's performance as needed
- ☐ Add site security measures with plug-ins such as "limit login attempts" or tools designed to thwart hacking
- ☐ Have a backup policy in place, with backups stored "off-site," meaning not on the same server. Make sure you know how to reinstall from the backup

TRY THIS

1. Visit one or more large commercial websites intended for the general public. Consider usability and accessibility. What features make the site accessible? What do you recommend for improving usability and accessibility?

2. Using a desktop browser, a tablet and a smart phone visit the website of a local news station. Do all site features function properly on all devices? How do the layouts differ? How are they the same?

3. *Part 1:* Go to your local school's website (high school, or department of your university or community college). Using a spreadsheet, create an inventory of the site's pages and primary assets. Don't forget to account for secondary navigation.

   Part 2: Use your spreadsheet data and put all your information on index cards or sticky notes. Working with a group of 3–5 classmates, do a card sorting exercise to come up with a new menu structure for your site. Or justify your reasons for *not* creating a new menu structure.

4. Explore UI patterns at UI-patterns.com. Go to your favorite e-commerce site. See how many UI patterns you can find. View the same site on different devices. Observe if and how patterns change. While you're there, see if the site displays best practices indicated by UX laws.

5. Create a portolio site for yourself following these steps:

   » Write a creative brief

   » Audit your available content (headshot, bio, work examples, etc.) and create an inventory. Turn your inventory into a sitemap.

   » Create at least two Style Tiles and an elemental collage to explore colors, fonts and overall design direction for your site. Choose a design direction and start a design system with your specific elements. Include fonts, font sizes, color palette, button styles and UI patterns.

   » Construct a working prototype using UI kits and a prototyping program (Figma, InVision). Apply styles and patterns from your design system. Recruit a friend to test your prototype by giving them tasks to complete and observing any sticking points they encounter. Strategize ways to correct for sticking points.

   » Build the final site using an online CMS-based website tool.

CHAPTER 14

CONCLUSION

NOW THAT YOU KNOW ENOUGH TO BE DANGEROUS, THANKS FOR STOPPING BY

If you're starting to annoy coworkers, friends and family with your constant design critiques, then congratulations. You've learned to recognize bad—and good—design when you see it. Our work here is done. Before you unleash the full force of your new powers to set the universe right, allow us to leave you with some final and somewhat contradictory thoughts.

> While industry turmoil may be inspiring innovation in visual styles and trends, the grammar of visual communication hasn't changed.

EVERYTHING IS CHANGING

We don't need to tell you the media business is in flux. That's old news. As the cliché goes, change is the only thing that doesn't change, especially in communications where we're all technophiles.

The new news is the contemporary assumption that everyone is a fluent multi-platform visual communication designer. And everyone means everyone. Sometimes the amateurs and the audiences are better visual communicators than the pros. Meanwhile, the media bosses operate as if anyone who wants to work in the business can produce effective visual communication across any platform. "Anyone" covers the self-described wordsmiths, too, such as journalists, copyeditors and copywriters.

This reality requires you, whatever your specialty, to develop the good eye that goes beyond memorizing layout rules. You also need to know why those conventions work—or don't work—and that means knowing something about art, design and formal composition. Otherwise, you show up for work with an embarrassingly poor visual aesthetic.

THERE'S NOTHING NEW UNDER THE SUN

Even as everything about the media professions from business models to technology is changing, when it comes to graphic design, there really is nothing new under the sun.

Advertising and marketing communication folks produce public relations materials. Public relations practitioners produce advertising, marketing and news materials. The news industry borrows visual conventions from the entertainment industry, which adopts innovation from the advertising industry. And vice versa and so on.

We're all visual communicators using and abusing the same rules of graphic design and layout. While industry turmoil may be inspiring innovation in visual styles and trends, the grammar of visual communication hasn't changed. Regardless of the platform or the format, the fundamentals don't change. Good design is good design. Form follows function. Use visuals and type to capture attention, control eye flow, convey information and evoke emotion. White space is not your enemy.

SOMETIMES YOU JUST NEED TO HIRE A PROFESSIONAL

If nothing else, you now have enough knowledge to work alongside visual experts without drawing their scorn.

Knowing enough to know the good stuff when you see it also means knowing your own limitations. Sometimes you do just need to hire a professional. Appreciate the talent, skill and experience of the full-timers—artists, designers, art directors, illustrators, photographers, videographers, cinematographers, web designers and developers, etc.

WORDS OF ENCOURAGEMENT

If our little book is your first foray into visual communication and design, there is way more to learn if you're interested. If you think graphic design might be your future, get busy. Take a class. Find some online tutorials. Read, read, read. Glom-on to a mentor. If, for you, some knowledge is plenty, we salute you for reading along with us this far.

Regardless, we hope you enjoy your new know-how. Try to avoid becoming an overzealous visual snob alienating colleagues and loved ones. Don't be afraid to break the rules with a purpose. Strive always to delight your audiences. Treat professional creatives with respect. Don't forget to have some fun.

Finally, as we say to our neighbors, thanks for stopping by.

GLOSSARY

Numerics

30-degree rule: In film and video, this rule says any change of camera angle relative to the focal point should represent at least 30 degrees of change. Anything less reads as an editing error.

180-degree rule: In film and video, to avoid disorienting viewers, the 180-degree rule cautions against crossing the imaginary line of action intersecting two characters, unless there is a narrative purpose for doing so.

A

Aesthetic Usability Effect: A law of usability, the aesthetic usability effect states that users often perceive aesthetically pleasing designs as easier to use than less attractive ones. Further, users are more tolerant of dysfunction in products that are attractively designed.

Alley: An alley is the negative space between columns, modules or units on a grid.

Alpha channel: Alpha channel, or "A," controls color transparency in the RGBa web color system. (See also RGB.)

Analogous color: Analogous colors sit next to each other on the color wheel and work well together in color palettes because they contain some of the colors sitting next to them.

ANNCR: The abbreviation for announcer is ANNCR.

App (application): Apps, short for "(software) applications," are programs designed to run on a computer, tablet, smart phone, website or social media. Since the introduction of smart phones and tablets, apps have become increasingly popular and accessible. Common types include calendars, mileage trackers, restaurant finders and games.

Ascenders: Ascenders are the tall parts of font glyphs that ascend above lowercase x-height, as in the lowercase letterforms b, d, f, h, k, l, t.

Aspect ratio: Aspect ratio refers to the ratio of width to height for electronic screens.

Assets, site: Site assets include all the items and materials used to populate a website, including copy, logos, photos, video, audio, external web links and code snippets from other online sources.

Asymmetrical balance: With its visual fulcrum or center of visual gravity moved off-center, asymmetrical balance is visually balanced but not symmetrical.

Atomic Design. A design methodology for building websites that combines basic building blocks (atoms) into larger components (molecules, organisms and templates) and ultimately into pages. Modularity encourages the reuse of individual components, which speeds up the design process and creates visual consistency in the final design.

B

B roll: B roll is file, extra or archival footage used as visual fill or for creating transitions between clips.

Backlight: A backlight is a light source used to highlight the focal point from behind in order to give it contrast and dimension.

Baseline: This sentence sits on the baseline, the line guiding the horizontal alignment of type at the bottoms of words.

Beauty shot: In camera work, a beauty shot frames the focal point, whether person or object, to show off its best visual features.

Beta site: A beta site is a working test version of a website that isn't available to the public.

Bleed: Bleed refers to content that runs beyond the specified live area or safe area into the margins and off the edge of the page or screen.

Brand standards: Think of brand standards as your organization's style book dictating how your logo may be used, in specified configurations, using approved fonts and colors.

Breadcrumb trail: As in fairytales about children lost in the forest, a breadcrumb trail in web design is a system for keeping users apprised of their location in cyberspace.

Brief, creative or design: The document that briefs the creative team on the project, the creative or design brief answers basic job order and research questions about the project.

Built color: Built color uses the CMYK 4-color or full-color printing process to build any color.

Burning & dodging: Burning and dodging refer to techniques that darken or lighten photographs, respectively. Traditionally achieved by increasing/decreasing exposure to prints in the darkroom, these techniques mostly now are accomplished digitally.

Byline: The byline is the name of the writer, artist or photographer given credit.

C

Callout: Also called labels, callouts "call out" or call attention to details of infographics.

Cap line: The invisible horizontal line against which the tops of capitalized glyphs align in a particular font.

Cascading Style Sheet (CSS): Although webpages are built with programming languages such as HTML, the appearance of webpages is dictated by Cascading Style Sheets or CSS.

Close-up: In framing video and film shots, a close-up frames the focal point as a detail shot. Variations on the close-up include extreme, medium, full and wide close-up shots, as well as close and medium close shots. These frames move from an extreme close-up framing only an actor's eyes to a medium close shot that frames an actor from the waist up.

Closure: The Gestalt law of closure predicts the way people mentally fill in gaps to complete a perceived shape.

CMYK: CMYK is the 4-color or full-color printing process of building any color with just four inks: cyan, magenta, yellow and black.

Color management: Color management is the formal term for getting your color to match properly across devices, from scanners to digital cameras to computer screens to printers.

Colorblind design: Accessible design accommodates varieties of colorblindness, conditions that alter the way people see some colors and color combinations.

Common fate: This Gestalt law says that we perceive objects moving in the same direction as part of the same group.

Common region: This Gestalt law says we perceive items in the same container or sharing the same background as belonging to the same group.

Comp or complimentary image: A comp image, short for complimentary image, is a low-resolution stock image, usually with a watermark, available to sample in a layout before purchasing.

Comp or comprehensive: A comp, short for comprehensive, is a mockup of the final design and is used for getting approvals before spending time and money on final production.

Compass: The compass establishes direction on a map.

Complementary color: Color complements sit opposite each other on the color wheel.

Concept: The concept is the big idea uniting and driving the design's message.

Condensed font: Condensed fonts are drawn to be narrower (condensed) to take up less space than standard fonts.

Content management system (CMS): A content management system or CMS is a web-based application that manages page content and generates pages on the fly from information stored in a database. CMSs allow people with no knowledge of coding to build visually consistent websites.

Content priority guide: A website sketching tool used for hierarchically organizing the content of a single webpage.

Continuity: The Gestalt law of continuity predicts the way the eye will follow the direction of a line.

Crawl: A crawl refers to superimposed moving type crawling across an electronic screen such as TV.

Creative or design brief: The document that briefs the creative team on the project, the creative or design brief answers basic job order and research questions about the project.

Crop: To crop is to trim excess from visuals such as photography.

CSS: Although webpages are built with programming languages such as HTML, the appearance of webpages is dictated by Cascading Style Sheets or CSS.

Curly quotes: Curly quotes or smart quotes are the correct punctuation marks for quotations. Curly quotes are curly, as opposed to prime marks, which are straight. Prime marks indicate feet and inches, not quotations. See also smart quotes and prime marks.

Cut: In film and video, part of continuity is transitioning or segueing between shots and scenes. The most common type of transition is the simple "cut" from one shot to the next.

Cutaway: In film and video, "cutting away" from the main action by inserting something else going on in the scene is called a cutaway.

Cut-in or insert: In film and video, "cutting in" or "inserting" a close-up shot of something significant in the scene is called a cut-in or insert.

Cutline: In news contexts, captions for photos and visuals are called cutlines.

D

Deck: In print news, the subhead between the main headline and the story's lead is called a deck.

Decorative fonts: Decorative fonts have no common feature other than they are mostly novelty fonts best used for "decorative" purposes.

Depth of field: In camera work, depth of field refers to what in the shot remains in focus, whether foreground, midground, background or some combination.

Descenders: Descenders are characters or glyphs with tails that descend below the baseline, such as the lowercase letterforms g, j, p, q, y.

Design or creative brief: The document that briefs the creative team on the project, the creative or design brief answers basic job order and research questions about the project.

Design pattern or UI pattern: A design pattern is a specific group of website building blocks (text, field, link, etc.) organized to solve a user-centered problem. A newsletter sign-up form is a design pattern that includes text labels, form fields and a button. Patterns are reusable and can be formatted to match any website or app design style.

Design system: A collection of modular, reusable, functional elements that allow web teams to rapidly design products. A design system also includes documentation, brand guidelines, content guidelines and libraries for logos, images, videos and other visuals.

Detail shot: In camera work, a detail shot is a close-up shot revealing detail about the focal point.

Diacritic: An accent mark added to a glyph indicating an alternate pronunciation of that glyph. Diacritics are more common in some languages than others.

Digital storytelling or scrollytelling. Longform stories displayed online that include audio, video and animation effects. These effects trigger as the user scrolls down the page.

Dingbats: Forms of type that can be styled like type, dingbats are the ornamental characters in a font, or they may comprise an entire font of nothing but picture glyphs.

Display fonts: Drawn specifically to appear proportionate at larger point sizes, display fonts work well in headlines and signs.

Dissolve: In video and film transitions, the dissolve simply dissolves the frame before cutting to the next one.

Dodging & burning: Dodging and burning refer to techniques that lighten or darken photographs, respectively. Traditionally achieved by decreasing/increasing exposure to prints in the darkroom, these techniques now mostly are accomplished digitally.

Dolly shot: In a dolly shot, the camera is positioned on a dolly that moves or pushes toward the focal point.

Drop cap or initial cap: Those really huge single letters (or words) that appear at the start of the first paragraph are called drop caps that might drop down into several lines of the paragraph or initial caps that sit at the baseline and rise upward well above the line.

Dummy: In print news, a dummy is the set of thumbnail sketches that lay out or paginate what goes on every page of the issue, including ads and stories with visuals.

E

Em and rem: Scalable CSS units of measurement for website design. Em values scale an element's size relative to its parent container, while rem values scale relative to the document (HTML).

Em dash: Historically the width of a lowercase m, the em dash adds emphasis by replacing punctuation such as commas, colons and parentheses.

En dash: Historically the width of a lowercase n, the en dash is the correct glyph for replacing the "to" with punctuation in expressions such as "2–4 weeks."

EPS: EPS (Encapsulated PostScript) is used for some specific kinds of images. Vector graphics, usually illustrations, are saved in EPS format, as are some photographs that have certain styling applied. EPS format is typically used for logos and, like GIF, supports transparency.

Establishing shot: In camera work, an establishing shot is a full or wide-angle shot designed to orient viewers to the overall scene.

Explainer: Also called chatter, the brief typeset explanatory copy on an infographic is called an explainer.

F

Fade: In video and film transitions, a fade simply fades the visual frame before cutting to the next one.

File Transfer Protocol: File Transfer Protocol or FTP enables you to upload and share very large files on the web.

Fill light: Fill light supplements the key light by filling in unwanted shadows for less contrast.

Fitts' Law: A usability law that states the time required to touch a target is a function of target size and proximity.

Flat plan: A minimal bird's eye sketch of all pages or spreads in a print layout. Flat plans are used for organizing the overall flow of pages.

Flexible or fluid web design: To avoid layouts, thus designs, that "break" across different types, sizes and aspect ratios of screens and browsers, designers build flexibility and fluidity into their designs' CSS by specifying sizes and measurements in percentages, ems, rems, view heights and view widths instead of fixed pixels.

Focal point: Sometimes called the principle of emphasis, the focal point is the visual center of attention in the design or layout because it focuses the eye's attention.

Folio: Usually appearing in the margins of serials and periodicals such as newspapers, magazines and newsletters, the folio identifies the publication, issue and date, as well as page number if hard copy.

Font: A font is a complete set of characters in a particular size and style of type.

Font family: A font family or typeface contains a series of related fonts, such as Times New Roman, Times Bold and Times Italic.

Foot space or footer: The bottom margin is the foot space or footer.

Four-color process: CMYK is the 4-color or full-color printing process of building any color with just four inks: cyan, magenta, yellow and black.

FTP: FTP or File Transfer Protocol enables you to upload and share very large files on the web.

Full-color process: CMYK is the 4-color or full-color printing process of building any color with just four inks: cyan, magenta, yellow and black.

Full shot: In framing video and film shots, a full shot reveals an actor head-to-foot. A medium full shot frames the actor from the knees up.

FX: FX is shorthand for special "effects."

G

Gamut: The range of colors within a color space a device can output or record.

Gestalt theory: In the early 20th century, a group of German psychologists studied the way the human brain interprets and organizes what the eyes see. The results of this research became the Gestalt laws. See: closure, continuity, proximity, similarity.

GIF (vs. JPG): GIF (Graphics Interchange Format) and JPG (Joint Photographic Experts Group) are file formats for saving images destined for the web or computer screens. Both are low-resolution image formats. A big difference between them is a GIF will support transparency and a JPG will not. Transparency by definition means see-through. In the case of web graphics, transparency is essentially the ability to make certain color groups invisible. If you've ever tried to put a logo in JPG format on top of a colored background and discovered that your logo has a white box around it, you've encountered lack of transparency. By creating your web graphic in the correct software application and saving it as a GIF image, you can eliminate the white box.

Glyph: A glyph is an individual character of a font, whether a letter, numeral, punctuation mark, dingbat or special symbol. Most fonts have 265 glyphs. OpenType fonts have up to 65,000 glyphs.

Golden proportion: The golden proportion, sometimes called the golden ratio or divine proportion, refers to a ratio—1:1.618—that results in a universally appealing aesthetic when applied to shapes such as rectangles.

Graphics package: In the newsroom, a graphics package reports a story by using multiple types of graphics together.

Grayscale: A graduated range of tones from black to gray to white is called grayscale.

Greek text: Greek text or greeking is dummy copy or type used as a temporary substitute for the actual copy or type.

Grid: A grid is a series of horizontal and vertical lines composing the skeletal template of a design.

Grid module or grid unit: Instead of columns, a grid structure may include squares or rectangles called modules or units.

Gutter: A gutter is the oversized margin between two facing pages. The gutter is designed to accommodate the fold or binding. Some design software applications refer to alleys between grid columns as gutters, too.

H

Hairline rule: A hairline rule is a very thin rule or border—as thin as a strand of hair.

Hairline strokes: The thin lines in characters or glyphs are hairline strokes. The thick lines are stem strokes.

Handheld: Handheld refers to the cameraperson holding the camera as they move through the scene shooting video or film.

Hanging indent: Hanging indents refer to indicators that hang out to the left in the margin, instead of indenting to the right into the paragraph or text. Hanging indents are required for bulleted and numbered lists, as well as for quotation marks on pull quotes.

Hard light or low key: Hard light or low key emphasizes shadows, thus contrast, including shadows on people's faces.

Headspace or header: The top margin is the headspace or header.

Hero: In web design, the hero is the large image or video that takes up a lot of real estate at the top of the webpage.

Hexadecimal code: A web-based color specification system, hexadecimal color uses sets of numbers and letters to designate RGB light formulae.

Hick's Law: Important to web design (and restaurant menus), Hick's Law reminds us that decisions get harder the more choices we have.

High key or soft light: High key or soft light evens out the shadows to decrease harsh contrasts. It makes people and products look more attractive.

High pixel density: This refers to the technology that allows tiny screens to display densely packed pixels at very small sizes for realistic effect.

Horizon line: The line separating land and sky is the horizon line, which communicates a sense of distance or perspective.

Horsey: Not a compliment in design, horsey means awkwardly large and lacking grace.

HTML: HTML stands for Hypertext Markup Language, the basic code that makes up most webpages.

Hue: In color, hue answers the "what color?" question.

Hypertext Markup Language: Hypertext Markup Language or HTML is the basic code that makes up most webpages.

I

Infographic: An infographic is a visual representation of information or numerical data that demonstrates a relationship among individual parts resulting in a map, chart, sequence, diagram, etc.

Infographic layout: An infographic layout is any print or online layout that includes one or more infographics, such as a chart, table, map or diagram.

Infographic-style layout: Not true infographics, infographic-style layouts mimic the visual style of infographics with colorful icons, figures, boxed content, etc., but these layouts don't demonstrate relationships among data the way true infographics do.

Information architecture: Information architecture is the practice of organizing, structuring and labeling website pages and content for maximum findability and usability. Sitemaps are a visual representation of information architecture.

Insert or cut-in: In film and video, "cutting in" or "inserting" a close-up shot of something significant in the scene is called a cut-in or insert.

Inset, map: On a map, an inset enlarges a section of the map to reveal more detail.

Inset & offset: Inset refers to the content of a box sitting in away from the box's edges, rule, border or frame. Offset refers to items outside the box sitting off away from the box's edges.

Isometric map: Popularized by the gaming industry, isometric maps are drawn as 3-dimensional objects on a 2-dimensional plane.

J

Jakob's Law: Users prefer that all websites they engage basically work in the same way so they don't have to continually figure things out, according to Jakob's Law.

JPG (vs. GIF): JPG (Joint Photographic Experts Group) and GIF (Graphics Interchange Format) are file formats for saving images destined for the web and electronic screens. Both are low-resolution image formats. A big difference between them is that a GIF will support transparency and a JPG will not. Transparency by definition means see-through. In the case of web graphics, transparency is essentially the ability to make certain color groups invisible. If you've ever tried to put a logo in JPG format on top of a colored background and discovered that your logo has a white box around it, you've encountered lack of transparency. By creating your web graphic in the correct software application and saving it as a GIF image, you can eliminate the white box.

Jump line: In journalism when a story "jumps" to another page, a jump line functions like a breadcrumb trail letting readers know where the story is jumping to and then where the story has jumped from.

Justification: Referring to how your text is aligned, justification might be flush left, flush right, centered or fully justified (tempting those ugly rivers of negative space).

K

Kerning: Kerning refers to the negative space between two characters or glyphs.

Key: On infographics, such as maps, the key identifies and defines symbols and other reference markers or icons used.

Key light: A key light is the main or "key" light source in the shot, whether natural or artificial.

L

Lead or lede: The first paragraph of the body copy is called the lead.

Leading: Leading refers to the negative space between lines of type.

Leg: A leg is a column of typeset copy.

Legibility: Legible text is easy-to-read with crisp, clear, glyphs, sufficient leading and proper kerning.

Lift-out: Also called a pull quote, a lift-out is a pithy quotation pulled from the body copy and then enlarged and embellished to become both a visual and a teaser.

Ligature: Ligatures are specially designed letter pairs—a single glyph meant to take the place of two traditional letters that may look awkward if typeset side-by-side, such as "fi."

Live area: Live area refers to the area of the page within which material should print safely. Anything outside of the live area may be cropped off. For the video equivalent, see safe area.

Long shot: In framing video and film shots, long shots and extreme long shots get long angles on the scene.

Loop: In video and animation, a loop endlessly repeats by circling the ending back to the beginning to start all over again.

Low key or hard light: Low key or hard light emphasizes shadows, thus contrast, including shadows on people's faces.

M

Matched color: Matched color is a premixed spot color of ink matched to a color swatch.

Mean line: The invisible horizontal line against which the x-height of lowercase glyphs align in a particular font.

Medium shot: In framing video and film shots, a medium shot frames the actor from the hips up. A medium full shot frames the actor from the knees up, and a medium close shot frames the actor from the belt up.

Miller's Law: One of the laws of usability, Miller's Law reminds us that we can only handle about 5–9 pieces of information at once so don't overwhelm users with too many items in any list, including navigation.

Mobile first: The concept of designing websites for mobile devices first instead of last, mobile first was introduced by Luke Wroblewski in 2011.

Modern fonts: Modern fonts have extremely thin serifs, and their stress lies on the vertical, unlike old style's diagonal stress. Choose modern fonts carefully for long copy situations, and avoid them for screen applications.

Modular page design: In modular page design, each story is arranged into a rectangle, and the rectangles are arranged onto rectangular units of the grid of the page. Modular design is popular with print and web news design.

Montage: The video/film version of the collage, a montage cuts together many images.

Motion Pictures Expert Group or MPEG-4 or MP4: Motion Pictures Expert Group (MPEG-4) is a popular video file format for the web that works well across platforms and is supported by most web browsers.

Mousetype: Mousetype means very small type often used in the tags of advertising.

Mug shot: A mug shot is a photographic close-up or headshot, usually of a person.

Music bed or track: A music bed or track is a background soundtrack over which the main video and/or audio are laid.

N

Navigation: In web design, navigation refers to the system that allows users to move through and among webpages, including hypertext links and buttons, etc.

Negative or white space: Negative or white space is the empty space in which design is created and by which any design achieves pleasing balance and composition. Negative or white space has visual weight. "White space is not your enemy."

O

Offset & inset: Offset refers to items outside of a box sitting off away from the box's edges. Inset refers to the content of the box sitting in away from the box's edges, rule, border or frame.

Old style figures: Old style figures treat numerals as old style glyphs with ascenders and descenders.

Old style fonts: Old style fonts have serifs, thick stem strokes, thin hairline strokes and a diagonal stress on o-shaped characters. Old style fonts have good readability.

OpenType®: Designed to be functional across both Mac and PC platforms, OpenType fonts may have as many as 65,000 characters each, including ligatures, swash alternates and old style figures.

Optical fonts: Some extended typefaces include optical fonts drawn for viewing at smaller or larger sizes. Caption fonts, for example, include spacing for viewing at smaller font sizes while display fonts would include detail enhancements for viewing at larger sizes.

Optimization: Optimization refers to balancing the resolution, thus appearance, of graphics with their generally large file sizes so that they load quickly but still look good.

Orphan: A typographic orphan refers to a few lonely words stranded at the top of a leg of type.

Over lighting: A key light shining directly from above is over lighting.

P

Pan: A pan or panning indicates a stationary camera that sweeps across the scene. The effect is that of turning your head to look around.

Perspective: In visual arts, such as painting, photography and film, perspective refers to the sense of distance in the scene, whether achieved by where the horizon line sits in the composition, the use of a linear vanishing point, the relative size of objects in the scene or atmospheric use of light and dark values that seem to recede or move forward, respectively.

Pixel: Pixels are smallest unit of a digital image, and the number of pixels affects the quality and downloading speed of an image.

Pixel density: This refers to the number of pixels a viewport is able to display. See also, high pixel density.

Plane: A plane is a flat surface, such as a piece of paper or a screen, but in design you can create the illusion of multi-dimensional planes demonstrating depth and height, etc.

Plug-in: A plug-in is code that gives a browser or website additional functionality, for example, when a website automatically displays the most recent posts from a separate blog, a plug-in is at work.

PNG (portable network graphics): PNG is a file format for web-destined graphics that must accommodate gradients and transparency, such as in drop shadows.

Pointer box: On a map or diagram, a pointer box literally is a box that points to some detail while offering additional information inside the box.

POV: POV is the abbreviation for point of view referring to the perspective of the camera lens, thus the audience.

Primary colors: The primary colors on the traditional color wheel are red, blue and yellow, which when variously combined produce every other color on the color wheel. Differing from the traditional color wheel, the RGB color wheel has different primary colors: red, green, blue.

Prime marks: Prime marks are the correct straight glyphs used to indicate feet and inches, as opposed to curly or smart quote glyphs used to punctuate quotations. See also curly quotes and smart quotes.

Prototyping: In web design, prototyping software is used in the planning process. It allows the designer to create a functional mockup of a whole website or parts of a website. Prototypes demonstrate a site's interactive components to a client.

Proximity: The Gestalt law of proximity predicts that the eye will perceive items physically grouped together as belonging to the same group.

Pull-down menu: In electronic environments such as webpages, a pull-down menu provides a form of navigation that remains hidden unless a user accesses it with the cursor/mouse.

Pull quote: Also called a lift-out quote, a pull quote is a pithy quotation pulled from the body copy and then enlarged and embellished to become both a visual and a teaser.

Push: In video and film, push shots push into the scene. In a zoom, a stationary camera pushes into the scene by using the lens to zoom in on the focal point. In a dolly shot, the camera itself, positioned on a dolly, moves or pushes toward the focal point.

R

Rack-focus: In film and video, a rack-focus uses a stationary camera to shift a scene's focal point simply by refocusing from one object to another.

Radial balance: Radial balance refers to circular designs in which the fulcrum lies at the center.

Readability: As it implies, readability refers to ease of reading, and design factors affecting readability include typeface choice, typeface styling, color, size, kerning/tracking, leading, and more.

Reference points: On a map, reference points are landmarks, either natural or built, that orient the viewer.

Registration: Registration refers to aligning material across color plates in commercial printing.

Rem and em: See "Em."

Rendered type: Rendered type is a character, a word or a string of words filled with an image or otherwise transformed using photo-editing software.

Resolution: Image resolution refers to the detail or crispness of an image and is measured in units per inch. Ink on paper requires images in specific *dots per inch (dpi)*. High-end printing requires 300 dpi, and newsprint requires 200 dpi. For screens, graphics are measured in *pixels per inch (ppi)*. Web graphics are prepared at 72 dpi.

Responsive web design: Responsive websites are coded to resize and rearrange their layouts to fit the size of the current viewport.

Reversing: A reverse literally reverses figure color with fill/field/background color. Reversed type refers to light type on a dark background, such as white type on a black field.

RGB: Standing for red, green and blue, RGB is the color wheel system for achieving color in electronic and digital screen environments by mixing red, green and blue light.

RGBa: A web color specification, RGBa adds "a" to "RGB." "A" stands for alpha channel, which controls color transparency in the RGBa web color system.

Rights-managed image: For a rights-managed image, you pay more to make sure other folks in your market don't use the same image, too. For a cheaper alternative, see royalty-free image.

Rough: A rough is a rough layout only slightly more detailed than a thumbnail sketch.

Royalty-free image: Royalty-free images are inexpensive stock images with no guarantees your competitor won't use them, too. For guarantees, see rights-managed image.

Rule: A rule is a graphic line, such as a border or a frame.

Rule of thirds: The rule of thirds says that dividing a layout or composition into thirds makes for a more interesting visual composition. The rule of thirds suggests that the four gridline intersections on a 3 × 3 grid offer the best locations to position a focal point in an asymmetrical layout.

S

Safe area: Action safe area and title safe area refer to the area of the screen within which material is visible. In video, title safe area refers to the area onscreen within which text and graphics will safely appear without cropping any content. Action safe area is a slightly larger area onscreen within which action appears without cropping content.

Sans serif fonts: Sans serif (French for "without serif") fonts have no serifs, and their strokes have uniform thickness. They are the most readable fonts for screen applications.

Saturation: Saturation refers to the amount or intensity of a hue.

Scalability: The ability of images, fonts and other web design components to adjust size in response to different viewing devices.

Scale: Scale refers to relative size and proportion.

Scale, map: The scale on a map establishes the reduced proportions of distance, i.e., an inch equals a mile, etc.

Script fonts: Script fonts resemble cursive handwriting. They can be quite elegant in decorative situations, but they are not a good choice for readability.

Scrollytelling: See Digital storytelling.

Search engine optimization (SEO): Search engine optimization or SEO refers to making your website search-engine friendly to rank well in user web searches.

Secondary colors: Mixing any two primary colors produces the secondary complement of the third primary color.

SEO, or search engine optimization: SEO or search engine optimization refers to making your website search-engine friendly to rank well in user web searches.

Serial position effect: This usability law, also known as "primacy-recency," predicts that people remember the first and last thing in a list or group. In web design, that means placing the most important navigation or content items first or last in the list.

Serif: Serifs are those little feet or flags at the tips of glyphs.

SFX: SFX is shorthand for "sound effects."

Sidebar: Simply a separate block of type with a solid background, a stroked outline or an ample border of negative space, a sidebar provides content related to its adjacent copy.

Side lighting: Side lighting casts long shadows and increases the sense of three-dimensional space, as opposed to the flattening effect of soft light.

Similarity: The Gestalt law of similarity predicts that people will group items with similar properties such as shape, size or color.

Site asset: Site assets include all the items and materials used to populate a website, including copy, logos, photos, video, audio, external web links and code snippets from other online sources.

Site map: In web design, a site map literally maps out the site to show the links between and flow among pages in the form of something that resembles either a family tree or a flowchart.

Slab serif fonts: Slab serif fonts are similar to old style fonts, but the serifs on slab serif fonts start thick and stay thick. Invented for display advertising, slab serif fonts are excellent for headlines and signage.

Small caps: Small caps capitalize the entire word, although the initial cap is slightly larger than the rest of the letters, which are slightly smaller than a regular capitalized glyph.

Smart quotes: Smart quotes are the correct "curly" punctuation marks for quotations. See also curly quotes and prime marks.

Soft light or high key: Soft light or high key evens out the shadows to decrease harsh contrasts. It makes people and products look more attractive.

Source line: The source line identifies the origin or source of data. In an infographic, the source line usually appears on the lower left under the infographic.

Split screen: A split screen divides the screen into two different images.

Spot color in design: Not to be confused with spot color ink in printing, spot color in design refers to designing with a few well-chosen spots or splashes of color to highlight items such as a focal point or to draw the eye around the layout.

Spot color printing: Instead of building color using the 4-color CMYK printing process, spot color printing uses premixed ink colors chosen from a swatch book. See also matched color.

Spread: Two facing pages part of the same design are called a spread, such as one magazine story spreading across the gutter in two facing pages or a two-page advertisement spanning the gutter.

Steadicam: A steadicam is a kind of harness the cameraperson wears to hold the camera steady as they shoot handheld video or film.

Stem strokes: The thick lines in characters or glyphs are stem strokes. The thin lines are hairline strokes.

Storyboard: A storyboard lays out the moving-picture or animated stories of planned film, video and electronic media in the form of scenes or shots arranged on a grid.

Stroked type: Stroked type or stroking is when the type characters or glyphs are outlined.

Super: A super is any on-screen type or graphic superimposed over another image.

SVG (scalable vector graphics): Scalable vector graphics are a file format for the web. They are an excellent format for charts and graphs.

Swash alternates: Swash alternates are decorative alternatives to traditional italic letterforms.

Symmetrical balance: With symmetrical balance, if you bisect the design, each side will be a mirror image of the other in terms of visual weight.

T

Tags: Tags refer to all the information typically found at the bottom of an advertisement, such as the logo, themeline or slogan, URL, physical address and map, phone number and sometimes, unfortunately, disclaimer and legalese.

Tertiary colors: Tertiary colors result from combining a primary and a secondary color.

Thumbnail sketch: Thumbnail sketches or thumbnails are tiny thumbnail-sized layout sketches that you can draw—and reject—quickly.

Thumb space: Sometimes margins are called thumb space because, if you were holding a hardcopy, margins leave enough negative space at the edges of the layout to accommodate your thumb without covering any visual material.

TIF: Choose TIF (Tagged Image Format) file formats to save images for print or video purposes (as opposed to GIF or JPG for web purposes). TIF images are larger in file size, but the TIF format does not lose data.

Tilt: In film and video, a tilt shot is a vertical up-and-down pan of the camera. See also, pan.

Tombstoning: In news design, as the name implies, two or more adjacent single-column stacked headlines look rather like tombstones lining up. They cause confusion about whether to read down or across columns making it difficult to distinguish between discrete stories.

Track or music bed: A track or music bed is the background soundtrack over which the main video and/or audio are laid.

Tracking shot: In a tracking shot for film or video, a stationary camera tracks along with a moving focal point.

Tracking, type: Tracking refers to the negative space across a string of characters, such as a word, sentence or paragraph.

Transitional fonts: Transitional fonts evolved from old style fonts and have serifs, thick stem strokes and thin hairline strokes. But transitional fonts may have a less pronounced diagonal stress or no diagonal stress at all. Transitional fonts have good readability.

Trapped space: A puddle of landlocked negative space with no apparent layout function in the design is called trapped space.

Triads, color: Color triads are colors on the 12-point color wheel that form any triangle 4 hours apart. Triads make pleasing color palettes.

Trim size: In commercial printing, trim size refers to the finished size of the page after the printer has trimmed away the excess paper.

Truck: In video and film, a truck refers to the camera trucking sideways across the scene. This is usually accomplished with a camera on a dolly. The effect is like rubbernecking from a moving car.

Tweened animation: In tweened animation, the artist illustrates only key changes in motion or shape. Then the software application automatically generates animation to fill "between" the artist's illustrated frames.

Typeface: A typeface or font family contains a series of related fonts, such as Times New Roman, Times Bold and Times Italic.

U

Under lighting: A key light shining directly from below.

User experience or UX: User experience refers to the total interaction with a product, including ease of use, level of satisfaction and overall feelings about the product.

User interface or UI: User interface is about the mechanics of interaction. It is the buttons, icons, and other visual elements that allow the user to interact with a website, app or other device.

V

Value: Value refers to the lightness or darkness of a hue.

Vanishing point: In linear perspective, the vanishing point is where two lines converge in the distance.

Vector image: Vector images use geometry and math to produce and preserve the proportions and quality of line-art illustrations as digital files. They can be scaled up or down infinitely without loss of image quality.

vh and vw: Scalable CSS units of measurement for website design. vh refers to viewport height and vw refers to viewport width.

Visual hierarchy: As a tactic for visually communicating a hierarchy of visual items in terms of visual importance, visual hierarchy conventions include making important information large and putting it at the top of the composition. In multiple screen and page designs, as well as in designs with multiple items on the same screen or page, it's important to establish a hierarchy of fonts and point sizes, in addition to placing important items at the top of the screen or page.

VO, voiceover: A VO or voiceover is a disembodied voice speaking over video or audio.

W

Web safe palette: The idea of the web safe color palette was to provide designers a way of getting consistent color. As a project, the web safe palette mostly has failed because of constant advances in hardware and monitors, not to mention the garish color choices of the palette.

WebP: An image file format providing superior compression for web applications while maintaining image integrity. WebP requires a tool for converting JPG and PNG files.

White or negative space: White or negative space is the empty space in which design is created and by which any design achieves pleasing balance and composition. White or negative space has visual weight. "White space is not your enemy."

Widget: Widgets are the visible user-friendly expression of the existence of a plug-in. Not all plug-ins have widgets, but all widgets require plug-ins as their invisible engines.

Widow: A typographic widow refers to a few lonely words stranded at the bottom of a leg of type. A hyphenated word ending the last line of a leg counts as a widow, too.

Wipe: In video and film, a wipe transitions between screens with the effect of wiping the picture from the screen.

Wireframe: In web design, a wireframe is the equivalent of a thumbnail sketch. Wireframes show the functional areas of the planned website.

X

X-height: In a given typeface, x-height refers to the height of a lowercase "x" relative to the length of ascenders and descenders.

Z

Zoom: In a zoom, a stationary camera pushes into the scene by using the lens to zoom in on the focal point.

INDEX

A

B

C

D

E

F

G

H

I

J

L

M

N

O

P

R

S

T

U

V

W

For Product Safety Concerns and Information please contact our EU representative GPSR@taylorandfrancis.com Taylor & Francis Verlag GmbH, Kaufingerstraße 24, 80331 München, Germany

Batch number: 10733643

Printed by Printforce, the Netherlands